SUICIDE ACROSS THE LIFE SPAN

SUICIDE ACROSS THE LIFE SPAN
Premature Exits
Second Edition

Judith M. Stillion, Ph.D.
Western Carolina University
Cullowhee, North Carolina

Eugene E. McDowell, Ph.D.
University of North Carolina
Asheville Graduate Center
Asheville, North Carolina

Taylor & Francis
Publishers since 1798

USA	Publishing Office:	Taylor & Francis 1101 Vermont Avenue, N.W., Suite 200 Washington, D.C. 20005-3521 Tel: (202) 289-2174 Fax: (202) 289-3665
	Distribution Center:	Taylor & Francis 1900 Frost Road, Suite 101 Bristol, PA 19007-1598 Tel: (215) 785-5800 Fax: (215) 785-5515
UK		Taylor & Francis Ltd. 1 Gunpowder Square London EC4A 3DE, UK Tel: 171 583 0490 Fax: 171 583 0581

SUICIDE ACROSS THE LIFE SPAN: Premature Exits, Second Edition

1 2 3 4 5 6 7 8 9 0 BRBR 9 8 7 6

This book was set in Baskerville by Graphic Composition, Inc. The editors were Alice Rowan and Holly Seltzer. Cover design by Michelle Fleitz. Interior text design by Bonny Gaston. Printing and binding by Braun-Brumfield, Inc.

A CIP catalog for this book is available from the British Library.
⊗ The paper in this publication meets the requirements of the ANSI Standard Z39.48-1984 (Permanence of Paper)

Library of Congress Cataloging-in-Publication Data

Stillion, Judith M.,
    Suicide across the life span:premature exits / Judith M. Stillion, Eugene E. McDowell.—
2nd ed.
      p. cm.—(Series in death education, aging, health care, ISSN 0275-3510)
    Includes bibliographical references.

    1. Suicide.   2. Life cycle, Human—Psychological aspects.   I. McDowell, Eugene E.   II. Title.   III. Series.
HV6545.S797   1996
362.2′8—dc20

96-338
CIP

ISBN 1-56032-303-5 (case)
ISBN 1-56032-304-3 (paper)
ISSN 0275-3510

Dedication

Barbara Morton Lord and Nancy McDowell Newton.
Our sisters, teachers, and friends.

Contents

Preface

We began contemplating a second edition of *Suicide Across the Life Span: Premature Exits* soon after the first edition appeared. As we read the burgeoning literature about suicide and the exciting new theories about cohort effects on the peer personality of entire generations, we began to reconceptualize the book and to prepare for this edition.

This edition is markedly different from the first one. To begin with, we have used the suicide trajectory model proposed in the final chapter of the first edition as an organizing principle for this volume. Consequently, beginning with chapter 1 and following throughout the developmental chapters, we present our review of the literature using the structure of the suicide trajectory to bring order out of the chaos of the interdisciplinary research.

A second major difference lies in our detailing of the cohort effect for each age group. Based on the seminal work of Strauss and Howe (1991), we have provided in this edition a thumbnail sketch of each currently living cohort. We believe that cohort differences form a rich backdrop against which suicide statistics and projections can be better understood. Furthermore, as developmental psychologists we applaud the added dimension of understanding that examination of the peer personality of living cohorts brings to the issue of suicide.

A third difference in this edition is the expanded coverage of several subtopics. For example, we have found that the literature on adolescent and young adult suicide has increased greatly, so we have given each of these topics a separate chapter (chapters 4 and 5). We have also added a full chapter on intervention (chapter 9), separating it from the chapter on prevention and postvention (chapter 8). This has enabled us to provide a more systematic review of the literature on suicide attitudes and on prevention and postvention approaches, as well as to examine in more depth differing approaches to the ongoing treatment of suicidal people. We have added one totally new chapter that focuses on physician-assisted suicide and end-of-life issues (chapter 10) because we believe these matters are becoming more salient every day. All of the chapters have been updated, adding to the currency and timeliness of the volume. Finally, we have added an exercise in empathy as an afterword.

We have retained what we think were the strengths of the first edition. Specifically, we continue to believe that examining suicide from a life-span perspective adds greatly to the understanding of suicidal people. So we also endorse the view that true understanding of suicide cannot be achieved through a single lens and that students of suicide must have a historical perspective as well as an interdisciplinary approach. Therefore, we have included in chapter 1 a history of suicide in the Western world as well as an

overview of the suicide trajectory model that demands interdisciplinary application. Chapter 2 retains its focus on examining suicide from the disciplines
of psychology, sociology, and biology, reinforcing the elements of the model
presented in the preceding chapter. Chapters 3 through 7 continue to be the
heart of the book, reviewing the literature by age group and presenting case
studies that invite the reader to apply what is known from the literature to
specific individual cases. Chapter 8 discusses current attitudes toward suicide,
as well as the roles that society, the family, and the schools play in the prevention and postvention of suicide.

Chapter 9 examines suicide intervention and treatment from several perspectives, expanding greatly on the coverage of these topics in the earlier
edition. Chapter 10 provides a short history of the recent developments in
assisted suicide with special emphasis on physician-assisted suicide.

Many of the people who helped with the first edition deserve our thanks
again. Our editor, Elaine Pirrone, has been most supportive and helpful as
we have struggled to meet deadlines and when we have had to change them.
She also took on the detail work in seeking permission for use of copyrighted
material in this edition, a task above and beyond her regular duties. Readers
of the first edition have cheered us on and made valuable suggestions for
reorganization. More importantly, knowing that they found the first edition
useful gave us the energy to attempt a second book. Library personnel at
Western Carolina University have been invaluable as always in their assistance
with procuring materials. Cameron Stillion, a new addition to the Stillion
family, added her expertise in art history by helping us select art for this
edition. John McIntosh, whose scholarly work is cited frequently throughout
the book, has provided special assistance with figures. Wanda Ashe and Jan
Scroggs typed several versions of this manuscript, checked references, and
proofread with their usual invaluable competence and good humor. Most of
all, our spouses, Glenn W. Stillion and Suzanne Hill McDowell, have been
exceptionally supportive of our devotion to this work by once again assuming
more than their share of responsibilities at home while also pursuing their
own professional careers. Finally, we wish to acknowledge our sisters, Barbara
Morton Lord and Nancy McDowell Newton, who died while this work was in
progress. They have enriched our lives immeasurably since childhood and
we continue to miss their presence.

Suicide Then and Now

Those who cannot remember the past are condemned to repeat it.

George Santayana

Suicide may be one of the most puzzling subjects in the history of the human species. For many years most people have believed that the desire to live is so deeply implanted in humans that it might be considered an instinctive behavior. In opposition to this idea is the recognition that human beings have an ancient tradition of self-murder. This chapter begins with a history of suicide throughout Western culture that will show that suicidal behavior has had different meanings at different times and in different circumstances. The chapter then turns to a definition of suicide for our times and gives an overview of the current problem in the United States and in several other developed nations. It ends with a model for understanding suicidal behavior that we will use in later chapters as a framework for understanding suicide at different ages.

A SUMMARY OF SUICIDE IN WESTERN HISTORY

Suicide as self-sacrifice has probably existed ever since humans banded together in clans. In primitive hunting practices, it was not uncommon for one individual to volunteer to draw the attention of a herd of animals to himself (men were generally the hunters) in order to turn them in a direction that would allow the tribe to trap and kill them more easily. The probability that the hunter would survive the onrushing herd was low. The reward if he did survive must have been very high. The reward for the tribe was often survival itself. Thus, the early acts of self-sacrifice for the good of the many added to the survival of the species. Such suicidal behavior is now called *altruistic suicide* (i.e., a person gives up his or her life for others or for a greater good).

Modern remnants of this urge toward altruistic suicide are found in battlefront accounts of people who have sacrificed their lives for the lives of their fellow soldiers, as well as in 20th century records of Eskimo tribes whose elders sacrificed their lives by wandering alone into the freezing countryside when they felt they could no longer be of use to the social system in which they lived. Such voluntary deaths also had species-survival value in that they freed the tribes of the burden of caring for elderly who would inevitably become increasingly dependent. Bromberg and Cassel (1983) reported that many primitive cultures encouraged suicide among the elderly as a means to avoid the pains of old age and to earn honor from their people. These authors pointed out that cultures as diverse as those of the Norseman, the polar Eskimos, the Crow Indians, and the Samoans all had traditions that promoted suicide with honor.

Although altruistic suicide and suicide by the elderly can be seen to have species-survival value, the history of Western civilization is marked by self-killings done for other reasons. An examination of some of these reasons may help us to attain the broadest view possible of what suicide has meant throughout the ages. A time line describing selected milestones in the history of suicide in the Western world is included in Table 1.1. Assembled from multiple sources (Alvarez, 1970; Donne, 1644/1982; Farberow, 1975; Farberow & Shneidman, 1961; The Holy Bible, 1949; Shneidman, 1985; Van Hoof, 1990; Harmet, 1984), it presents a shorthand version of the discussion that follows.

Suicide in the Old Testament

There are four instances of suicide recorded in the Old Testament, only two of which appear on the time line. These two, the suicides of Samson and King Saul, took place in roughly the same period, around 1000 B.C. It is interesting to note that no scriptural judgment is expressed about either of these suicides; both are merely described factually. Samson killed himself after violating his faith, being captured and blinded by his enemies, and suffering a long period of physical labor as a prisoner. Those who are familiar with the story might recognize retribution against enemies, atonement for behavior that violated deep religious beliefs, and sacrifice for principle as possible motivating elements in that suicide. Looking beneath the surface, there may also have been elements of helplessness and hopelessness involved since Samson had no likelihood of being freed or of being able to reclaim his former quality of life. It is noteworthy that this suicide resulted in the death of many of Samson's enemies as well as the destruction of their temple. It may well be regarded as the first case of murder-suicide in recorded history.

The suicide of King Saul seems to have occurred as a reaction to loss and pain and as an escape from an intolerable situation. The loss was the death of his three sons, who died in the same battle in which Saul was wounded. Saul apparently sought by his suicide to ward off worse wounds; he asked his armor bearer to kill him "lest these uncircumcised come and thrust me through and abuse me" (I Sam. 31:4). When his armor bearer refused to kill him, Saul fell on his own sword. There is also an element of prophecy fulfillment in this suicide: Saul's death had been foretold earlier by the witch of Endor. The third suicide recorded in the Old Testament was Saul's servant and armor bearer, who also took his own life, apparently overcome with grief and loss at Saul's death, in a show of loyalty to his sovereign.

The fourth suicide mentioned in the Old Testament was that of Ahito-

TABLE 1.1   Selected Milestones in the History of Suicide in the Western World

Event & Approximate Date	Description
1000 B.C. Deaths of Samson and Saul	Reported without comment. Possible causes: retribution, self-punishment, justification of God and beliefs, reaction to death of sons, despair, fulfillment of prophecy.
399 B.C. Death of Socrates	Honorable exit; rational control over death.
350 B.C. Proclamation of Aristotle	Established suicide as unlawful.
300 B.C. to **300** A.D. Development of Greek & Roman Stoicism	Concept of rational suicide was developed fully.
33 A.D. Death of Judas Iscariot	Reported without comment. Possible causes: guilt, remorse, self-punishment, fulfillment of prophecy.
33 A.D. Death of Jesus of Nazareth	Martyrdom (i.e., allowing oneself to be killed for one's faith) became a major moral lesson for Christians.
65 A.D. Death of Seneca and his wife Paulina	Reinforced concept of rational suicide; quality rather than quantity of life emphasized.
73 A.D. Mass suicide at Masada	960 defenders of Masada died rather than surrender to the enemy.
300–400 A.D. Donatism flourished	Martyrdom established as a goal for fervent Christians.
400 A.D. St. Augustine condemned self-killing	Censured martyrdom to ensure future of Christianity.
533 A.D. Council of Orleans	Denied funeral rites to suicides accused of crime.
563 A.D. Council of Braga	Denied funeral rites to all suicides.
590 A.D. Council of Antisidor	Added system of penalties for suicide.
693 A.D. Council of Toledo	Adopted excommunication as punishment for suicide or attempted suicide.
1265–1272 A.D. Thomas Aquinas published *Summa Theologica*	Presented detailed arguments against suicide. Added to the idea that suicide is sinful.
1284 A.D. Synod of Nimes	Denied Christian burial to suicides.
1647 A.D. John Donne publishes *Biathanatos*	Questioned whether self-murder always is a sin.
1651 A.D. Word *suicide* entered English language	
1670 A.D. Secular laws were passed against suicide	Suicide became triple crime: murder, high treason, heresy.
1763 A.D. Merian published medical work on suicide.	Introduced concept of suicide as illness.
1783 A.D. Hume published *Essay on Suicide*	Argued that suicide is not a crime against God, neighbors, or self.
1838 A.D. Esquirol published chapter describing suicide as a symptom of mental illness.	Added support to the interpretation of suicide as an illness.
1897 A.D. Durkheim published *Le Suicide*	Beginning of study of suicide as a sociological phenomenon.
1800–1900 A.D. Rise of existentialism (e.g., Kierkegaard, Nietzsche, et al.)	Stressed individual freedom to act and responsibility for that action. Suicide seen as merely one more decision that individuals must face throughout their lifetimes.
1917 A.D. Freud published *Mourning and Melancholia*	Established modern foundation for viewing suicide as evidence of mental illness.
1958 A.D. First suicide prevention center established in Los Angeles	Based on the view that suicidal thoughts are temporary and that intervention effects a cure.

The Death of Socrates, **Jacques Louis David. (The Metropolitan Museum of Art, Wolfe Fund, 1931. Catherine Lorillard Wolfe Collection, 31.45.)**

phel, whose plan to attack and kill King David went awry. When Ahitophel realized this, he went home, put his affairs in order, and hanged himself. The Scripture once again passes no judgment on his act. The motivation in this case might have been a sense of shame and disgrace over his failure, or a fear of retribution from David or his captain, Absalom. It might also be regarded as the fatalistic acceptance of the inevitable, since death would probably have been his punishment for treason.

From these four cases of suicide, which occurred during the same general period, little can be discerned about the attitudes of the populace at the time toward the act of suicide. All four stories contain elements of morality, however, which seem to point to the expectation that suicide might be appropriate for those who are less than faithful to their beliefs or who face imminent death, or as a show of loyalty to one's sovereign.

Suicide in Ancient Greece and Rome

Perhaps the best known suicide in history is the next one depicted on the time line in Table 1.1, the suicide of Socrates. This suicide, which occurred in 399 B.C., is the epitome of taking one's life out of a sense of duty and enduring loyalty to one's philosophy of life. Socrates chose to drink poison rather than to moderate or renounce his teachings. If he had renounced his teachings or moderated them at an earlier date, he most likely could have avoided the situation leading to his death. Once in the situation, he could also have chosen not to take the hemlock and thus forced his accusers to murder him. But Socrates chose to die as he had lived, teaching right up to the moment of his death and in control of his own fate until the last. His death has long been regarded as an example of honorable death.

The next major milestone on the suicide time line occurred around 350 B.C. when Aristotle, the intellectual heir of Socrates via his teacher, Plato, proclaimed that suicide is or should be unlawful because it injures the community. This could be most clearly seen in the case of a suicide by a slave or servant, which would result in the deprivation of services to the master's household. It is also evident, however, that in a culture where community welfare is a strong value, the life of any one individual would be viewed as secondary in importance to the needs of the community as a whole. In such a situation, suicide would be condemned, since it would result in a weakening of the community by the loss of the talents and energies of the suicidal individual.

During the period of 300 B.C. to 300 A.D., the concept of self-murder as a rational act was developed fully by followers of the philosophy known as Stoicism. Stoicism flourished first in Greece and then in Rome. The Stoics placed a high value on reason and on the control of all aspects of life, including death. Self-murder was seen as a rational act that enabled a human to have control over the time and nature of his or her death. It could even have been considered a preferred method of dying, since it permitted a rational review of one's past life and future options as well as recognition that death is in the natural order of things. Stoicism had nothing to say, however, about those humans who took their own lives in an emotional state or as a result of nonrational motivations. It follows that the Stoics would easily understand, accept, and approve of the suicide of Socrates but would reject that of Saul.

One of the most famous Stoic suicides occurred in 65 A.D. when Seneca, a former teacher of the Roman Emperor Nero, was forced by his mad former pupil to take his own life. This suicide was noteworthy for two reasons: First, it seemed a fitting death for a man who was well known for his teaching that it is the quality rather than quantity of life that counts. Second, it led to the suicide of Seneca's wife, Paulina, which further underlined the quality-of-life arguments, since Paulina chose to die rather than experience the reduced quality of life she expected after her husband's death.

In a book that examined concrete cases of suicide in classical antiquity, Van Hoof (1990) detailed the complexity with which suicide was viewed in

---

Just as I shall select my ship when I am about to go on a voyage, or my house when I propose to take a residence, so I shall choose my death when I am about to depart from life. Seneca

Greek and Roman societies. He noted that the act of suicide could be met with the extremes of indifference and outspoken respect, but it was generally viewed with horror, condemnation, and disapproval. He reviewed cases of suicide and classified them into 11 categories of causation or motivation. According to Van Hoof, people in ancient Greece and Rome committed suicide out of despair or madness; because they were forced to take their own lives; because they were grieving or realized that they were no longer the beings they used to be; because of guilt; because of age or unbearable suffering; out of devotion to a cause or a person; or because they were showing off.

Suicide in Christianity

The beginning of the Christian era was marked by a famous suicide. Judas Iscariot, one of the twelve disciples of Jesus of Nazareth, hanged himself after the priests refused to take back the "blood money" they had paid him for his betrayal of Jesus. Once again, the Scriptures are noncommittal about this suicide, merely recording it as a historical fact. Possible motivations for the act include remorse for the betrayal, an attempt at atonement for his breach of faith (similar to the case of Samson), and an element of fulfilling prophecy (similar to the case of King Saul). Judas had heard Jesus predict the betrayal and had heard the accompanying observation: "But woe unto that man by whom the Son of Man is betrayed! It had been good for that man if he had not been born" (Matt. 26:24). For Judas, acting emotionally, and for millions of readers of the Gospel of Matthew over the centuries, this act of self-murder may represent just punishment for traitorous behavior.

The most controversial suicide by far included on the time line occurred at almost the exact moment in history as the suicide of Judas: the death of Jesus of Nazareth. Donne (1644/1982) was the first to assert that this death contained many elements of suicide. Donne, a devout Christian, maintained that Jesus of Nazareth, like Socrates, could have abandoned behaviors that led to his death. Moreover, Donne maintained that Jesus, unlike Socrates, could also have avoided death because of his divine nature. As a true divinity, he was all-powerful, Donne reasoned, and therefore could have chosen not to die. The fact that he did not choose to avoid death makes this particular death one of the earliest in recorded Christian history that might be classified as an altruistic suicide.

An alternative and more traditional view of the death of Jesus is that he was martyred, that is, that he was a victim of the wrath of others and that he chose to die for his principles. Those who hold this view take martyrdom to be clearly different from suicide. Martyrdom, they would suggest, occurs when an individual is put to death by others for his or her beliefs; suicide, on the other hand, occurs when an individual takes his or her own life for personal reasons. Given this distinction and discounting the argument that

Christ could have avoided death and therefore permitted himself to be killed, the death of Jesus would not be considered a suicide.

Regardless of whether one classifies the death of Jesus of Nazareth as altruistic suicide (following Donne's reasoning) or as martyrdom (following more traditional Christian thought), we include this death on our suicide time line because of its impact on attitudes toward suicide over the centuries. Jesus' death set in motion a series of historical events that caused the Catholic Church and, later, secular law to condemn suicide.

Because of the example inherent in the death of Jesus, many of the early Christians sought martyrdom as a way of asserting their belief and demonstrating the strength of their faith. By 400 A.D., the practice had grown to such dimensions that it could not be ignored. Alvarez (1970) pictured the early Christians as glorifying martyrdom, often seeking even flimsy reasons for which to give their lives in the faith. He concluded that "Christian teaching was at first a powerful incitement to suicide" (p. 68). The practice went so far that members of a sect called the Donatists killed themselves out of respect for martyrdom.

The frequency of martyrdom, as well as its growing appeal to early Christians, led St. Augustine around 400 A.D. to condemn self-killing, proclaiming it to be a sin. Some recent writers (e.g., Shneidman, 1985) have maintained that the basic reason for this condemnation was political: Augustine was concerned about the future of a religious movement that approved or even encouraged martyrdom. Augustine, however, took as the authority for viewing self-killing as sin the Sixth Commandment ("Thou shalt not kill"). He also argued that self-killing took the power of life and death out of the purview of the Creator and indicated a desire to avoid accepting the Divine Will in one's life.

Following Augustine's pronouncements, the Catholic Church, in a series of councils held across a period of 160 years, began to attach consequences to the act of suicide by Christians. The Council of Orleans in 533 denied funeral rites to people who killed themselves while accused of a crime; the Council of Braga in 563 refused funeral rites to all suicides regardless of social position, reason, or method; and the Council of Toledo in 693 passed a ruling excommunicating people who attempted or committed suicide (Alvarez, 1970).

For the next 500 years, organized Christianity continued to regard suicide as a mortal sin and to punish attempters, completers, and their families in various ways. Survivors could not inherit an estate from a suicide victim. The victim was excommunicated from the church, and burial was conducted in nonhallowed ground. Punishments were also inflicted on the corpses of suicide victims in order to impress upon others the deeply sinful nature of the act.

The next important milestone in the Church's view of suicide is found in the writings of St. Thomas Aquinas (1225–1274 A.D.). Aquinas tried to incorporate the teachings of Aristotle into prevailing Christian thought in his massive exposition *Summa Theologica* (1265–1272/1975). In this work, Aquinas gave three reasons to support his view that suicide is wrong. The first reason was that suicide is against natural inclination and therefore violates the physical and biological laws set down by the Creator. The second reason echoes Aristotle: Suicide damages the community, by depriving the community of the talents and energies of the suicide victim and by setting a bad example for others. The third reason is that suicide does not show proper respect for the most precious of all God-given gifts, life itself.

Growing out of these arguments against suicide came more specific doctrinal statements. For example, self-killing came to be viewed as a mortal sin because the individual who killed himself or herself could not confess the sin, atone for it, or benefit from the final sacrament of extreme unction. Suicide also came to be viewed as a sin because it revealed a lack of faith that God would provide for the needs of humans; the depression and despair often seen in suicidal people were thus interpreted as evidence of lack of hope brought about by a weakened or nonexistent faith in God. The desperation accompanying impulsive suicides was viewed either as the work of the devil or as final evidence that the victim had discounted the power of the Divine Saviour. In either case, the act itself was considered sinful—so sinful, in fact, that in 1284 at the Synod of Nimes, Christian burial was denied to suicides and they were forced to be buried in nonhallowed ground (Hutton & Valente, 1984). Soon after this statute was enforced, more punitive customs began to gain popularity. For example, it was not unusual for the bodies of suicide victims to be dragged behind carts or buried at crossroads with stakes in their hearts (Farberow, 1975).

By the time John Donne wrote *Biathanatos*, in the middle of the 17th century, church teaching about suicide had become rigid, and there was no doubt that suicide was considered one of the worst sins, perhaps the very worst, that humans could commit. In *Biathanatos*, Donne reexamined the case of self-killing and specifically argued against the points raised by the Christian church in declaring suicide a sin. It is telling that the book was shared with only a few close friends while Donne lived and that it was not published until after his death.

In their commentary, modern authors credit Donne with being the first to suggest that human beings have a natural desire to die as well as a desire to live. For this reason, Donne rather than Freud should perhaps be credited

---

Suicide is the worst form of murder, because it leaves no opportunity for repentance. Churton Collins, *Aphorisms*

as the first person to explicate the concept of Thanatos (the death wish). To support his claim that humans are attracted to death, Donne cited examples of group suicides as well as almost two dozen individual suicides. In a wide-ranging, well-informed discussion, he highlighted the practice of suttee in India, the group suicides of Jews at Masada, the suicides of New World Indians, and perhaps most tellingly, the suicides of the early Christian martyrs. Donne's modern interpreters argue that for Donne the desire to die on the part of the Christian martyrs was less a wish for self-destruction than a measure of their faith, their desire to change their current pattern of existence, and their belief in the "spiritual comforts of the afterlife" (Donne, 1644/1982, p. 111).

Donne did not endorse widespread self-murder, but he did recognize that suicide occurs for many reasons, and he argued that individuals who kill themselves in order to promote the glory of God do not sin. In this way, Donne is perhaps the first author to call attention to the motivation for or intention behind a given suicide as a determining factor in whether it should be considered right or wrong. Donne also foreshadowed one side of a current ethical debate when he proclaimed that there is no moral difference between acts of omission and acts of commission in taking one's own life. Donne thus would label as suicidal a man who allowed himself to be killed by an enemy without trying to defend himself, a woman who starved herself for a principle, a man who chose to go without medical care for an increasingly serious physical condition, or a woman who shot or poisoned herself. He would not, however, necessarily judge any of them as sinners. Rather, the *intention* behind the act would determine the sinfulness of the act. In this context, Donne also foreshadowed some of the elements of Kohlberg's (1976) modern theory of moral development, which maintains that it is not the behavior but the reason behind the behavior that determines the level of morality of an act. In the end, however, *Biathanatos* did not argue for a legalization of suicide or even a lessening of the strictures against suicidal people and their families. Donne finally approved only one kind of suicide, that carried out for the glory of God. Suicides of all other kinds seemed to Donne to be based on the suicidal person's own desire for comfort rather than on God's will; he therefore concluded that such suicides should not be allowed.

The next date on the time line is 1651, which until recently has been thought to be the year when the word *suicide* was introduced into the English language. Van Hoof (1990) has recently documented, however, that the word

---

Death may be called in vain, and cannot come, Tyrants can tie him up from your relief: Nor has a Christian privilege to die. Alas, thou art too young in thy new faith. Brutus and Cato might discharge their souls: But we like sentries are obliged to stand in starless nights, and wait th' appointed hour. Dryden, *Don Sebastian,* Act II, Sc. 1

was used by the writer Gauthier of Saint-Victor in the 12th century. Regardless of the date it was first introduced, the word did not come into widespread use until the debates that took place during the middle of the 17th century concerning the morality of suicide (Barraclough & Shepherd, 1994). There is some difference of opinion about the origin of the word. Farberow (1975) suggests two possible derivations: first, that it derives from the word *suist*, meaning "a selfish man." The second suggestion, perhaps more believable, is that it derives from the Latin word *suicidium*. The Latin roots of this word seem clear: *sui*, a pronoun meaning "himself" or "herself," and *cedo*, a verb meaning "to give up."

In 1670, under the influence of the Christian religion, legislation was passed making suicide a triple crime: murder, treason, and heresy (Farberow, 1975). This was the period in which punishment became common both for the deceased and for his or her family. Aries (1981) pointed out that

> *men of the middle ages and of early modern times did not believe that the cause of justice or of legal action stopped with the death of the defendant. In the case of a suicide, they prosecuted the dead man in court, and his body was ejected from the cemetery. (p. 44)*

Suicide in Secular Society

An important milestone in the history of suicide occurred in 1763, when Merian, a Frenchman, published a treatise that attempted to establish that suicide was neither a crime nor a sin but resulted from emotional illness (Merian, 1763). This was followed by Hume's *An Essay on Suicide* (1783/1929). In this work, Hume argued that suicide was not a crime against God, neighbors, or self, and therefore did not deserve the extreme punishments common at that time.

The 19th century witnessed writings on the topic of suicide by philosophers as well as by scientists and medical doctors. In 1838, Esquirol, writing from a medical perspective, echoed Merian's earlier sentiment that people who commit suicide suffer from a mental condition or are insane. With the rise of existentialism, philosophers such as Kierkegaard and Nietzsche (followed by Heidegger, Sartre, and Camus in the 20th century) introduced the idea that individual freedom to act and responsibility for one's acts are fundamental characteristics of the human condition. Many considered suicide merely one more act that a human being had to make a decision about (or a

---

To attempt suicide is a criminal offense. Any man who, of his own will, tries to escape the treadmill to which the rest of us feel chained incites our envy, and therefore our fury. We do not suffer him to go unpunished. Alexander Chase, *Perspectives*

The Suicide, **Thomas Rowlandson. Pen and watercolor drawing. (Courtesy of the Boston Public Library, Print Department, Albert H. Wiggin Collection.)**

series of decisions over a lifetime), weighing both freedom and responsibility to self and others.

In all countries for which data existed, suicidal behavior increased throughout the 19th century, largely as a result of the industrial revolution (Chesnais, 1992). As the industrial revolution grew in strength and spread geographically across Europe and the United States, old patterns of living were disrupted, workers were exploited, and extended families and community structures disintegrated. In short, people were left to face a changed, more hostile world with fewer supports than they could previously have expected from family, community, and church. The more industrialization occurred, the more widespread the dislocation in society became and the higher the suicide rate climbed. For example, Anderson (1987) observed that in the middle of the 19th century,

London seems to have been a place where those who took their own lives were very often neither sober nor in good health; where both their living and their dying were improvised and rough; where the strains of close relationships had been very familiar but not those of loneliness; where the humblest and most destitute suicides of all were women, not men; and where in their last moments those who destroyed themselves rarely fully knew what they were doing. (p. 420)

The 19th century closed with the publication of one of the most influential books of all time on the subject of suicide, Emile Durkheim's *Le Suicide* (1897/1951). The content of this work is discussed in detail in chapter 2. It remains an influential work to this day for two reasons: First, it made a case for using sociological methods to understand an individual phenomenon. According to Durkheim, when a person commits suicide, one must investigate not only the particulars of the individual situation but also the values of the society and the amount of integration or isolation the suicidal individual experienced. Second, Durkheim introduced the first widely discussed typology for classifying suicides, a practice that would proliferate in the 20th century.

The 20th century witnessed a major turnabout in attitudes toward suicide. Christianity began to consider routinely the state of mind of a suicide victim at the time of the act as an extenuating circumstance. In this way, the church could be less judgmental toward a suicide victim and the survivors because the victim could be viewed not as a sinner condemned to hell but as someone whose mind was unclear and therefore not subject to judgment. Although the philosophy of crisis intervention had already begun, attitudes toward suicide remained contradictory well after the midpoint of the century. Still officially condemned by the Catholic Church as a mortal sin, suicide was also viewed as the ultimate evil by many other religious sects. For example, the Church of Jesus Christ of Latter Day Saints (commonly known as the Mormons), one of the fastest growing denominations in the 20th century, maintained that

mortal life is a gift of God; it comes according to the divine will, is appointed to endure for such time as Deity decrees, and is designed to serve as the chief testing period of man's [sic] eternal existence. No man has the right to run away from these tests, no matter how severe they may be, by taking his own life. (McConkie, 1966, p. 771). [Copyright © by Bookcraft, Inc. Used by permission.]

The treatise went on to make the now common exception based on mental condition: "Obviously persons subject to great stresses may lose control of themselves and become mentally clouded to the point that they are no longer accountable for their acts. Such are not to be condemned for taking their own lives" (p. 771).

In contrast, one of the oldest non-Christian religions in the world, Judaism, has relied on its historical traditions for its interpretations. The Jewish position throughout history has been to abhor suicide and to relegate the punishment for suicide to God in the hereafter. However, the Talmudic tradition has recognized and accepted (if not approved) suicides that fit in two different categories: The first encompasses suicides that occur when death is imminent and that enable people to avoid a painful or disgraceful demise. Examples of such suicides include King Saul and the deaths of 960 Jewish defenders of Masada in 73 A.D. The second category contains suicides that are committed to avoid abandoning the Jewish faith.

Cohn (1976) reviewed suicide in the Jewish legal and religious tradition and concluded that it is difficult to prove that any given death is a suicide. He stated that "suicide can be proved only by two eyewitnesses who saw the actor committing the act after having been warned by them, or after having declared to them, that it was forbidden and unlawful to do so" (p. 36). Thus, in the Jewish tradition, both the motivation for suicide and the state of mind of the individual committing the act are taken into consideration. In addition, the term suicide is not applied to minors, because they are not capable of forming the necessary criminal intent, or to depressed or mentally disturbed persons. Although it is difficult to determine when a suicide has occurred, the Jewish tradition still employs some punishments for the act when it can be documented:

> *Still, Jewish ritual denies the suicide certain honours due to the dead: suicides are given no funeration orations, and the mourners' clothes may not be rent for them. In many places it has become customary to set aside a particular portion of the cemetery for the burial of suicides, so as not to bury the wicked next to the righteous. The general rule is that on the death of the suicide you do everything in honour of the surviving, such as visit, comfort, and console them, but you do nothing in honour of the dead apart from burying them. (Cohn, 1976, pp. 135–136)*

Not only has the act of suicide been condemned less heartily by the Christian church in the 20th century, it has also come to be viewed less harshly from other perspectives. As secularism increased, suicide came to be regarded less as a sin and more as a sign of mental illness. This change in view was not altogether positive, however, as families of suicide victims often found themselves trying to cover up the cause of the death rather than face the disgrace of having to admit "insanity" in the family.

Freud published two important works that added to the understanding of suicide as mental illness. The first was *Mourning and Melancholia* (1917/1961a), in which he introduced intrapsychic reasons for suicide. He maintained that suicide results when anger, harbored by the id toward some outside force, is turned inward upon the ego. In this work, he also laid the foundation for his concept of Thanatos, the death instinct. In a later work, *The Ego and the Id* (1923/1961b), Freud returned to the theme, stating in effect that suicide could be caused because the superego for many complex reasons could become "a pure culture of the death instinct" and turn its full strength against the ego (p. 53).

At the same time that Freud's theories were spreading throughout the Western world, the influence of the scientific method was also spreading. Inevitably, that methodology was directed toward the study of suicide. In 1958, with the aid of a five-year grant from the U.S. Public Health Service, Shneidman and his colleagues established the first suicide prevention center in the United States. That center was designed to address the nonmedical needs of suicidal people. It had three major goals: (1) to save lives, (2) to serve as a major public health agency for the Los Angeles community, and (3) to test various hypotheses concerning suicidal phenomena. Thus, this center had a clinical mission, a community service mission, and a research mission. The Los Angeles center quickly became the model for suicide intervention and prevention centers throughout the United States during the last half of the 20th century.

The importance of the Los Angeles Suicide Prevention Center cannot be overstated in any history of suicide. In addition to its critical lifesaving work, this important center carried out studies and began to build a wealth of factual material. The center marked the beginning of research into suicide using the scientific method of inquiry, a process that has yielded a great deal of the information shared in later chapters of this book. The work begun in that center by Shneidman and his associates and expanded upon later, when Shneidman became director of the National Institute of Mental Health, changed the nation's view of suicide and suicidal behavior. The most important change was a shift away from seeing suicide as an act committed by an insane person or a lost sinner to seeing it as an act committed by a person who felt overwhelming ambivalence toward life. Suicidal people came to be regarded as individuals who needed help to find reasons to live, and the view of suicide as a cry for help became common. The major implication of this new view was that an interruption in the trajectory toward suicide might result in an individual changing his or her mind; as a result, crisis intervention centers became commonplace in urban areas. Many were and still are staffed by volunteers trained to handle the emergency situation until longer-term supportive therapy can be arranged.

As the twentieth century nears its end, the research orientation begun by Shneidman at the Los Angeles Suicide Prevention Center has been extended by other researchers into the biological and chemical realms. For example, research into the chemistry of the brain is making valuable contributions to our understanding of suicide. Chapter 2 documents some of the major findings to date. Another major avenue of research and theory formation, also discussed in chapter 2, has emerged from the work of Beck and his colleagues into the cognitive characteristics of depression (Beck, Rush, Show, & Emery, 1979). Building upon the techniques of the behavioral school of psychology, these therapists have attempted in practice to modify the rigid and perfectionistic thinking patterns common to depressed, suicidal people.

Still another influence on attitudes toward suicide in the latter half of the 20th century has been the spectacular increase in medical discoveries and the rapid development of medical technology. Beginning with the discovery of penicillin by Fleming in 1928, medicine has become increasingly able to prolong life. Life expectancy increased by almost 30 years from the beginning of the 20th century until the present because of improved understanding of the disease process, improvements in childbirth procedures, advances in the prevention and treatment of disease, and technological advances in the treatment of traumas and terminal illness. Ironically, the capability to prolong life beyond any useful function with the aid of such devices as respirators has set the stage for heated ethical debates about the right to die and has blurred the lines between suicide and euthanasia, a subject that will be discussed in detail in chapter 10.

While many people differentiate between euthanasia and suicide, many others think the purported distinction is a matter of splitting hairs, questioning whether there is any real difference between actively taking your own life and creating the conditions for your own death. John Brantner, for example, an early leader in the study of death and dying, actively took his own life early in the 1990s. His suicide seemed to be a response to the knowledge that he was terminally ill and to be based on a wish to retain control of his life and the mode of his death. Because he had been a public figure in the so-called death movement, his suicide was widely publicized. Some people assumed that his suicide was a form of self-performed euthanasia, that he had chosen what for him was "an appropriate death," that he had indeed "died with dignity." Some critics, however, condemned his action, stating that suicide under any circumstance is wrong and that the principle of the sanctity of life must be defended no matter what the situation. These same critics would insist that a terminally ill woman who carefully orders her affairs, enters a hospital stating that her wish is to die, and declines nourishment is as guilty of suicide as was Brantner since she too arranged the conditions of her death. To these critics, terminating life or allowing it to be terminated violates the principle that God is the only judge of when and how a person should die.

The majority of people probably hold a moderate position on the subject. Two principles seem to be important in the thinking of the moderates: The first is that the rights of the individual are primary in any situation; the second is that death is both natural and inevitable, and that it is not necessarily the province of God alone. In support of these principles, every state in the

United States has passed some form of "right to die" legislation (National Council for the Right to Die, personal communication, 1994). Such legislation, while differing in language from state to state, endorses the right of persons to refuse treatment as well as the right to establish the conditions under which they would wish to die. It is clear that many of the legislators in these states, since they ascribe to both of these laws, do not believe that arranging the circumstances of one's death under controlled conditions and while one is in good mental health is a form of suicide. One key to understanding the difference between suicide and euthanasia, according to the moderates, lies in the action necessary to bring about death. Passive euthanasia (i.e., allowing an individual to die by withholding treatment, food, or water) is allowable; active euthanasia (i.e., helping an individual to die by injecting a lethal dose of pain killing drugs or by cutting off life support systems) is not allowable. Active euthanasia is covered by the laws against aiding and abetting suicide.

It is clear that in the closing years of the 20th century, the issues of suicide and euthanasia are intertwined and controversial. Organizations such as Concern for Dying and EXIT are vocal in their insistence on the individual's right to death with dignity. The Hemlock Society, established in England, has introduced the term *rational suicide* into their publications. Derek Humphrey's book *Final Exits* (1991), which describes both the rationale for and methods of suicide, made the best-seller list in the United States for 18 successive weeks. Thomas Szasz (1986) has argued that suicide should be given the "status of a basic human right" and that the "power of the state should not be legitimately involved or deployed to prohibit or prevent persons from killing themselves" (p. 811). At the time of this writing, Dr. Jack Kevorkian, a physician who has assisted with or been present at the death of more than a score of critically ill people, has become the symbol of the national debate in the United States on physician-assisted suicide. *The Congressional Quarterly* devoted a full issue in 1992 to the topic of assisted suicide (Worsnop, 1992; see chapter 10 for a review). The vigor of the debate raging internationally attests to the confusion that still exists about these topics.

The debate on this question will not be easily settled because it is rooted in the centuries-old emotionally laden negative attitudes toward suicide that this chapter has so far examined. Although the controversy is not likely to be entirely settled in the remaining years of the 20th century, it has provoked much thought and discussion and has created the conditions for a reexamination of all facets of suicide.

TOWARD A DEFINITION OF SUICIDE

Thus far, we have examined suicide across time and to a lesser extent across cultures. It is clear that attitudes toward the act of suicide are dependent upon many factors. For example, the dominant religion of a given period may embrace martyrs for the faith, as in the early days of Christianity, or condemn suicidal persons to posthumous punishments, as in the years between St. Thomas Aquinas's writings and the advent of science in the 1900s. Also, in this century as in the time of the Stoics, before passing judgment many people seek to discover the motivation of an individual who commits or tries to commit suicide. Is the individual aged and infirm, in the throes of terminal pain, psychotic, depressed, or emotionally overwrought and impulsive? The answers to such questions now color our reaction and response to any given suicide.

Up to this point, we have discussed suicide without defining the term. In our historical overview we have mentioned suicides that today might be viewed as active euthanasia (e.g., King Saul), forced suicides that today might be considered substitutes for murder (e.g., Socrates), and altruistic suicides, wherein an individual lays down his or her life for a greater good or for another person (e.g., Jesus and the early Christian martyrs). We have also regarded all of these types of self-induced death as forms of suicide.

For the purposes of the remainder of this book, we will adopt a broad definition for the term *suicide*. Shneidman (1985) devoted a whole book to defining suicide, concluding with a definition that is perhaps the clearest to date: "Currently in the Western world, suicide is a conscious act of self-induced annihilation, best understood as a multidimensional malaise in a needful individual who defines an issue for which the suicide is perceived as the best solution" (p. 203). We accept Shneidman's definition with one addition: We believe that a broad definition of suicide should be consistent with the moderate view of euthanasia. A terminally ill person may not manifest "multidimensional malaise" as he or she actively seeks to terminate life, yet we view active euthanasia but not passive euthanasia as suicide. We accept Shneidman's definition because it clearly recognizes that any definition of suicide is "time bound" and relative to the society in which it takes place. A 10-year-old child who knowingly stands in the path of oncoming traffic and is killed would be classified as a suicide according to this definition. So would an airplane pilot who chooses to go down with her plane rather than ditch it over a heavily populated area. So would an elderly man who takes an overdose of medication, thus hastening his death. So, obviously, would people who shoot or hang themselves or find other ways of shortening their lives.

THE STATISTICAL PICTURE

Even as awareness of the complexities surrounding suicide grows, the number of suicides continues to increase throughout the world. One of the central features of the information age we live in is our ability to collect reliable data about any phenomenon that occurs, at least in developed countries.

Table 1.2 lists suicide rates for selected countries by sex and age group. It shows that suicide remains an issue in the 13 countries that reported their suicide statistics between 1988 and 1990, and that suicide rates vary widely among these countries, with Italy, the geographical home of the Catholic Church, reporting the lowest figures for males and Austria reporting the highest figures for males. For females, the lowest rates are reported by the United Kingdom and the highest rates by Denmark. The United States ranks 10th among the countries in its rate of both male and female suicide.

Table 1.2 also shows that the patterns of suicide vary by sex and age among the countries reporting suicide statistics, a point that is pertinent to the focus of this volume. In every country reporting, males show higher suicide rates than females at every age level. In general, suicide tends to increase with age. Closer examination of the pattern of suicide by age in Table 1.2 shows that for males the pattern is generally linear. With only a few exceptions in the middle years, suicide increases across the life span for males in all countries. For females, the pattern is more variable. In Canada, women aged 35 to 44 show the highest rates. In three countries (the United States, the Netherlands, and Sweden), suicide among women peaks during the age range between 45 and 54. In three other countries (Australia, Denmark, and Poland), suicide among women peaks during the period from 55 to 64. In the remaining six countries (Austria, France, Italy, Japan, the United Kingdom, and West Germany), the suicide rate of women mirrors that of men, increasing in frequency across the life span. Having established that suicide is a worldwide phenomenon, we will now turn our attention to a detailed picture of suicide in the United States.

The combined U.S. suicide rates for whites and blacks, males and females, and for the sexes and races in 1992 are presented in Table 1.3. As shown in this table, the suicide rate for whites is approximately double that of the African American rate, and the ratio of male to female suicides is approximately 4:1. Upon closer examination, the table shows that the sex difference in suicide rates is greater for African Americans than for whites, primarily because of the very low suicide rate for African American women. Also, as will be illustrated repeatedly throughout this book, white males have the highest suicide rates of any group.

It is clear from our discussion that suicide is an immensely complex and relatively common human behavior. Motivations for taking one's life have differed across the centuries, from the ancient Eskimos permitting themselves to freeze to death for the good of the community to the Greek Stoics supporting rational suicide as a "proper" way to die to the early Christian martyrs who sought death to imitate their Lord to depressed young people in today's culture killing themselves out of a sense of hopelessness and despair. When suicide is a threat, it is not enough simply to examine the individual's mental state. We must begin to look at the culture in which the individual is raised,

TABLE 1.2 Suicide Rates per 100,000 Population for Selected Countries, by Sex and Age Group

Sex and Age	United States 1989	Australia 1988	Austria 1990	Canada 1990	Denmark 1990	France 1989	Italy 1988	Japan 1990	Netherlands 1989	Poland 1990	Sweden 1988	United Kingdom[1] 1990	West Germany 1989
Male													
Total[2]	20.0	21.0	34.8	20.4	32.2	30.5	11.1	20.4	13.0	22.0	26.4	12.1	23.5
15–24 yrs. old	22.0	27.8	25.0	25.2	14.1	15.8	4.9	9.2	8.9	16.2	18.2	11.7	14.7
25–34 yrs. old	24.4	28.2	32.7	29.3	26.7	32.2	9.1	18.4	15.4	30.4	29.8	16.0	22.7
35–44 yrs. old	22.4	26.0	37.3	26.3	44.5	37.4	9.9	21.5	15.6	33.0	31.8	17.1	21.6
45–54 yrs. old	22.7	24.4	47.7	22.7	53.0	39.2	12.1	32.0	17.3	38.4	38.2	16.4	30.8
55–64 yrs. old	24.8	23.8	44.0	22.9	43.7	38.9	16.2	32.5	19.9	36.3	37.0	18.3	31.5
65–74 yrs. old	33.6	27.7	66.8	20.8	47.3	52.9	28.3	36.6	21.1	28.0	36.4	13.6	39.4
75 yrs. old and over	54.5	39.8	107.6	32.7	76.7	107.2	47.4	62.9	29.0	27.3	47.2	19.4	75.6
Female													
Total[2]	4.8	5.6	13.4	5.3	16.3	11.7	4.4	12.4	7.5	4.5	11.5	3.7	10.0
15–24 yrs. old	4.2	4.5	5.5	5.1	4.0	4.6	1.4	4.7	4.4	2.8	5.9	2.0	4.2
25–34 yrs. old	5.6	7.2	8.4	6.5	6.9	9.2	2.7	9.0	7.2	4.3	11.3	3.8	6.9
35–44 yrs. old	6.6	7.5	13.9	8.9	18.4	13.0	3.6	9.2	7.5	6.0	17.1	4.5	7.9
45–54 yrs. old	7.4	8.2	16.5	7.3	27.3	17.4	5.7	15.0	13.8	7.4	20.5	5.1	13.0
55–64 yrs. old	7.3	8.7	20.8	5.5	31.5	19.4	7.3	17.6	12.6	8.7	14.5	5.3	13.7
65–74 yrs. old	5.9	7.4	22.0	6.0	30.0	20.2	9.7	25.3	13.4	7.2	15.3	6.1	18.2
75 yrs. old and over	6.0	10.0	35.5	4.2	32.2	25.7	11.1	48.6	10.8	7.4	13.8	6.2	22.7

[1]England and Wales only   [2]Includes under 15 years old not shown separately.

Source: U.S. Bureau of the Census, (1994). *Statistical Abstract of the United States.* 114th Ed. Washington, DC: U.S. Government Printing Office.

TABLE 1.3   U.S. Suicide Rates per
100,000 population for 1992 by Sex and
Race

	Both Sexes	Males	Females
All Races	11.1	18.4	4.3
Whites	11.8	19.5	4.6
Blacks	6.9	11.8	2.5

Source: National Center for Health Statistics
(1994). Advance report of final mortality statistics,
1992. *Monthly Vital Statistics Report, 43.* Hyattsville,
MD: Public Health Service.

the family environment, the biological constitution the person inherited, the
relationships the individual has experienced throughout his or her lifetime,
the current physical and psychological health of the individual, the religious
beliefs that he or she holds, and the messages he or she gives himself or herself on a minute-to-minute basis about the value of his or her personal existence. Certainly, keeping all of these circumstances in mind is difficult. What
is needed is a model of suicide that imposes order on the disparate strands
of the research while capturing the complexity of the suicidal act. The model
that follows organizes the literature into four major categories of risk factors
that contribute to suicidal ideation and behavior.

THE SUICIDE TRAJECTORY

Figure 1.1 presents the Suicide Trajectory Model, which we believe cap-
tures and organizes much of the burgeoning literature that attempts to explain suicidal behavior. Each of this book's developmental chapters (chapters
three to seven) organizes its review and discussion of the literature using this
model. In the remainder of this chapter, we will examine each of the elements
of the model and discuss the commonalities that exist in suicidal behavior
regardless of age.

The model suggests that there are four major categories of risk factors
that must be examined whenever one is attempting to study or work with
suicidal individuals. The risk factor categories are biological, psychological,
cognitive, and environmental (McDowell & Stillion, 1994; Stillion & McDowell, 1991; Stillion, McDowell, & May, 1989).

---

*Suicidal phenomena ARE enormously complex.—In suicidology, no one specialty has a strangle-
hold on truth. We must listen to several voices, each of which may represent legitimate aspects among
the relevant specialties.* E.S. Shneidman, *Suicide: Understanding and responding*

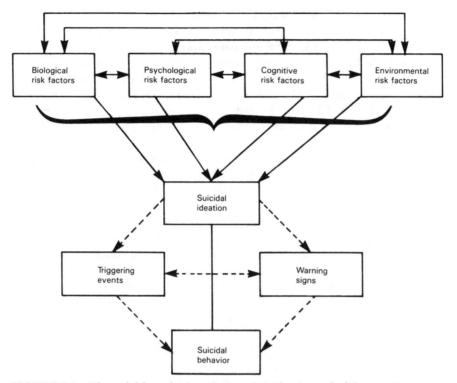

FIGURE 1.1   The suicide trajectory *Source: Suicide across the life span: Premature exits*, **(p. 240) by J. M. Stillion, E. E. McDowell, and J. H. May, 1989, New York: Hemisphere.**

These risk factors may influence each other, as shown by the interconnecting arrows in the figure. As we move through life, we encounter situations and events that add their weight to each risk factor category. When the combined weight of these risk factors reaches the point where coping skills are threatened with collapse, suicidal ideation is born. Once present, suicidal ideation seems to feed upon itself. It may be exhibited in warning signs and may be intensified by triggering events. In the final analysis, however, when the suicide attempt is made, it occurs because of the contributions of the four risk categories. Understanding any individual suicidal person requires probing into and exposing the life experiences of patients in each of these risk factor categories. A general understanding of suicidal risk requires a knowledge of the ways in which these risk factors contribute to suicide across the life span, as well as the ways in which predictable life events may increase suicidal risk at various stages across the life cycle.

Commonalities in Risk Factors Across the Life Span

The risk factors, warning signs, and triggering events that have been found to be common in suicidal behavior among people of all ages are presented in Table 1.4. The material presented in this section will be confined to the commonalities in the suicide trajectory; comparable tables and discussions for specific age groups will be presented in chapters three through seven.

Biological Risk Factors Evidence of a biological base or substrate to suicidal behavior is accumulating from three separate types of research: research on brain functioning at the cellular level, research into possible genetic bases of suicidal behavior, and research into behaviors associated with being male or female. Much of this research has been carried out with depressed patients who may or may not have reached the point of being suicidal. While nondepressed people may take their lives, the great majority of suicidal people report depression as a major symptom. One psychiatrist has estimated that "direct suicide claims the lives of at least 15% of depressed patients" (Gold, 1986, p. 205). It is important, therefore, to review what is known about the biological basis of depression in order to shed light on suicide.

Depression is listed in Table 1.4 as a biological risk factor for suicide because a growing body of research indicates that neurotransmitters in the brains of depressed people may play a role in depression and, indirectly, in suicide (Asberg & Traskman, 1981; Banki & Arato, 1983; Schildkraut, 1965). Although research is continuing on a number of these chemicals, such as acetylcholine and norepinephrine, the most provocative research for students of suicide has been conducted on serotonin. Serotonin is a substance that has been implicated in the regulation of emotion. A deficiency of serotonin has been found in the brains of some people who have committed suicide (Asberg, Traskman, & Thoren, 1976). In addition, one of the main metabolic products of serotonin (5-HIAA) has been shown to be correlated both with depression and with the seriousness of suicide attempts. Two major studies have shown that among groups of patients hospitalized for a suicide attempt, those who had lower levels of 5-HIAA during hospitalization were significantly more likely to have died from suicide a year later than were those who had higher levels (Asberg, Traskman, & Thoren, 1976; Nordstrom et al., 1994). This research, while clearly in its early stages, has lent credibility to drug approaches for treating suicidal people.

A second line of research into the biological basis of suicide has attempted to tease out possible genetic components by studying monozygotic twins and suicide across generations in the same family. In a review of this research, Blumenthal and Kupfer (1986) cited three intriguing findings: First, they reviewed data that showed that half of a sample of psychiatric inpatients who had a family history of suicide had attempted suicide themselves. They then reviewed a study that reported 10 cases of identical twins who committed suicide compared to no recorded cases of fraternal twins in which both had

TABLE 1.4 Life Cycle Commonalities in the Suicide Trajectory

Age Group	Biological Risk Factors	Psychological Risk Factors	Cognitive Risk Factors	Environmental Risk Factors	Warning Signs	Triggering Events	Suicidal Behavior
Life Cycle commonalities	Depression Genetic factors Male sex	Depression Low self-esteem Hopelessness Existential issues Poor coping strategies	Developmental level Negative self-talk Cognitive rigidity Generalization Selective abstraction Inexact labeling	Negative family experiences Negative life events (loss) Presence of firearms	Verbal threats Previous suicide attempts	"Final straw" life event	Ambivalence

committed suicide. Finally, they reviewed a study of 57 adoptees who had committed suicide. Among their biological relatives, 12 (4.5%) had also committed suicide, while no adopting relatives had committed suicide. Among a matched group of 57 adoptees who did not commit suicide, only two (0.7%) of their biological relatives and none of their adoptive relatives had committed suicide. Later work reported by Gold (1986) showed a familiar pattern in suicide among the Amish, who have strict religious taboos against suicide. Researchers found a total of 26 suicides across the last century in a Pennsylvania Amish group. Of these, 73% occurred within four families. The researchers have suggested that, since other Amish families experiencing mood disorders did not have suicides, their findings provide support for the inheritability of suicide. While this line of research is by its very nature indirect, it does indicate some support for a genetic component in suicidal behavior.

The third area of research into biological bases of suicide began with the observation that, in all developed countries where suicide statistics are kept, males complete suicide more often than females. Table 1.2 showed comparative figures for male and female suicide across cultures, indicating that male deaths by suicide are three to five times more common than female deaths by suicide.

When a behavior shows consistent sex differences across cultures, there is reason to suspect that biology may play a role in establishing a threshold or susceptibility for that behavior. A cursory examination of the literature on sex differences finds support for the idea that the differences in suicide rates by sex may be related to other well-documented sex differences. Human males, as well as the males of other species, display higher levels of aggression at earlier ages than do females (Goy & Resko, 1972; Hoyenga & Hoyenga, 1979; Maccoby & Jacklin, 1974; Mitchell, 1979; Money & Ehrhardt, 1972; Svare & Gandelman, 1975; Unger, 1979). If suicide can be viewed as aggression turned inward, it would follow that male suicides would outnumber those of females. Since the Y chromosome inherited from the father defines maleness, this line of research has been interpreted as indirect support for a genetic component in suicidal behavior.

Perhaps the most important insight in the area of biology as it relates to suicide can be gleaned from Akiskal and McKinney's work on depressive disorders (1973). These authors maintain that there is always a biological component to true depression. Whether the individual inherits a genetic tendency toward depression or not, when there are sufficient environmental, psychological and/or cognitive reasons, the resulting stress comes to be expressed biologically, changing the chemistry of the brain and adding a physical component, which they call the "final, common pathway," to depressive and suicidal behavior. One young college student described his dramatic recovery from a serious depression in the following manner:

I knew the minute that the drugs took hold. It was as though someone turned the lights on in a darkened room. My life's situation hadn't changed. I still was hopelessly behind in my courses and my social life was caput, but it didn't seem so grim anymore. I could handle it again. Nothing had changed and yet everything had changed.

While not all improvements are as spectacular as this, the success of drugs in counteracting the biological bases of depression mandates that therapists learn about drugs used to combat depression and work closely with physicians in monitoring the effects of drugs as an adjunct to therapy.

Psychological Risk Factors Psychological risk factors form the second category to be explored with suicidal patients. As shown in Table 1.4, we include within the psychological category such elements as depressed mood, feelings of helplessness and hopelessness, poor self-concept and low self-esteem, poorly developed ego defense mechanisms and coping strategies, and existential questions concerning the meaning in life.

Although we have stated that there is a biological component to most if not all severe depression, depression must also be discussed as a psychological risk factor. Depression tends to be perceived by those suffering from it as a psychological rather than a physiological syndrome; that is, depressed people talk more about their feelings than about their physical condition. Also, inherent in a diagnosis of depression are the elements of poor self-concept and low self-esteem. Individuals who see themselves positively and value themselves highly are rarely depressed.

A growing body of research, however, supports the idea that hopelessness outweighs depression, poor self-concept, and low self-esteem as the major psychological factor leading to suicide (Goldney, 1981; Kazdin, French, Unis, Esveldt-Dawson, & Sherick, 1983; Wetzel, 1976). One study found that the level of hopelessness was a stronger predictor of attempted and completed suicide than the level of depression (Beck, Steer, Kovacs, & Garrison, 1985). While hopelessness may be associated with depression, it is possible to be depressed and still have hope. When hopelessness is high, however, and especially when it is coupled with feelings of helplessness, suicidal risk greatly increases.

Suicidal people also have reached the limit of their coping strategies. The ego defense mechanisms they have learned to use have not been effective and have left them without adequate tools to confront their present life situations. People working with suicidal persons should be willing to explore the types of defense mechanisms the person used in the past and the reasons they are no longer effective. They may also have to teach new coping strategies directly.

Finally, depressed and suicidal persons generally struggle at some level with existential issues, questioning the meaning of life. "From the existential perspective under the *best* conditions life is short, painful, fickle, often lonely, and anxiety generating" (Maris, 1981, pp. xviii–xix). Suicidal people often view living as an empty exercise. One suicidal woman expressed it this way:

> *I don't think I'll ever feel better. But even if I do, what's the use? It's all illusion anyway. All those people thinking that their little lives mean something. They'll all be dead in 100 years. In 200, nobody will even remember that they lived. What's it all about anyway?*

Care givers need to be prepared to face and deal with such nihilism in the suicidal people with whom they work.

Cognitive Risk Factors   The category of cognitive risk factors is assuming growing importance as we come to realize the power our thoughts and words have to maintain or change mental states. This category can best be viewed as consisting of three major parts: The first is the cognitive level that a person has attained. From a Piagetian point of view, we attain our understandings of the world slowly, passing through stages that include sensorimotor, preoperational, concrete operational, and formal operational thinking (Piaget & Inhelder, 1969). Understanding which stage a child or adolescent is at is important in assessing their suicide risk as well as in deciding strategies for treatment. For example, a suicidal child who is in the preoperational stage of cognitive development may be at special risk for suicide because children at this stage do not understand that death is permanent and irreversible.

A second component of the cognitive risk factor lies in the messages we tell ourselves about ourselves and the way we fit into the larger world. Meichenbaum (1985) has identified these messages as "self-talk." He maintains that poor adjustment is fostered by negative self-talk and that positive self-talk can promote better adjustment. Suicidal people tend to carry on continuous negative self-talk, which reinforces an already negative mind-set and accelerates suicidal ideation.

The third and most important category of cognitions influencing depression and suicide has been elaborated by Beck and his colleagues (Beck, Rush, Show, & Emery, 1979). They have shown that depressed people develop rigidity of thought. Individuals who think in this way tend to see the world as presenting black or white, good or bad, live or die choices. They are unable to see the shades of gray or to imagine multiple outcomes in a situation. In addition, cognitively rigid people typically engage in three types of thinking that may predispose them to developing suicidal ideation. These include overgeneralization, selective abstraction, and inexact labeling. Overgeneralization is the tendency to view the world pessimistically and to pile negatives upon negatives. Selective abstraction is the tendency to focus on the negative and to ignore or deemphasize the positives in one's life. Inexact labeling occurs when an individual places a negative label on himself or herself and reacts to the label rather than to the situation at hand.

Environmental Risk Factors   The final category of risk factors is environmental. Much research exists to show that environmental factors do influence suicidal behavior. Negative family experiences have been shown to be correlated with suicidal thoughts and behavior (Bock & Webber, 1972a; Garfinkel, Froese, & Hood, 1982; Pfeffer, 1986). In the families of suicidal children, abuse and neglect are common, as are parental discord and disorganization in the homes of suicidal adolescents (Pfeffer, 1991). Suicidal adults are much more likely to be living in a discordant home or to be single, divorced, or widowed than to be happily married (Stephens, 1985). Suicidal elderly people are more likely than their peers to suffer loneliness and isolation from their families and others (Darbonne, 1969). We have evidence, then, that across the life span poor home environments are important elements feeding into suicide.

A second environmental factor associated with suicide is the occurrence of negative life events, especially those involving loss. Loss of any kind, whether a relationship, a job, prestige, or a loved one through death, triggers a depressive reaction in nonsuicidal people. For those already considering suicide, such losses, particularly if they come close together, may be the final blows in destroying their weakened or fragmented coping techniques.

A final environmental factor related to suicidal behavior is the easy access to instruments of self-destruction. In many suicides, it is the availability of firearms that makes a suicide attempt easy—and fatal. One authority has gone so far as to point out that the rise in suicide during the last three decades can be accounted for almost entirely by the rise in deaths caused by handguns (Hudgens, 1983).

Suicidal Ideation   All four of the risk categories just discussed work together to increase an individual's likelihood of attempting suicide. In order to make such an attempt, however, in all but the most impulsive suicides there is a period of suicidal ideation.

For some, suicidal ideation takes on an almost compulsive quality. One middle-aged suicidal woman confessed that she "couldn't shake" her suicidal thoughts. They intruded again and again as she went about her everyday tasks, finally taking on the clarity of a vision of a place where she could commit suicide by driving off a cliff. The period during which suicidal ideation is forming may vary in length from a few minutes to a few years, but it is an intensely important period in the final definition of the suicidal act. The contemplation of the prospective suicide builds upon itself until suicide is seen as "the solution to the problem of life—of having to eat, to breathe, to work, to get up each morning, to shave, to move about, to go to school, to cope with other humans, to experience pain, anxiety, and so on" (Maris, 1989, p. 450).

Triggering Events and Warning Signs   Also shown in Table 1.4 are triggering events and warning signs. Triggering events can best be understood as "last straw" phenomena. The events need not necessarily be the worst losses or most dramatic events in a person's life. The crucial element in a triggering event is that it occurs after suicidal ideation has begun. Warning signs may or may not be exhibited by suicidal people; however, those presented in Table 1.4 are the most common across all ages. Verbal threats are by far the most common suicide warning sign. People often tell others, in more or less subtle ways, about their suicide plans. The most lethal warning sign, however, is previous suicidal behavior. Farberow (1991) has reviewed a number of studies showing that prior self-destructive behavior (especially a suicide attempt) is a powerful predictor of later completed suicide for many age groups.

Suicidal Behavior   There is one commonality in suicidal behavior. In all but the most impulsive suicides, the individual experiences ambivalence. Even when suicidal ideation is well advanced, some ambivalence remains (Shneidman, 1973, 1985). Although the decision to commit suicide may have been reached and the details of the suicide plan may be complete, care givers may call up ambivalence with questions such as "What would it take for you to change your mind? What specifics in your life would have to change for you to choose to go on living? Under what circumstances can you see a future for yourself?" Such questions may move suicidal persons back from the brink as their essential ambivalence is reengendered and they are forced to consider possible alternatives for the present and the future.

THE COHORT PERSPECTIVE

The suicide trajectory model described in this chapter will be heavily utilized throughout the book to organize research findings as they apply to particular age groups. However, developmental psychologists have long known that the value of research findings must be considered in the light of cohort effects. A cohort can be defined as a unique birth group that passes through life's milestones together (McGraw, 1987). Cohorts that are distinguishable from each other tend to be born at 20- to 25-year intervals; thus, there are four or five cohorts born in every century.

We believe that the timeless developmental changes in an individual's life (e.g., moving from childhood into adolescence) are strongly influenced by the cultural conditions or "zeitgeist" in which they occur. For example, adolescents who came of age in the early 1940s and were drafted to serve in World War II were different in important ways from adolescents who became draft eligible during the Vietnam conflict. Although both groups had experienced the same biological processes inherent in growth and maturation, the different cultural contexts in which they were raised caused very different

Six Living Generations, Wanda Ashe, 1995. Computer generated drawing. (Adapted from Strauss, W. & Howe, N., 1991. *Generations: The History of America's future 1584–2069.* New York: William Morrow and Company, Inc.)

responses to the two wars. Because of the differing impact of varied cultural influences, in addition to examining age-related differences in suicidal behavior we will discuss suicide from a cohort perspective in order to understand more fully the self-destructive behavior in the world today.

Strauss and Howe (1991) put forward a thought-provoking historical analysis of cohort effects. They used the term "generation" to refer to a cohort, and we will use these terms interchangeably in the discussion that follows. Strauss and Howe argued that understanding cohort differences is an important component in the study of any phenomenon within the social sciences because cohort membership influences the attitudes and values of entire generations of citizens. In particular, the period in which a group of people "comes of age" (i.e., moves from adolescence into adulthood) shapes their "peer personality." Strauss and Howe describe the peer personality as the way in which generations see and describe themselves as well as the way in which they will react to the world around them throughout their generational life span. We believe that the understanding of suicidal attitudes and behavior in various age groups today can be facilitated by examining the individual against the background of the peer personality of the cohort in which he or she is a member. No doubt, attitudes toward suicide among today's adolescents are different from those of earlier generations partially because the youth of today have grown up in a world where the specter of AIDS is a daily death threat, suicide is a topic included in music and the media, and television and newspaper accounts present serious considerations of physician-assisted suicide.

According to Strauss and Howe, there are six cohorts living today that collectively constitute the five age groups that we will discuss in chapters 3 through 7. The members of the youngest cohort living today were born in 1982 or later and began reaching their teen years in 1995. This group, which we will discuss in detail in the child suicide chapter, has been labeled the "Millennials" because its members will come of age in the second millennium (Strauss & Howe, 1991).

Because they are a new generation, we know relatively little about the Millennials. They are, however, projected by Strauss and Howe to be a "civic" generation or cohort. The "civics" throughout American history have been groups that are committed to doing the right thing for the public good. Previous generations of young civics fought in the American Revolution and in World War II. We also know that Millennials may be enjoying better parenting than some other recent generations. For example, they are being raised in the smallest child-per-family households in recent history. The parents of Millennials appear to have a renewed interest in and commitment to strong education, and Millennials are growing up in an environment in which both the divorce rate and the child poverty rate appear to be on the decline. These facts suggest that the Millennials should be a relatively healthy group of children.

The second living cohort, born between 1961 and 1981 is called the "13th Generation" by Strauss and Howe because they are the 13th generation born in America since the American Revolution. This group, which in 1995 ranged in age from 14 to 34 years of age, will be discussed in detail in chapters 4 and 5, where we deal with adolescent and young adult suicide. According to Strauss and Howe, the 13ers are a "reactive" generation that has responded negatively to the perceived excesses of their "boomer" parents. They are a conservative group with a stronger commitment to economic success than their parents. The 13th Generation has suffered from relatively poor parenting and education compared with the millennials. During their coming-of-age period, child abuse and neglect have increased dramatically, as has the incidence of divorce; the quality of public education has declined; and the incidence of school violence has increased. This generation's response to these circumstances has been declining SAT scores and performance on other academic achievement tests. Particularly pertinent to the thesis of this book, the 13ers have accounted for the significant growth in adolescent suicide over the past 20 years.

The third cohort of individuals alive today has been labeled by Strauss and Howe as the Baby Boom Generation, or the Boomers. The members of this group, born between 1943 and 1960, were between 35 and 52 years of age in 1995 and therefore constitute the largest group we will focus on in chapter 6, where we deal with suicide among middle-aged individuals. This large generation came of age during the Vietnam conflict. Strauss and Howe described them as idealists who brought about a new awakening of the spirit. This group was heavily responsible for putting one of its own generation in the White House in 1993 and in so doing reflected their concern for better health care and life circumstances for everyone. Although the Boomers had a high suicide rate in their youth, there are reasons to believe that they may be a relatively healthy and insightful group as they age.

The fourth generation, known as the Silent Generation, was born between 1925 and 1942. The members of this group, who were between the ages of 53 and 70 in 1995, constitute the oldest of the middle-agers discussed in chapter 6 and the youngest of the elderly presented in chapter 7. Strauss and Howe characterized the Silent Generation as an adaptive group of people who, except for a few years in their mid 30s, have worked hard and followed the rules of clean living set down by their parents. This group has shown a relatively low suicide rate, especially in their teenage years.

The second oldest group alive today is the "GI" Generation, born between 1901 and 1924. The members of this group, who in 1995 ranged in age from 71 to 94, constitute almost all of the elderly group that will be discussed in chapter 7. According to Strauss and Howe, the GIs are a civic generation that has always been committed to doing one's duty and sacrificing for the common good. The GIs are presently the healthiest and wealthiest group of elders that has ever lived. They have given much to their country but have received a great deal in special programs in return. The GI Generation is noted also for having strong expectations about gender roles. Their sex role stereotyping may have contributed to the fact that this group shows very large sex differences in elderly suicidal behavior.

The last and oldest cohort alive today is the rapidly disappearing Lost Generation. Born between 1883 and 1900, the members of this group ranged in age from 95 to 112 in 1995 and constitute what many sociologists refer to as the "old-old." The Lost are a reactive generation that has come to elderhood rather stoically, demanding and expecting very little social or financial support. They have been characterized as having very little fear of death, which may help account for the fact that suicide rates are the highest for this generation.

It is against this cohort or generational background that we will examine the differences in suicidal behavior across the life span. We trust that this backdrop will provide both a historical and a sociological dimension to the understanding of suicide at different ages.

PRINCIPLES OF LIFE SPAN DEVELOPMENT

We believe that studying suicide from a life-span perspective carries with it specific benefits. It enables us to focus in more detail on suicidal individuals at a particular time within their life journeys and to illuminate the interpersonal, intrapersonal, and environmental conditions that might be leading them to consider suicide. This perspective becomes especially valuable against the backdrop of their cohort's peer personality as illuminated by Strauss and Howe. However, to increase the usefulness of the developmental perspective, a few additional principles of life-span psychology are needed.

The first principle is that genetics forms a core component of all growth. The genetic information inherited from our parents at conception affects subsequent development in two major ways: First, it sets limits beyond which an individual cannot go, regardless of stimulation or education. For example, a child who is born with a genetic disease that causes severe retardation will not become a college graduate. Second, it establishes thresholds for reacting to the environment. For example, Brazelton (1969) has shown that even newborn babies exhibit differences in startle responses to the noises in their environment. Infants seem to have built-in levels of arousal and irritability. These biological thresholds probably account for individual differences in endurance of pain and stress and may well contribute to differential predispositions to depression and, indirectly, to suicidal behavior. Development at any stage from conception onward can only be understood as a product of these biological limits and thresholds as they interact with a changing environment.

A second important principle of life-span psychology is that change is a constant throughout life. Terenzini (1987) defines change as a value-free term that refers to alterations that occur over time in the affective and cognitive characteristics of an individual. It is important to note that merely recognizing that change is a constant neither allows one to infer the direction or rate of change nor, most importantly, sets a value on the changes that occur. There is evidence, however, that change by itself, regardless of whether it evokes positive or negative reactions, is a stressor and that rapidly accumulating change, especially of a negative nature, enhances the anxiety and depression that frequently accompany suicide attempts (Holmes & Rahe, 1967).

The third principle is that development, unlike simple change, is a continuous, organized, and systematic process. Many developmental psychologists take the term "development" to have an evaluative connotation, assuming that development involves a movement from immaturity to maturity and that such movement is inevitably positive. Development is also often thought to consist of a succession of changes that have survival value for the individual. Life-span theorists, however, do not necessarily agree that development always connotes positive growth. They point out that development in the later years may involve loss of earlier modes of functioning in some areas, whereas other areas may continue to show improvement. Some characteristics, such as crystallized intelligence, may continue to grow over the entire life span; other traits, such as short-term memory, may have a normal distribution across time, increasing during the early years and then declining. In our life-span model, we use the term "development" to include changes that lead to more complex and mature functioning as well as changes that reflect the principles of entropy, including deterioration in both structure and function.

A fourth basic tenet of developmental psychology is known as the dialectic principle. According to this principle, all development occurs as a result of imbalance. Freud endorsed this principle when he pointed out that children grow from one psychosexual stage to another as a result of being frustrated by the external environment. Perfect satisfaction at any given stage, Freud maintained, could lead to fixation, because there would be no incentive to grow. Piaget and Kohlberg also recognized this principle in the intellectual and moral development of children. They believed that development is dependent upon external stimulation that confronts the child with unknown material and challenges him or her to master new knowledge. Piaget (1926) pointed out that there are two modes of learning: assimilation and accommodation. Assimilation involves taking in new information and adding it to already existing categories of knowledge, whereas accommodation involves changing existing knowledge structures to incorporate conflicting information. Both assimilation and accommodation occur when an individual reacts to a stimulus or intellectual challenge from the environment. Building on Piaget's theory, Kohlberg (1976) believed that people pass from a lower stage in moral development to a higher one by being confronted with moral dilemmas or examples of moral reasoning that require higher levels of cognitive functioning than they currently possess. Adult developmental theorists like Gould (1978) recognize this principle when they suggest that development occurs as short periods of equilibrium give way to periods of turbulence. Implied in the concept of passages or transformations is the idea that advanced development occurs from working one's way through a challenging period and that balance attained as a result of such work is delicate, transient, and subject to assault from new environmental demands, life accidents, opportunities, and challenges.

The dialectic principle lends credence to Shneidman's (1976) view that suicidal behavior is the result of a temporary crisis rather than of an internal personality trait of the individual. The principle also supports crisis intervention as a method for temporarily reestablishing balance until the individual can marshal his or her coping skills and move to a more mature level of functioning. Furthermore, the dialectic principle suggests that a suicidal crisis, once resolved, may actually cause the person to become stronger and better equipped to meet the stresses of life. The principle also recognizes that suicidal crises may recur at other periods in an individual's life and that these later recurrences may be resolved through growth or may lead to death.

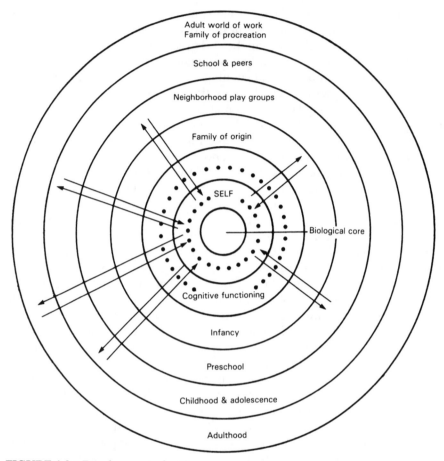

FIGURE 1.2   Development of self

The fifth principle of development, based on humanistic theories, is that there is a central organizing force within every person that governs change proactively. That force is known as the self. Of all the developmental principles presented in this chapter, we believe that the organization and operation of the self is the most critical for thoroughly understanding suicidal behavior. Therefore, we will devote more space to this topic than to the other developmental principles.

Figure 1.2 depicts our understanding of the way the self develops and regulates behavior across the life span. At birth, the self consists only of the inherited traits and tendencies that set genetic limits and establish thresholds of reaction. In the figure, this dimension is labeled the biological core. As the child grows and develops, the environment starts to impact on the self through widening circles of influence, beginning with the family of origin and later spreading to neighborhood groups, then to the school environment, and finally to the adult world of work and the family of procreation. It is important to note that the self does not merely react to the stimuli in the environment. Instead, the self acts on the environment in increasingly complex and organized ways. As the self becomes more firmly established, it provides a consistent core for interpreting and acting on the environment (Lecky, 1973).

One major element shaping the self is the expanding cognitive repertoire of the growing child. Messages from the environment are mediated by the cognitive processes and accepted or rejected based on goodness of fit. As the child grows, he or she learns to accept some of these messages and ignore others. This is called selective perception. Perhaps initially because of genetic predispositions and later also because of environmental experiences humans tend to perceive the world differentially and to assign different meanings to the same stimuli.

Cognitive theorists point out that one's belief system is important in establishing and maintaining a consistent picture of oneself (e.g., Ellis, 1962). This belief system is an accumulation of perceptions about oneself and one's place in the world that are consistent with one's experience of self. One theory suggests we create personal constructs for important events and activities (Kelly, 1955). Those constructs then become our own unique way of viewing the world. Other theorists suggest that, once established, our belief systems and view of self are maintained by the self-talk we engage in to interpret the external world meaningfully (Meichenbaum, 1985). By suggesting this, they are essentially asserting the importance of cognition in helping to maintain or enhance our self-concepts. In the same way, an individual's potential behaviors, including suicidal behavior, are mediated by cognitive processes, and these processes determine the actions in which the individual chooses to engage.

Three other elements shaping the self should be noted. These are the processes of imitation, modeling, and identification. Behaviorists have shown that humans imitate the behavior of other humans. They have even discovered some rules that govern the process. For example, humans are more likely to imitate the behavior of models who are powerful, attractive, and of the same sex (Bandura, 1977). Throughout our lives we focus on other people as important sources of learning. As children, we may blindly imitate the gestures or actions of adults. As teens, we engage in idol worship. Much of faddish adolescent behavior is imitative of a style set by an admired performer, sports star, or local teen leader. Young adults continue imitating others in the process of being mentored. A young adult will focus on a successful person in his or her occupational field, develop a relationship with that person, and attempt to become as much like the mentor as possible. Every academic recognizes this behavior as basically imitative. New male graduate students, advised by a powerful, attractive male faculty member who has a beard and long hair, are apt to sprout beards and long tresses themselves before the end of the first semester. The process of imitation not only allows us to try out different types of behaviors and ways of being and to learn from them, it also forms the basis for the deeper process of identification. Identification is the taking on of qualities that others possess, making them a part of us. In this process we incorporate into our growing concept of self the admired, respected, or even negative qualities that are modeled by others.

Imitation, modeling, and identification have all been shown to be important in suicidal behavior. The incidence of suicide increases after a powerful role model commits suicide. Parents who model suicidal behavior often have children who imitate their actions. Finally, suicidal behavior as a coping technique can be incorporated into our sense of who we are. Like Jerry W. in chapter 2, whose suicide attempt occurred when he was the age at which his father killed himself, we may identify with a suicidal parent so completely that we feel compelled to attempt suicide ourselves at a certain age.

As the self becomes an identifiable entity, it also assumes an organizing function. The major organizing principle of self theory is that at any given time a person acts so as to maintain or enhance his or her self-concept (Lecky, 1973). Thus, the person's individual view of self becomes the guiding force in determining the direction of his or her future development. Once established, a view of self as competent and worthy is strengthened by acting on the environment and accepting messages from the environment that maintain or enhance that positive self-concept. Unfortunately, the opposite is also true. Many suicidal individuals, like Marian in chapter 2, have such poor self-concepts that they cannot accept positive feedback from those around them.

A final important concept in self theory is that of self-esteem. Self-esteem refers to the value that an individual places on himself or herself. At any given time across the life span, an individual's behavior can be understood as a function of the way in which the individual views himself or herself and by the assessment of worth that such a self-concept inspires. The literature we have reviewed in this book clearly links suicidal behavior to depression. We would maintain that it is impossible to have a positive self-concept, to value oneself highly, and at the same time to be depressed enough to consider suicide. We therefore suggest that a positive self-concept and high self-esteem are important variables inoculating individuals against suicide at any age and, conversely, that people with low self-esteem are at higher risk for committing suicide. Indeed, the literature of depression frequently defines depression in terms of low self-esteem, which is almost a tautology.

A sixth principle of development is the principle of individuation. According to this principle, people develop toward their unique potentials across the life span. Carl Jung, who has been called the father of adult development, was the first to popularize the term. He believed that the process of individuation begins when a person is in his or her 40s. He described it as a process that requires us to recognize the complexities of our inner selves and to try to find a balance between competing forces (Jung, 1960). Erikson (1959) interpreted this process of individuation as movement toward ego integrity. Levinson, Darrow, Klein, Levinson, and McKee (1978) recognized it as a process of clarifying the boundaries between our inner selves and the external world, as well as a process of balancing conflicting internal demands. To Levinson et al., individuation is a process of coming to know who one is, what one wants, what the world is really like, and how much one values these things. Proponents of the humanistic school of thought would recognize the principle of individuation in the drive toward self-actualization. Although their point of view is more clearly evaluative than some, the basic idea is the same. Individuation helps a person to move toward his or her uniqueness, to become more clearly the person he or she is capable of becoming.

The principle of individuation contains the idea of unfolding. Walt Disney's film *The Living Desert* showed in a spectacular way the process by which a plant breaks through the soil, attains full growth, buds, comes to full flower, fades, and disintegrates. According to the principle of individuation, the process applies to humans in all their complexity. The analogy holds up well. Just as the full beauty of the blossom depends on both the caliber of the seed planted and the characteristics of the environment (e.g., soil, sun, and rain), the quality of an individual life depends on both the genetic inheritance and the external demands, opportunities, and nurturance available. Suicidal behavior is generally the result of the accumulation of environmental insults by predisposed individuals who have not been able to develop adequate self-concepts and coping techniques.

The seventh important principle of a life span perspective is that cohort differences should be taken into account when trying to understand and explain the behavior of any age group. For example, people who were adolescents during the depression learned a dramatic lesson about limited opportunity and harsh economic reality. People who were children at the time may not have been affected so heavily, whereas middle-aged people, perhaps reacting to the lack of time for beginning anew, committed suicide at unprecedented rates. In order to understand fully the reasons for an individual suicide, characteristics of the cohort of which the suicide is a part should be examined.

In conclusion, the life span developmental perspective we endorse views development as the product of genetics and biology interacting with the social and physical environment as they are mediated by increasingly sophisticated cognitive skills. The gyroscope in the process of development, the factor that accounts for the consistency we see in personalities across time, is the self. We believe that all behavior can best be understood by taking into account biology, psychological development, cognitive abilities and habits, and environmental pressures, challenges, and opportunities. Suicidal behavior is no exception. In the remainder of this book, we will suggest a model for viewing suicidal behavior that incorporates each of these categories.

SUMMARY

In this chapter we have examined suicide both historically and in the present. We began by reviewing the history of suicide in the Western world. It is clear from this brief history that suicide has occurred in all ages of which we have a record. The historical perspective also revealed that suicide has been viewed differently by different cultures at different times. Depending upon the dominant thinking in any given society, the act of suicide has been deemed a crime, a rational and honorable act, evidence of insanity, a sin, and a failure to cope. The existence of all of these views of suicide points up both the complexities inherent in understanding an individual act of suicide and the need for examining the context within which suicide is studied.

Moving to the present day, we presented statistics that show that students of suicide must take into account such demographic factors as the age, sex, and ethnic origin of those who take their own lives. Current statistics in the United States show that males are more likely than females to commit suicide, whites are more likely than African Americans to take their own lives, and suicide rates generally increase with age.

Shneidman's definition of suicide was accepted for use in this book, with one addition. We believe that active euthanasia must be included in any complete discussion of suicide.

In order to begin to address the complexities in understanding suicidal behavior, we have introduced a model called the suicide trajectory. The suicide trajectory provides a method of organizing the research literature as well as a way of conceptualizing the sequence leading to suicidal behavior. It maintains that the four major risk categories feeding into suicidal ideation are biological, psychological, cognitive, and environmental in nature. Interacting with each other, these risk factors may lead to suicidal ideation in susceptible individuals. Suicidal ideation consists of thinking through a plan for attempting suicide, including method, place, and time. As suicidal ideation becomes more firmly established, people may reveal warning signs. Triggering events may also occur, leading to the actual suicidal behavior. Commonalities across the life span in each risk category as well as in suicidal ideation, warning signs, triggering events, and suicidal behavior were detailed.

Finally, we recognized the importance of understanding suicide within a cohort or generational setting. We accepted and reviewed Strauss and Howe's definitions for each of the existing cohorts alive today: the Millennials, the

13ers, the Boomers, the Silent Generation, the GIs, and the Lost Generation. We promised that these cohort differences will be reviewed in each of the developmental chapters that follow. We ended this chapter by describing seven principles of developmental psychology, which may help to illuminate suicidal behavior.

2

Perspectives on the Nature and Causes of Suicide

> There is but one truly serious philosophical problem, and that is suicide. Judging whether life is or is not worth living amounts to answering the fundamental questions of philosophy.
>
> Albert Camus, *The Myth of Sisyphus*

As we have seen in chapter 1, suicide has long been and continues to be a salient issue. What makes individuals take their own lives? Some of the best thinkers in every human-oriented field of study have puzzled over this question. In this chapter we will examine four major psychological perspectives and their insights into and implications for the phenomenon of suicide: psychoanalytic theory, behaviorism, humanistic psychology, and cognitive psychology. Sociologists also have speculated about the nature and causes of suicide. We will explore the most influential sociological theory, that of Emile Durkheim. Although his theory is more than a century old, it continues to generate thought and empirical research today. Finally, in recent years it has become obvious that biology plays a role in at least some suicides. We will therefore also present evidence for a biological substrate or correlate of suicidal behavior.

Because each of these perspectives could easily justify several books, the discussion of each theoretical perspective will be general in nature and will focus primarily on implications for the study of suicide. A list of additional readings for each perspective is provided at the end of the chapter.

THE PSYCHOANALYTIC PERSPECTIVE

The psychoanalytic perspective has been a strong force throughout the 20th century in shaping the way many people view individual behavior. Its founder, Sigmund Freud, is still recognized as a sensitive and insightful pioneer in the investigation of human personality. Many of the elements of Freud's theory are so well known that they have become part of the common parlance. His theory is summarized in every introductory psychology text and in many personality theory and abnormal psychology texts. We will include here only those aspects of Freud's theory that have implications for the study of suicide.

Freud was educated as a biologist and a physician. Every aspect of his theory is rooted in the notion that each human being is a closed energy system. He believed that humans have only a certain amount of psychic energy, which he called *libido*, available to them at any given time. Furthermore, he believed that there is a dynamic balance between two major forces in the lives of humans. These two forces came to be known as *Eros* and *Thanatos*. Eros is the name that was given to the life instinct, the purpose of which is individual survival and species propagation. The death instinct, Thanatos, was regarded as the psychological embodiment of the drive to return to an inorganic state. Freud believed that Thanatos is universal in humans and is based on the constancy principle, which, simply put, proposes that the goal of all living beings is to return to the stability of the inorganic world (Freud 1920/1961).

Later theorists have attached additional meanings to the constructs of Eros and Thanatos. They have described eros as consisting of all the positive influences in a person's life that urge that person on to become all he or she can be. Humor, compassion, altruism, and sexual intimacy are all aspects of Eros. Thanatos has come to be viewed as consisting of those negative traits (e.g., hatred, anger, jealousy, and guilt) that cause humans to become less than they can be. The interplay between Eros and Thanatos represents a lifelong struggle. When individuals are growing and developing in a positive way, Eros is dominant in their personalities. When, however, individuals feel stagnant, depressed, or hopeless, Thanatos is in control of their lives. The implications of the Eros-Thanatos dichotomy for suicidal individuals are obvious: persons contemplating or attempting suicide are acting under the influence of Thanatos.

A more recent adaptation of the Eros-Thanatos continuum was proposed by Orbach (1988). He suggested that an individual's orientation toward suicide can be assessed by measuring his or her attraction to and repulsion from life and death. Orbach's descriptions of attraction to death and repulsion from life bear marked resemblance to Freud's concept of Thanatos; likewise, Orbach's description of attraction to life and repulsion from death echo the essence of Freud's concept of Eros. It would seem that these notions continue to have some utility in present-day research, as we will see in chapter 3.

A second major contribution of Freudian psychology is its construction of a topography of the mind. Freud envisioned the human mind as made up of the conscious, the preconscious, and the unconscious. Of the three components, the conscious is by far the smallest part. The *conscious* consists of all those things of which an individual is aware at the present moment. For example, for an individual who is engrossed in reading an absorbing novel the conscious would include only the words on the page and the mental images those words are evoking in the reader's mind. If, however, the story becomes less absorbing, the reader may become aware of background noises, physical sensations such as hunger or an itch, and psychological sensations such as boredom. At any given time, then, the field of attention of the conscious is narrow and subject to change. The topography of the mind is commonly likened to the topography of an iceberg. In this metaphor, the conscious is like the tip of the iceberg. It is the only part visible, but it signals that much more is hiding beneath the surface.

The *preconscious* is a reservoir of material of which we are not usually aware but which can become conscious given appropriate circumstances. For

Depression, Jacob Lawrence. Tempera on paper, 22 × 30 ½ in. (From the collection of the Whitney Museum of American Art, New York. Gift of David M. Solinger, 66.98.)

example, if you were asked to identify a specific song that was popular in the 1960s, you might have some difficulty unless you were given more clues. If you were told that the song was made popular by a young group of male singers from Liverpool, you might begin to make reasonable guesses provided that you are a fan of the Beatles. If you were then told that the title of the song included the name of a color, you might well be able to guess its identity. Perhaps a final clue would be necessary: The name of the color preceded the name of a type of boat. At this point, you would probably know that the song was "Yellow Submarine." Freudian-oriented psychologists would probably agree that the song was buried in your preconscious just awaiting adequate environmental cues to bring it to mind. The same kind of exercise can occur when you are asked to remember nursery rhymes (e.g., "The Cow Jumped Over the Moon") and fairy tales (e.g., *Cinderella*). The preconscious has much material stored in it that can be accessed fairly easily. Using the iceberg metaphor, the preconscious can be likened to that portion of an iceberg that is just below the surface and is made visible as tides grow lower or as waves wash up and down over the surface.

The third component of the topography of the mind is the *unconscious.*

From the point of view of Freudian theorists, the unconscious is the most important component of the triad. Like the nine-tenths of the iceberg that is never seen, it is the part of the mind that can present the most danger to navigation through life. The unconscious contains material that is threatening and painful, including memories of incidents that would cause anger, grief, guilt, or anxiety if we admitted them into consciousness. People protect themselves from these feelings by repressing such material. Because keeping repressed material in the unconscious, thereby keeping it from being known by the conscious, uses up some of the libidinal energy, which at any point in time is limited, less energy is available to the human being for growth and development. It fllows that an excess of repressed unconscious negative material can lead to a strengthening of Thanatos.

When Thanatos threatens to envelop Eros within an individual, suicide is a natural alternative, according to the Freudian view. Many psychoanalytic theorists believe that suicide is a manifestation of anger turned inward. Shneidman (1985) made the claim that, according to Freud, suicide "was essentially within the mind. The major psychoanalytical position on suicide was that it represented unconscious hostility directed toward the introjected (ambivalently viewed) love object. Psychodynamically, suicide was seen as murder in the 180th degree" (p. 34).

The third major Freudian construct related to suicide is the concept of the triad of personality. Freud believed that personality is composed of three entities: the id, the ego, and the superego. According to Freud, most mental illness comes about as a result of intrapsychic conflict between these three aspects of the personality. Once again adhering to his biological roots, Freud felt that at birth all energy is invested in the *id*, which has been described as the "spoiled brat" of the personality. The id is represented as the now-centered, demanding portion of a person that insists, "I want what I want and I want it now." Because of this emphasis on immediate gratification the id has been described as operating according to the pleasure principle; that is, its guiding rule is to seek pleasure and avoid pain. Only gradually, as humans leave the infant stage, does the id surrender some energy to the ego.

The *ego* can best be viewed as the executive of the personality. The ego mediates between the id and the component of the triad that develops last, the superego. It also mediates between the id and the superego on the one hand and the realities of the outside world on the other. Among the questions the ego asks in its mediating function when confronted by a desire of the id are: "Is it safe? Is it available? Is it to my long-term good?"

The *superego*, which begins to develop around five or six years of age, is composed of two components: the conscience and the ego ideal. The conscience is, of course, that part of the personality that is composed of all the no-no's taught at home and school and by religion and other socializing forces. It is that part of the personality that metes out psychological punishment in the form of guilt. The ego ideal, on the other hand, is that part of the personality that is composed of all we would like to be (i.e., our idealized self). It is the one part of the personality that is self-created. Each person's ego ideal is unique and changes as the person grows and matures.

The ongoing utility of Freud's triad of personality conception is reflected in more modern theories such as transactional analysis theory. Readers familiar with transactional analysis will recognize the constructs of "parent," "adult," and "child" as corresponding closely to the "superego," "ego," and "id" (Harris, 1969).

Many Freudians believe that an overdeveloped superego may be implicated in some suicides. They suggest that people who have adopted perfectionist standards and whose ego ideal is out of reach set themselves up for constant intrapsychic conflict. Such conflict uses up so much of their available energy that they have less and less available for coping with everyday demands and for growth. They thus become even less like their ego ideal, are further from meeting their own standards each day, suffer more guilt and anxiety, and experience more intrapsychic conflict. This type of downward spiral may be difficult to break and may account, at least in part, for the narrow, rigid, and unrealistic thinking seen among some potential suicides. The superego is said to operate according to the perfection principle: that is, its governing rule is to seek out the perfect and to reject anything less than absolute perfection. A case in point might clarify the relationship between superego and suicide.

> Marian N. was a 38-year-old married mother of two. She was also a successful career woman and had recently accepted a position as director of nursing at the local urban hospital. She had the respect of the doctors and other nurses, and many patients spoke of her with gratitude. Her 18-year marriage was stable, and her teenage children seemed happy and productive. Yet Marian N. appeared in a psychiatrist's office, deeply depressed and harboring active suicidal thoughts.
>
> She confided that she was really a failure; that her life was not what it should be. As a young child she had set high standards for herself in every area of life. She had wanted to be the perfect wife and mother. It was clear to her that she was neither. She had wanted to help people in her career and to excel at it in every way. She continually recalled and dwelled on rather minor errors she had made in each of her roles. She summed up her failures by saying, "It's just never enough. I never have enough to give to everyone who needs it. I always fail everyone sometime in some way." She felt "sinful and inadequate," al-

---

Our greatest foes, and whom we must chiefly combat, are within. Cervantes, *Don Quixote*

though she could not verbalize any real reasons for feeling this way. She felt that she could never live up to what "should be" and that the future was bleak and hopeless. She had few avenues of pleasure in her life, and she felt guilty on the rare occasions when she discovered she was having a good time.

Both in her words and in her appearance she betrayed a great deal of anger and disgust directed at herself for failing in her own eyes to live up to what she should be. When confronted with the realities of her patients' esteem and her family's love, she retorted irrationally, "It's because they don't really know the real me. If they did, they'd know the truth—that I am a failure in everything."

It is clear from the Freudian perspective that Marian suffers from unrealistic anxiety and guilt inflicted by an overdeveloped superego. Such an individual may be using rigid, perfectionistic standards to cover deep-seated feelings of inferiority or self-contempt. In any case, it takes little imagination to relate to the intense negative feelings that might lead to suicidal thoughts and actions. Such negative thoughts and emotions might be addressed by psychoanalytic therapists by trying to provide insight or by bolstering Marian's *defense mechanisms*.

Freud hypothesized that all of us attempt to protect our egos from anxiety and guilt by employing defense mechanisms. Defense mechanisms allow us to distort or selectively perceive reality in ways that protect our self-esteem. Table 2.1 presents the most common defense mechanisms, their definitions, and an example of each. The utilization of defense mechanisms is almost always unconscious. If we use defense mechanisms too often, we use up the energy available for day-to-day functioning and growth. When this happens, we become overwhelmed by the demands of the environment and/or by the material in the unconscious that we no longer have energy to repress. As our customary defense mechanisms begin to fail, we may become overwhelmed with feelings of helplessness and inability to cope. In the case study just presented, Marian shows a failure to cope with feelings of inadequacy and inferiority. Bolstering defense mechanisms might help temporarily—until real insight and change could be achieved. But overuse of defense mechanisms would obviously be nonproductive in the long run, since it would decrease the amount of energy left for positive growth.

The fourth major contribution of Freudian theory that has implications for suicidal behavior is the concept of developmental stages. Freud was the first psychologist to popularize the existence of age-related stages of development. In keeping with his ideas about libidinal energy, he hypothesized that the focus of each stage was a specific erogenous zone. Table 2.2. presents the psychosexual stages with their appropriate ages, the erogenous zone identified by Freud, and the personality outcomes that might occur if fixation or regression occurred at a given stage.

Freud believed that during the first two years of life children are in the

TABLE 2.1 Common Defense Mechanisms

Defense mechanism	Definition	Example
Repression	Forgetting or unconsciously denying emotionally laden material	Amnesia; fugue states; missing appointments, deadlines, etc., because they were "forgotten"
Denial	Rejecting or ignoring unacceptable impulses and refuse to act on those that do reach awareness	A man who continues to smoke in spite of multiple warnings, believing that lung cancer, heart disease, etc., happen only to others
Projection	Attributing unacceptable impulses and ideas to others	A young adolescent who has overwhelming aggressive feelings and maintains that "people are out to get him"
Reaction formation	Reversing an impulse so that the original anxiety-evoking impulse is replaced by its opposite	Dealing with someone you dislike by treating him or her with exaggerated warmth and friendliness
Regression	Returning to an earlier stage of development in an attempt to cope with anxiety	Taking up thumb sucking again when a new baby is born after not sucking one's thumb for a year
Fixation	Becoming stuck at a given stage of development	A child who throws temper tantrums becomes an adult given to rages in anxious situations
Sublimation	Turning unacceptable impulses and ideas into socially acceptable avenues	An artist who uses repressed sexual feelings to create a statue of a beautiful nude body
Displacement	Diverting negative feelings onto innocent people or objects	A man who is scolded by his boss comes home and yells at his wife and children
Identification	Modeling oneself on an admired person; taking on his or her valued attitudes and behaviors and making them a part of one's own personality	Children's acquisition of habits and mannerisms of their parents; students' imitation of mentor figures

oral stage of development, in which they learn major lessons about the environment through their mouths. He described people whose development becomes fixated at this stage or who later regress to this stage as either oral dependent or oral aggressive. According to Freud, oral dependent people have great problems with decision making and tend to depend on others for their happiness and identity. Oral aggressive people tend to use their mouths as weapons, engaging in sarcasm and gossip and making vicious remarks about others. Both types have high oral needs and often use oral habits such as smoking or overeating to help them cope.

TABLE 2.2 Freudian Psychosexual Stages of Development

Stage	Age	Erogenous zone	Outcome of fixation or regression at this stage
Oral	0–2	Mouth	Oral dependence Oral aggression
Anal	2–4	Anal area	Anal retentive personality Anal expulsive personality
Phallic	4–6	Genitalia	Unresolved Oedipus conflict Castration anxiety Penis envy
Latency	6–12	None	Delayed maturity Possible homosexuality
Genital	12–18	Genitalia	None

During the *anal stage*, children learn control over their bodily waste products. At that time, they gain pleasure, according to Freud, by consciously retaining or expelling feces. The psychological costs of becoming fixated at or regressing to this stage again take two forms: the anal retentive personality and the anal expulsive personality. Freud described these two personality types as opposites. He described the anal retentive personality as almost compulsively clean, parsimonious, and orderly, while picturing the anal expulsive personality as generous, disorderly, and gregarious. Those familiar with the play *The Odd Couple* might recognize Freud's descriptions in the two main characters, Felix Unger and Oscar Madison.

In traditional Freudian theory, the *phallic stage* presents the most danger to a child's developing personality. Freud believed that a child at this stage falls in love with the parent of the opposite sex and wishes to take the place of the parent of the same sex within the parental relationship. For boys this conflict, which Freud called the *Oedipus Complex*, is resolved by identifying with the father, which permits a healthy boy to move into the latency period with little difficulty. A young boy who does not move through this stage appropriately will experience problems in the masculine identification process. A girl, however, has far deeper problems during this stage, according to traditional Freudians. She cannot identify with her mother because of her growing "realization" that females are inferior because of their lack of male anatomy (Freud dubbed this realization *penis envy*). The girl child therefore is more liable to suffer from arrested development and to have less energy available for moving into the latency stage. As a result, females, according to Freud, are most likely to have weaker superegos than males and also to be more dependent, narcissistic, and masochistic as adults. This aspect of Freud's theory has been soundly criticized by feminist writers for obvious reasons.

Freud suggested that during the *latency stage* of development children are freed from sexual urgings and are thus able to devote their energy to learning and to socializing. This stage, he intimated, is important for the development of sexual identity and for healthy superego development. The latency stage will be described in more detail in chapter 3.

The final psychosexual stage, the *genital stage*, begins around age 12. Its central theme is the development of procreative sexuality, which is fully achieved at approximately age 18. Although the focus is once again on the genitalia, this stage differs from the phallic stage in that the young person becomes increasingly capable of relating to nonfamily members of the opposite sex, thus closing the distance between the sexes that typifies the latency stage. Toward the end of this stage, people are able to make specific choices regarding sexual partners, to build ongoing relationships, and to create the next generation of human beings.

Although Freud's psychosexual stages do not in themselves relate directly to suicide, it is important to acknowledge them as they may help us to understand children and adolescents who are considering suicide. It is also important to be familiar with these stages because so many helping professionals in a variety of fields use them as part of their frame of reference in dealing with troubled children and adolescents.

In summary, Freudian theory views suicide as a failure to cope. The failure may arise out of a collapse of ego defense mechanisms; out of an overdeveloped, demanding superego; out of prolonged intrapsychic conflict; or out of regression to or fixation at a particular psychosexual stage. All of these causes have two things in common: They use up energy, and they result in a disequilibrium between Thanatos and Eros, a situation in which Thanatos takes command. The direct result might be a suicide attempt. The Freudian emphasis on the early years of life as all-important in determining personality makes the psychoanalytic perspective a gloomy one for those intent on helping suicidal persons. The theory suggests that only through in-depth analysis can a person obtain the insight necessary to understand and cope with unconscious material and with energy-draining intrapsychic conflict.

THE PSYCHOSOCIAL PERSPECTIVE

One exception to the generally dark picture presented by Freudian psychoanalytic theory is found in the writings of Erik Erikson, who extended Freudian theory to allow for the social nature of human beings (Erikson, 1959). Erikson did not reject most of the Freudian constructs; however, he did suggest that Freud had not given adequate recognition to the fact that humans are social beings. Erikson also believed that human beings continue to develop in important ways throughout their lifetimes rather than cease their development in adolescence, as Freudian theory suggests. Erikson's

TABLE 2.3   Erikson's Stages of Psychosocial Development

Stage	Most sensitive ages	Task Positive pole		Negative pole
Sensory stage	0–2	Trust	vs.	Mistrust
Muscular development stage	2–4	Autonomy	vs.	Shame, doubt
Locomotor stage	4–6	Initiative	vs.	Guilt
Latency stage	6–12	Industry	vs.	Inferiority
Puberty stage	12–18	Identity	vs.	Role diffusion
Young adult stage	15–20	Intimacy	vs.	Isolation
Adulthood stage	30–65	Generativity	vs.	Stagnation
Maturity	65+	Ego integrity	vs.	Despair, disgust

Source: Table adapted from Byrne, B. F., & Kelley, K. (© 1991), *An introduction to personality*, 3rd ed., Englewood Cliffs, N.J.: Prentice-Hall, p. 70. Used with permission.

well-known eight stages of psychosocial development are presented in Table 2.3. Each stage is bipolar in nature. The table portrays the major tasks and dangers at each stage.

Erikson believed that there are special developmental periods during which specific psychosocial lessons are most likely to be learned. These periods are closely related to the developing capabilities of the individual, but they are also dependent upon the conditions in the environment. A physically healthy person in a positive, nurturing social environment learns each lesson well, emerging from the stage at the positive end of the continuum. No matter how physically healthy they are, people who are in unhealthy social environments learn negative lessons and are less likely to learn lessons well during subsequent stages.

According to Erikson, in the first stage, between birth and age two, infants work primarily to develop a basic sense of security in the world. Children who develop positive feelings of *trust* view the world as more pleasant than unpleasant, more predictable than unpredictable, and they also view themselves as having some control over their own world. This developmental stage is particularly important since it is preverbal and the child is not able to mediate with words such negative experiences as abuse, neglect, or psychological trauma.

The development of a basic sense of *autonomy* (roughly equivalent to independence) or of *shame and doubt* is the central developmental outcome of the second stage. Children between the ages of two and four are working on their growing sense of identity (or "me-ness"). All parents recognize the autonomy of the "terrible twos," for this is when healthy children insist on doing things their own way. Erikson, like Freud, recognized that conflict with parents over toilet training can lead to deeply ingrained feelings of shame. He also maintained that children who experience major problems in any aspect of their social world during this stage are apt to emerge with high levels of self-doubt and accompanying feelings of shame about self.

During the period from ages four to six, children are involved in the process of developing either a healthy sense of *initiative* or feelings of *guilt*. During this stage, children often use their newly developed independence to move out into neighborhood, preschool, and other group settings. Children suffering from self-doubt are not able to move with assurance in these circles and thus may feel guilty about their inability to participate as fully in their social worlds as can some of their peers.

According to Erikson, the long childhood period between ages 6 and 12 permits a great deal of exploration regarding the extremes of *industry* versus *inferiority*. Healthy children who have developed trust in their worlds, independence, and a positive sense of initiative are in good positions to try out new relationships, activities, and skills. Those who do not trust their world, who doubt themselves, and who have high levels of guilt will find it hard to develop a positive sense of industry. Instead, dragging their burdens of previous negative development they are likely to not try very hard, to doubt their abilities, and to perceive themselves (and be perceived in turn by teachers and peers) as inferior.

Identity and *role diffusion* are the extremes of the next stage hypothesized by Erikson. The most sensitive period for beginning to explore this continuum is during the early teen years, although such exploration, like the earlier explorations, is likely to be repeated at intervals throughout the life span. Identity and a positive sense of self, including both strengths and weaknesses, form the positive end of the continuum, while role diffusion leaves the adolescent lost in the worlds of school and vocation.

The next stage, with the extremes of *intimacy* and *isolation*, occurs during the middle teens and extends into young adulthood. The central goal of this stage is to develop the ability to maintain an ongoing intimate relationship with another human being that becomes more meaningful with time. Psychological isolation, with its accompanying loneliness and depression, is a significant danger.

Erikson believed that most adults from early adulthood until old age are in a period of *generativity* rather than *stagnation*. The central task of the generative period is to find ways to give back something to the society that has nurtured them. Being productive on the job, parenting, writing books, painting pictures, and carrying out community service are all ways of being generative. Erikson pointed out that people who do not find ways of contributing to society are likely to stop growing, to lose their zest for living, to turn inward in a futile effort to nurture themselves—in short, to stagnate.

The final psychosocial stage Erikson proposed has *ego integrity* at one extreme and *despair and disgust* at the other. He viewed this stage as attainable only after a lifetime of positive or negative experiences. Those with ego integrity have developed a positive sense of their life histories, while those who arrive at old age at the negative end of the continuum view their lives as lacking in meaning and question the reasons for existence.

Erikson's theory provides a helpful framework for viewing suicide from a developmental perspective. It is important to note that Erikson believed that individuals are able to move back and forth across the bipolar continuum regardless of their age. In this way, young people who have developed negatively during the first few stages could, with proper attention and guidance in a changed social environment, establish a sense of basic trust in the world that would allow them to reexamine negative lessons like self-doubt, guilt, and inferiority. Erikson's theory thus is more hopeful than Freud's and provides a framework both for understanding and for working with suicidal persons. The following case study illustrates negative psychosocial learning.

> *Robin S. is a 16-year-old boy who was admitted to a psychiatric institution following a moderately serious suicide attempt. Robin took several Quaaludes and washed them down with bourbon. Upon his recovery, he admitted knowing that the combination could be fatal. He said he had learned that from reading about Karen Quinlan's case. "But," he said sadly, "I guess I wasn't as lucky as her."*
>
> *Upon questioning, the following facts were revealed: Robin was born into a lower-middle-class family. He was the fourth of five children. Before the last child was born, Robin's father deserted the family. Robin's mother went to work as a carder in a local textile mill. The three older siblings also worked as soon as they were able to in order to help out with expenses. Even as a baby, Robin's care was frequently left to his oldest sister, then eight years old, who was at best casual in caring for him. Robin learned three specific lessons: (1) the world was not a comfortable, warm, and secure place; (2) he could not predict consequences (when he cried, he was sometimes attended to and sometimes not); and (3) he was powerless to affect the outcome of any situation in a consistent way. In short, he learned mistrust.*
>
> *When Robin began talking, he lisped. As he grew older and other children made fun of him, he stopped talking almost completely. His shyness made him the target of still more neighborhood teasing and Robin developed a strong sense of shame and self-doubt. These feelings became overlaid with a sense of guilt concerning his own inadequacy as he watched his preschool friends move confidently into a world he dared not approach.*
>
> *When he entered school, he was labeled as "slow" and placed in the slow-learning group. His boredom with the group coupled with his unwillingness to talk caused his teachers to lose patience with him, to write him off, and to communicate in a variety of ways to parents, peers, and other teachers their convictions that Robin was stupid. They also communicated this to Robin, who learned, "I am inferior."*

As a result of his feelings of inferiority, Robin seldom entered into any activities. He did only what was absolutely required and withdrew into himself. He had no friends and rarely talked to his siblings. When his oldest sister suggested that he get involved in something he could do well, Robin said, "There ain't no such thing." He had no clear understanding of his strengths and weaknesses and almost no interpersonal connections. In short, he suffered from role diffusion and isolation.

Clearly, Robin is someone who at 16 has gone through the first five stages delineated by Erikson's theory at the extreme negative end of each continuum. However, if Erikson is correct, it would be possible for a counselor to work with Robin and, by proving to be trustworthy, help him regain a sense of trust in his environment. He could be helped through speech therapy to overcome his sense of shame and self-doubt by developing competence and confidence in speaking. He could be supported and rewarded for expressing himself in safe situations. In addition, he could be encouraged to try out new situations in which he could expect to succeed (and even be accompanied for added support). In this way, as Robin developed increasing competence he would be likely to overcome self-doubt and feelings of inferiority and to move toward the positive poles of autonomy and industry. As his feelings of competence and self-esteem grew, he would be in a good position to move toward a self-defined identity as expressed in the pursuit of a vocation or in the development of positive relationships with others. While such developments take time, energy, and support, from an Eriksonian perspective they pay off. They allow a person to develop the psychosocial foundation on which to build an adult life of generativity and integrity. From the Eriksonian perspective, then, suicidal individuals are people who must be helped to move from the negative to the positive poles in the psychosocial tasks of life.

Erikson's theory has been the source of a great deal of rich discussion since the 1950s and has been used by many authors (e.g., Levinson, 1980; Vaillant, 1977) as an organizational framework for analyzing research findings concerning adult development. Erikson was the first major theorist to postulate that development continues after sexual maturity is attained, extending through the long period of generativity and into old age when successful adults may experience ego integrity. Because Erikson's theory has been so influential to thinking about behavior in different age groups across the life span, we will rely on it heavily in the developmental chapters that follow.

THE BEHAVIORAL PERSPECTIVE

The third major psychological perspective is that of behaviorism, which traces its roots to Pavlov and his famous conditioning experiments with dogs (Pavlov, 1927). Pavlov and others showed that principles of learning could be gleaned from research with animals. These principles were later shown to be applicable to the more complex behavior of human beings. For example, certain phobic responses, such as claustrophobia, were shown to have their roots in early traumatic experiences, such as being punished by confinement. Such phobic reactions in adulthood could be traced to even a single traumatic experience in childhood, suggesting the powerful influence of *classical conditioning*.

Perhaps the best known form of behaviorism in the United States is Skinnerian *operant conditioning* (Skinner, 1953). The most basic principle in this model is the principle of reinforcement. Skinnerians believe that reinforcement is the key to controlling behavior and that behavior can be understood by identifying the contingencies that have shaped it and that maintain it. Even more than Eriksonians, behaviorists believe in the plasticity of human beings. In its purest form, behaviorism holds that all behavior is learned and that anything that is learned can be unlearned and relearned.

Social learning theory is a third type of behaviorism, one that places an emphasis on modeling and imitation as prime factors in learning. Bandura and Walters (1963) are two of the leading exponents of this theory. Bandura in particular has attempted to modify learning theory to include the principles of modeling and self-efficacy as they interact within a social context (Bandura, 1977). In accordance with most behavioral approaches to personality, social learning theory is based on the premise that human behavior is largely acquired or learned. The following case study illustrates some of the principles of suicidal behavior from the perspective of behaviorists.

> *Jerry W. was a 42-year-old man referred to therapy after an unsuccessful but very serious suicide attempt. He had waited until his wife and teenage children had gone to visit the grandparents. Then he had systematically sealed the windows in the garage and the air space under the door with rags and fed a hose from the exhaust pipe into the car. He had then taken the evening paper with him into the car. Only the unexpected visit of a golf partner, who was returning a borrowed club and who heard the engine running as he got out of his car, prevented the completion of this suicide.*
>
> *Jerry had no obvious reason for attempting suicide. His 15-year-old marriage was a success. He was considered to be a leader in his job. He had been successful at a very young age in a computer software company and now was earning a salary of six figures. His children, while not models of adolescent development, seemed to be well adjusted and reasonably loving.*
>
> *Upon probing, his therapist discovered that Jerry had been feeling anxious for a couple of years, "like everything was going to go wrong." Just lately, within the last month, he had felt that everything was over, that he "was just going through the motions, that he had no right to go on living." After several therapy sessions Jerry admitted that his father had committed suicide at exactly*

The Scream, **Edvard Munch. Tempera and casein on paper. (Courtesy of Nasjonalgalleriet, Oslo. Photograph by Jacques Lathion.)**

age 42, leaving a very confused and angry 15-year-old Jerry trying to understand why. After a while, he gave up trying to understand, stopped talking about his father, and went on to become a "wunderkind" in the computer software business. Jerry took quiet pride in his success, particularly when older family members told him that his intelligence and hard work reminded them of his father.

Supporters of the social learning view would claim that Jerry's attempt was an example of an "anniversary" suicide attempt and that both anniversary suicides and cluster suicides are examples of suicides that result from imitation and modeling. Jerry's attempt was rooted in the traumatic experience of observing his father commit suicide. Jerry's father modeled suicide as an acceptable behavior. It is worthwhile to note that the power of modeling is increased when the model performing the behavior is the same sex as the learner and is regarded by the learner as powerful. Both of these conditions were met in Jerry's case.

A special case of social learning theory is particularly appropriate in any discussion of suicide. It is the research generated by Martin Seligman (1975), which applies learning principles originally established in the laboratory with animals to a special emotional reaction among humans: depression. Seligman was trained as an experimental psychologist in the behavioral tradition, and his initial work followed the principles of experimental research with animals. Seligman and his colleagues carried out a series of experiments that placed dogs in a device called a shuttlebox, which essentially is a large box with two compartments. Seligman then administered a series of shocks accompanied by a tone. In their anxiety to escape the shock the dogs would eventually jump over the barrier dividing the box. When they did, both the shock and the tone would stop. Eventually the animals would jump over the barrier at the first sound of the tone, thus avoiding the shock altogether. In another experiment, dogs were placed in restraining harnesses in the first compartment of the shuttlebox and given a series of brief shocks that they could not escape. In subsequent trials, even with no restraint, the dogs did not attempt to escape from the compartment. They lay whimpering in the first compartment until both the tone and the shocks ended. Their response of passive acceptance of painful stimuli was labeled *learned helplessness*.

Seligman and his colleagues soon investigated this phenomenon with college students. In a series of experiments, they showed that when students were faced with unsolvable problems coupled with noxious stimuli (noise) the students were later unable to learn to escape the stimuli. In other experimental conditions, students confronted with solvable problems or with no problems quickly learned in later sessions to escape or avoid the noxious stimuli. Seligman pointed out that in both kinds of situations later learning was dependent upon antecedent events. He drew parallels between reactive depression brought on by a major loss or failure and learned helplessness. Table 2.4 shows the features common to learned helplessness and depression. Seligman believed that at least some forms of depression that often lead to suicidal behavior could be explained as the result of traumatic events that could not be controlled or warded off, even by the best efforts of those involved.

Again the voice spake unto me: "Thou are so steep'd in misery, surely 'twere better not to be."
Tennyson, The *Two Voices*

TABLE 2.4 Summary of Features Common to Learned Helplessness and Depression

	Learned helplessness	Depression
Symptoms	Passivity	Passivity
	Difficulty learning that responses produce relief	Negative cognitive set
		Time course
	Dissipates in time	Introjected hostility (hostility turned inward)
	Lack of aggression	
	Weight loss, appetite loss, social and sexual deficits	Weight loss, appetite loss, social and sexual deficits
	Ulcers and stress	Ulcers (?) and stress
Cause	Learning that responding and reinforcement are independent	Belief that responding is useless
Cure	Directive therapy: forced exposure to responses that produce reinforcement	Recovery of belief that responding produces reinforcement
	Electroconvulsive shock	Electroconvulsive shock
	Time	Time
Prevention	Immunization by mastery over reinforcement	(?)

Source: From Martin E. P. Seligman, *Helplessness: On depression, development, and death,* p. 106, W. H. Freeman and Company, (© 1975). Reprinted with the permission of W. H. Freeman and Company.

One approach to helping individuals who evidence learned helplessness and its accompanying depression is to teach a more "internal locus of control," that is, to help them see that they do have control over many aspects of their lives and do not have to be entirely at the mercy of the environment in all situations. Identification of controllable elements and rational acceptance of those that cannot be controlled might also help alleviate depression. Another approach, which will be described in chapter 9, is to use cognitive techniques to develop "learned optimism" as a defense against depression.

In summary, the behavioral perspective would maintain that suicidal behavior, like all behavior, is learned. Whether it is learned by imitation and modeling or through unavoidable loss (which can lead to learned helplessness), it can be manipulated. What is learned can be unlearned and relearned. It is clear that the proper role of the therapist in the behavioral model is as a teacher, utilizing the powerful principles of learning to help clients develop new and healthier ways of coping.

THE HUMANISTIC PERSPECTIVE

The fourth major school of thought in psychology is the humanistic or *humanistic-existential* perspective. It was developed during the middle part of the 20th century as a response to the pessimistic view of human growth held by Freudian psychoanalysts and the more mechanistic view of humans held by the early behaviorists. The basic emphasis in this school is on the human potential for growth. It also stresses essential human characteristics, those that separate humans from other animals. Thus, humanistic psychologists feel free to focus on the inner experience of the individual. They frequently use such tools as humor and visualization in working with people. Central to most humanistic-existential theories of applied psychology is the belief that the client should be at the center of the process and that the client can, with minimal intervention, approach the realization of his or her potential.

Two of the major figures early in the development of humanistic psychology in the United States were Abraham Maslow and Carl Rogers. Maslow is also known as the father of *transpersonal psychology*, an approach that focuses specifically on such subjective experiences as ecstasy, mystical experiences, awe, wonder, and cosmic awareness. Rogers, the father of *client-centered* therapy, derived his positive theory of human development from his clinical work. We shall examine here only the early work of Maslow, with special reference to its similarities to Roger's therapeutic approach (self-theory) and to its relevance for suicidal behavior.

Maslow conceived of human behavior as operating on a hierarchical basis (Maslow, 1954). Table 2.5 presents Maslow's now-famous hierarchy of needs, as well as corresponding conditions of deficiency and fulfillment and an example for each level. The column entitled "conditions of deficiency" can be regarded as a summary of the feelings of suicidal people. Maslow believed in two basically different types of needs, the D, or drive, needs and the B, or being, needs. Maslow felt that we are pushed by our drive needs to eliminate a deficiency and by our being needs to become more completely all that we are capable of becoming.

Similarities between Maslow's theory and Rogers's theory are many. In particular, both would agree that provided basic needs are met humans are essentially growth-oriented creatures whose nature is directed toward realizing their potential if external conditions permit. Both theorists are also basically optimistic about human nature. That is, rather than view human development as a product of basic energies and conflicts (as do psychoanalytic theorists) or as a result of learning imposed largely by environmental conditions (as do behaviorists), these theorists believe that humans are essentially good and that there are higher levels of development that most of us can hope to achieve (Maslow, 1971). Aspiring to these levels helps humans to live "authentic" lives and to find meaning in their lives.

Inability to discover meaning in life can lead to feelings of uselessness, hopelessness, and depression. Frankl (1963), an existential neurologist, described this state as *noogenic neurosis* and claimed that it was one of the most widespread illnesses of Western societies in the 20th century. People who can-

TABLE 2.5 Maslow's Needs Hierarchy and Levels of Personality Functioning

Need hierarchy	Condition of deficiency	Fulfillment	Illustration	
Self-actualization	Alienation Metapathologies Absence of meaning in life Boredom	Healthy curiosity Peak experiences Realization of potentials Work that is pleasurable and embodies values	Experiencing a profound insight	
	Limited activities	Creative living		B needs
Esteem	Feeling of incompetence Negativism Feeling of inferiority	Confidence Sense of mastery Positive self-regard	Receiving an award for an outstanding performance on some project	
Love	Self-consciousness Feeling of being unwanted Feeling of worthlessness	Free expression of emotion Sense of wholeness Sense of warmth	Experiencing total acceptance in love relationship	
	Emptiness Loneliness	Renewed sense of life and strength Sense of growing together		
Safety	Insecurity Yearning Sense of loss Fear Poise Obsession Compulsion	Security Comfort Balance Calm Tranquility	Being secure in a full-time job	D needs
Physiological	Hunger, thirst Sexual frustration Tension	Relaxation Release from tension Experiences of pleasure from senses	Feeling satisfied after a good meal	
	Illness Lack of proper shelter	Physical well-being Comfort		

Source: Adapted from Nicholas S. DiCaprio, *Personality theories: Guide to living.* (© 1974). Philadelphia, PA: W. B. Saunders Company. Reprinted by permission of Saunders College Publishing/CBS College Publishing.

not see any meaning in living are prime targets for suicide from the point of view of humanists and existentialists. The following case study exemplifies some of the elements thought to be important in suicidal behavior by proponents of the humanistic-existential school of psychology.

> *Lynn B. was a successful 28-year-old high school English teacher. She had always been a good student, finishing college with honors. She had taught for six years and described her experience in muted, solemn tones. "I guess I was convinced that the two greatest goods in the world were knowledge and helping people. That's what attracted me to teaching. I thought that was the one field where my two highest goods in life could be realized together. I guess I really bought into the old "Mr. Chips" stereotype. I thought I would go through life learning more and more and sharing it with eager young people, who would be properly appreciative. It seems funny now. My students have taught me more than I've ever taught them. They've taught me that reading poetry is a waste of time, that literature is only millions of meaningless words written by dead people who thought they had something to say. For the first few years, I thought the students were wrong. Then I began to ask what was so great about the stuff I was teaching, and it came to me that the students were right. Much of literature is as dead as the people who wrote it. It doesn't speak to humans today. Learning it is just an exercise of neurons. When we die, will it make any difference if we've read Beowulf? Or Canterbury Tales? Will it make any difference to us before we die? I see no difference in the lives of my students who take my old English course and those who don't, except maybe that those who don't are not so bored for one hour a day. If you ask me why I live, I guess the best answer I can give you is, why not? Sometimes it almost scares me. I'd like to believe in something again, but I know better now."*

According to humanists, Lynn is in psychological trouble. If she does not find something that she feels has real meaning, she will go through life in a kind of fog of meaninglessness and ennui. If and when things get too difficult for her and an existential crisis of major proportions occurs, she is likely to attempt suicide. At the very least, her life will be an emotional desert, lacking passion and commitment.

Humanists speak of self-actualization as the highest attainment of humans, the ideal mental health criterion. Self-actualization is the process whereby we each realize our own unique potential. It is a lifelong process, marked by discovering our own version of what gives life meaning and living that to its fullest. Self-actualized people are well adjusted and productive. They are also capable of having a rich inner life. Suicide is highly unlikely among self-actualized people—unless it is a response to a terminal illness.

THE COGNITIVE PERSPECTIVE

Beginning in the late 1950s, many psychologists became disillusioned with behaviorism, the prevailing theory in psychology at that time. The primary reason for their disillusionment was that strict behaviorists thought that psychologists should study only observable behaviors. Such topics as motivation, will, desire, even learning (except as it could be observed) were considered to be outside the purview of psychology. In fact, the behaviorism of the early and middle 20th century became known as "black box" psychology, since in its purest form it regarded the individual as a black box, the internal workings of which could never be known. Black box psychology restricted itself to studying the stimuli that acted upon the black box, the behavior emitted from the black box, and the results of reinforcing or punishing that behavior.

Since the goal of psychology as a social science is to understand, predict, and control behavior, and since much behavior is rooted in motivations that are not visible, many psychologists began midcentury to broaden their field of study to include the thinking of the individual. This broadening of research has resulted in the establishment of a fourth school of psychology, known as *cognitive psychology*. It is the fastest growing theoretical perspective in psychology in the United States. It has been greatly influenced by the work of the Swiss psychologist, Jean Piaget.

Piaget was the foremost 20th-century theorist regarding the development of cognitive abilities in children and young adults. He proposed that cognitive development occurs in an orderly manner that is less open to environmental manipulation than the behaviorists believe. Piaget thought that all children move through stages of cognitive development in a particular order and that each stage is associated with specific qualitative aspects of thinking and problem solving (Piaget, 1926; Piaget & Inhelder, 1969). His stages of cognitive development, the ages in which children typically progress through them, and some major characteristics of each stage are presented in Table 2.6.

According to Piaget, the first stage of cognitive development, the period of *sensorimotor* intelligence, occurs between birth and two years of age for most children. The sensorimotor period was so named by Piaget because children in this age group typically learn about the world through their sensory and motor experiences. Young children have little or no symbolic representations of the world until the end of this stage. As they progress through the first two years of life, children move from a very immature level (in which mental capabilities are limited to reflexive activities such as sucking and grasping) to a more mature level (which includes the ability to distinguish between self and others and the performance of intentional acts). A special milestone that typically occurs about halfway through the sensorimotor period is the development of *object permanence,* which is indicated when a child searches for an object that has been moved out of his or her visual field. Object permanence

TABLE 2.6   Piaget's System of Cognitive Development

Period and stage	Life period	Some major characteristics
I. Period of sensorimotor	Infancy (0–2)	"Intelligence" consists of sensory and motor actions. No conscious thinking. Limited language. No concept of reality.
II. Period of preoperational	Early childhood (2–7)	Egocentric orientation. Magical, animistic, and artificialistic thinking. Thinking is irreversible. Reality is subjective.
III. Period of concrete operations	Middle childhood/ preadolescence (7–11/12)	Orientation ego-decentered. Thinking is bound to concrete. Naturalistic thinking. Recognition of laws of conservation and reversibility.
IV. Period of formal operations	Adolescence and adulthood (12+)	Propositional and hypo-deductive thinking. Generality of thinking. Reality is objective.

Source: Adapted from Wass and Corr, *Childhood and death,* p. 4, New York, Hemisphere and McGraw-Hill International, 1984.

is very important, because it reflects the rudiments of the capability for symbolic representation of objects in the world. Toward the end of the sensorimotor period, children show evidence of learning through trial and error and even some capacity for insight learning through mental combinations.

The second stage of cognitive development is the *preoperational* period, which occurs between ages two and seven. These preschool years are marked by very rapid development of language skills and symbolic capabilities in general. Young children are very impressive when they begin to develop language and can for the first time actually communicate their thoughts to another person. However, Piaget in some ways characterized the preoperational period more in terms of what children are unable to do rather than in terms of what they are able to do. The term *preoperational* was chosen by Piaget to reflect the fact that children in this age group are typically unable to utilize certain logical thinking techniques in problem solving. For example, the preoperational child is unable to deal effectively with part-whole relationships. When presented with a jar filled with red beads and white beads, he or she has difficulty understanding that there are more beads than either red or white beads.

The preoperational child also has great difficulty solving conservation problems. In Piaget's now-famous experiment testing conservation of volume, the young child is presented with two identical glasses filled to the same level with water. As the child watches, the liquid from one glass is poured into another, differently shaped container, resulting in a higher or lower water level than in the original glass. The preoperational child does not understand that the volume of liquid is unchanged by this operation and reports that the amount of water in the new glass is more (or less) than the amount in the original glass.

Preoperational children show their intellectual immaturity in other ways as well. They are, for example, very susceptible to animistic thinking, investing inanimate objects with lifelike characteristics. For example, their teddy bears or blankets may have names and personalities and be capable of action in the eyes of the preschool child. Preoperational children also tend to be incapable of understanding more than one point of view in a complex situation. This characteristic, called egocentric thinking by Piagetians, has been blamed for much of the argumentativeness and negativism of younger children in the preoperational stage.

The *concrete operations* child, between ages 6 and 12, possesses many logical-thinking characteristics that younger children do not. Children in the stage of concrete operations can easily solve conservation problems, have no difficulty with part-whole relationships, and show mature understandings of time, space, and causality. Their thinking and problem solving closely approximate adult reasoning except for one important limitation: their understanding is limited to real-world facts. They have great difficulty following a hypothetical line of reasoning and understanding highly abstract concepts such as justice. The elementary school child works best in the real and the here and now. This stage has been called the stage of the natural scientist, because children's thinking is so bound to the concrete aspects of their world.

The *formal operations* period begins during adolescence and develops more fully in young adulthood. Unlike children in younger age groups, individuals at the formal operations stage can think hypothetically and deal with higher levels of abstraction. Also during this period, adolescents and young adults begin intuitively to utilize certain aspects of the scientific method in solving problems. This stage has been called the stage of the philosopher because young people can begin to ask questions regarding abstract principles such as truth and justice and can begin to face issues of meaning in their intellectual lives.

Piaget's detailed descriptions of the qualitative changes in thinking that occur as children develop help to explain the different ways in which various age groups view the world. Some of the developmental changes have implications for the study of suicide. For example, children in the preoperational and concrete operational periods understand death differently than adults, whose formal operational thinking is richer and more abstract. The thinking patterns of these children are, in fact, evidence that children younger than age 10 have a tendency to see death as a temporary and reversible state much like sleep. This and other age-related cognitive differences described by Piaget will be discussed in detail as we explore the suicidal behavior of different age groups in chapters 3 through 7.

Piaget's stages of cognitive development have done more than reveal patterns in children's increasingly sophisticated thinking. They have helped other theorists and clinicians to understand the powerful influences thought and language have on the developing personality and on all types of behavior. Moreover, Piaget's work demonstrated conclusively that it is possible to study the thinking of individuals. In this way, it laid the groundwork for cognitive therapists like Albert Ellis, Aaron Beck, and Donald Meichenbaum to target the thought patterns of depressed and suicidal people.

In the section on behaviorism, we reviewed the early work of Martin Seligman, which led to the notion of learned helplessness. For the past several decades, Seligman has moved fully into the cognitive perspective and has proposed that the way we think about life affects our psychology and our biology. In an important book entitled *Learned Optimism*, Seligman (1991) posed the following questions:

- What if depression arises from mistaken inferences we make from the tragedies and setbacks we all experience over the course of a life?
- What if depression occurs merely when we harbor pessimistic beliefs about the causes of our setbacks?
- What if we can unlearn pessimism and acquire the skills of looking at setbacks optimistically?

In a wide-ranging and readable review of the literature on depression with references to suicide, Seligman has suggested that we can have more control over our depressed and suicidal thoughts by learning some simple methods to control our thoughts, ruminations, and reactions to negative events. In short, Seligman suggests that we can choose to be helpless or not, to be pessimistic or optimistic, to become depressed or to become capable of resisting depression, to embrace suicide or to be inoculated against it. In chapter 9 we will examine some of his suggestions in more detail, along with those of other cognitive therapists as they treat people suffering from suicidal depression.

THE SOCIOLOGICAL PERSPECTIVE

Sociologists maintain that suicidal behavior cannot be viewed outside of the context in which it occurs. As evidence, they point to the fact that people in different cultures have had different psychological problems at different times. For example, hysterical symptoms, such as spontaneous blindness,

---

Razors pain you; rivers are damp; acids stain you; and drugs cause cramp. Guns aren't lawful; nooses give; gas smells awful; you might as well live. Dorothy Parker, *Résumé*, 1926

deafness, or loss of feeling in a part of the body, were far more common in the early part of this century than they are today. Sociologists would maintain that greater understanding of the way the body works, coupled with widespread reading of psychoanalytic literature, has led to a decrease in the number of people presenting with this type of artificial physiological problem.

As we discussed in chapter 1, sociology first began to examine suicidal behavior and its causes in the latter part of the 19th century. Emile Durkheim (1897–1951), a major figure in sociology, hypothesized that suicides occur as a result of the kind of "fit" that an individual experiences in his or her society. He postulated four different types of suicide: The first type he labeled *egoistic suicide*, which occurs when "the bond attaching man to life relaxes because that attaching him to society is itself slack. The individual becomes remote from social life and suffers from an excess of individualism" (Taylor, 1982). Durkheim took pains to point out that the suicide rate of his time was higher among Protestants than among Catholics; his explanation was that Catholics received more support from their church while Protestants were left more to their individual devices. Other supportive evidence for egoistic suicide at that time was that more single people committed suicide than married people and that fewer married women with children committed suicide than unmarried women. Durkheim believed that the incidence of egoistic suicide is inversely related to family density.

Durkheim labeled the second type of suicide *altruistic suicide*, which according to Durkheim occurs when there is an overintegration of the individual into society. The person then kills himself or herself in an attempt to conform to social imperatives. Suttee, the ritualistic suicide that an Indian widow committed by throwing herself on her husband's funeral pyre, which was practiced until the early part of this century, is an example of such suicide. More recent examples can be found in the Japanese kamikaze pilots of World War II. These young boys, some under 15 years of age, volunteered near the end of the war to fly planes on one-way missions to destroy U.S. ships. The planes they were given did not have enough fuel for a return trip. In addition, the landing gear on some of them was altered to dislodge on takeoff so that no safe landing could be carried out. These young idealists are good examples of people who had so thoroughly assimilated their society's values that they were willing to commit suicide for love of country. The opposing side in that war offered similar examples. Roger Young, an infantry officer, was immortalized in song because he threw himself on a grenade to save other infantrymen sharing the same foxhole: "Roger Young. Roger Young. Fought and died for the men he marched among. To the everlasting glory of the Infantry, shines the courage of Private Roger Young." Roger Young's sacrifice was a model of altruistic suicide.

The third type of suicide discussed by Durkheim was called *anomic suicide*, which results from a person's activity "lacking regulation." Evidence for this type of suicide is found in the fact that suicide rates rise both in times of economic depression and in times of greater prosperity. Regardless of what is going on in the larger society, the suicidal individual feels cut off from it, "out of sync." In addition, the individual has a great deal of freedom to express himself or herself. The drug-related suicides of the late 1960s might be good examples of this type of suicide. During that decade, many young people were not comfortable with society's mainstream values. Their behavior lacked regulation. They experimented wildly, sometimes fatally, with toxic substances.

The final type of suicide discussed by Durkheim was called *fatalistic suicide*. He viewed this as almost the opposite of the anomic type of suicide. It results from overregulation and oppressive discipline by a society, directed at a particular segment of that society. Evidence for this type of suicide might be found in the suicide rates among slaves or prisoners in barbaric and punitive conditions, such as those in concentration camps.

The sociological view of suicide calls for a broader perspective than that found in most psychological approaches. It challenges people to look at conditions in their cultures at any given point in history as factors that can directly influence the suicide rate. In this way, sociologists provide a major service to students of suicide. An analogy that is useful in understanding the utility of this perspective is that of an anthill. A child watching an individual ant busily wander back and forth across a path carrying a bit of sand can infer little meaning from the behavior. If, however, the child stands up and regards the broader scene, he or she may observe a nearly finished anthill. While the individual behavior is not explainable, it becomes meaningful as a part of the larger picture. In just such a way, individual suicidal behavior may become more meaningful when examined against the social fabric of society.

THE BIOLOGICAL PERSPECTIVE

No discussion about perspectives for viewing suicide would be complete without a brief review of the remarkable progress being made in understanding the biological correlates of depression. Although depression is not synonymous with suicide (for a person can commit suicide without being depressed), the relationship between the two is sufficiently close to justify an examination of the research on the biological bases of depression.

During the past three decades, major insights have been gained into the way the brain functions and into how specific brain dysfunctions may relate to depression. In order to appreciate these findings, some understanding of the way the brain functions is helpful.

The nervous system of human beings is composed of two parts: the central nervous system and the peripheral nervous system. The *central nervous system*, which includes the nerves of the brain and spinal cord, governs behavior by interpreting informational or sensory input that comes to it from the *peripheral nervous system*—the nerves outside the brain and spinal cord—and by sending messages to the muscles and glands.

The most central part of the nervous system is the brain, which is composed of billions of individual nerve cells called *neurons*. Figure 2.1 depicts the anatomy of a neuron. Neurons are composed of a cell body, a nucleus, impulse receptors (dendrites), and impulse transmitters (axons). Each neuron is capable of "firing," that is, of producing an electrical impulse in the cell body that is sent through the axon to the receptor site of the next neuron. Figure 2.2 illustrates the synaptic transmission processes. Chemical changes at the synaptic junction between the transmitting and receiving neurons determine whether the signal will complete the connection or be stopped. The discovery of the effects of these chemicals on behavior was largely accidental.

In the 1950s, many physicians used the drug reserpine to control high blood pressure. They noted that a high percentage of their patients reported depressive symptoms while on the drug. At the same time, animal studies showed that reserpine depleted nerve endings in the brain of several important neurotransmitter substances. Subsequent studies over a 20-year period have determined that the substances most involved in depression are the neurotransmitters serotonin and norepinephrine (Asberg & Traskman, 1981; Banki & Arato, 1983; Schildkraut, 1965).

As discussed in chapter 1, deficiency of serotonin has been found in the brains of some people who have completed suicide and in the cerebrospinal fluid of suicide attempters (Asberg, Nordstrom, & Traskman-Bendz, 1986). Since serotonin is instrumental in regulating emotion, some researchers have suggested that a deficiency of serotonin may be implicated both in depression and in suicide attempts, especially impulsive suicide attempts. Researchers have found that low serotonin, as measured by one of its main metabolic products (5-HIAA), was correlated with both depression and the seriousness of suicide attempts (Asberg, Traskman, & Thoren, 1973; Nordstrom et al., 1994). Furthermore, these studies showed that among patients who had been hospitalized in conjunction with a suicide attempt those who had less 5-HIAA were more likely to have died from suicide a year later than were those who had higher levels of the substance.

When chemical deficiencies are found to be related to mood or behavior, a natural development is to try to erase the deficiency by means of the development of drugs. Over the past three decades the pharmaceutical industry has developed three major groups of medications for the treatment of unipolar depression. The actions of these three types of psychotropic drug have

---

—Most researchers and clinicians again believe that the serious mental disorders [including depression] reflect abnormalities in brain structure or biochemistry. Physiology of Behavior

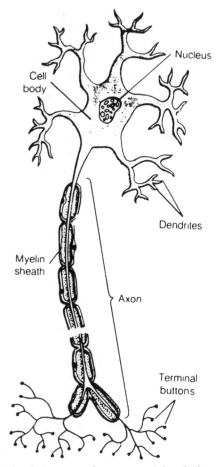

FIGURE 2.1   An idealized diagram of a neuron. Stimulation of the dendrites or of the cell body activates an electrochemical nerve impulse that travels along the axon to the terminal buttons. The myelin sheath covers the axons of some but not all neurons; it helps to increase the speed of nerve impulse conduction.

Source: Introduction to Psychology, Eighth Edition (p. 32), by R. L. Atkinson, R. C. Atkinson, & E. R. Hilgard, 1983 New York: Harcourt Brace Jovanovich, Inc. Copyright © by Harcourt Brace Jovanovich, Inc. Used with permission.

been recounted in a recently published handbook (Bezchlibnyk-Butler, Jeffries, & Martin, 1994). Although each drug has a different biochemical effect on the central nervous system, the functional result is to increase the level of serotonin at the synaptic junctions of the neurons in the brain. The first type consists of *monoamine oxidase (MAO) inhibitors* (e.g., moclobemide), which block the action of the MAO enzyme that metabolizes serotonin and several other neurotransmitters. The second group of antidepressants is known as *tricyclics*

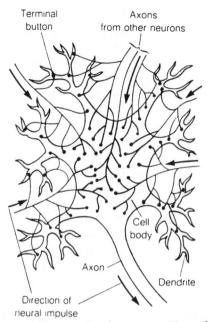

Terminal button

Axons from other neurons

Cell body

Axon

Dendrite

Direction of neural impulse

FIGURE 2.2   Synapses at the cell body of a neuron. Many different axons, each of which branches repeatedly, synapse on the dendrites and cell body of a single neuron. Each branch of an axon ends in a swelling called a terminal button, which contains the chemical that is released and transmits the nerve impulse across the synapse to the dendrites or cell body of the next cell.
Source: Introduction to Psychology, Eighth Edition (p. 33), by R. L. Atkinson, R. C. Atkinson, & E. R. Hilgard, 1983 New York: Harcourt Brace Jovanovich, Inc. Copyright © by Harcourt Brace Jovanovich, Inc. Used with permission.

(e.g., amitriptyline). The exact pharmacological action of tricyclics that results in the lifting of depression is uncertain; however, recent evidence suggests that this class of drugs acts by increasing the sensitivity of the receiving neuron to serotonin. The third and most recently developed group of antidepressant medications is known as *selective serotonin-reuptake inhibitors (SSRIs)*. SSRIs such as fluoxetine (Prozac) increase the effectiveness of serotonin by inhibiting the reuptake process when the neurotransmitter substance is in the synaptic junction. This new class of antidepressants has been widely prescribed (perhaps too widely) because their action appears to have fewer side effects (e.g., constipation, dryness of mouth, drowsiness) than many of the MAO inhibitors and tricyclics. A fourth type of medication discussed in the clinical handbook is *lithium,* which is used in cases of bipolar or manic-depressive affective disorder but appears to be relatively ineffective in the treatment of unipolar depression.

A second area of research on the biology of suicide involves examining its genetic bases. As reported in chapter 1, Blumenthal and Kupfer (1986) reviewed the literature on family history and genetics and reported that the incidence of suicidal behavior is higher than usual in relatives of persons who exhibit suicidal behavior. Also, the closer these genetic relationships are (i.e., identical twins), the higher are the suicide concordance rates. Lester (1986), in another review of the literature on genetics, twin studies, and suicide, concluded that "it is clear that the concordance rate for completed suicide is higher in monozygotic twin pairs raised together than in dizygotic twin pairs raised together" (p. 200). While these studies are far from definitive, they are suggestive of the biological position that maintains that at least a portion of suicidal behavior may be attributed to genetic traits interacting with biology.

Examining suicide from many different perspectives provides a richness that is impossible to achieve from a single perspective. It also establishes an appreciation of the complexities involved in any suicidal gesture. Finally, it reminds us that human beings are multifaceted creatures. Those who would understand suicidal individuals must begin to see them as persons who may have been born with a biological inclination toward depression and whose internal personality needs and drives may or may not be able to be expressed within their environment. Moreover, those studying suicide must recognize that the cognitive set of the individual and his or her thoughts about the current situation can serve to increase or decrease suicide susceptibility. Caring people must try to understand the mind-body connections within suicidal people. Stressful environments change body chemistry. In susceptible people, increased stress can result in changes that increase the likelihood of depression. When these chemical changes occur, an increase in depression-related cognitions may result. Such negative cognitions may well increase the subjective impression of stress, which in turn will have a continuing effect on the chemistry of the brain. In short, biology, psychology, cognitions, and environment all interact to produce a suicidal individual. The mind and the body are indeed a unity. We are only beginning to discover the nature of their connections, which the study of depression and of suicidal persons is helping to illuminate.

SUMMARY

In this chapter, we have reviewed the major psychological and sociological perspectives on the nature and causes of suicide and we have provided case studies to illustrate these perspectives. Freud's psychoanalytic perspective was presented, with emphasis on the view of suicide as resulting from an imbalance between Thanatos and Eros. Erikson's psychosocial perspective was discussed, stressing the importance of the social environment in contributing to the development of both healthy and unhealthy personalities. This book owes a major theoretical debt to Erikson's theory with its emphasis on personality development over the life span.

The behavioristic perspective, which considers suicide to be a form of learned behavior, was presented in a discussion of reinforcement, modeling, and learned helplessness. Seligman's theory of learned helplessness was described as a model for depression. The humanistic theories of Maslow and Rogers were noted, with attention given to their belief in the human potential for growth. The universal search for meaningfulness in our lives was discussed, especially on how failure to discover such meaning can lead to feelings of uselessness, hopelessness, and depression.

The importance of the cognitive perspective was discussed. Piaget's theory for understanding the development of concepts of death was described, and Seligman's cognitive approach to teaching optimism was presented as an example of a further application of cognitive theory.

The sociological perspective and Durkheim's suicide classification system were presented to emphasize the fact that suicidal behavior is influenced by the social context within which a person lives. We noted the importance of Durkheim's work in understanding suicide, both historically and presently.

Finally, we reported several recent discoveries of biological correlates of depression. There is now a new understanding of the role of serotonin in depression and of the implications for antidepressant medications. Evidence for the role of genetics in depression is increasing.

We concluded that suicidal behavior results from a complex interaction of biology, psychology, cognitions, and environmental forces. Biology forms the core of who we are, but biology does not exist in a vacuum. It exists in a psychological-social-spiritual human being who lives at a particular time within a material environment and complex culture. We must therefore examine each of these elements and their interactions as we attempt to understand humans moving through their life cycles.

SUGGESTED ADDITIONAL READINGS

The Psychoanalytic Perspective

Bowlby, J. (1973). Separation. In *Attachment and loss* (Vol. 2). New York: Basic Books.

Freud, A. (1946). *The ego and the mechanisms of defense.* New York: International Universities Press.

Freud, A. (1967). *The ego and the mechanisms of defense* (2nd ed.). London: Hogarth Press.

Freud, S. (1961). Mourning and melancholia. In J. Strachey (Ed. and Trans.), *The standard edition of the complete psychological works of Sigmund Freud* (Vol. 14, pp. 243–258). London: Hogarth Press. (Original work published 1917)

Horney, K. (1937). *The collected works of Karen Horney.* New York: Norton.

The Psychosocial Perspective

Erikson, E. H. (1963). *Childhood and society* (2nd ed.). New York: Norton.

Erikson, E. H. (1980). *Identity and the life cycle.* New York: Norton. (Original work published in 1959)

Erikson, E. H. (1982). *The life cycle completed.* New York: Norton.

Gould, R. L. (1978). *Transformations: Growth and change in adult life.* New York: Simon & Schuster.

Levinson, D. J., Darrow, C. N., Klein, E. B., Levinson, M. H., & McKee, B. (1978). *The seasons of a man's life.* New York: Knopf.
Vaillant, G. E. (1977). *Adaptation to life: How the best and brightest came of age.* Boston: Little, Brown.

The Behavioral Perspective

Bandura, A. (1969). *Principles of behavior modification.* New York: Holt, Rinehart, & Winston.
Bandura, A. (1977). *Social learning theory.* Englewood Cliffs, NJ: Prentice-Hall.
Bandura, A. & Walters, R. H. (1963). *Social Learning and Personality Development.* NY: Holt Rinehart and Winston.
Craighead, W. E., Kazdin, A. E., & Mahoney, M. J. (1981). *Behavior modification: Principles, issues, and applications* (2nd ed.). Boston: Houghton Mifflin.
Rotter, J. B., Chance, J. E., & Phares, E. J. (1972). *Applications of a social learning theory of personality.* New York: Holt, Rinehart & Winston.
Seligman, M.E.P. (1975). *Helplessness.* San Francisco: Freeman.
Skinner, B. F. (1971). *Beyond freedom and dignity.* New York: Knopf.

The Cognitive Perspective

Beck, A. T. (1976). *Cognitive therapy and the emotional disorders.* New York: International Universities Press.
Elkind, D. (1981). *The hurried child: Growing up too fast too soon.* Reading, MA: Addison-Wesley.
Kohlberg, L. (1969). Stage and sequence: The cognitive-developmental approach to socialization. In D. A. Goslin (Ed.), *Handbook of socialization theory and research.* Chicago: Rand McNally.
Meichenbaum, D. H., & Jaremko, M. (1982). *Stress prevention and management.* New York: Plenum Press.
Piaget, J. (1952). *The origins of intelligence in children.* New York: International Universities Press.
Piaget, J., & Inhelder, B. (1969). *The psychology of the child.* New York: Basic Books.
Seligman, M. (1990). *Learned Optimism.* New York: Pocket Books.

The Humanistic Perspective

Frankl, V. E. (1963). *Man's search for meaning: An introduction to logotherapy* (I. Lasch, Trans). New York: Washington Square Press.
Maslow, A. H. (1967). Self-actualization and beyond. In J.F.T. Bugental (Ed.), *Challenges of humanistic psychology.* New York: McGraw-Hill.
Maslow, A. H. (1970). *Motivation and personality* (2nd ed.). New York: Harper & Row.
Maslow, A. H. (1971). *The farther reaches of human nature.* New York: Viking Press.
Rogers, C. R. (1970). *On becoming a person: A therapist's view of psychotherapy.* Boston: Houghton Mifflin.
Rogers, C. R. (1951). *Client-centered therapy.* Boston: Houghton Mifflin.

The Biological Perspective

Deakin, J.F.W. (1986). *The biology of depression.* Oxford: Alden Press.
Geschwind, N. (1979, September) Specializations of the human brain. *Scientific American, 241,* 180–199.
Restak, R. M. (1984). *The brain.* New York: Bantam Books.
Rossi, E. L. (1986). *The psychobiology of mind-body healing.* New York: Norton.
Roy, A. (1994). Recent biological studies on suicide. *Suicide and Life-Threatening Behavior, 24,* 10–14.
Teuting, P., & Koslow, S. H. (1981). Special report on depression research. In *Science Reports.* Rockville, MD: National Institute of Mental Health.

3

Suicide in Childhood

A simple child,
That lightly draws its breath
And feels its life in every limb,
What should it know of death?

Wordsworth

New York, June 17, 1992, *The New York Times:*

*An 8-year-old boy: "Sometimes when I'm really upset, I say I will shoot myself.
When my brother gets on me, I feel like dying."*

*A 10-year-old boy: "I think about dying a lot. I thought of hurting myself,
cutting my wrist. I think about how it's going to be when I die. It keeps coming
back."*

*Adults commonly dismiss such talk as foolish or fleeting notions, manipula-
tive scare tactics or exaggerations born of immaturity. But Dr. Cynthia R. Pfeffer, a child psychiatrist at the Westchester division of Cornell University Medical Center, urges parents, teachers, health professionals and the youngster's
friends to take seriously all suicidal statements by children. . . . (p. C12)*

The reality of suicide in childhood has only recently been recognized.
Most adults in the United States find it almost impossible to contemplate a
child committing suicide. As a culture we have long shared the belief that
childhood should ideally be a happy and secure time lived under the protection of parents and other caring adults, a time in which children should be
free to explore actively, to learn, and to develop toward their maximum potential. However, as the article quoted above indicates, child suicide is a growing reality in the United States. The purpose of this chapter is to expose the
full reality of suicide by children aged 5 to 14, a reality that is in direct contrast to our cultural ideal. In order to lay the framework for the discussion
that follows, we will begin with a profile of childhood based on the psychological perspectives discussed in chapter 2.

PROFILE OF CHILDHOOD

According to psychoanalytic theory, the elementary school child is in the
latency stage of personality development. The latency stage was so named by
Freud because libido is believed to be relatively quiet during this period as
the child represses sexual urges. Freud (1953) believed that children in the
latency stage continue to work on the resolution of their incestuous wishes
that arose from the Oedipus conflict during the preceding phallic period. He

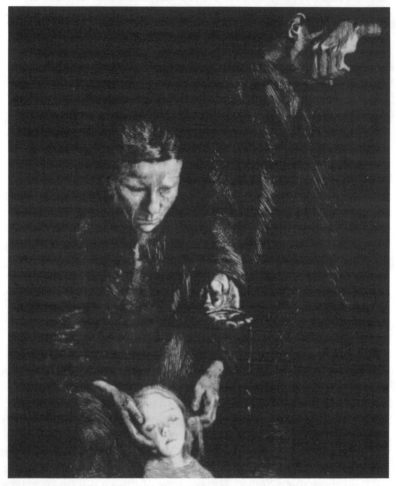

The Downtrodden, **Käthe Kollowitz, 1900. Etching on paper. (The National Museum of Women in the Arts. Gift of Wallace and Wilhelmina Holladay.)**

believed that in order to give up the parent of the opposite sex as the pre-ferred love object, latency stage children identify with members of the same sex and often show a clear preference for interaction with their own sex and a disdain for the other. Children in this stage are typically concerned with making and upholding rules in their various organizations, both formal and informal. Freud believed that this appreciation for sticking by the rules helps children in this stage to repress their sexual urges. Children's emphasis on "playing by the rules" is also evidence of a continuation of conscience devel-opment begun in the previous stage. Like all developmental personality theo-rists, Freud believed that unresolved problems from an earlier stage can affect later stages. He expressed special concern for children who enter the latency period overburdened with sexual guilt from the preceding period.

Erikson (1968) held that children between ages 6 and 12 are in the personality development stage that has industry and inferiority as the two extremes. Erikson believed that the major developmental task of children in this stage is the rapid accumulation of new skills and abilities associated with beginning school. When children enter school, performance expectations increase dramatically. Also, children begin to get feedback on their performance from teachers and peers, who tend to be more objective than their families could be during the preschool years. The child who is able to invest energy in learning new school-related and interpersonal skills is likely to experience considerable success and become an industrious individual with high self-esteem. In contrast, the child who is unprepared for the challenges of this stage of development because of guilt-ridden psychological baggage resulting from poor parenting and unhealthy relationships within the family is highly likely to fail in school and with his or her peers as well as to suffer significant feelings of depression and inferiority. Erikson pointed out that industry during childhood is generally characterized by joining organizations, making collections of everything from coins to baseball cards, and being open to new experiences. The child on the positive end of the continuum of industry versus inferiority embarks on new experiences with enthusiasm and confidence, expects success, and interprets failure as feedback rather than as personal inadequacy. The child on the negative end of the continuum is reluctant to open himself or herself to new experiences, expects failure, and develops an ever-deepening sense of inferiority.

As discussed in chapter 2, the behavioral perspective, instead of focusing on orderly stages of development, focuses on reinforcement, punishment, and modeling as major influences on behavior at any age. The behaviorists would therefore predict that children who enter the elementary school years having learned the appropriate habits and skills to meet the many challenges of this age will enjoy a great deal of success, while children who begin school poorly prepared for its challenges will very likely fail. In addition, the punishment that failing children receive from teachers and peers may create a negative spiral leading to learned helplessness and its analog, depression. Parental modeling is also very important for this age group. The child whose parents are confident and industrious is much better prepared for success than the child whose parents are not. The research literature shows that suicidal children often have parental models who are avoidant, impulsive, and suicidal.

The humanistic perspective does not specify a particular stage of development for children between ages 6 and 12. Writers such as Rogers and Maslow do believe, however, that these are important years for the development of self-concept. Healthy children in good homes and schools develop, like plants in good soil, toward their potential. The most important fruit of that development is positive self-regard. Children who do not experience healthy, nurturing, and supportive environments may not prosper and will suffer low self-esteem.

Cognitive development theory also is helpful in understanding the suicidal child. According to Piaget, the child between ages 6 and 12 is in the concrete operations stage of development. During the concrete operations years the child shows impressive development in thinking and problem solving. Having just emerged from the preoperational period, when thinking and problem solving are characterized by egocentrism and an absence of logic, the concrete operations child can correctly solve conservation problems, think logically, and understand time, space, and causality. In many ways the concrete operations child who is developing on schedule is well prepared for the challenges of this stage. He or she spends much time and energy developing an understanding of cause-effect relationships and categorizing and classifying the external world. These developing understandings allow the child to have a growing sense of competence and control, which in turn fuels his or her sense of industry.

The child whose developmental pattern is delayed because of genetic factors or life experiences is likely to manifest some of the problems and failures of a younger child in this situation. Even for the child whose development is appropriate for this age, however, there are some special pitfalls associated with this stage. Although the child's logical thinking develops significantly across this period, the child, especially in the early stage of concrete operations, is incapable of abstraction and hypothetical thinking and therefore fails to understand fully certain concepts, such as death. It is not uncharacteristic for some children, especially those under age 10, to believe that death is a temporary and reversible state (Wass, 1984). Such thinking may increase a child's vulnerability to suicide when other predisposing factors are in operation.

The theoretical perspectives we have presented in this section illuminate different aspects of child development. It is important, however, to bear in mind that children who grow up in different time periods are exposed to special cultural influences that affect the peer personality of each generation idiosyncratically. In the following section we will present Strauss and Howe's (1991) description of the present-day cohort of children from the "generations" perspective introduced in chapter 1.

TODAY'S CHILDREN

The youngest generation living in the United States today has been labeled the Millennial Generation. The oldest members of this group were born in 1982 and the age of members in 1995 was 13 or younger. These children are called Millennials because their generation will come of age in the third millennium. Strauss and Howe (1991) have characterized the Millennial children as a civic generation, like the GI elders we will discuss in detail in chapter 7. If this label proves to be prophetic for today's children, we can expect that many will develop into dutiful, selfless, team-oriented, patriotic adults who will collectively accomplish great things for the world.

Although it is too soon to know for certain how the present generation of children will turn out as adults, there are signs that this group is living in a more child-friendly world than the world of their predecessors, the "13ers," who will be discussed in detail in chapter 4. Strauss and Howe (1991) have pointed out that the early 1980s marked a transition in the United States toward more child-centeredness that, in some circles, has been labeled a "child fad." The antiabortion movement has flourished during the brief life span of the Millennials. Movies and sitcoms about babies and children (e.g. *Three Men and a Baby*) have become very popular during this period; such programs were almost unheard of during the preceding 20 years.

There is growing evidence that today's youth are better protected from the adult world and presented with more positive role models than preceding generations. Parents in the Silent Generation took their 13er children to R-rated movies about bad children who promote death and desecration (e.g. *The Exorcist*), while today's Boomer parents are more likely to take their children to see G- or PG-rated movies about good children who improve the quality of their parents' lives (e.g. *Sleepless in Seattle*). In addition, we have witnessed a resurgence of a propensity to hold parents responsible for their children's behavior, as illustrated by the 1989 California legislation that provides for the prosecution of parents of children who participate in illegal gang activities.

In spite of this optimistic scenario, all is not well with today's children. For example, evidence exists that middle-grade and elementary-grade students are bringing weapons to school in growing numbers (Celis, 1994). Children have become increasingly involved in adult crimes ranging from vandalism to theft to murder. Also, the suicide rate for children, although low relative to other age groups, continues to rise among the Millennial Generation. Perhaps it is because the youth-nurturing trend is relatively recent that positive outcomes, including a reduced youth suicide rate, are not yet in evidence. If this is indeed the case, we can expect to see a reduction in the youth suicide rate in the future. In the next section we will review the most recent information about child suicide rates and trends.

Millenial babies frequently arrive to parents who want them desperately. Strauss and Howe, *Generations*

THE STATISTICAL PICTURE FOR CHILD SUICIDE

The suicide rate is lower for children than for any other age group. Recent statistical data show that 314 children below the age of 15 killed themselves in the United States in 1992. These suicides constituted approximately 1% of the 30,484 suicides that occurred in the United States that year (National Center for Health Statistics, 1994).

The good news about a low rate of child suicide is offset by the bad news that suicide is increasing in this age group. The incidence of child suicide was not officially reported in the United States or Canada until 1970. In that year, the National Center for Health Statistics reported that the suicide rate among 5- to 14-year-olds was 0.3 per 100,000 population. In 1992, the last year for which official statistics were available, the comparable rate had tripled to .9 per 100,000 population (National Center for Health Statistics, 1994). Although Canadian statistics do not include the same age divisions as those from the United States, the findings from these countries regarding an increase in the child suicide rate parallel one another. For example, a recent study reported a doubling of the child suicide rate for Canadian males (aged 10 to 14) between 1960 and 1985 and a sixfold increase for females in this age group for the same period (Joffe & Offord, 1990).

While completed suicide may be relatively rare among children, suicidal behavior is not. Two studies by Pfeffer and associates reported that 33% of a group of 39 outpatient psychiatric children (aged 6 to 12) and 78.5% of a comparable group of 65 inpatient children had contemplated, attempted, or threatened suicide (Pfeffer, 1981a; Pfeffer, Solomon, Plutchik, Mizruchi, & Weiner, 1982). In contrast, in the 1960s only 10% of similar groups of children were reported to have suicidal symptoms or ideations (Mattisson, Hawkins, & Seese, 1969). Further evidence of suicidal behavior in children is documented in a report by Turkington (1983) that showed that 12,000 children between the ages of 5 and 14 were admitted to psychiatric hospitals for suicidal behavior annually.

There have been only a few investigations of the incidence of suicidal behavior among nonclinical populations of children. However, the research that has been done shows that suicidal ideation and attempts do occur in this group also. For example, one study of 101 school children (aged 6 to 12) who had never been psychiatric patients found that 11.9% revealed suicidal ideas, threats, or attempts (Pfeffer, Zuckerman, Plutchik, & Mizruchi, 1984). Another study of a nonpsychiatric population involved a survey of a large cross-sectional sample of Canadian children and their families. Findings from this study showed that 5 to 10% of males and 10 to 20% of females between 12

Childhood is the kingdom where nobody dies. Edna St. Vincent Millay, *Wine From These Grapes*

and 16 years of age had engaged in suicidal behavior (Offord et al., 1987). Perhaps most revealing about the extent to which "ordinary" children think about suicide are the remarkable findings from a study on attitudes toward suicide conducted with 116 junior high school students in Tucson, Arizona (Domino, Domino, Berry, 1986–87). Twenty-three percent of the girls in this study and 22% of the boys answered yes to the question: "Have you ever seriously thought about killing yourself?"

Both suicide rates and suicidal behavior are grossly underreported in all age groups (Berman & Carroll, 1984). Because there is still a stigma attached to suicide, many families hide evidence, and many doctors and coroners are reluctant to classify a death as a suicide if there is the slightest doubt. This tendency to deny suicide is extremely powerful in the case of a child. Turkington (1983) has estimated that no more than 1% of the actual incidence of self-destructive behavior among children is officially reported each year.

An explanation for the fact that suicide in childhood is more underreported than suicide at other ages may be found in our human tendency to defend the "just world" hypothesis. This hypothesis, held by most of us though not often examined, is that there is a natural and proper order in the universe. In this predictable and orderly universe, parents die before their children. When children precede their parents in death, the just world hypothesis is challenged. The death of a child seems all the more unnatural when it is self-inflicted, and defense mechanisms such as denial understandably come into play.

Having established that suicidal behavior does in fact occur among children, we will now turn our attention to what is known about the causes of self-destructive behavior in this age group. In the following section we will apply the Suicide Trajectory Model that was introduced in chapter 1 to research findings concerning the causes of suicidal behavior in children.

THE SUICIDE TRAJECTORY APPLIED
TO CHILDHOOD SUICIDE

In Chapter 1 we used the Suicide Trajectory Model to explain the commonalities that characterize suicide in every age group (see Table 1.4). The model is presented again in Table 3.1 but includes only those risk factors, triggering events, and warning signs that are idiosyncratic to childhood. In discussing Table 3.1 we will, however, remind the reader of relevant common risk factors that apply to all age groups.

Biological Risk Factors

Table 3.1 shows that impulsivity is a risk factor that may have its roots in biology and that may predispose children to suicide. Children are more impulsive in their suicidal behavior than any other age group (Joffe & Of-

TABLE 3.1 The Suicide Trajectory Model Applied to Child Suicide

Age Group	Biological Risk Factors	Psychological Risk Factors	Cognitive Risk Factors	Environmental Risk Factors	Warning Signs	Triggering Events	Suicidal Behavior
Childhood (5–14)	Impulsivity	Feelings of inferiority Expendable child syndrome	Immature views of death Concrete operational thinking Attraction to and repulsion from life and death	Early loss Parent conflict Inflexible family structure Unclear family member roles Abuse & neglect Parent suicidal behavior	Truancy Poor school performance Anxiety Sleep disturbance Aggression Impulsiveness Low frustration tolerance	Minor life events	Impulsivity High lethality Lowest completion rate Males attempt and complete more

ford, 1983, 1990; Kosky, 1982; Pfeffer, Conte, Plutchik, & Jerrett, 1980). They are also more likely than members of older age groups to commit an impetuous self-destructive act such as jumping from a high place or running in front of a car, and they are less likely to engage in suicidal behavior that involves planning, such as hoarding and ingesting drugs.

The impulsive nature of suicide in this age group is especially evident in a particular type of suicidal child who is greatly at risk (Carlson & Cantwell, 1982; Pfeffer, Plutchik, & Mizruchi, 1983). Such children are described as angry and impulsive and as having a tendency to approach problems in an assaultive manner. Children with these characteristics have been given various labels including "brain damage," "attention deficit hyperactive disorder," "antisocial personality disorder," "behavior disorder," and so on. Many of these children appear to be born with their impulsive, hyperactive, and destructive natures. It also is not unusual for them to have parental models who are impulsive and suicidal themselves. Therefore, when these children exhibit suicidal behaviors, they may be manifesting a biological predisposition or an overlearned approach to problem solving that has been observed in the home. The case of Tony L. reflects this type of suicidal behavior:

> Tony, the oldest of three children, was born into a lower-middle-class home. Tony's mother described him as a "live wire." As a baby he seemed to never sleep. He cried a great deal and always seemed to be hungry or uncomfortable in some way. As a toddler he was into everything. He would rummage through the cabinets, pull the cloth off the kitchen table, or demolish the linen closet. He had to be watched every waking moment or he would be into something potentially dangerous. His parents had made numerous trips to the emergency room to pump household cleaner from his stomach, to treat a burn from the iron or stove, or to have a cut sutured.
>
> Tony's father was an aggressive and impulsive individual. Although he was a skillful carpenter and made a good salary when he worked, he had difficulty keeping jobs. He frequently developed conflicts with the foremen that resulted in his either quitting or getting fired.
>
> The father's impulsiveness and temper caused problems at home as well as at work. Once when the family was accidentally locked out of the house, Tony's father kicked the front door down instead of searching for an unlocked window. Another time, when he locked his keys in the car, he broke one of the windows rather than search for the spare key.
>
> Tony's mother was very unhappy but felt unable to deal constructively with

---

Children have never been very good at listening to their elders, but they have never failed to imitate them. James Baldwin, *Fifth Avenue Uptown*

her family's problems. She worked part-time as a receptionist in her father's business. Her husband's angry and impulsive outbursts and her son's overactive behaviors upset her greatly. She had frequent and severe headaches that sent her to bed for days at a time. She wanted to leave her husband but was afraid of what he might do in retaliation. She was frequently depressed and cried often. Once, when suffering from a particularly severe headache, she took so many aspirin that her stomach had to be pumped.

Tony's problems seemed to escalate when he entered school. He could not get along with the other children in his class. When the teacher reported that Tony fought with the other children, his mother became upset but took no action. His father spanked him.

By the time Tony entered the third grade, he had been labeled a behavior problem by teachers in the school. His relations with other students degenerated to the point where physical fighting occurred almost daily in the classroom or on the playground. One day when the teacher was scolding him for fighting, Tony broke away from her, ran to the window, and jumped from the second floor.

Tony's suicidal behavior can best be viewed as a product of both his temperament and his environment. There is evidence that Tony was a "difficult" baby. Such babies seem to come into the world with more sensitive biological systems (Derryberry & Rothbart, 1984). Highly active and irritable babies are difficult for parents in the best of situations. In Tony's case, his parents were poor models of coping behaviors. Tony's father modeled impulsive and aggressive behaviors, while his mother modeled weak, dependent, and escapist behaviors. Those two models, in combination with Tony's biological predisposition to act out, help to explain his suicidal reaction to the frustration of the teacher's scolding.

Psychological Risk Factors

It is obvious that happy, well-adjusted children do not attempt suicide. A variety of mental illness diagnoses have been found to be applicable to suicidal children; however, depression is the one category that has consistently been shown to be related to suicidal behavior (Asarnow, 1992; Bettes & Walker, 1986; Myers, McCauley, Calderon, & Treder, 1991; Orbach, 1984; Pfeffer, 1981a; Rosenthal & Rosenthal, 1984; Shaffer, 1974). You will note that depression is not one of the childhood-specific risk factors listed in Table 3.1. Depression is a general risk factor that predisposes suicidal behavior in every age group; it was discussed in detail in chapter 1. In this chapter we will limit our discussion of depression to its influence on child suicide.

Children do get depressed, and they get depressed as frequently and as profoundly as adults do.
Seligman, *Learned Optimism*, p. 126

At least three studies have shown that depression is more prevalent among suicidal children than among nonsuicidal children (Asarnow & Guthrie, 1989; Orbach, 1984; Pfeffer, Conte, Plutchik, & Jerrett, 1979). Other studies with children have shown strong relationships between depression and suicidal ideation (Brent et al., 1986; Carlsen & Cantwell, 1982). It is apparent that severely depressed children think about suicide and that they think about it more often than nondepressed children or those who are suffering only mild depression.

One element of severe depression in all age groups is a sense of hopelessness. Studies with both children and adults have shown hopelessness to be a stronger predictor of suicidal ideation and behavior than is generalized depression alone (Asarnow & Guthrie, 1989; Beck, Steer, Kovacs, & Garrison, 1985). Kazdin and his colleagues compared suicidal and nonsuicidal children on separate measures of hopelessness, depression, and self-esteem. The researchers found that although all three variables were interrelated, feelings of hopelessness correlated significantly with the lethality (seriousness) of the suicide intent, even when the general level of depression was taken into consideration by using the statistical techniques of partial correlation (Kazdin, French, Unis, Esveldt-Dawson, & Sherick, 1983). These findings indicate that children who dislike themselves and are generally depressed may contemplate suicide. However, the seriousness of such contemplations is increased greatly in children who also feel hopeless about the future.

Noted in Table 3.1 are two childhood-specific psychological factors that, in addition to the more general risk factors of depression and hopelessness, increase the risk of suicide. The first such factor is a *sense of inferiority*. Erikson (1968) pointed out that children need to develop feelings of confidence and positive self-regard, which he called a sense of industry. Children who fail to develop a sense of industry experience strong feelings of inferiority and develop poor self-concepts and low self-esteem. Although there is no direct evidence that low self-esteem leads to suicide in children, the study by Kazdin and associates (1983) discussed in the preceding paragraph found a relationship between negative self-concept and suicidal ideation. Pfeffer (1986) has pointed out that the family systems of suicidal children produce low self-esteem in addition to depression and hopelessness. Also, our research dealing with attitudes toward suicide has shown that children and adolescents with low self-esteem, as measured by the Tennessee Self-Concept Scale, agree more with all reasons for suicide than others their age (Stillion, McDowell, & Shamblin, 1984).

The second psychological risk factor specific to childhood is the *expendable child syndrome* (Sabbath, 1969). While many children experience loss of love, the expendable child experiences loss of love in the most extreme form. Parents of expendable children communicate low personal regard, hostility, withdrawal of love, and even hatred. These children believe that they are unworthy and that their deaths will not matter to anyone. Patros and Shamoo (1989) have presented case studies to illustrate how the expendable child syndrome may activate a wish to die. It is not unusual for the child who perceives himself or herself in this way to consider suicide as a way to stop being a burden to a parent.

Many children are unable to interpret parental hostility accurately. Children born to parents who dislike them and who treat them with hostility are likely to introject (absorb into themselves) those feelings, turning them into self-hatred and hostility against self. These children frequently feel responsible for parents' negative emotions and sometimes feel they should be punished for the role they play in making their parents unhappy. Suicidal behavior may represent a natural consequence of such negative feelings.

Cognitive Risk Factors

Table 3.1 shows that holding onto an immature view of death is an important cognitive risk factor in child suicidal behavior. Over the past 50 years, a rich body of literature has been accumulated that indicates that children's concepts of death develop slowly in accordance with the Piagetian stages of cognitive development (Gartley & Bernasconi, 1967; Koocher, 1973; Nagy, 1948; Pfeffer, 1984; Speece & Brent, 1984; Stillion & Wass, 1979; Swain, 1979; Wass, 1984; Wass, 1995; Wass & Stillion, 1988). It is generally believed that children under 7 years of age have an immature and egocentric view of death. They think of death as being a transient and reversible state. Between ages 7 and 12, most children develop increasing understanding of the facts of death. By age 12, almost all children understand that death is universal, inevitable, and final.

Some writers have suggested that the immature view that younger children have about death protects them against suicide (Gould, 1965; Shaffer & Fisher, 1981). They point to the relatively low incidence of suicide in childhood to support their position. People holding this view believe that because children do not have a clear understanding of what death is they are reluctant to attempt suicide for fear of the unknown.

Other writers disagree, however, with the assumption that children's immature views of death protect them from suicide. There is evidence that suicidal children conceptualize death differently than nonsuicidal children do. Joffe and Offord (1983) have shown that suicidal children have less-well-defined concepts of death. Other authors have suggested that suicidal children may view death as a transient and pleasant state (Carlson, Asarnow, & Orbach, 1987; McIntire & Angle, 1971; McIntire, Angle, & Struempler, 1972). A recent study by Carlson, Asarnow, and Orbach (1994) provided empirical support for this hypothesis. They found that a suicidal hospitalized group of 8- to 10-year-olds was less likely to understand the finality of death than a nonsuicidal hospitalized group of children the same age. Rather than protecting children against suicide, it would seem that less developed cognitions might make suicide a more attractive option. For children who lack a clear understanding of the finality of worldly existence in death, and especially for those who believe that death is the gateway to a more pleasant existence, suicide may be less frightening than it is for other children.

Orbach and Glaubman (1979) have suggested that even children who have a mature view of death may lose that maturity when they begin to consider suicide as a personal option. Older children who understand the finality of death in the abstract may regress to earlier forms of thinking that allow them to view their own deaths by suicide as pleasant and even transient. Pfeffer's (1986) clinical work with suicidal children has uncovered support for this position. She described children in a suicidal crisis as manifesting "ego constriction" that leads to a regression in their thinking about death.

A second cognitive factor affecting child suicide is the rigidity associated with concrete operational thinking that characterizes the mental processes of children. Concrete operational thinking resembles in many ways the characteristically rigid thought patterns associated with suicide at later ages. For example, children in the concrete operations stage are unable to consider multiple outcomes in a problem situation, including the possibility that things might get better. Children in this age group tend to think dichotomously and fail to see the shades of gray in a problem situation. Once these children reach the conclusion that suicide is the answer, other solutions receive very little attention. Since they have never experienced the stage of formal operations, they are literally locked into their black-white, life-death view of the world.

In an important study, Orbach (1984) compared a group of suicidal children with a chronically ill group and a normal control group on rigidity in solving life and death dilemmas. He found the suicidal children to be significantly more cognitively rigid in this type of problem solving than the other two groups. He also found that the degree of cognitive rigidity correlated positively with a measure of attraction to death among the suicidal children. Put another way, those suicidal children who were more cognitively rigid found death to be a more attractive alternative to life than did suicidal children who were less cognitively rigid. Orbach concluded from these findings that cognitive rigidity is an intervening process in the relationship between the stresses of life and suicidal behavior. Cognitively rigid children tend to

---

Whatever crazy sorrow saith, no life that breathes with human breath has ever truly longed for death. Tennyson, *The Two Voices*

overestimate the seriousness of their problems, to consider too few solutions, and to exaggerate the attractiveness of suicide as a solution (Orbach, 1984; Turkington, 1983).

One final perspective in understanding the cognitive aspects of child suicide was also developed by Orbach (1988). Orbach has proposed that understanding any child's suicidal orientation can be enhanced by a determination of his or her attraction to and repulsion from life and death. Attraction to life is influenced by personality strengths and by the support a child feels from the environment, while repulsion from life reflects characteristics growing out of experiences with pain and suffering. Attraction to death is associated with a belief in a serene and peaceful existence after life, and may also include the notion that death is reversible. As we have seen, this type of thinking is characteristic of many suicidal children. Repulsion from death reflects a frightening expectation of irreversible cessation. It is possible that some children in cultures that stress the afterlife concepts of heaven and hell may also experience repulsion from death because of their belief in punishment in the hereafter, particularly if the act of suicide is regarded as sinful.

Orbach's (1988) perspective is phenomenological: Attraction to and repulsion from life and death are salient only from the child's perspective. As environmental and other factors change, the child's orientation regarding each of these dimensions will be affected. Orbach's perspective also includes the notion of ambivalence toward suicide. Even the most seriously suicidal child shows some attraction to life. Orbach's concept of ambivalence is reminiscent of Freud's now-familiar concept of tension between Eros and Thanatos and it echoes Shneidman's well-known assertion that ambivalence exists in all suicides. The child whose life experiences cause him or her to have a strong repulsion from life and attraction to death and a weak attraction to life and repulsion from death could be characterized as showing a pathological imbalance between Eros and Thanatos and a dangerous level of ambivalence concerning life and death.

According to Orbach's theory, happy and well-adjusted children should show very positive attitudes toward life and hold negative views of death, and depressed, hopeless, and suicidal children should have the opposite views. In two different studies, Orbach and his associates compared groups of suicidal and nonsuicidal children on four different measures of attraction to and repulsion from life and death. Both studies found that suicidal children showed more repulsion from life, less attraction to life, more attraction to death, and less repulsion from death than nonsuicidal children (Orbach, 1984; Orbach, Feshbach, Carlson, & Ellenberg, 1984). Interestingly, the smallest difference between the suicidal and nonsuicidal groups was found on the measure of attraction to life. The suicidal children in these studies remained attracted to life even under the most negative circumstances. These findings support Orbach's belief in the ambivalence of suicidal children and have encouraging

Garino Tomb, A. Frilli. [Cemetery of Nice-Gairaut. Photograph from Images de l'homme devant la mort (Images of Man and Death) by Philippe Aries, Editions du Seuil, 1983, Janet Lloyd, Trans.]

implications for prevention and intervention techniques designed to move ambivalent suicidal children toward more positive views of life.

It is evident that cognitive factors are important influences on child suicide. The role that cognitive factors can play in attempted suicide is illustrated in the following case study.

> *Laura S. is an academically gifted nine-year-old who was born to professional parents. She was a much-wanted child who was born after her mother had experienced a succession of miscarriages. Laura's parents were deeply religious people who interpreted Laura's birth as a gift from God. They vowed to do everything possible to raise this child in an atmosphere of love.*
>
> *Laura was the centerpiece of the family. Her parents took her everywhere they went and included her in all activities. They discontinued many of their previous social activities that did not include children. They also broke off relationships with former friends who did not share their child-centered orientation.*
>
> *Laura's parents loved and cared for her to the point of overindulgence and*

overprotection. She was not allowed to have the usual kinds of experiences that promote the development of appropriate independence. She was not left in day care or with a baby-sitter, and she never stayed at other children's houses overnight.

When Laura was eight and a half, she and her parents took a vacation. While traveling there was an accident that resulted in the death of both of Laura's parents. Laura was not badly injured and she moved into her grandparents' home, where she was loved and cared for.

Laura's grandparents tried to console her by assuring her that her parents were "happy in Jesus." As the months went on, Laura became increasingly withdrawn, spending her time alone reading Bible stories about heaven and staring at pictures of her parents. One day her grandmother found her standing on a chair with a belt around her neck in an obvious attempt at suicide. Laura tearfully told her grandmother and grandfather that, while she loved them very much, she missed her parents terribly and wanted to be with them and Jesus in heaven. She said that the Bible told her that heaven is a lovely place where she and her parents will live together in peace and happiness.

Laura's story reveals that levels of cognitive understanding play a real role in suicidal behavior. Laura, yearning for her dead parents, was attracted to death as the best way to reclaim her lost happiness. Once she considered this possibility, it seemed the only solution to her. Her thinking reflects the immature conceptualization of death and the cognitive rigidity that are characteristic of suicidal children, and the attraction to death described by Orbach.

Environmental Risk Factors

Laura's suicide attempt also illustrates the first environmental risk factor listed in Table 3.1. Suicidal children have experienced more frequent and earlier loss than others. Several studies show that these children have lost parents through death and divorce before 11 years of age more often than others (Corder & Haizlip, 1984; Matter & Matter, 1984; Pfeffer, 1981b). The separation and divorce rates for parents of suicidal children are higher than the national average (Garfinkel, Froese, & Hood, 1982; Murphy & Wetzel, 1982; Tishler, McKenry, & Morgan, 1981). Throughout their childhood, suicidal children experience more stress related to loss than other children do, and their suicidal behavior is to some extent a response to accumulated loss (Cohen-Sandler, Berman, and King, 1982). The relationship between loss and suicide in children was reflected in a study by Morrison and Collier (1969) which found that 76% of a group of 34 outpatient children experienced a significant family loss or the anniversary of a loss within a few weeks of a suicide attempt. Further evidence of a relationship between early loss and child suicide was provided by a retrospective study of suicidal ideation with college students. An event history revealed that parental absence was the most frequently remembered occurrence related to suicidal ideation during childhood (Bolger, Downey, Walker, & Steininger, 1989).

Environmental factors within the family may influence the suicidal behavior of children more directly than any other age group. The family environments of suicidal children are less healthy and more likely to be dysfunctional than those of other children (Joffe, Offord, & Boyle, 1988; Pfeffer & Trad, 1988). High levels of turbulence and crises of all types seem to occur more often in these families. The incidence of parental conflict, including physical violence, is greater than usual in the homes of suicidal children (Kosky, 1982; Orbach, Gross, & Glaubman, 1981). Many suicidal children are aware of the pathological aspects of their family lives. A recent study by Asarnow (1992) found that a group of 6- to 13-year-old inpatients who had attempted or thought about suicide characterized their homes as being higher in conflict, less cohesive, and less expressive than a comparison group of inpatient children who were not suicidal.

As shown in Table 3.1, family inflexibility and resistance to change as well as unclear parent/child role definitions are additional home environment characteristics of suicidal children (Pfeffer, 1981b, 1982). These families are often intractable in their refusal to consider new ways of dealing with problems. The relationship between the parents and children often is one of mutual dependency, almost symbiotic in nature. The children within these homes too often find themselves carrying out adult responsibilities for siblings or even parents. Their own needs are likely to be overlooked, even by themselves, as they try to cope with rigid, inflexible demands of parents who cannot or will not change their views of the world.

Future research is likely to show increasing evidence of a relationship between child abuse (especially child sexual abuse) and suicidal behavior in all age groups (Berman, 1993). Several studies have already found that child abuse and neglect are characteristic of the families of suicidal children (Briere, Evans, Runtz, Wall, 1988; Joffe & Offord, 1983; McLaren & Brown, 1989; Orbach, 1984; Pfeffer, 1990; Rosenthal & Rosenthal, 1984). Perhaps the most definitive work relating child abuse and neglect to self-destructive behavior in children was carried out by Green (1978). In a study comparing the incidence of suicidal behavior among abused and nonabused children, he found that 40% of the physically abused children and 17% of the neglected children demonstrated suicidal behavior, compared with only 7% of a group of nonabused and nonneglected children. The self-destructive behavior of the abused children often occurred in response to a beating. Another study showing a relationship between child abuse and suicide found suicide and self-destructive behavior to be the most common pathological outcome for 28 children who were sexually abused (Adams-Tucker, 1982). Pfeffer (1986) has pointed out that the victim of child abuse suffers both the stress of the abusive action and the low self-esteem associated with the belief that his or her "bad" behavior caused the abuse. We would also suggest that such children may have high levels of learned helplessness and accompanying depression as explained in chapter 2. No doubt each of these consequences contributes to the relationship between child abuse and child suicide.

There are some questions, however, regarding the specific nature of the relationship between child abuse and neglect on the one hand and suicidal behavior on the other. At least two carefully controlled studies have shown that child abuse is a significant factor in the family histories of many psychologically disturbed children, but abuse does not specifically differentiate suicidal children from other disturbed children (Pfeffer, Conte, Plutchik, & Jerrett, 1979, 1980). It is possible, however, that rather than any single factor, a particular combination of family characteristics (e.g., abuse and neglect, conflict, the modeling of suicidal behavior, inflexibility, and unclear roles) is needed to predispose a child to suicide.

All of these environmental risk factors result in increased stress for children, whose coping mechanisms are not yet mature. With increasing stress come depression and heightened feelings of hopelessness, the twin harbingers of suicidal behavior. Often a child will attempt suicide when the family is in the midst of a crisis that does not directly involve the child. In retrospect, such suicidal behavior can be seen to be a product of accumulated stress that finally overwhelms the child's endurance. The case of John P. illustrates this situation.

> John was an 11-year-old child whose family had a long history of turbulence. There had been frequent threats of separation and numerous actual separations throughout the marriage. John's younger brother had been born as a result of one of the many reunions. Social workers who became involved with the family described their situation as follows: Most of the frequent arguments centered around money. John's father's income as a sporadically employed day laborer was never enough to support a family of four. John's mother had worked in a department store before marriage but was now forbidden to do so by her husband, who said repeatedly, "A wife's place is in the home with the children."
>
> Although there was only occasional physical violence between the parents, shouting matches occurred weekly. During these emotional arguments—almost always witnessed by John—John's parents said terrible things to and about each other. After the arguments, John's mother often tried to persuade him to take her side against his father, to be her protector, her "little man." Also, on two occasions she took overdoses of sleep medication in the wake of fights with her husband and was hospitalized briefly.
>
> As the stress increased in the home, John's mother spent more and more time in bed, abdicating her role as wife and mother. John became more a parent than a sibling to his younger brother. It was John who had to be sure that his younger

brother had something to eat for dinner, took a bath, had his lunch packed, and was appropriately dressed for school.

When he was much younger, John had tearfully told a friend that when his parents argued, it "hurt my stomach and made me feel scared." He described running from the house when his parents fought, or hiding in his bedroom and using his pillow to muffle the sound of their shouting. As his parents' fighting accelerated, John spent more and more time away from home, often staying away all night. This resulted in his skipping school in order to rest during the day. When his teacher questioned him about his absences, her questions were met with stony silence. When she threatened to call his parents, John screamed, "Do it," and ran from the classroom. The teacher's call to the parents provoked a major fight, during which John's father packed his clothes and left the house. Before school the next day, on the school grounds, John set his clothes on fire.

John's story involves many of the family characteristics typical of the homes of suicidal children. Crisis, turbulence, separation, and the threat of divorce were pervasive. The socioeconomic status of the family was low, and money problems exacerbated the already weak relationship between the parents. The parental roles, in terms of responsibilities inside and outside the home, were inflexible. John's mother vacillated between ignoring his presence and expecting him to play an adult role in helping her deal with her husband and in raising his younger brother. She also occasionally modeled self-destructive behavior as a means of dealing with stress. John's suicide attempt followed a final crisis for which he felt partially responsible and clearly marked a total collapse of his ability to cope.

Warning Signs

Table 3.1 lists a number of warning signs that may alert us to the possibility that a child is suicidal. Truancy and poor school performance have been repeatedly shown to be associated with child suicide (Connell, 1972; Joffe & Offord, 1983; Lewis, Johnson, Cohen, Garcia, Velez, 1988; Pfeffer, 1981a). There is considerable evidence, however, that the poor school performance of suicidal children is seldom related to low intelligence (Ackerly, 1967; Connell, 1972; Joffe & Offord, 1983; Rosenberg & Latimer, 1966). At least two studies have shown that many children who attempt suicide are of above average intelligence (Kosky, 1982; Shaffer, 1974).

Although the poor school performance of suicidal children is well documented, these studies typically do not examine suicidal children's school performance in comparison with other emotionally disturbed children. One study that did make such a comparison found no differences in school performance between suicidal and other psychologically disturbed children (Pfeffer, 1981b). Apparently, poor school performance is associated with childhood psychopathology but is not specific to suicidal behavior (Joffe & Offord, 1983).

The remaining warning signs presented in Table 3.1 reflect the many ways in which children demonstrate depression. The symptom picture for childhood depression is often somewhat different from that of adults. Depressive symptoms in children often include anxiety and sleep disturbance, which are found in depressed adults, but they also include age-specific symptoms such as aggressive acting out, impulsiveness, and low frustration tolerance (Kosky, 1982; Orbach, 1984; Patros & Shamoo, 1989; Rosenthal & Rosenthal, 1984).

Triggering Events

Suicidal behavior in children is often triggered by minor events that appear to be trivial according to adult standards. A denied privilege or a spanking or harsh words from a teacher may trigger suicidal ideation or a self-destructive act in a child who is predisposed to suicide and/or lacks adequate coping skills.

Suicidal Behavior

We have already discussed the first two behavioral characteristics of child suicide, its impulsive nature and the highly lethal methods used by this age group. Fortunately, however, in spite of the deadly nature of child suicide, children have the lowest completion rate of any age group.

One surprising fact about child suicide concerns sex differences. In all age groups above 14 (with perhaps the exception of old age—see chapter 7), females attempt suicide more often than males while males complete suicide more often than females. This is not true for children aged 5 to 14. For this age group, males both attempt and complete suicide more often than females (Joffe & Offord, 1990).

Developmental psychologists have long held that childhood is more difficult for males than for females. Females seem to mature faster than males from birth through puberty (Mussen, Conger, & Kagan, 1974). Females are also physically healthier than males. Death rates for males are higher at every age from conception onward (Stillion, 1985). In addition, the world of school seems to be a better fit for girls than for boys, perhaps because of girls' greater verbal facility (Maccoby & Jacklin, 1974). These developmental differences must surely contribute to the fact that boy children are at higher risk for suicide than are girl children.

As Stillion (1995) has discussed in a recent publication, the gender differentiation that is inherent in socialization practices in the United States may also predispose boys to be at greater risk than girls for death by suicide. The socialization of boys includes emotional inhibition ("big boys don't cry"), demands for independence ("if he hits you, hit him back"), and above all, remonstrances against any behavior that smacks of femininity ("don't be a sissy"). Boys are socialized to be competitive at an early age—often learning to endure physical punishment and pain as part of "having fun." Girls, on the other hand, are freer to engage in cooperative and imaginative play. Demands for competitiveness and winning are not typically a part of the socialization process of young girls. Tolerance of emotional expressiveness and of dependence on parents is maintained longer for girls. There are, of course, negative consequences of these female socialization processes that impede development. However, so far as life and death matters are concerned, traditional socialization practices make the world a more dangerous and less supportive place for boys than girls and no doubt contribute to the fact that boy children are at greater risk for attempted and completed suicide than girl children.

SUMMARY

The suicide rate for children is lower than that of any other age group. Approximately 300 children in the United States between the ages of 5 and 15 kill themselves each year. Children account for less than 1% of the total number of suicides in the United States in a single year; however, the suicide rate for this age group has grown significantly during the past two decades. Although completed suicide is relatively rare among children, suicidal ideation and suicide attempts are not. Suicidality is frequently a factor in the referral of children for mental health services. Children are more likely than other age groups to attempt suicide in an impulsive and impetuous manner. Those with biologically predisposed (and/or learned) impulsive, aggressive, and destructive natures tend to be especially at risk.

Psychological risk factors for suicide in children include depression and hopelessness as well as feelings of inferiority, which in their most dramatic form may be a manifestation of the expendable child syndrome. Cognitive risk factors for child suicide include the tendency to hold immature views of death, denying its finality and irreversibility, which is typical of the concrete operations stage of development. Even older children, who have a more mature understanding of death, may regress in their conceptualizations of death when experiencing the stress of a suicidal crisis. Another aspect of concrete operations thinking that adds to the suicide risk of children is the natural tendency toward dichotomous thinking that limits the exploration of possible outcomes in a problem situation.

Many of the environmental risk factors that influence suicidal behavior in children are related to the home environment. Suicidal children often come from pathological families in which patterns of interaction inhibit growth and development among the members. The homes of suicidal children are likely to involve considerable parental conflict, abuse and neglect, and the modeling of self-destructive behavior. The structure of these families tends to be inflexible, but the roles of individual members are often unclear. In addition, suicidal children experience more frequent and early loss of family members through death and divorce than other children.

The warning signs that should alert us to the fact that a child might be considering suicide are those generally associated with poor adjustment as well as more specific manifestations of childhood depression. Among the behavior characteristics that should raise concerns about suicidality in children are truancy, poor school performance, anxiety, sleep disturbance, aggression, impulsiveness, and low frustration tolerance.

Unlike the members of other age groups, with the exception of the elderly, male children both attempt and complete suicide more frequently than female children. There is considerable evidence that the roots of the enhanced vulnerability of male children to suicide lie both in biological development and in socialization practices, especially those that promote traditional gender differentiation.

4

Suicide in Adolescence

So much of adolescence is an ill-defined dying,
An intolerable waiting,
A longing for another place and time,
Another condition.

Theodore Roethke, "I'm Here"

Adolescent suicide has received a great deal of attention in recent years. In fact, suicide among those aged 15 to 24 has been the subject of numerous magazine and newspaper articles, radio and television reports, and made-for-TV movies. The special media attention given to adolescent suicide is not a reflection of an exceptionally high rate—although the rate is high. It has resulted from a remarkable increase in the self-destructive behavior of this age group over the last half of the 20th century. The big news about adolescent suicide is that young people, who prior to the mid 1950s were relatively immune to self-destruction, have joined the adult world of suicide.

In this chapter, we will review the changing statistics on suicide among adolescents since midcentury in the United States and other developed countries. We will also, as in the preceding chapter, apply the Suicide Trajectory Model to research findings concerning risk factors, warning signs, and triggering events that influence suicidal behavior in this age group. We will first examine normative events and cohort-specific generational factors associated with this period of life. Our discussion will begin with a profile of adolescence in today's world.

PROFILE OF ADOLESCENCE

The hallmark of adolescence is physical growth. Formally, the period of adolescence begins at puberty, when increased levels of hormones entering the bloodstream result in the appearance of the first menstrual period in girls (around 12-1/2 years) and the first nocturnal emission for boys (around 14 years). Puberty is preceded by a period of rapid physical growth. It is not unusual for young people to grow four or five inches in a single year. Primary and secondary sex characteristics are also triggered by the increase in hormone production. In boys, secondary sex characteristics (those not directly involved in propagating the species) include pubic, axillary (underarm), and facial hair; a deeper voice as the larynx and vocal cords lengthen; and changed body and facial contours as shoulders widen, the rib cage expands, the face becomes angular and the body more muscular. Girls at this time experience the growth of pubic and axillary hair and the rounding of the body as breasts develop and hips and thighs grow wider. Primary sex characteristics (those directly related to procreation) in boys include the development of the penis and testes and the ability to produce live sperm. Girls experience their first menstrual period, which signals their ability to conceive and bear children.

The rapid, asynchronous (uneven) growth in adolescence, coupled with the effect of relatively high levels of hormones, causes both boys and girls to become more self-conscious and introspective than they were in childhood. They focus on their changing body image and often develop negative feelings about themselves. This restricted focus can feed into a rise in egocentrism that may result in adolescents feeling unique, misunderstood, and lonely. The common adolescent complaint "No one understands me" is evidence of the kind of idiosyncratic emotions that may play a role in the rising suicide statistics among adolescents. The suicide note that will appear later in this chapter illustrates the egocentrism, isolation, and depressive preoccupation with self that is common among young people contemplating suicide.

The period of adolescence is considered to be formally over when the individual has become an independent adult and begins to function on his or her own without the help of parents. The period of adolescence has lengthened in the United States during the 20th century. Puberty now occurs two years earlier in both boys and girls than it did at the end of the 19th century. In addition, many young people remain in college for a longer period of time or return home after college, thus remaining in or reentering the semidependent world of adolescence. The fact that the period of dependency has lengthened at the upper end in recent years lends support to our decision to define adolescence as the period from 15 to 24 years of age.

In terms of psychological growth, according to psychoanalytic theory adolescents are in the final stage of personality development—the genital stage. Because Freud strongly believed that the early years are more important than the later years in personality development, he wrote less about this stage than he did about the previous ones. During the genital stage, in response to increased hormones the libidinal drives reappear after the hibernation of the latency period, and sexual motivation and activity take on more adult forms. The adolescent seeks more adult sexual experiences, in dramatic contrast to the preference for nonsexual interactions with one's own sex that characterizes the preceding stage.

The healthy adolescent enters the adult sexual world through a variety of group experiences involving both boys and girls. The group experiences gradually give way to deeper and more exclusive relationships with a member

---

The imagination of a boy is healthy, and the mature imagination of a man is healthy; but there is a space of life between, in which the soul is in a ferment, the character undecided, the way of life uncertain, the ambition thicksighted. Keats, *Endymion*, preface

of the opposite sex. According to psychoanalytic theory, the poorly adjusted adolescent brings many unresolved problems from earlier stages of development into the genital period. Early conflicts related to trust (from the oral stage), difficulty with authority (from the anal stage), or sexual identification problems (from the phallic stage) all have specific implications for adult personality. As indicated in chapter 2, when the adolescent must expend too much energy in repressing or otherwise defending against problems from earlier stages, the balance between Eros and Thanatos is disturbed; this creates the possibility for the strengthening of the death wish, which is sometimes manifested in suicidal behavior.

In contrast to Freud, who showed relatively little interest in this age group, Erikson described personality development in adolescence in great detail (Erikson, 1968; Thomas, 1979). Erikson proposed two polar stages of personality development for this age group: (1) identity as opposed to role diffusion, for young adolescents, and (2) intimacy as opposed to isolation, for older adolescents and young adults.

In the stage of identity as opposed to role diffusion, young adolescents struggle to determine who they are and who they want to become while at the same time experiencing major physical changes and the development of adult-like sexual interests. They must synthesize what they have learned about themselves during the preceding 12 to 14 years and incorporate the rapid physical and psychological changes of adolescence into an understanding of self (or self-concept) that will be an important part of their adult personality.

Adolescents typically cope with this struggle toward identity by turning to peers, popular heroes, and causes. They usually engage in a process of trying out various ways of being, under the critical eyes of their peers. Successful adolescents gradually glean a growing sense of identity through this trial and error process. Those who are unsuccessful become involved in the cliquish and critical world of adolescence without being able to discern what can and cannot be incorporated into their growing sense of self. As these individuals grow older they continue to show the clannishness and intolerance of adolescence. They remain confused concerning their identity and their role in life, and they are not prepared to meet the challenges of adulthood. They are likely to fail in the adult responsibilities of intimacy and generativity and to suffer low self-esteem and depression (which have repeatedly been associated with suicide).

The next psychosocial stage, intimacy as opposed to isolation, occurs as the adolescent moves into young adulthood. In this stage the young person must deal with the issue of establishing an adult, sharing, nonexploitive relationship with another person. The young person who emerges from adolescence with a strong sense of personal identity is well prepared to establish a meaningful, loving, trusting, intimate relationship. The young person who is still struggling with the issue of identity will be unable to establish a truly intimate relationship and will be likely to retreat into self-absorption. These individuals tend to become increasingly isolated and unconnected as they grow older. As we will learn in chapters 6 and 7, middle-aged and older adults who lack the support systems that develop from intimate relationships with others are a group at high risk for suicide.

While the behavioral perspective does not include specific age-related stages of development, the principle of modeling does have special significance for adolescents. Imitation and modeling are prevalent behaviors among this age group. Adolescents are especially likely to copy the dress, speech, mannerisms, and other behavior of their peers and of popular public figures such as rock stars. They are also more vulnerable to cluster suicides, a phenomenon in which a group of people who are similar demographically and live in the same general geographic location commit suicide over a relatively short time span. Adolescents are also vulnerable to the "copy cat" suicide phenomenon, in which several suicides of a similar nature occur following a single highly publicized suicide. Both of these phenomena can be understood as examples of modeling.

The humanistic perspective, like the behavioral perspective, does not specify stages of development. It does, however, maintain that human beings are growth oriented and continuously in the process of seeking meaning and purpose in life. The search for meaning and purpose is especially prominent during the adolescent and young adult years. Young people are heavily involved in preparation for their adult lives and in setting goals and establishing a dream for lifetime accomplishments. Because of youth's heavy orientation toward the future, the existential claim that the future determines the present is likely to be more true for this age group than for any other. Young people who for any reason are unable to establish and work toward important lifetime goals are likely to develop feelings of uselessness, hopelessness, and depression. As discussed in chapter 2, these individuals will be the victims of noogenic neurosis, which Frankl (1963) believed to be widespread in 20th-century Western societies.

According to cognitive development theory, the adolescent is in the formal operations stage. As discussed earlier, this stage is marked by the development of hypothetical and abstract thinking capabilities as well as by the intuitive use of the scientific method in problem solving. Piaget believed that young people's ability to form hypotheses is particularly relevant in explaining certain characteristics of adolescent thinking (Piaget & Inhelder,

Don't laugh at a youth for his affectations: he is only trying on one face after another to find a face of his own. Logan Pearsall Smith, *Afterthoughts*

1969). For the first time in their lives, adolescents are capable of dreaming of idealized worlds that do not exist. However, because their development has not yet progressed to a level where they can impose reality constraints upon their hypothetical "better" worlds, they are often disappointed with life as it really is. This type of thinking among adolescents may result in considerable disillusionment and unhappiness with the world and may also lead to the consideration of other hypothetical possibilities, one of which is death.

In summary, the adolescent years tend to be characterized by rapid physical growth and major psychological changes. Adolescents must cope not only with a rapidly changing physical body but also with hormonal changes that promote adult sexual responses and with cognitive changes that permit more abstract and hypothetical analyses. In addition, adolescents become more influenced by the behavior and attitudes of their peer group even as they strive to develop their own personal identity. The stress resulting from such major life changes undoubtedly taxes the adolescent's coping skills and contributes to the rates of suicide and attempted suicide among individuals aged 15 to 24. The developmental characteristics of adolescents are important contributors to behavior in this age group; however, as we saw in the preceding chapter, development interacts in special ways with *zeitgeist,* the culture and period in which a person lives. Therefore, in the following section, we will look more closely at the adolescent in today's world.

TODAY'S ADOLESCENT

Each generation of adolescents adopts norms and behaviors that differ from those of earlier cohorts. Hairstyles, clothes, speech, and pastimes are all eligible to be included in the persona that distinguishes the generation that is coming of age. As discussed in Chapter One, according to Strauss and Howe (1991) today's adolescents (and young adults) are members of the 13th Generation, so named because they are the 13th group to call themselves Americans. In 1995, 13ers ranged in age from 14 to 34, encompassing both adolescents (15- to 24-year-olds), discussed in this chapter, and young adults (25–34 year olds), who will be the focus of chapter 5.

The 13ers, according to Strauss and Howe (1991), are a reactive generation that spends much time and energy reacting against the values and norms of the Baby Boom Generation of their parents. They are in many ways the antithesis of their younger counterparts described in Chapter 3, who constitute a civic generation. Thirteeners, also known as Generation X, have been characterized as uninspired, poorly prepared, and unproductive. Strauss and Howe (1991) believe that these negative characteristics are a natural outcome of the fact that 13ers have been one of the least wanted and most poorly parented groups in recent times. The first wave of 13ers was born at the advent of the birth control pill in the early 1960s, and those born ten years later in the early 70s arrived at the time of the Supreme Court ruling on Roe vs. Wade and quickly became the most aborted generation in history. 13ers were the true children of the 1960s and 1970s—a time that was marked by self-indulgence for many young adult Boomers but that was negative for many children, who often received poor quality parenting. Even slightly older Silent Generation parents of the 1960s and 1970s, envious of the freedom enjoyed by Boomer hippies, often saw their children as a hindrance to their own self-exploration. The last wave of 13ers, born in the early 1980s, saw an already growing divorce rate reach its zenith with record numbers of single-parent and blended families.

The 13ers have not distinguished themselves academically—at least not in a positive way. SAT scores have declined steadily with each wave of 13ers, a trend that did not begin to reverse itself until the birth of the following generation (the Millenials). The 13ers are a college-going group, but their graduation rates are below that of their Boomer elders at the same age—which threatens to make this the first generation in history to have a lower graduation rate than their predecessors. The undistinguished academic careers of this group have been chronicled in a number of best-seller publications such as Allan Bloom's *The Closing of the American Mind* (1987). Clearly this group has not been served well by the American education system. The prevailing educational philosophy when they entered the schools during the 1960s was that there is no single indispensable body of knowledge to be learned. After many years of cafeteria-style curricula, which included more electives than required courses, many 13ers exited the system with the prevailing educational philosophy that there is essential knowledge, and "you missed it" (Strauss & Howe, 1991).

Finally, unlike the Millenials, many 13ers have been raised on a diet of sex and violence. As children they were taken to adult movies about bad children (e.g. *Rosemary's Baby, The Exorcist, Damien*). This group was also exposed to more real-life crime and violence early in life than preceding generations. During their coming-of-age years, between 1965 and 1992, crime victimization in the United States rose from 2,177 per 100,000 population to 9,120 per 100,000, an increase of approximately 500% (U.S. Bureau of the Census, 1970, 1994). They learned early that the world is a dangerous place.

Predictably, significant numbers of 13er adolescents, have experienced adjustment problems. These difficulties have been reflected in the highest youth suicide rate ever recorded. Although the growth in adolescent suicide started with the Baby BoomGeneration, the 13ers carried the trend to record levels that peaked for older adolescents (20- to 24-year-olds) in the late 1970s but continues to climb for younger adolescents (15- to 19-year-olds), who represent the last wave of this generation.

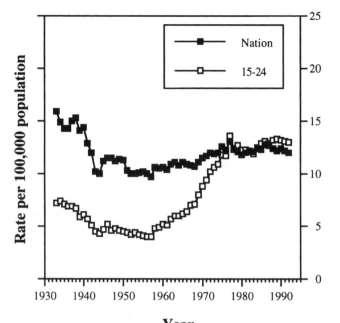

Year

FIGURE 4.1   U.S. suicide rates 1932–1992 for the nation and for those aged 15 to 24.

Source: Generated by John L. McIntosh, Ph.D., professor of psychology, Indiana University South Bend, based on annual data published by the National Center for Health Statistics.

THE STATISTICAL PICTURE FOR ADOLESCENT SUICIDE

The latest statistics available show that 4,693 of the 30,484 suicides in the United States in 1992 were completed by individuals between the ages of 15 and 24. These data reflect a suicide rate of 13.0 per 100,000 population— slightly higher than the national average of 12.0 for all age groups (National Center for Health Statistics, 1994).

Figure 4.1 shows the annual suicide rates in the United States between 1932 and 1992 for the nation and for those aged 15 to 24. The figure shows that the adolescent suicide rate remained low and more or less paralleled the overall U.S. rate until the late 1950s. During the 1960s and 1970s, however, the adolescent suicide rate rose precipitously while the rates for the general population remained fairly constant. In 1957, when adolescent suicide was at its lowest recorded level, the suicide rate for 15- to 24-year-olds was 4.0 per 100,000 population. Twenty years later, in 1977, the adolescent suicide rate peaked at 13.3 per 100,000 population, an increase of more than 300 percent (National Center for Health Statistics, 1994).

Suicide rates for adolescents have differed over time and by age, sex, and

TABLE 4.1   Adolescent Suicide Rates per 100,000 Population for 1970, 1980, & 1990 by Age, Sex, and Race

| | White Males | | | | Black Males | | | |
Age	1970	1980	1990	% Change	1970	1980	1990	% Change
15–19	9.4	15.0	19.3	+105	4.7	5.6	11.5	+145
20–24	19.3	27.8	26.8	+39	18.7	20.0	19.0	+2
	White Females				Black Females			
Age	1970	1980	1990	% Change	1970	1980	1990	% Change
15–19	2.9	3.3	4.0	+38	2.9	1.6	1.9	−34
20–24	5.7	5.9	4.4	−23	4.9	3.1	2.6	−47

Source: U.S. Bureau of the Census (1992). Statistical Abstract of the United States (112 th. ed.): Washington, DC, p. 90.

race. Suicide rates for 1970, 1980, and 1990 for younger and older, male and female, and black and white adolescents are presented in Table 4.1. The table shows that older adolescents (20- to 24-year-olds) of both sexes and races have higher suicide rates than younger adolescents (15- to 19-year-olds). Also, male suicide rates are significantly higher than female rates (on the order of four or five to one), and suicide rates for white adolescents are higher than those for African Americans.

Primary among the findings indicated in Table 4.1 is the dramatic sex difference in the adolescent suicide rate trends over the 20-year period. Males (both white and black) have accounted for the lion's share of the suicide rate increase for this age group over the past two decades. In fact, with the single exception of 15- to 19-year-old white females, all other female groups have shown a decrease in suicide since 1970. In contrast, all male groups experienced a significant increase in suicide during the same period. It is noteworthy that among white and black males, younger adolescents (15- to 19-year-olds) have experienced larger increases in suicide rate than older adolescents (20- to 24-year-olds). In other words, young teenage males (especially African Americans) have shown the largest increase in suicide rate of any group over the past two decades.

A further concern about the suicide rate of African American adolescents is the possibility that their's may be more underestimated than other groups. Homicide victimization peaks for 15- to 24-year-old nonwhites (mostly African Americans) at an incredible rate of 109.1 per 100,000 population, far greater than that of any other age or ethnic group (National Center for Health Statistics, 1994). In an extensive study of suicide and homicide among adolescents, Holinger, Offer, Barter, and Bell (1994) have made a strong case for the possibility that many of the homicides of African American youth may include elements of suicide, that is to say, a number of these victims may have behaved in ways that placed themselves in greater danger. This possibility will be developed further in chapter 5, where we discuss suicide (and homicide) in young adults.

The incidence of suicide among adolescents is dwarfed by the number of attempted suicides. Precise information is impossible to obtain because the great majority of youth suicide attempts occur at home, often undiscovered and unreported, and of low lethality, requiring no medical attention (Berman & Jobes, 1991). Farberow and Schneidman (1961) developed the most widely accepted general population estimate of an 8:1 ratio of suicide attempts to completions. Although this ratio appears to be realistic for the population as a whole, there is considerable variability among age groups. The ratios of attempted to completed suicides vary inversely with age (i.e., adolescents have a higher rate of unsuccessful suicide attempts relative to successful attempts than young, middle-aged, and older adults). Estimates of the ratio of attempts to completed suicide for 15- to 24-year-olds vary from 100:1 (Jacobzinzer, 1965) to 200:1 (Angle, O'Brien, & McIntire, 1983).

The increasing adolescent suicide rate during the last half-century has not been confined to the United States, but rather reflects an international trend (Sainsbury, Jenkins, & Levy, 1980). Studies have shown significant increases in the adolescent suicide rate in a number of countries, including Canada (Pettifor, Perry, Plowman, & Pitcher, 1983), Great Britain (McClure, 1984), Australia (Goldney & Katsikitis, 1983), and Micronesia (Rubenstein, 1983). Other similarities between the United States and other countries include higher rates among older adolescents than younger adolescents, more suicides by males, and more attempts by females.

The suicide rates of adolescents and other age groups in 13 developed countries was presented in Chapter 1. Table 1.2 showed that the United States ranks fourth in suicide rate for 15- to 24-year-old males and eighth for female suicides in this age group. A further examination of Table 1.2 shows that the suicide rates for adolescent males are higher than those for adolescent females in all 13 countries reporting.

In summary, the adolescent suicide rate increased more rapidly than the rate for any other age group during the last half of the 20th century. The increasing rate for this age group has been primarily a male phenomenon—especially younger adolescent males. Suicide rates for male adolescents are approximately four times higher than those for females, and the rates for white adolescents are approximately double the African American adolescent rate.

The dramatic changes in adolescent suicide over the last few decades have stimulated a great deal of research and theory to better understand the causes of self-destructive behavior in this age group. We will discuss some of the important findings from this research and the theoretical conclusions in the following sections as we apply the Suicide Trajectory Model to adolescents.

THE SUICIDE TRAJECTORY APPLIED
TO ADOLESCENT SUICIDE

The Suicide Trajectory as it applies to adolescent suicide is presented in Table 4.2. This now-familiar model includes biological, psychological, cognitive, and environmental risk factors as well as warning signs and triggering events that contribute to suicidal behavior in this age group.

Biological Risk Factors

As shown in Table 4.2, the onset of puberty, triggered by the increased production of hormones that bring about sexual maturation, is a biological risk factor that may influence suicide among adolescents. The process of maturation occurs over a period of years, and its onset may occur any time between the preteen and midteen years. Whenever these biological changes occur, they add weight to the tumult of this period and, we believe, increase suicide risk. Although there is no direct evidence that the onset of puberty increases suicide risk, the fact that the suicide rate for postpubescent teenagers is higher than that for preteens strongly suggests at least an indirect influence.

Psychological Risk Factors

Table 4.2 shows that problems with identity and fluctuating mood states are psychological risk factors that may contribute to suicidality among adolescents. As Erikson (1968) has explained, the establishment of a sense of identity is a major developmental task of adolescence. Teenagers who develop some consistent understanding of who they are and who they are becoming will have a foundation of competence in coping with the stresses of this period. In contrast, adolescents who struggle with their identities are less likely to develop the coping skills needed to deal effectively with these challenges. Moodiness, which is experienced by all adolescents, may also contribute to suicidality in this age group. Moodiness is partially rooted in biology; it may be extreme, reflecting a significant amount of depression, which repeatedly has been shown to be associated with increased suicide risk in all age groups. At least one study has shown that adolescents who experience excessive moodiness are more likely than other young people to show patterns of disturbed affect (Golombek & Marton, 1989).

Suicidal adolescents have been shown to exhibit many symptoms of psychopathology (Berman & Jobes, 1991; Shaffer, Garland, Gould, Fisher, & Trautman, 1988). The association between suicidal behavior and psychopathology has been demonstrated repeatedly in both the clinical and research

TABLE 4.2 The Suicide Trajectory Model Applied to Adolescent Suicide

Age Group	Biological Risk Factors	Psychological Risk Factors	Cognitive Risk Factors	Environmental Risk Factors	Warning Signs	Triggering Events	Suicidal Behavior
Adolescence (15–24)	Puberty Hormonal changes	Identity crisis Fluctuating mood states Psychopathology: depression, substance abuse, personality disorder, comorbidity Gay or lesbian orientation	Formal operational thinking Idealism Egocentrism Imaginary audience Illusion of invulnerability Reduced problem-solving skills Absence of future-time perspective	Parent conflict Anomic family Drug/alcohol abuse Sexual abuse Social isolation Poor peer relationships Population characteristics	Change in habits Self-mutilation Preparation for death Truancy Poor school performance	Failure experiences Problems with peers, parents, opposite sex, legal authorities Suicides by peers or famous people	Largest increase in 40 years Most dramatic sex difference in attempts vs. completions

literature. A variety of pathologies have been found to be associated with suicidality among adolescents; however, the three disorders listed in Table 4.2—depression, substance abuse, and personality disorder—are the predominant ones (Berman & Jobes, 1991).

As indicated in chapter 1, *depression* is the most common pathological symptom of suicidal individuals in all age groups (Goldberg, 1981; Linehan, 1981). Many studies have shown that depression is associated with adolescent suicidal ideation, suicide attempts, and suicide completion (Berman & Carroll, 1984; Berman & Jobes, 1991; Bettes & Walker, 1986; Borst & Noam, 1991; Cole, 1989; Kienhorst, DeWilde, Diekstra, & Wolters, 1992; Shaffer, 1974). These studies underscore the fact that the depressed adolescent, especially one who also has suicidal thoughts, is greatly at risk for suicide. The importance of depressive symptoms in adolescent suicide was demonstrated in a study that found a positive correlation between the level of depression and the lethality of suicide attempts among 505 adolescents admitted to a hospital emergency room (Garfinkel, Froese, and Hood, 1982). The adolescents in this study, whose suicide attempts had placed them in the greatest physical jeopardy, showed the highest level of depression.

Several studies that included adolescents and other age groups have found that feelings of hopelessness constitute an important variable linking depression to suicide (Beck, Kovacs, & Weissman, 1979; Lester, Beck, & Mitchell, 1979; Minkoff, Bergman, Beck, & Beck, 1973; Morano, Cisler, & Lemerond, 1993; Peck, 1987; and Rotheram-Boris & Trautman, 1988). These studies have shown that feelings of hopelessness are stronger determiners than generalized depression of lethality of intent among suicide attempters.

A study by Wetzel (1976) found that hopelessness relates to actual suicidal behavior as well as to lethality of intent. He compared three groups of hospitalized psychiatric patients (suicide attempters, suicide ideators, and a nonsuicidal group) on measures of depression, hopelessness, and suicidal intent. Wetzel found that the suicide attempters scored higher on the measure of hopelessness than either the suicide ideators or the nonsuicidal group. He also found that the suicide attempters with high lethality-of-intent scores reported greater feelings of hopelessness than attempters with low lethality-of-intent scores.

Finally, a study by Beck, Steer, Kovacs, and Garrison (1985) found that hopelessness can predict future suicidal behavior. In a 10-year follow up of 207 patients previously hospitalized because of suicidal ideation, level of hopelessness at the time of hospitalization was found to differentiate the 14 individuals who later committed suicide from the 193 who did not.

Numerous studies have shown that *alcohol and drug abuse* are related to attempted suicide and suicide completion in adolescents (Downey, 1990; Garfinkel, Froese, & Hood, 1982; McKenry, Tishler, & Kelly, 1983; Schuckit &

Schuckit, 1991). In their review of risk factors associated with adolescent suicide, Berman and Jobes (1991) have reported that 15 to 33% of adolescent suicide completers have a history of substance abuse. In addition to their role in predisposing suicide among adolescents, drugs are frequently used in suicide attempts (especially among teenage girls), and alcohol is often taken as a prelude to a suicidal act (Grueling & DeBlassie, 1980).

Personality disorder is a third type of pathology commonly found among adolescent suicide attempters and completers (Borst & Noam, 1991; Shafii, Carrigan, Whittinghill, & Derrick, 1985). One study of institutionalized adolescents found evidence of a stronger relationship between suicidality and personality disorder (particularly antisocial personality type) than between suicidality and major depressive disorder (Apter, Bleich, Plutchik, Mendelsohn, & Tyano, 1988). Young people with this disorder fail to develop adequate internal controls over their behavior. They frequently engage in antisocial behaviors that bring them into conflict with legal authorities. A recent study of conduct-disordered and substance-abusing adolescent suicide victims found that this group had commonly experienced legal and disciplinary problems less than a year before taking their lives (Brent et al., 1993). More research is needed in order to ferret out the specific aspects of personality disorder that contribute to suicide risk in this group. It is likely that the impulsive and aggressive nature of these young people may enhance the likelihood of a self-destructive act, especially when their antisocial behavior increases their stress by bringing them into conflict with legal authorities.

You will recall from chapter 3 that depressed children and hyperactive, aggressive, conduct-disordered children have been found to be the two major groups at risk for suicide among children. It is interesting to speculate that the association between depression (and conduct disorder, and perhaps substance abuse) and suicide among adolescents may be an upward extension of the child-suicide phenomenon. It should be noted, however, that Cynthia Pfeffer, the best known authority on child suicide in the United States today, characterizes depressed children and conduct-disordered children as two different suicidal groups. In contrast, recent research concerning the psychopathology of suicidal adolescents focuses more on comorbidity involving depression, conduct disorder, and substance abuse. Recent research has shown that adolescents who manifest two of these types of mental illness engage in more frequent and lethal suicidal behavior than adolescents who show evidence of only one of these disorders (Runeson & Rich, 1992). Further evidence of the importance of comorbidity in adolescent suicide was provided

---

It is an illusion that youth is happy, an illusion of those who have lost it. W. Somerset Maugham, *Of Human Bondage*, 1915

by a psychological autopsy study of 21 adolescent suicides in Louisville, Kentucky. Postmortem reviews of official records and extensive interviews with close relatives and friends revealed that 81% of the suicides manifested two or more DSM III mental disorders (Shafii, Steltz-Lenarsky, Derrick, Beckner, & Whittinghill, 1988).

It is important to note here again that other types of abnormal behavior have also been found to accompany suicidal behavior in adolescents, although less frequently. Berman and Jobes (1991) have pointed out that, in addition to the big three—depression, substance abuse, and personality disorder—two other pathologies that are related to adolescent suicide are *anxiety disorder* and *borderline personality disorder.*

Table 4.2 indicates that one final psychological risk factor is gay or lesbian orientation. Several studies have found that gay and lesbian adolescents are more at risk for suicide than others in this age group (Harry, 1983; Remafedi, 1987; Roesler & Deishmer, 1972; and Rothblum, 1990). Although for more than a decade homosexuality itself has not been considered to be psychopathological (American Psychiatric Association, 1987), psychosocial stressors associated with establishing a gay identity and lifestyle are believed to be factors contributing to suicide in this group. In a very important study of suicidal behavior among gay adolescent males, Schneider, Farberow, and Kruks (1989) found that many of the stressors that affect suicidal ideation among gays (e.g., a family background of alcoholism and physical abuse) are the same stressors that influence such thinking among heterosexuals. Their study also showed, however, that additional stressors, including perceived rejection of homosexuality by social supports and difficulties in coming to terms with an emerging homosexual identity, were significant factors affecting suicidal ideation and suicide attempts among gay adolescent males. It is particularly noteworthy that Schneider, Farberow, and Kruks found elevated incidences of suicidal ideation (55%) and suicide attempts (20%) among their particular sample of 108 gay adolescents. The subjects in this study were recruited from several gay and lesbian support organizations. It is reasonable to assume that the incidence of suicidality among members of support groups may provide an underestimation of the suicide risk for gay and lesbian adolescents who do not have these types of social supports available.

Cognitive Risk Factors

Adolescence brings rapid developmental changes in the cognitive realm. Some of these changes, we believe, may increase adolescent risk of suicide. As indicated earlier in this chapter, most adolescents are entering the early stages of the formal operations period of cognitive development, which is reflected in their beginning ability to engage in hypothetical and abstract thinking (Piaget & Inhelder, 1969). Hypothetical thinking in this age group manifests itself in the imagining of idealized worlds that do not, and often cannot, exist. This type of thinking, coupled with the absence of ability to impose reality constraints upon what could be, creates a special opportunity for disillusionment and unhappiness. Any parent or professional who has regular contact with adolescents is frequently perplexed by the young person's apparent lack of perspective regarding the issues that distress him or her. Additionally, adolescents experience a renewed period of egocentrism, as they believe they are the first ones to really understand the world from this new perspective. This egocentrism fuels their sense of performing for an imaginary audience and increases their feelings of self-consciousness, making small embarrassments seem like major traumas. Also, members of this age group have great difficulty accepting their own mortality. Adolescents often hold an illusion of invulnerability that contributes to high risk taking (Elkind, 1967). Although there is no evidence of a direct relationship between enhanced disillusionment, self-consciousness, and risk taking and suicidality, we believe that these are risk factors that add to the perturbation of adolescents and affect vulnerability to suicide.

In addition to these inherent cognitive characteristics, Table 4.2 also includes two special deficiencies that may be of special significance to suicidal adolescents: (1) problem-solving difficulties and (2) absence of future-time perspective. Clum, Patsiokas, and Luscomb (1979) have speculated that adolescents with limited problem-solving skills are at greater risk for suicide when experiencing significant life stress than those who are better problem solvers. These researchers believe that, because adolescents have fewer life experiences to draw on than adults, problem solving capabilities are especially essential for this age group. A study by Levenson and Neuringer (1971) compared the performances of a group of suicidal adolescents with those of a nonsuicidal psychiatric group and those of a nonsuicidal nonpsychiatric group on the arithmetic subtest of the Wechsler Adult Intelligence Scale and on the Rokeach Map Reading Problems Test. The suicidal adolescents scored significantly lower than the other two groups on both of these tests. In another study investigating this phenomenon, the problem-solving abilities of a group of female minority adolescents who had attempted suicide were compared with those of a non-suicide-attempting group of minority, adolescent, psychiatric outpatients and those of a nonpsychiatric community group (Rotheram-Boyus, Trautman, Dopkins, & Shrout, 1990). The suicide-

---

There is a feeling of Eternity in youth which makes amends for everything. To be young is to be as one of the Immortals. No young man believes he shall ever die. William Hazlitt

attempting group of adolescents showed significantly poorer interpersonal problem-solving skills than either of the control groups as measured by the Means-Ends Problem Solving Procedures Test.

Compared with nonsuicidal adolescents, suicidal adolescents have been found to have a reduced future-time perspective and goal orientation (Corder, Shorr, & Corder, 1974). It is easy to understand how young people who deal with problems ineffectively and are also unable to imagine better times might be more inclined to consider suicide when experiencing a great deal of stress. Like Jason in the next case study, they do not believe that the situation will improve.

The following suicide note was found in a college student's dormitory room after he took an overdose of pills. The content of the note reveals several of the cognitive characteristics of suicidal adolescents. Although the names, places, and dates are fictitious, the essential features and language of the note are unchanged.

Jason Kelvin Joyner
(July 16, 1968—April 30, 1989)

To Whom It May Concern:

Why?! Because my life has been nothing but misery and sorrow for 20 3/4 years! Going backwards: I thought Susan loved me, but I suppose not. "I love you Jason" was only a lie. I base my happiness on relationships with girls—when I'm "going steady," I'm happy. When a girl dumps me (which is always the case) I'm terribly depressed. In fact, over the last three years I've been in love at least four times seriously, but only to have my heart shattered—like so many icicles falling from a roof. But I've tried to go out with at least 30 to 40 girls in the last few years—none of them ever fell in love with me. My fate was: "To love, but not be loved."

My mother threw me out of the house in March. I guess she must really hate me; she doesn't even write me letters. I think she always hated me.

In high school, and even before that, nobody liked me. They all made fun of me and no girl would ever go to the proms with me.

I haven't anything to live for. Hope? Five years ago I wanted to end my life—I've been hoping for five years! Susan was just the straw that broke the camel's back. I simply cannot take it anymore! I only wanted someone to love; someone who would love me back as much as I loved her.

Yeah, I had pretty good grades, but the way my luck runs, I wouldn't have gotten a job anyway. I got fired over the summer cause the boss said, "Jason, you don't have any common sense." Gee, that really made my day.

I walk down the streets of Madison and people call out of dorm windows: "Hey Asshole!" What did I do to them? I don't even know them!

I've been pretty miserable lately (since 1979), so I think I will change the scenery.

What's the big deal? I was gonna die in 40 or 50 years anyway. (Maybe sooner: when George decides to push the button in Washington, D.C.!)

Good-bye Susan, Sean, Wendy, Joe, Mr. Montgomery, Dr. Johnston, Jack, and everyone else who made my life a little more bearable while it lasted.

Jason Kelvin Joyner
April 30, 1989

P.S. You might want to print this in the campus newspaper. It would make excellent reading!

Last Will
(Only will. I never made one before.)

I probably am wasting my time, because you need a lawyer or a witness for a will to be legal, but here goes:

To Sean—go my records, tapes, cassette player, clock/radio, and my camera (in the doctor's bag in closet).
To Wendy—I leave my car (if you want it, if not, give it to ET), my big black coat and my military school uniform—you said you wanted them.
To Joe and Wendy—all my posters, if you want them.
To Jack—miscellaneous items left over (that's still a lot, so don't complain).
To Susan—I leave memories of nice times we had. Also my airbrush (in doctor bag w/ camera), and all my love; I'll miss you forever.
If I've forgotten anyone—I'm sorry.

Jason Kelvin Joyner
April 30, 1989

Please: No autopsy.

Jason's suicide note reveals a number of cognitive characteristics that have been shown to be associated with adolescent suicide. He certainly has idealized expectations about love relationships, apparently on the occasion of each first date. His egocentrism is reflected in the importance he attaches to failed relationships with girlfriends and with his mother. Although the suicide note does not include details, it would seem likely that his interpersonal problem-solving skills leave something to be desired. Clearly, there is an absence of future-time perspective in the suicide note. Jason does not believe that his situation will eventually improve.

The note also includes several of the cognitive characteristics introduced by Aaron Beck (1967) and discussed in chapter 1 that apply to depressed and suicidal individuals of all ages. For example, a few instances of rejection have been selectively abstracted and overgeneralized by Jason into a lifetime of "nothing but misery." Clearly, Jason's suicide note reflects a great deal of what Albert Ellis calls "awfulizing." The note also reflects the characteristic cognitive constriction that eventually leads to only two choices—live or die.

Jason's note illustrates a number of other important characteristics of suicidal people. He is obviously depressed from a series of significant interpersonal losses. His self-esteem is low, and he is hopeless about the future.

Environmental Risk Factors

In the fifth column of Table 4.2 are listed a variety of environmental factors that have been found to be associated with increased risk of suicide among adolescents. Many suicidal adolescents, like the children described in chapter 3, come from highly conflicted homes that are unresponsive to the young person's needs (Berman & Carroll, 1984; Pfeffer, 1991). There is a higher than average incidence of family dysfunctions of all types among the parents of suicidal adolescents. The homes of suicide attempters in this age group are more likely to be disrupted by parental separation and divorce than the national average (McAnarney, 1979; Walker, 1980). Even within intact families, suicide-attempting adolescents see their parents as less cohesive (Miller, King, Shain, & Naylor, 1992) and more conflicted (Tishler, McKenry, & Morgan, 1981) than nonsuicidal adolescents.

Although there are many exceptions, families of suicide attempters tend to be anomic (that is, not accepting of the usual standards of conduct) more often than would be expected by chance. These families have higher incidences of medical and psychiatric problems (Garfinkel, Froese, & Hood, 1982). There is also a higher than usual incidence of alcoholism and drug abuse among the parents of suicide attempters (Jacobs, 1971).

There is a growing body of evidence that sexual abuse is an environmental stressor that may affect suicide risk among adolescents. A number of studies have shown that adolescents who report a history of sexual abuse have a higher incidence of suicidal ideation and suicide attempts than those who have not been sexually abused (Harrison, Hoffmann, Edwall, 1989; Kienhorst, DeWilde, Diekstra, & Wolters, 1992; Shaunesey, Cohen, Plummer, Berman, 1993). The specific nature of the relationship between sexual abuse and suicidal behavior is not well understood; however, a number of studies have provided some additional insight. We do know, for example, that sexually abused adolescents show a higher incidence of depression, substance abuse, and conduct disorder, all of which have been shown repeatedly to be associated with suicidality (Bayatpour, Wells, & Holoford, 1992; Sansonnet-Hayden,

Haley, Marriage, Fine, 1987). Additional research will be necessary in order to fully understand the complex relationships among these causal factors.

Table 4.2 shows that social isolation and poor peer relationships are two additional environmental risk factors that affect suicidality in adolescents. Suicidal adolescents are often alienated both within their families and among their peers. Modern-day youth, who generally live in nuclear or single-parent families, do not enjoy the support that was provided for earlier generations by extended families, neighborhood churches, and small communities. Contributing further to this sense of social isolation is the fact that family mobility is at an all-time high. Twenty-seven percent of all 15- to 24-year-olds in the United States relocated between 1989 and 1990 (U.S. Bureau of the Census, 1994). Although 17% moved within the same geographic region, 10% (35,000 adolescents) relocated to a totally different place, thus breaking friendships and family ties.

Several studies have shown that suicidal adolescents have poor interpersonal relationships within the family (McKenry, Tishler, & Kelly, 1983; Morano, Cisler, & Lemerond, 1993; Slap, Vorters, Chaudhuri, & Centor, 1989; and Topol & Reznikoff, 1982). These young people regularly report poor familial relationships that include low levels of affection, little enjoyment of time spent with other family members, and negative views of parents. Farberow (1991) has reviewed a number of studies showing that suicidal adolescents are often socially isolated and alienated among their peers. Suicidal adolescents are more likely than others to have poor peer relationships, to be nonjoiners, and to be generally unpopular.

As shown in Table 4.2, population characteristics may also influence adolescent suicide. Holinger and Offer (1991) have hypothesized that the adolescent suicide rate will increase as this age group constitutes a larger percent of the total population and will decrease as their relative numbers decline. Holinger and Offer believe that larger numbers of adolescents increase competition for relatively fewer societal rewards (e.g. class president, valedictorian, team captain) and result in more "failure" and lost self-esteem. Studies over periods of approximately 20 years have shown significant relationships between adolescent representation in the total U.S. population and the suicide rate for this age group (Holinger, Offer, & Zola, 1988; Holinger & Offer, 1991). Predictably, the 15- to 24-year-old suicide rate peaked in 1977, when this age group's population representation reached its zenith, and both statistics have correspondingly declined since. Although the data are not available at this writing, Holinger and Offer have predicted that the adolescent suicide rate will start to climb again in 1995 as this age group begins to claim a higher percentage of the total population.

We have seen in this section that many biological, psychological, and cognitive characteristics of adolescents place them at risk for suicide when environmental stressors strain their coping mechanisms. The following case study of Joe and Lenora illustrates several of the environmental risk factors that have been shown to be associated with adolescent suicide.

> Joe was 18 and Lenora was 17 when they attempted suicide together. They drove their old car into a garage, closed the door, and turned on the radio. Local police patrolling the area heard the radio and saw the exhaust fumes escaping from cracks in the garage. They interrupted the suicide attempt and took Joe and Lenora to the hospital, where they were treated for drug overdoses and for carbon monoxide poisoning. From statements made at the hospital and later at the police station, the following facts emerged.
>
> Both Joe and Lenora came from troubled homes. Joe lived with an alcoholic father, and Lenora lived with her mother and younger sister in a rundown tenement building. She and her sister did not get along, and her mother seemed to have given up on both of them.
>
> Joe and Lenora's relationship was heavily based on their common use of drugs. They were sporadic students who considered themselves to be loners. Since they had no other friends, they soon found themselves inseparable. Joe took the responsibility for supplying the drugs for both of their growing habits. He began dealing drugs and was arrested once and put on probation. Both young people tried to stop using drugs after Joe's arrest. However, when they were not high, they were irritable and fought a great deal with each other. After several weeks of trying to be straight, they began using drugs again. Within two weeks, Joe was dealing again in order to supply their needs.
>
> Joe was arrested again. This time it took several days to raise the bail. Once he was out on bail, the couple discussed their future. It was clear that Joe would be imprisoned for some time. He dreaded prison and separation from the one friend he considered loyal. Lenora would be alone once again with a drug habit and no supplier.
>
> Joe and Lenora later reported that suicide seemed to be the only solution to their problems. Joe gathered together what cocaine and marijuana he had left, and the couple drove around town until they found an unlocked, vacant garage.

This suicide attempt contains many of the elements common to adolescent suicides. Drug abuse and difficulty with legal authorities were discussed earlier in this chapter as risk factors frequently associated with youth suicide. Neither Joe nor Lenora came from a stable home. Joe's alcoholic father was a model for self-destructive behavior, and Lenora's mother seemed depressed and hopeless. Both young people were socially isolated from their peer groups and at home, making their relationship with each other all the more important. The inevitability of a long-term separation as a result of Joe's impending incarceration was the "final straw" environmental stressor that triggered the double suicide attempt.

Warning Signs

Many of the warning signs for adolescent suicide listed in Table 4.2 differ from those of other age groups. Unlike adults, adolescents are likely to show dramatic changes in established habits or behaviors, such as no longer going to movies, participating in extracurricular activities, or watching television. Self-mutilators are at increased risk for suicide (Favazza, 1989). Many adolescents manifest the early stages of self-mutilation by carving initials on their arms with penknives. Finally, adolescents more than any other age group tend to make final preparations for death by giving away prized possessions such as record, tape, or CD collections.

Numerous studies have found that suicidal adolescents are likely to have school records that reflect poor performance and frequent truancy (Berman & Carroll, 1984; Corder, Shorr, & Corder, 1974; Garfinkel, Froese, & Hood, 1982). As with their younger counterparts, however, research using better control groups shows that poor school performance and truancy are characteristics of emotionally disturbed adolescents in general (especially depressed adolescents) and do not specifically differentiate the suicidal adolescents from the others (Berman and Jobes, 1991).

Triggering Events

Triggering events for adolescent suicide often seem trivial to adults. The previously mentioned egocentrism of this age group often inflates the importance of such occurrences as minor failure experiences or problems with peers, parents, or the opposite sex (Spirito, Overholser, & Stark, 1989). One recent well-designed study compared the stressful life events that had occurred within 12 months of the suicides of 67 adolescents with those of a matched group of community controls (Brent et al., 1993). Findings revealed that the adolescent suicide completers were more likely than the control group to have experienced (1) interpersonal conflict with parents and with boyfriends or girlfriends, (2) disruption of a romantic attachment, and (3) legal or disciplinary problems. The study also found that certain types of psychopathology (conduct disorder and substance abuse) interacted with particular types of stressors. For example, they found that legal or disciplinary problems were more commonly associated with suicide in conduct disordered and substance abuse disordered youth while interpersonal loss was more commonly associated with suicide in substance abuse alone. However, even when controlling for psychopathology, the life stressors were still found to be significant variables associated with suicide in this age group.

Table 4.2 shows that two triggering events of special importance for ado-

Lovers in the Waves, **Edvard Munch. Lithograph. (Munchmuseet, Oslo Kommuns Kunstsamlinger, Norway.)**

lescents are suicides by peers and highly publicized suicides, either factual accounts of famous people or fictional stories, usually on television. It would appear, however, that the suicides of peers have special modeling effects on adolescents as the following newspaper article attests:

> *Cary, N.C., Nov. 16—Less than two weeks after two teenage girls killed themselves in a garage, another Cary High School student was found dead Monday morning after failing to show up for classes.*
>
> *Christopher Kyle Glover, 17, who was described as distraught over the deaths of Christa Jones and Lindsay Rankin, died after rigging hoses from his car's exhaust pipes to the interior of the car, authorities said.*
>
> *Kyle was last seen by his parents about 7:15 A.M. His father found the body after returning to the family's home in the Preston development about 11:15 A.M., Cary police said.*

Adolescents tend to be passionate people, and passion is no less real because it is directed toward a hot-rod, a commercialized popular singer, or the leader of a black-jacketed gang. Edgar F. Friedenberg, *Emotional Development in Adolescents,* 1959

News of the death came as a hard jolt to a school that is now struggling with the fourth suicide in one year. In addition to the two girls, a 17-year-old boy killed himself one year ago. (The News & Observer, *November 16, 1993, p. 1*)

Highly publicized cluster suicides have occurred in places as diverse as Plano, Texas; Westchester, New York; Omaha, Nebraska; and Bergenfield, New Jersey. In each of these situations, a single or group suicide served as a prelude to others in a tragic episode of adolescent conformity. The specific dynamics of suicide clustering are not well understood. Berman and Jobes (1991) believe that perceived similarity between the model and the cluster victim and the victim's interpretation of the model's behavior as granting permission are significant factors. Other researchers have stressed the common pathology among suicide cluster victims rather than the modeling effect (Davidson, Rosenberg, Mercy, Franklin, & Simmons, 1989). These writers believe that many young people who become involved in cluster suicides already manifest several high risk characteristics and are as likely to respond self-destructively to other types of triggering events (e.g., failure experiences) as to suicides by peers.

The suicide cluster that occurred in Plano, Texas, in the early 1980s reflects a number of the modern-day factors that may contribute to the growing suicide problem among the young in our country. Plano is a very rapidly growing suburb of Dallas with a highly mobile population that grew by 18,000 residents to a total of 90,000 during the three years preceding a 1983 suicide cluster. Plano became primarily a community of white collar families with both parents employed in middle management positions. As the town was transformed from a farming village to a metropolitan bedroom community, the incidence of divorce, drug abuse, and alcoholism also increased significantly. The dramatic influx of adolescents from highly mobile, success-oriented families greatly increased pressure and competition in the local high school, which included approximately 1000 students per grade level. The epidemic of teenage suicides began with the deaths of two best friends in February 1983 and grew to a total of six suicides within a one-year period (Coleman, 1987). It should be noted that Cary, North Carolina, like Plano, was recently transformed from a small rural town into a bedroom community serving the rapidly growing "research triangle" that includes Raleigh, Durham, and Chapel Hill. Commensurate with this precipitous transformation have been a dramatic influx of highly mobile, professional families and an associated rise in the high school population.

Cary, N.C., Nov. 21—Ten years ago, Plano, Texas, was a booming Dallas suburb that had everything: wealth, beautiful homes, good schools. A Texas magazine proclaimed it "the perfect city," though most of America would never hear of Plano until 1983—the year six of its children died by their own hands.

> *The string of teen suicides that started in February would continue into the following spring. By May 1984, eight high school students would be dead, and a new phrase, "suicide clusters," would enter the national vocabulary.*
>
> *A decade later, Plano's nightmare has become Cary's painful reality. Four teens in the past year chose to end their lives in a picture-perfect suburb where, as the town slogan goes, "better living begins."*
>
> *Multiple teen suicides are profoundly disturbing, wherever they occur. But somehow, they seem even more shocking in towns like Cary and Plano—places where kids aren't supposed to have serious problems.* (The News & Observer, November 21, 1993, p. 1)

Highly publicized accounts of real-life suicides by famous people and televised fictional suicide stories have long been believed to increase suicide risk among young people. Empirical research in this area has led to conflicting findings, however. Several studies have shown that news publications and fictionalized television accounts of suicide temporarily increase the adolescent suicide rate (Gould & Shaffer, 1986; Phillips & Carstensen, 1986). Other researchers have found no significant increase in the adolescent suicide rate after a highly publicized true or fictional account (Kessler, Downey, Milavsky, & Stipp, 1988; Phillips & Paight, 1987). Although more definitive research is needed to better understand these conflicting findings, anecdotal clinical reports such as the following raise serious concerns among practitioners:

> *Sayreville, NJ—two teenagers despondent over the death of rock star Kurt Cobain were found dead in an apparent double suicide, police said.*
>
> *Thomas Rodriguez, 15, and Nicholas Camperi, 14, died from blasts from a shotgun that had been locked in a gun locker at Rodriguez's house, Middlesex County Prosecutor Robert Gluck said Saturday.*
>
> *Two suicide notes "indicated that they were depressed over his [Cobain's] death," Gluck said. He did not elaborate.*
>
> *Cobain, lead singer of rock band Nirvana, killed himself with a shotgun in his Seattle home on April 8. He was 27.* (Asheville Citizen-Times, Sunday, July 17, 1994, p. 6)

Suicidal Behavior

The final column of Table 4.2 lists two characteristics of adolescent suicidal behavior that need special attention. First, the suicide rate for adolescents has increased more rapidly than that of any other age group during the last half of the 20th century. Because this phenomenon was discussed earlier in the chapter, no more detail will be provided here except to note our belief that many of the reasons for this dramatic increase in the adolescent suicide rate are related to the changing demographics of the various environmental risk factors listed in Table 4.2 (e.g. parent conflict, drug and alcohol abuse, population characteristics, etc.).

The second important characteristic of adolescent suicidal behavior is the dramatic sex difference in suicide attempts versus completions. It is widely known that in the general population attempted suicide is more a female phenomenon while completed suicide is more characteristic of male behavior. Actuarial data show that across the life span females attempt suicide four times for every single male suicide attempt. In contrast, four males actually kill themselves for every one female suicide. There is evidence, however, that sex differences in the suicidal behavior of young people may be greater than those for the general population. For example, 90% of all adolescent suicide attempters are female, while 80% of adolescent suicide completers are male (Berman & Carroll, 1984). Furthermore, the ratio of male to female adolescent suicides in the United States has steadily increased since the early 1970s (McIntosh & Jewell, 1986; Stafford & Weisheit, 1988).

As we explore the causes of these sex differences in suicidal behavior, we must look beyond the adolescent risk factors listed in Table 4.2. In fact, many of the risk factors, such as hormonal change, fluctuating mood states, idealism and egocentrism, dysfunctional home environment, and poor peer relationships, are as prevalent among adolescent females as among adolescent males. Furthermore, at least one important risk factor, depression, is more prevalent among adolescent girls than among boys (Nolen-Hoeksema, 1987). We must therefore consider other gender-related behavior differences in order to better understand sex differences in suicide.

Developmental psychologists have shown well-documented gender-related behavior differences in aggressiveness, activity level, competitiveness, help seeking, and problem solving orientation that we believe are helpful in understanding sex differences in suicidal behavior. We will discuss the sources of these gender differences and their impact on the suicidal behavior of males and females in chapter 8 when we address attitudes toward suicide.

SUMMARY

Although the United States has long been identified as a youth-oriented society, actuarial data for adolescent suicide indicate that many young people are very unhappy. The suicide rate has increased more rapidly for adolescents (aged 15 to 24) than for any other age group during the past half century. Cluster suicides are a special problem in dealing with this age group. Application of the Suicide Trajectory Model to adolescent suicide reveals several risk factors that are especially important in working with this age group. Depression, substance abuse, and personality disorder are psychopathologies that greatly enhance suicide risk for adolescents. Also, there is growing evidence that gay and lesbian adolescents are at greater risk for suicide because of the special stresses associated with establishing a homosexual identity and lifestyle.

Formal operational thinking, which contributes to idealism and disillusionment in this age group, may enhance unhappiness and depression. Reduced problem-solving skills and absence of future-time perspective have been shown to be cognitive weaknesses that also contribute to suicide risk in this age group.

Like their younger counterparts, adolescents who are at risk for suicide tend to come from homes that have numerous problems and that are unresponsive to the young person's needs. Parental conflict, drug and alcohol abuse, and sexual abuse occur more often in the homes of suicidal adolescents than they do in other homes. Suicidal adolescents are less likely than other adolescents to have supportive interpersonal relationships either inside or outside the home. They often have poor peer relationships and are socially isolated. The school performance of suicidal adolescents is often poor, and they tend to be truant more frequently than other students.

There are dramatic sex differences in the suicidal behavior of adolescents, with a mirror-image reversal in suicide attempts and completions. We believe that these sex differences are to a great extent a product of gender socialization.

5

Suicide in Young Adulthood

Sometimes I sit down with myself and say, "Look, you're thirty now. At best, you've got fifty years more. But what are you doing with it? You drag yourself from day to day, you spend most of your time wanting, wanting, but what you have is never any good and what you don't have is marvelous. Why don't you eat your cutlet, man? Eat it with pleasure and joy. Love your wife. Make your babies. Love your friends and have the courage to tell those who seek to diminish you that they are the devil and you want no part of them. Courage, man, courage and appetite!"

George Belcher, "The Death of the Russian Novel"

The period that we call young adulthood includes the years from 25 to 34. Little empirical research is available regarding developmental changes or factors influencing suicide within this age group; however, there is a small but growing body of evidence that suggests that this 10-year period is characterized by the need to make major commitments regarding work, marriage, and parenthood as well as by rigorous reevaluation of those commitments.

In this chapter we will consider the possibility that the stresses of work, marriage, and parenthood have special impacts on the suicidal behavior of today's young adult men and women. We will review the statistical picture for suicide in young adulthood and apply the Suicide Trajectory Model to research findings about factors affecting suicide in this age group. Also, because young adults suffer the highest incidence of Acquired Immune Deficiency Syndrome, we will explore the growing controversy concerning the relationship between AIDS and suicide in this chapter. We will begin with a profile of early adulthood in order to illuminate the paradoxical and demanding normative and cohort-related issues of this stage of life.

PROFILE OF YOUNG ADULTHOOD

Young adults have reached the peak of their physical development. Indeed, there is reason to believe that, from about age 18, small but constant declines begin in sensory functioning. Hearing in particular begins to decline in measurable ways, but generally the changes are so small that they go unnoticed. Male sexuality also peaks around age 18, although female sexuality seems to peak later, around age 36 (Masters & Johnson, 1966). However, once again the changes are so slight that they do not affect quality of functioning or life satisfaction.

As we have seen, Freud had little to say about the pattern of development after individuals enter the genital stage. However, he did indicate that people who become fixated at or regress to earlier psychosexual stages of development because of stress or trauma are likely to be maladjusted as adults. When asked about the characteristics of well-adjusted adults, he maintained that healthy adults are capable of directing their energy toward two important adult activities: love and work (Freud, 1953).

Erikson (1980) underscored the importance of Freud's characteristics of healthy adulthood by suggesting that young adults, building upon their still-developing sense of identity, need to invest in an ongoing intimate relationship with another human being. The healthy young adult relationship is intimate both sexually and intellectually. Healthy young adult couples are able to share their thoughts, beliefs, and hopes, as well as their sexuality, with one another. Thus, they are in a better position than adolescents to make permanent commitments to relationships and activities. In contrast, young adults who continue to struggle with identity issues will be unable to develop authentic intimacy and therefore will inhabit a world of psychological isolation.

In the cognitive realm, young adults are at their peak of performance. Because they have assimilated much knowledge in the first two and one-half decades of life, they have developed many cognitive schemas that promote ease of learning. This is fortunate because young adults typically encounter many situations that require much new learning within a short time. Marriage, pregnancy, parenthood, new jobs, and job promotions are only a few of the situations that require young adults to master new information. They continue to operate at the level of formal operations in many cognitive areas; however, the novelty of this mode of thinking has worn off, freeing them to adopt a less egocentric world view. This development results in the ability to balance individual needs and goals with community welfare, and it often results in the involvement of young adults in some form of community service.

Although the humanistic-existential theories do not speak specifically about the stage of young adulthood, it would appear that young adults seek meaning from the types of commitments they make to relationships, to work, and to their communities. From the point of view of Maslow, healthy young adults are working to satisfy both belonging and esteem needs. Belonging needs are satisfied as they marry and begin their own families. As one young man said, "I knew Laura was the woman for me when I realized I felt more at home when I was with her than when I was in my old bedroom in my parents' home." Esteem needs are satisfied as young people complete school, begin their careers, and are rewarded by salaries and perhaps their first promotions. The assertion of competence helps young adults to meet their needs for self-esteem and to acquire the esteem of others.

From the behaviorist perspective, young adults continue to learn through reinforcement and modeling. Reinforcement takes on new meaning as salaries and promotions increase the young adult's buying power and make possible the visible symbols of success. A special instance of modeling that occurs primarily during the stage of young adulthood is mentoring. Studies have shown that young adults who have mentors (i.e., teacher-sponsors who guide them through the early years of their careers) get ahead more quickly and with less stress than do those who do not have mentors (Levinson, Darrow, Klein, Levinson, & McKee, 1978; Walsh, 1983).

CONTEMPORARY RESEARCH ON YOUNG ADULTHOOD

Three researchers who have added to our understanding of young adulthood are Vaillant, Levinson, and Gould. Drawing heavily on Erikson's theory, each researcher conducted research on adults that led to the conclusion that there are identifiable themes in adult development.

Vaillant (1977) conducted a longitudinal study with a group of male Harvard students. His work suggested that the early adult years constitute a time of career consolidation in which most men are concerned with progress in their chosen profession. Vaillant characterized career consolidation as a stable and conforming process marked by assimilation into the working world. Although this period is seemingly very stable, there is an unexamined paradox in career consolidation that can be very problematic for young adults. Vaillant has pointed out that during this period difficulties often arise as young adults try to establish a proper balance between striving to get ahead and putting down roots. Progress in an individual's career often necessitates moving and thus sacrificing stable relationships. Choices between career and family welfare, as well as between financial gains and personal losses, are common causes of stress during this period (Walsh, 1983).

Vaillant has noted that both the rate and the direction of development can be affected during this stage of life by the availability of opportunities, by life events and accidents, and by the quality of the resources and relationships the individual develops. Thus, the amount of life stress experienced by young adults is a function of the fit between the life events that occur and the normative developmental processes of evaluation, commitment, and reevaluation that characterize the young adult period. Even the best-adjusted young adults experience stress, especially toward the end of this stage. Those who are less well-adjusted tend to experience higher levels of stress and failure to cope.

Levinson's work, based on extensive interviews with 40 middle-aged men, suggested that in contrast to the late adolescent years, which focus on the problems of escaping parental control and leaving the family, the early adult years (ages 22 to 28) are characterized by the development of a mature sense of independence and by the making of basic commitments to a career and children (Levinson, Darrow, Klein, Levinson, & McKee, 1978). Levinson suggests that between the ages of 29 and 34 there is the first in a series of reevaluations of life commitments. He found that this period of evaluation, which he called the "age-30 transition," was reported by approximately 80%

of the men studied. It involves a reexamination of the choices of mate, work, and lifestyle, and it sometimes results in divorce, return to school, change of occupation, or reorganization of priorities in other aspects of life. Levinson's subjects reported experiencing mild to moderate stress during this period. Healthy young people frequently emerge from this transitional stage with a deeper commitment to original choices or with fresh energy generated by their commitment to new and more carefully thought-out careers and relationships. Less healthy young adults, unable to establish commitments and make productive contributions, find themselves experiencing increasing stress as they realize they are on the brink of middle adulthood and have no clearly developed life goals.

Gould (1978) echoed Levinson's emphasis on stability and change based on his observations of both a clinical and a nonclinical population of men and women. His research revealed essentially the same developmental tasks for early adulthood suggested by Levinson, but Gould added the observation that individuals who face the crises of this and other life stages and work them through are in a better position to make healthy adjustments in the future than those who attempt to avoid or escape the central issues of any life stage. The title of Gould's major work, *Transformation: Growth and Change in Adult Life*, reveals his belief that individuals can be transformed for the better by successfully coping with the transitional periods inherent in adulthood.

As we have seen, the young adult period, especially the age-30 transition, is potentially a very stressful time of life. The new challenges faced by young adults, coupled with a reevaluation of life goals, may begin to overwhelm coping skills. There is reason to believe that young adulthood may be even more stressful for the present generation than for their recent predecessors. As stated in chapter 4, modern day young adults are the older counterparts of the adolescent 13th Generation, a group that has received less than its share of quality parenting and has thus far failed to distinguish itself with many outstanding accomplishments. In the following section we will consider further the young adult in today's world by reviewing Strauss and Howe's (1991) description of this group whose birth years include 1961 through 1981.

TODAY'S YOUNG ADULTS

As young adults, the 13ers have continued to receive negative attributions as they did during their teen years. As if the name "13th Generation" were not a negative enough accolade, the modern-day press has labeled this group

---

A young man is so strong, so mad, so certain, and so lost. He has everything and he is able to use nothing. Thomas Wolfe, *Of Time and the River*, 1935

"Generation X." Young adult 13ers, like their adolescent counterparts, continue to be described as poorly motivated, underprepared, and underachieving. They have been characterized as whiners who complain about older generations using up resources, saddling them with an impossible national debt, and refusing to retire at a reasonable age in order to create career opportunities for them. There is indeed some likelihood that 13ers may be the first generation in American history to fail to enjoy a better standard of living than their parents. Thus far, for example, a smaller percentage of young adult 13ers in their late 20s and early 30s have been able to achieve the "American dream" of home ownership than their Boomer predecessors did at the same age (U.S. Bureau of the Census, 1994). As a personal example, both Silent Generation writers of this book had bought and sold two houses and purchased a third by the time they reached their early 30s. In contrast, none of our seven 13er, young adult children is presently a home owner.

Not all writers are so negative about the 13th Generation. A *Newsweek* feature article, for example, has challenged several beliefs about Generation X (Giles, 1994). The cover story labeled as myths the beliefs that young adult Xers are slackers, whiners, and psychologically damaged children of divorce. Writers who have taken a closer look at this group of young adults have begun to recognize a number of positive characteristics. Although young adult 13ers do not tend to be dreamers of a better world, many are realists with definite goals concerning careers and relationships. Although 13ers tend to distrust organizations and government, they are a rather generous and altruistic group whose members are very willing to get involved in grassroots community endeavors. Strauss and Howe (1991) have characterized them as survivors who are "streetwise" about the ways of the world. They grew up fast and learned their lessons well, lessons that may be essential in the world of the future. A mildly encouraging sign that 13ers may be functioning better as young adults than they did as children and adolescents is the fact that suicide rates for 25- to 34-year-old women have declined slightly over the past decade, and corresponding rates for males have remained stable rather than continuing to increase. In the following section we will examine more closely the most recent data on young adult suicide rates.

THE STATISTICAL PICTURE FOR YOUNG ADULT SUICIDE

The U.S. suicide rate for young adults is somewhat higher than the rate for adolescents and the rate for the general population. Of the 30,484 official

---

We as a generation have yet to produce any defining traits, except perhaps to show a defeatest belief that we will do worse than our parents. Joshua Janoff, "Generation X." *Newsweek*, April 24, 1994

TABLE 5.1   Suicide Rates Per 100,000 Population Among Young Adults by Sex and Race for 1991

Age	All Groups	Males	Females	White Males	Black Males	White Females	Black Females
25–34	15.2	25.0	5.4	26.1	21.1	5.8	3.3

Source: U.S. Bureau of the Census (1994). Statistical Abstract of the United States (114th ed.): Washington, DC, Pp. 96 & 101.

suicides reported in 1992, 6,172 were completed by young adults (National Center for Health Statistics, 1994). Although the suicide rate for young adults has increased during the past 30 years, the increase has not been as great as that for adolescents, and as mentioned in the preceding section, this trend has recently begun to slowly reverse.

The young adult suicide rates are presented by sex and race in Table 5.1. The table shows that the statistical picture for young adult suicide reflects the same gender and racial patterns that are found among other age groups. Young adult white males have the highest rate, followed by African American males, white females, and African American females. It is noteworthy that the suicide rate for African American males peaks during the young adult years and does not again reach this level until the 75 to 84 age range (U.S. Bureau of the Census, 1994).

Although young adult suicide rates are high throughout the world, the U.S. rate for this age group compares favorably with other developed countries. Data presented in Table 1.2 in chapter 1 show that the U.S. suicide rate for young adult males ranks 8th among the 13 countries reporting, and the U.S. female suicide rate for this age group ranks 10th among the same 13 countries. Only West Germany, Japan, the United Kingdom, the Netherlands, and Italy report lower male suicide rates, and only Poland, the United Kingdom, and Italy have lower female suicide rates than the U.S.

In spite of findings that reflect a lower young adult suicide rate in the United States than in many other countries, and in spite of the recent trend reflecting a slight reduction in the suicide rate for females in this age group, the overall incidence of self-destructive behavior among young adults continues to be high and necessitates careful consideration of causal factors in an effort to develop effective prevention and intervention strategies. In the next section we will apply the Suicide Trajectory Model to what is known about the causes of suicide in young adults.

THE SUICIDE TRAJECTORY APPLIED TO YOUNG ADULT SUICIDE

Research that attempts to uncover factors related to suicide rarely studies isolated groups of young adults. Young adults typically do not belong to easily identifiable groups, such as college classes, and therefore are difficult to gather together for a single study. Also, young adults tend to be absorbed in the demands of their stage of life and have little interest in participating in research studies. Much of the material in this section has been synthesized from studies that have included young adults as well as adolescents and/or older adults. In our reporting, however, we will emphasize findings that are idiosyncratic to the young adult age group. The major findings that relate the Suicide Trajectory Model to young adult suicide are summarized in Table 5.2 utilizing the usual categories of the model.

Biological Risk Factors

Young adults generally experience their life's peak of biological well being. For young women, however, two biological conditions, premenstrual syndrome (PMS) and postpartum depression, may impact upon suicidal tendencies. Rooted in the hormonal changes that occur across the menstrual cycle, PMS can cause women to feel depressed and/or anxious, to experience low self-esteem, and to question their abilities to cope during the premenstrual phase. Also, the changing hormonal state that occurs in postpartum depression, or the "baby blues," in its severe form may lead to painful feelings of depression, hopelessness, and low self-esteem. We believe that these biological conditions may cause a minority of susceptible women to consider suicide. Although there is presently no empirical evidence showing direct linkages, there are case studies of women who experienced onset of depression and suicidality during the postpartum period with later premenstrual recurrences (Platz & Kendell, 1988; Schenck, Mandell, & Lewis, 1992).

Psychological Risk Factors

The first psychological risk factor listed in Table 5.2 is the now-familiar one of depression. Although depression was discussed in detail in chapter 1, where we presented risk factors that are common to all age groups, it is included again here in order to illuminate special stresses for young adults. The special stresses in young adulthood, including changing roles (from student to wife or husband to parent to wage-earner) and the stresses inherent in beginning a career, exacerbate depression in this age group. This may be especially true for those who have a biological predisposition to depression or who may have arrived at this age with much unfinished business from earlier stages. There is evidence of changing demographics of depression that

---

We're not Generation X, we're Generation Depressed. Unnamed Respondents, in "Generation Depressed," *Newsweek,* July 10, 1995

TABLE 5.2 The Suicide Trajectory Model Applied to Young Adult Suicide

Age Group	Biological Risk Factors	Psychological Risk Factors	Cognitive Risk Factors	Environmental Risk Factors	Warning Signs	Triggering Events	Suicidal Behavior
Young Adulthood (25–34)	Premenstrual syndrome (W) Postpartum depression (W)	Depression (W) Lack of intimate relationships	Reevaluation of life choices	Marital problems (W) Presence of children (W) Mobility (W) Occupational problems (M) AIDS	Marital problems (W) Child care stress (W) Occupational stress (M)	Marital difficulty Occupational setback AIDS diagnosis	Small suicide rate reduction Peak suicide rate for African American males

supports the notion that young adulthood is a difficult period in the lives of many men and women. Depression has historically been an older person's disorder. During the past 50 years, however, the typical age of onset has steadily declined. Recent findings indicate that depression is now more prevalent among those aged 20 to 30 than among those aged 50 to 60 (Reich, Rice, & Mullaney, 1986). Depression is more common among women than men in all age groups; however, the incidence of depression is especially high for young adult women and peaks for this group in their mid 30s, while the highest rates for men do not occur until old age (Hirshfeld & Cross, 1982).

Lack of intimate interpersonal relationships is a second psychological risk factor for suicide in this age group. Young adults are working on the task of establishing intimacy and avoiding isolation (Erikson, 1980). Young adulthood is a critical time for forming bonds of intimacy with mates and friends that will protect one against isolation and the accompanying sense of loneliness. Research has shown that marital difficulties leading to separation and divorce are associated with depression in both women and men; however, women seem to be more affected by these types of problems. For example, one study found that women are more likely than men to seek counseling for depression during marital breakdown (Weissman, 1986). An important study by Goldney (1981) investigated the influence of personal relationships on depression, hopelessness, and self-destructive behavior among 110 suicidal women aged 18 to 30. A major finding of the study was that those women who had no significant personal relationships exhibited more frequent and more highly lethal suicide attempts.

Cognitive Risk Factors

As shown in Table 5.2, the cognitive risk factor that is most prevalent for young adults is the reevaluation of life choices that characterizes this age group, which for many young adults is the first in a series of reevaluations they will make during their lives. Whether it is called "the age-30 transition," as labeled by Levinson and his associates (1978), or "catch 30," as popularized by Gail Sheehy (1976) in *Passages*, this process calls for a cognitive examination of all aspects of life to date, including marital choice, parenthood, and occupational selections, and it may lead to a great deal of distress and disruptive life changes. The changing demographics of depression, which show a growing incidence of this problem among young adults, support the notion that the age-30 transition is a difficult period for men and women and that the natural review of important life decisions may increase suicide risk.

Environmental Risk Factors

The environmental variables that increase the risk of suicide among young adults may differ for men and women. The major environmental risk

Melancholy, **Edgar Degas. Oil on Canvas, 7½ × 9¾. (The Phillips Collection, Washington, D.C.)**

factors for women include marital problems, the presence of children in the
home, and family mobility while men are more often placed at risk by occupational problems.

Evidence supporting the role that conflict in the home plays in women's
suicide was provided by findings of a study that investigated the relationships
between 50 suicidal women (aged 18 to 63) and their husbands or boyfriends
(Stephens, 1985). Extensive interviews with these women, which focused on
the nature of their relationships, revealed four major suicide-related themes.
The first theme included "smothering love" and the suicidal female's unrealistic expectations regarding the love relationship. The second theme involved
sexual infidelity by the spouse or boyfriend that severely aggravated an already strained relationship. The third theme was physical abuse by the partner. Many of the suicide attempts by these women were followed by another
battering experience as punishment for the suicidal behavior. The fourth and
most common pattern associated with suicidal behavior in women involved
an uncaring and emotionally indifferent relationship created by their partners. Two-thirds of the women in this study characterized their partners as
being unwilling to express even rudimentary affection for them. The re-

ported feelings resulting from these relationships included loneliness, power-lessness, and low self-esteem, which are common preludes to significant de-pression. Although a history of marital problems may increase tendencies toward suicide among men and women, the relationship appears to be sig-nificantly stronger for women (Rygnestad, 1982).

The presence of young children in the home can further stress women's coping abilities, especially in the presence of other stressful life events. For example, Brown and Harris (1978) found that mothers who had three or more young children in the home, no full-time outside employment, and no supportive relationship with a husband or boyfriend were more at risk for depression than other women.

The growing mobility of our society appears to take a special toll on women. Because young women, especially young professionals, are more mo-bile than other age groups, they are particularly vulnerable. One study has shown that moving increases the risk for depression among women, even if the move is voluntary; results in greater financial reward; and leads to a bet-ter standard of living (Hull, 1979).

Occupational stress has historically been a larger factor in male suicide than female suicide (Illfeld, 1977). The traditional sex-role socialization of males to fulfill the instrumental role (i.e., to be the bread winners) has placed men at greater risk for depression due to occupational failure, stress on the job, or unemployment. There is evidence that unemployment and downward occupational mobility are factors in adult suicide (Breed, 1963; Maris, 1981; Powell, 1958). Although rapidly changing gender roles in our society may lead to similar relationships between occupational problems and suicidality for women, there are presently no data available to confirm a spread of this phenomenon across the sexes. The following case study illustrates the power-ful influence of occupational stress on suicide in young adult men.

> *Gary F. was only 32 when he died. Ever since he was a child, Gary had been in a hurry. His grieving parents described him as a child who "ran before he walked." Impatient, energetic, and charming, Gary had experienced almost nothing but success throughout high school and college.*
>
> *Although Gary had never been a serious student, he had impressed his col-lege teachers with his willingness to undertake a task and his political "savvy" in getting things done. He completed his bachelor of science in business admin-istration with a respectable 2.3 grade point average. One of his professors wrote about him that "Gary would take a back seat to no one." Gary was hired by a major brokerage firm. He married his college girlfriend, Beth, and began to rise swiftly up the management ladder.*
>
> *When the stock market crashed in 1987, Gary was among the first in his firm to be dismissed. After a few weeks of looking for work, Gary came to realize that he probably would not get work soon, certainly not as good a job as he had*

lost. Although Beth worked, their debts soon reached a point where her salary could not cover their expenses. Beth and Gary began to argue over money.

They were paying for a home in a wealthy suburb and for two expensive cars. While Beth quietly began to figure how to get along on her salary, Gary was busy trying to dream up get-rich-quick schemes. Beth sold one car to make the payments for the house and other car. From that time on, Gary became quiet and contemplative. He no longer dreamed big or discussed material goods. He began to refer to himself as a "loser." On the day of his death, he and Beth argued once again about money. Gary slammed out of the house, yelling, "We've still got my insurance policy. I'm worth more dead than alive."

The police report filed after the accident revealed that Gary was driving over 85 miles per hour on a narrow two-lane country road. The car was traveling so fast that it actually became airborne. The two front wheels were suspended over a branch of a tree 20 yards from a curve in the road. Gary, who was not wearing his seat belt, was thrown from the car and killed instantly.

No one will ever know with certainty whether Gary committed suicide or whether his death was a result of angry, impulsive behavior, but Beth told her therapist that she thought Gary had meant to die. "At some level," Beth said quietly through her tears, "he knew he was going to have to slow down, to take stock, to think things through. I was trying to talk to him about having a baby before the stock market crashed. Even that seemed to bother him. It was as though he was afraid of what he might see if he took time to really evaluate our life. When everything crashed, he found it too painful to look at. He just tried to escape—from failure, from me, from himself."

Gary's case reflects the effect that a life accident—in this case, the crash of the stock market—can have, especially when it occurs during a period of reevaluation. At 32, Gary might naturally have begun to examine where he was going and what he wanted out of life. This was especially likely because Beth was suggesting parenthood. However, faced with the disintegration of his career and the loss of material things by which he had defined his life, Gary probably found reevaluation too painful. Instead, he regressed to an earlier stage of dreaming big dreams. When these were not realized, he became depressed and hostile. Whether suicide or accident, Gary's death was undoubtedly due, at least in part, to his inability to reevaluate life choices and to set new goals for himself when the first young dreams died.

Gary's case and others like it point up the danger of assuming that self-worth is indicated by employment status. The literature is less clear about the relationship between occupational status and suicide. Gibbs and Martin (1964) proposed that high-status jobs are inherently more stressful than low-status jobs because of the responsibilities and competition inherent in the former. Breed (1963) argued that low-status jobs are more stressful because of the limited wages and the poor self-esteem that tend to be associated with them. In a definitive study, Lampert, Bourque, and Kraus (1984) examined the relationship between occupational status and suicide by calculating age-specific suicide rates for men in various occupational categories in Sacramento County, California, over three decades. They found a highly significant inverse relationship between occupational status and suicide rate for all age groups, including those aged 25 to 44 (among whom are young adults as we have defined them). In this age group, the suicide rates were highest for the low-status occupations of laborer, farm laborer, and service worker. The lowest suicide rates occurred among the highest-status occupations, including professional-technical ones.

Warning Signs, Triggering Events, and Suicidal Behavior

Warning signs and triggering events for suicide among young adults include many of the common stressors of this stage of life: marital difficulties, parenting problems, and occupational setbacks. Although these stressors are present in the lives of many young adults, they may become deadly for people with limited coping skills and a predisposition to self-destruction.

As reported in the statistical portion of this chapter, the overall suicide rate for young adults has declined slightly over the past decade. This reduction has occurred exclusively for females; however, it is somewhat gratifying to note that the suicide rate for young adult males has also leveled off during this period and is no longer increasing.

In spite of this leveling effect, however, suicide and homicide statistics show that the world is a dangerous place for young black men. Table 5.2 shows the previously reported fact that the suicide rate for African American males peaks during the young adult years. In addition, African American men between the ages of 25 and 34 become victims of homicide at the remarkable rate of 96.5 per 100,000 population, exceeded only by the non-white adolescent rate that was discussed in chapter 4 (National Center for Health Statistics, 1994). As in chapter 4, we maintain that homicide victimization in this group may also include many elements of suicide. Holinger, Offer, Barter, and Bell (1994) have noted that suicide and homicide victimization have a number of similar demographics. For example, suicide and homicide rates for older adolescents and young adults are higher than those for younger adolescents; male suicide and homicide rates are higher than those for females; suicide and homicide show similar time trends, with low rates in the 1950s and high rates in the 1970s and 1980s; and both tend to increase and decrease with the availability of firearms. The common elements in suicide and homicide become especially evident in cases of victim-precipitated homicide, where the victim's behavior elicits an aggressive act by the assailant, or when, as in the following case study, a gunman opens fire against impossible odds and dies in a hail of bullets.

The headlines read, "Stickup Man Killed in Shootout with Police." The associated story told how Demetre Brown, a 25-year-old unemployed warehouse stock clerk, was shot while allegedly in the process of robbing a convenience store when he was surprised by the arrival of two patrol cars that had been summoned by a silent alarm activated by an employee. The police officer in charge was quoted as saying, "We ordered the suspect to drop his weapon and come out with his hands on top of his head; but he suddenly ran from the store firing rapidly. Our officers had no choice but to shoot to kill."

Demetre had begun a criminal career at an early age. His school record was littered with notations of in-school suspensions and expulsions for infractions including fighting, stealing, insubordination, and truancy. His record also included entries from teachers and guidance counselors lamenting the fact that a great deal of academic potential was going to waste in this young man. So much of his energy was invested in anger and defiance that he was unable to apply himself.

Demetre quit school at the age of 16 and went to work as a laborer on a downtown construction project, but minimum wage and lost days in bad weather didn't leave much to live on after his car payment. He began to pick up a few dollars by providing some "muscle" to collect on gambling debts. Soon he was making more money on his part-time criminal job than from working every day on his dead-end regular job.

Demetre's criminal activities escalated to getaway car driver for a gang by the time he was in his early 20s. One night, a robbery attempt resulted in a store clerk being shot and three men, including Demetre, were arrested. The district attorney offered to reduce the charges against Demetre from "murder one" to "accessory" if he would testify to what he knew as the driver. He did, and drew a reduced sentence. He quickly learned that life in prison is not an easy one for a "snitch." He endured countless beatings and sexual abuses that went unnoticed or ignored by the guards.

When Demetre left prison, he was surprised to learn there was a job waiting as a clerk in a warehouse. Although Demetre was pleased to have a regular income, he never felt comfortable at the warehouse. The foreman always seemed to be watching him. Any time something suspicious happened, the "ex-con" was the first to be questioned. One night, a truckload of television sets was stolen. The next morning, Demetre was grilled by the foreman, who said, "I don't care if you didn't have anything to do with it; I believe you know who did, and you're fired!"

Out of work with no prospect of another job, Demetre became more angry and bitter than ever. There was no place for him. He couldn't even return to his former gang, whose members had sworn to kill him when they got out of prison. Demetre decided to use his last paycheck to invest in a semiautomatic pistol and go into business for himself. He staked out the perfect place to hit, a 24-hour convenience store with only one clerk after midnight. The robbery went smoothly until the police cars appeared. Demetre barricaded himself inside, but soon determined that there was no possibility of escape. As he briefly considered his situation, everything looked hopeless. He could never return to the abuse of prison, an inevitability if he were captured. There seemed no alternative but to make a break. "I'll kill any of you sons of bitches that get in my way," he shouted as he ran from the store firing rapidly.

Demetre's case provides an example of *equivocal,* or *subintended, death.* We cannot determine with certainty whether Demetre intended to die in the shoot-out or whether he believed he had a reasonable chance to escape. It would seem, however, that this case includes many suicidal elements. Demetre was angry and bitter about his life, and probably significantly depressed. Perhaps more important, he was hopeless about the future. He did not expect things to get better. We believe that, as in Demetre's case, the lives of many African American young men are made more perilous by the specter of suicide often disguised as macho aggressiveness.

We will now consider one final triggering event that has already adversely affected the lives of many white and African American young adults. The presence of AIDS, a fatal infectious disease that entered the United States in the mid 1970s, has raised many new and difficult issues regarding sexuality, civil rights, health care, euthanasia, and suicide, among others. There is a very recent but already burgeoning literature relating the AIDS epidemic to suicide risk. Because of the timely, conflicting, and highly emotional nature of this literature and because the modal age of victims falls within the young adult years, we decided to devote a special section of this chapter to the discussion of this risk factor.

THE SPECIAL CASE OF AIDS AND SUICIDE

Acquired Immune Deficiency Syndrome (AIDS) is a relatively new, yet already well-known, fatal infectious disease caused by the human immunodeficiency virus (HIV). AIDS was introduced into the United States in 1976, ironically the year smallpox was eradicated worldwide. The first U.S. clinical case was discovered in 1978, and the Center for Disease Control began tracking AIDS in 1981. More than 200,000 cases of AIDS have been reported in the past decade, with the number increasing every year. The great majority of AIDS victims have been male; however, the female percentage has gradually increased over the years to a high of 14% in 1992. A total of 166,467 people had died from AIDS by 1992. The number of deaths from AIDS has increased every year since its discovery to a high of 30,593 in 1991 followed

---

"I never thought I'd lose, I always thought I'd win" Elton John, *The Last Song*

by the first ever decline in 1992 (U.S. Bureau of the Census, 1994). In 1994, AIDS reached another negative milestone when it became the number one killer of Americans between the ages of 24 and 44.

Because AIDS is a blood-transmitted disease, certain groups (e.g., gay and bisexual men and intravenous drug users) are especially vulnerable. Anal intercourse and shared needles are especially high-risk behaviors; however, AIDS is also transmitted through heterosexual intercourse, which is believed to be the primary source of the gradually increasing number of women with this diagnosis. Smaller numbers of AIDS victims have contracted the disease in other ways, such as through blood transfusions, during birth, or by infection from contaminated medical or dental instruments.

Because the presence of HIV can be readily detected through blood tests, people may learn that they have this terrible disease long before the development of any symptoms. Indeed, many individuals who show HIV seropositivity are symptom free and remain so for periods of two to five years. It is important, therefore, that we examine the impact of both an HIV-positive diagnosis and full blown AIDS on the risk of suicide.

The particular nature of the relationship between AIDS and suicide is not completely understood and, frankly, fraught with controversy. Many investigators have presented evidence to support the contention that the presence of AIDS or an HIV positive diagnosis may serve as a triggering event for suicide. Others, however, are less sanguine about the AIDS—suicide connection and have questioned the evidence suggesting such a relationship. In the remaining pages of this chapter we will present the evidence from both sides of this controversy in hopes of drawing some conclusions.

Since the early days of the AIDS epidemic, a number of publications have alerted clinicians to the risk of suicide among their clients who either are HIV positive or have developed AIDS (Flavin, Franklin, & Frances, 1986; Frierson & Lippmann, 1988; Fryer, 1987; McKusick, 1993; Nichols, 1987; Werth, 1992; Whiteford & Csernasky, 1986). Most of this advice has been based on the speculation that the presence of a condition that will result in a slow and terrible death increases the likelihood that a suicide solution will be considered. In fact, as the horrors of death due to advanced stages of this disease have become more widely known, AIDS has begun to replace terminal cancer as the prototypic scenario for a discussion of rational suicide. A paper by James Werth, Jr. soon to be published in *Death Studies,* the major scholarly publication of the Association for Death Education and Counseling, is illustrative (Werth, 1996). In this paper, Werth proposed that counselors consider supporting the suicidal ideation and plans of counselees with AIDS when certain conditions of rationality are met. Werth believes that this type of support from counselors can be a means of empowering and returning some autonomy to people with AIDS.

Since the mid 1980s there has been a series of studies seeking to show a relationship between HIV/AIDS and suicide. Perhaps the best known is a study conducted by Marzuk and associates with an HIV-positive population (Marzuk et al., 1988). Marzuk and his colleagues calculated the suicide rate of 3,828 New York City residents who lived with an HIV positive diagnosis at some time during the year of the study (1985). The suicide rate for this group was found to be 36.3 times higher than the suicide rate for men in the same age range (20 to 59) who were not diagnosed as having HIV and 66 times higher than the rate for the general population. The suicide rate for the AIDS patients was also found to be significantly higher than that of other terminally ill patients, whose rates are usually only slightly elevated. It is important to note that all suicides among the AIDS patients in this study occurred early in the disease process and before the onset of significant symptomatology.

Other U.S. studies have replicated the Marzuk findings (Cote, Biggar, & Dannenberg, 1992; Kizer, Green, Perkins, Doebbert, & Hughes, 1988). Rajs & Fugelstad (1992) reported similar findings for a group of AIDS patients in Stockholm between 1985 and 1990. These findings strongly indicate that the admonition of counseling groups to pay special attention to suicide risk among counselees with either HIV positive diagnoses or full-blown AIDS is well founded.

Research by Schneider and his associates has shown that several AIDS-related factors contribute to suicidal ideation among gay and bisexual men (Schneider, Taylor, Kemeny, & Hammen, 1991). Their research found higher levels of suicidal ideation among individuals who were experiencing the following AIDS-related stressors: (1) recent bereavement of a partner, (2) recent AIDS-related complex (ARC) diagnosis, and (3) multiple close friends with ARC. Their research showed also that among suicidal ideators those individuals with higher levels of suicide intent had experienced a larger number of AIDS-related stressors. The AIDS-related factors most closely associated with high intent included (1) having a partner with AIDS or ARC, (2) having multiple close friends with AIDS, or (3) having ARC themselves. In contrast, receiving an HIV-positive diagnosis was associated with low levels of suicide intent.

In spite of evidence of elevated suicide rates among people with AIDS, as well as findings of elevated suicidal ideation in conjunction with AIDS-related stressors and a plethora of clinical literature that admonishes practitioners to be alert to the danger of suicide among clients with HIV/AIDS, some critics have questioned whether the presence of AIDS has in fact increased the suicide rate. The most significant challenge to the assumption of an AIDS/suicide relationship has been raised by David Phillips (1993), a noted sociologist at the University of California at San Diego who was cited in chapter 4 for his research on suicide contagion. Phillips has pointed out that much of the previously reported research showing a relationship between AIDS and suicide is problematic methodologically. This research, he believes, tends to overestimate the relative risk of suicide among AIDS patients because of consistently using inappropriate comparison groups that do not control for the effects of marital status and sexual proclivity. Phillips has noted that single homosexual men have been overrepresented in the HIV/AIDS diagnosed experimental groups and underrepresented among the control groups. It is well-known that single men and gay men are at greater risk for suicide than married men and straight men, even when AIDS is not a consideration. Also, intravenous drug users, who are heavily represented among people with AIDS, are a high-risk group for suicide. Phillips has pointed out that the type of research needed to show a definitive relationship between AIDS and the suicide rate must adequately control for these factors.

Employing a different experimental design, Phillips (1993) used computerized death certificates to calculate mortality rates for males and females in the United States between 1969 and 1988 in order to precede and include the years of the AIDS epidemic. The annual mortality rates were calculated separately for males and females in four different age groups (20 to 29, 30 to 39, 40 to 49, and 50 to 59). Trend lines across the years of the study were plotted for these groups for deaths by infectious and parasitic diseases (the method of reporting AIDS deaths until 1988). Comparable trend lines were also plotted for suicides and for accidental poisonings.

The trend lines for deaths by infectious and parasitic diseases reflected the AIDS epidemic in predictable fashion. The lines for both males and females in each age group showed an upward trend beginning in 1981 and continuing through 1988. Predictably, the curve was the steepest for males in the 30- to 39-year-old group, where the AIDS epidemic is most severe. Contrary to what one would predict from the assumption of a relationship between the presence of AIDS and the suicide rate, the trend line for male and female suicides showed no evidence of an increasing trend coincident with the rise of infectious- and parasitic-disease-related deaths. The steep increase in AIDS-related deaths since 1981 was accompanied by a very gradually increasing trend for male suicides that began long before the AIDS epidemic and a decreasing trend for female suicides.

Phillips's data are consistent with findings from another recent study using similar methodology, which showed no relationship between the growing AIDS epidemic and suicide rates for the same time period (Buehler, Devine, Berkelman, & Chevarlay, 1990). The Phillips study expanded and amplified the findings from the Buehler study, however, by including data for women as well as men.

At present, then, the literature on the AIDS/suicide relationship is unclear. There is evidence suggesting that AIDS increases suicide risk. Several studies have found high suicide rates among gay men with HIV positive diagnoses or full-blown AIDS. Also, several AIDS-related stressors, such as bereavement of a partner, have been found to be associated with increased suicidal ideation among gay and bisexual men. The interpretations of these studies have been challenged, however, because of methodology that does not control for the possibility of elevated suicide rates among gay men who do not have HIV/AIDS. Recent research comparing trend lines for the AIDS epidemic and suicide rates during the same time period have not found parallel relationships between these two variables. One possibility is that the presence of HIV/AIDS increases suicidal ideation in victims but not completed suicide. Additional research will be necessary for a clearer understanding of these complex relationships.

SUMMARY

The suicide rate for young adults (aged 25 to 34) is higher than that for adolescents and has increased significantly since the mid 1950s. During the past decade, however, the young adult suicide rate for men has plateaued and the rate for women has gradually declined. Like other age groups, young adult males have higher suicide rates than females, and whites have higher rates than blacks, although this age range reflects peak suicide rates for African American males. Young adult African American men are especially at risk for homicide as well as suicide. It has been speculated that homicide victimization in this group may include many elements of suicide.

The suicide risk factors that are most prevalent for young adults appear to be those related to the special challenges of this stage of life. The stressors of marriage, parenting, and occupation take on special significance during this period and are often exacerbated by the age-30 transition, when many young adults become heavily involved in reviewing their previous decisions in these areas. The special stressors of young adulthood appear to have differential effects on men and women. Young adult women appear to be placed at greater risk for depression and suicide by marital problems, by stressors associated with having young children in the home, and by family mobility. Young adult men, in contrast, appear to be at greater risk for depression and suicide when suffering occupational problems.

The presence of AIDS has created a special new concern for suicide risk among young adults. Several findings have shown significantly elevated suicide rates among people with HIV-positive diagnoses or the presence of full-blown AIDS. Other investigators have raised methodological questions concerning these earlier studies, particularly with regard to the control groups used. Research comparing the yearly incidences of AIDS and the corresponding suicide rates has shown no parallel relationships. Further research will be necessary in order to more fully understand the relationship between AIDS and suicide.

Suicide in Middle Adulthood

The years of middle adulthood bring special opportunities and challenges. They offer perhaps more opportunities for significant accomplishments than any other period of development. Middle adulthood is a time when many people reach the zenith of their careers, with the accompanying power and influence that allow noteworthy accomplishments. Although high levels of responsibility are often self-actualizing, they may also be stressful and anxiety provoking. Reaching the pinnacle of any career may also provide the first glimpse of the other side and the growing realization that what lies ahead may be less pleasing. In addition, the realization that one has gone about as far as one is ever going to go makes one wonder if this is all there is or if, perhaps, another career choice would have been wiser.

Middle adulthood constitutes the largest age span discussed in the developmental chapters of this book, with the possible exception of old age. The middle adult years constitute the three decades between the ages of 35 and 64. For the purpose of understanding suicide during the middle years, we will examine the changes that adults are most likely to experience within this period and their possible impact on personality and life satisfaction. The clear implication is that people who are happy with their own growth and development and who are experiencing high levels of satisfaction and low levels of anxiety are poor candidates for suicide, while those who are struggling with predictable midlife concerns are at risk. Because there are special problems inherent in the study of middle adulthood, we will address these methodological issues before providing a profile of this age group.

METHODOLOGICAL ISSUES IN RESEARCH
WITH MIDDLE ADULTS

Middle age is truly the terra incognita of developmental psychology. There are at least four reasons why we know less about the life experience of people between ages 35 and 65 than we do about people in any other age group. First, developmental psychology began by studying the periods of life in which the most dramatic changes occur—childhood and adolescence. Indeed, until recently, developmental psychologists seemed to be saying that

The Subway, **George Tooker, 1950. Egg tempera on composition board, 18 × 36 in. (Collection of the Whitney Museum of Modern Art, New York. Juliana Force Purchase, Acq. #50.23.)**

human growth and development are completed by age 18 and that the next 50 years constitute merely a "playing out" of the learning or mislearning of the first 18 years. The first 5 or 6 years of life were thought by many of the early psychologists to be the most important. This bias toward the early years probably delayed the study of normative changes in adulthood more than any other single factor.

The second reason that we know little about middle adulthood is that it is difficult to gather data on adults between the ages of 35 and 65. Unlike children, adolescents, and even college-going young adults, middle-aged adults do not attend school on a regular basis. In addition, the middle years are typically so full of activity (e.g., parenting, caring for aging parents, promoting careers, providing leadership in community activities) that it is difficult to find groups of middle-aged adults who are willing to take the time to participate in developmental studies. In short, middle-aged adults are living Erikson's stage of generativity, and their too-full lives leave little time for participating in research.

Third, even when groups of middle-aged adults do agree to participate in research, the results are almost always less than satisfactory, because there is no one group of people that can be said to be representative of middle-aged adults. There are no organizations for middle-aged people that provide a microcosm of this age group with all demographic characteristics proportionally represented. We know of no study of middle-aged adults that can claim a representative sample of all people in the middle years. For this reason alone, many fine researchers, loath to violate the basic tenet of representativeness, have eliminated studies of middle-aged adults from their research agendas. Although the issue of representativeness also exists within the elderly population, it is less problematic because elderly people have groups organized around age (e.g., the American Association of Retired Persons), and many can be found living together in retirement communities. In addition, elderly people often have more time than the middle-aged do to participate in research. It is easier, then, to gather large samples of children, adolescents, young adults, and even elderly people from organized groups than it is to gather middle-aged adults.

The fourth major problem that exists within the literature on adulthood is the lack of comparability of age samples. We view middle age throughout this chapter as starting at age 35 and ending at age 64. Furthermore, we suggest that within the 30-year period called middle-age there should be three subdivisions: the early middle years (35 to 44), the middle middle years (45 to 54), and the late middle years (55 to 64). Such subdivisions are justifiable because the nature of individuals' lives seems to change in important ways over these years, and also because suicide rates are reported in government statistics according to those ranges. However, many of the studies examined in this chapter do not use our age ranges. Various studies operationally define middle age as starting as early as age 30 and as late as age 45. Some have studied only a segment of middle adulthood, and others have not identified the ages of the adults studied. In general, then, research on development in the middle adult years is methodologically more flawed than the research for any other age group.

In spite of the problems inherent in studying the middle aged, a minor explosion in both the quantity and quality of research about the middle years has occurred in the last two decades. Much of the research is based on open-ended interviews with members of groups acknowledged to be nonrepresentative. For example, the ongoing study of Terman's sample of gifted children has followed a group of 1,000 children and adolescents into old age (Sears, 1977). The Grant study by Vaillant followed a sample of male Harvard students for 30 years (Vaillant, 1977). Although blatantly biased with regard to sex, socioeconomic status, and education level, these studies have added to our understanding of the nature of middle age, as has the work of other developmental specialists, including Gould and Levinson (Gould, 1978; Levinson, Darrow, Klein, Levinson & McKee, 1978). Although none of these studies specifically addresses the topic of suicide among the middle-aged population, their findings are important to our understanding of self-destructive behavior in this age group. In this chapter we will utilize these landmark studies and others and review the few studies available that specifically address suicide and attitudes about suicide among the middle-aged in order to illuminate the circumstances of this period of development that may lead individuals to consider, attempt, or commit suicide.

PROFILE OF MIDDLE ADULTHOOD

Researchers in the field of adult development have engaged in an ongoing debate about continuity and change in the middle years. Some authorities maintain that development in the middle years consists primarily of continuing growth along lines begun in the young adult years (Neugarten, 1968; Vaillant, 1977). Others see the middle years as consisting of periods of intensive reflection and reevaluation, frequently resulting in major life changes growing out of a "midlife crisis" (Gould, 1978; Jaques, 1965; Levinson, Darrow, Klein, Levinson, & McKee, 1978; Sheehy, 1976).

Perhaps the best known research that supports the notion of a widespread midlife crisis was conducted by Levinson and his colleagues (Levinson, Darrow, Klein, Levinson, & McKee, 1978). Based on interviews with 40 working and middle-class white males aged 35 to 45, Levinson identified specific stages, which he called the "seasons of a man's life." These seasons consist of alternating periods of stability and transition. The longer stable periods occur when appropriate developmental tasks are performed and appropriate goals pursued. The transitional periods, which tend to last approximately five years, occur when men review their progress toward certain goals and question the direction of their lives. Levinson found that 80% of the men he interviewed reported the midlife transition that occurs between ages 40 and 45 to be stressful. His subjects frequently expressed disappointment that they were not "on schedule" in realizing the dreams they had as young adults. They experienced a growing sense of aging and for the first time became keenly aware of their own mortality.

A number of developmental psychologists are not in agreement with the "crisis" model of adult development. These writers support instead a model of change in which individuals progress across the life span in predictable, orderly ways, adhering reasonably well to a socially determined timetable without abrupt and tumultuous transitions. They believe that the difficulties experienced at various ages are the result of personal characteristics of the individuals interacting with environmental experiences and not universal products of a particular stage of development or transition. A well-known proponent of this position is George Vaillant (1977), who found in the previously mentioned study of Harvard graduates that although some men divorce, change jobs, and suffer depression at midlife, the frequency of these occurrences in this age group is no greater than at other stages of adulthood. Several studies in addition to Vaillant's research have also found very little evidence for widespread midlife crisis among either men or women (Clausen, 1981; Haan, 1981; McRae & Costa, 1983).

Regardless of whether change occurs as crisis or in some slower, more

---

Middle Age is that time in life when we hear two voices calling us. One says, "Why not?" and the other, "why bother?" Author Unknown

continuous manner, the central issue of the middle years is to find ways to remain productive in the face of multiple demands and losses. Erikson (1980) described people in the middle adult years as being in the stage of generativity versus stagnation in their personality development. People at the positive end of this continuum are productive, responsible, optimistic, and creative. The generative individual is active in giving back to his or her society through significant accomplishments and by mentoring members of younger generations to be future leaders. Middle-aged individuals at the opposite end of Erikson's continuum are stagnant and tend to be pessimistic, negative, and self-indulgent. These individuals do not feel good about their lifetime accomplishments. They envision diminishing opportunities for accomplishments in their chosen fields and are inflexible in their thinking about new and different ways to be productive.

One of the more recent books on midlife, entitled *In Our Fifties*, provides considerable insight concerning middle-aged people at the generative end of Erikson's continuum (Bergquist, Greenberg, & Klaum, 1993). The authors report findings from in-depth interviews with a selected group of 73 people between the ages of 50 and 60. The findings from these interviews show that many middle-aged individuals cope with the changes associated with this period of life by reinventing themselves. Life does not stay the same throughout the middle years, and coping requires flexibility as abilities, work-related opportunities, and relationships with family change. The successful middle-aged person must begin to get in touch with other interests and to develop new and different relationships in order to continue to be productive. The authors of this study claim that well-adjusted middle-aged individuals begin to listen to "voices from other rooms." Successful individuals in their 50s must be open to new roles and responsibilities. For many of the men in the study, these new roles often involved attending less to career building and more to family and new interpersonal relationships. Conversely, for many of the women in the study, the new activities included career development and less emphasis on home and family. The findings of the study promote the development of interests in generative activities of all sorts throughout the middle years. According to the authors, the four R's for generativity in the middle-age years are: (1) reexamining, (2) redefining, (3) renewing, and (4) reinventing.

Peck (1968) added to our understanding of generativity by conceptualizing four developmental tasks or challenges for people in their middle years. First, they must shift from *valuing physical capability* to *valuing wisdom*. The years of middle adulthood bring the first undeniable signs of physical deterioration for most people. Unavoidable physical changes include the graying

---

At thirty man suspects himself a fool; knows it at forty, and reforms his plan, at fifty chides his infamous delay, pushes his prudent purpose to resolve, in all the magnanimity of thought resolves, and re-resolves; then dies the same. Young. *Night Thoughts*

and loss of hair, the appearance of wrinkles, and a general decline in attractiveness. Speed, strength, and endurance also decline during this period, even when individuals attempt to moderate aging's effects by proper nutrition and exercise. Because of these inevitable declines, adults who are able to shift their focus from their physical appearance and functioning to their cognitive growth and development are likely to be better adjusted during the middle years. Those who cling to physical capabilities as their chief tool for coping with life and as the most important element in their value hierarchy and self-definition become increasingly depressed, bitter, and otherwise unhappy as they grow older.

The second task is to shift from *sexualizing* to *socializing*. During this 30-year period of midlife, females experience menopause, with its attendant hormonal changes and loss of child-bearing possibilities, and males notice a diminishment in the urgency of their sexual drive. In addition, sexual overtures among the middle-aged become less socially acceptable. Sometime during this period the "swinging bachelor" starts to be perceived as a "dirty old man" and the flirtatious young women becomes the middle-aged vamp, both figures to be avoided because of their continuing sexual overtures and exploitation of others. Learning to accept people and to appreciate them for their individuality rather than for sexual possibilities permits the development of deep friendships that promote adjustment throughout middle adulthood and old age. The shift from sexualizing to socializing may not be accomplished easily, however. Frequently such changes result in the need to reexamine one's identity, and they may be perceived as a loss of a highly valued aspect of one's younger life, thus contributing to a negative self-image and deepening depression.

The third shift discussed by Peck is from *cathectic impoverishment* to *cathectic flexibility*. Cathectic impoverishment is a state that results from having few or no meaningful relationships, while cathectic flexibility is the ability to build new relationships as old ones are lost. As individuals move through midlife, a number of important personal relationships must be given up. The adult who is able to cope with these inevitable losses and to build new relationships is in a good position to remain optimistic and generative.

The fourth shift is from *mental rigidity* to *mental flexibility*. One of the great dangers of midlife is that a person will become increasingly rigid and set in his or her own ways. In order to grow and be productive, middle-aged individuals must avoid the tendency to become rigid in their view of the world. People who are able to remain flexible in their thinking are less likely to develop the rigid, dichotomous thinking that has been shown to be characteristic of potential suicides (Beck, Rush, Show, & Emery, 1979).

In addition to the major developmental issues of generativity versus stagnation, middle-aged adults also often experience change in their encounters with death. Death, which for many fortunate people has been a stranger until the middle years, becomes first an acquaintance and then a well-known companion. Most people between the ages of 35 and 65 experience the death of their parents. With these deaths comes the clear realization that one belongs to the next generation to die. One 50-year-old reminded her five siblings at the funeral of their mother that "the next time we come together for a funeral, it will be one of us." Fulfilling this prophecy three short years later, the family gathered again at the funeral of the oldest sister. The middle-aged also become chillingly aware of deaths in their cohort group, as 40-year-old friends contract cancer and other terminal illnesses or die suddenly from heart attacks. Some middle-aged people experience the death of an adolescent or young-adult child, forcing them to reexamine their concept of a just world.

A popular book of the last decade that attempts to integrate the major studies of adult development against a background of life experiences is Judith Viorst's *Necessary Losses* (1986). In this book Viorst points out that middle-aged people experience many normative losses. The "necessary losses" of midlife detailed by Viorst include several already discussed in this chapter, such as the loss of the youthful self and the loss of parents and friends through death. Another necessary loss of midlife discussed by Viorst is the loss of the parenting role.

The middle years are a time when children grow up and leave home, resulting in either an "empty nest" or a "child-free home," depending on how the parents view this event. The status of parenthood can be very important to the self-definition of middle-aged people, and the loss of the parenting role can be very stressful. When children leave home, parents experience an additional shrinking of their interpersonal worlds as the children's friends also disappear. Parents may also experience a great deal of pain as a result of relinquishing certain illusions associated with parenthood—such as the belief that they can always protect their children from harm or that their adult children will lead the types of lives their parents planned for them.

The special pain associated with losing one's children is closely related to the loss of other young dreams and illusions, such as the illusion of oneself as a perfect parent. The loss of this illusion is poignantly described by Viorst in the following passage:

> Our fantasy is that if we are good and loving parents, we can hold the tigers and thorns at bay. Our fantasy is that we can save our children. Reality will find us late at night, when our children are out and the telephone rings. Reality

---

A lot of people—tried to figure out why he had taken his own life. Some of them asked if he had AIDS—. I don't know what he had, but I know what he didn't have: his health, his work, somebody to share his life with. Calvin Trillin, *Remembering Denny*

will remind us—in that heart-stopping moment before we pick up the phone—
that anything, that any horror, is possible. Yet although the world is perilous
and the lives of children are dangerous to their parents, they still must leave,
we still must let them go. Hoping that we have equipped them for their journey.
Hoping that they will wear their boots in the snow. Hoping that when they fall
down, they can get up again. Hoping. (Viorst, 1986, p. 247)

Sheehy (1995) has suggested that the middle-age period need not be all negative. She proposed that we begin to think of adulthood as being divided into three distinct periods: Provisional Adulthood from age 15 to 30, First Adulthood from 30 to 45, and Second Adulthood from 45 to 85 and beyond. She suggested also that Second Adulthood should be viewed as having two divisions: an Age of Mastery from 45 to 65 and an Age of Integrity from 65 to 85. Students of Erikson will see that Sheehy's paradigm reinforces his psychosocial theory.

In summary, the literature on adult development seems to be consistent in documenting change and the necessity for growth in the middle years. These are important years for developing new interests and relationships and for being generative in many ways. Middle-aged adults must come to terms with a changing time perspective brought about by the growing realization of their own mortality. The successful individual during this period must begin to cope with the first of a parade of inevitable losses by developing new and generative interests to replace them. In contrast, individuals who are unable to cope with the losses and disappointments inherent in the middle years will experience significant stagnation. Feelings of regret for lost opportunities, grief over the deaths of close friends and loved ones, sorrow over lack of time to begin anew or to realize one's dreams all feed into the sense of despair that may cause some people to attempt or commit suicide during the middle years.

The challenges and pitfalls of the middle years that were chronicled by Erikson and embellished by other researchers, including Gould, Levinson, Peck, Sheehy, and Vaillant, are timeless and have applied to countless generations of middle-aged men and women and will continue to do so. However, we also believe, like Strauss and Howe (1991), that each generation brings its particular peer personality to this stage of development drawn from its own unique encounters with the world. Therefore, as in the preceding three chapters, we will now discuss several characteristics of the present generation of middle-agers within the context of their own particular *zeitgeist*.

TODAY'S MIDDLE-AGED COHORTS

Two of Strauss and Howe's (1991) cohorts constitute the middle adulthood population of the United States in the mid 1990s. The younger half of middle-aged Americans belong to the baby boom or Boom Generation, a group born between 1943 and 1960 that ranged in age from 35 to 52 in 1995. The older half of today's midlife Americans belong to the Silent Generation, a group born between 1925 and 1942 who were between 53 and 70 years of age in 1995. Because the age range of the Silent generation includes both the latter years of midlife and the early years of elderhood, this group has the unusual possibility of being either middle-agers or the parents of middle-agers or even both.

The Boomers have been described by Strauss and Howe (1991) as an "idealist" generation that has been the cultural and spiritual focal point of America since they came on the scene in the post–World War II years. They are the largest generation in American history because they are the product of both late-nesting GI's and early-nesting Silent Generationers. As children, the Boomers received a great deal of attention from their parents, who religiously followed the liberal parenting practices espoused by Dr. Spock. Their adolescence brought about the greatest youth upheaval of the 20th century, much of which was a manifestation of their historic efforts to avoid service in Vietnam. Boomer adolescents were more responsible than any other group for the sexual revolution, especially among women.

Many social ills, including youthful drunken driving, crime, teen pregnancy, drug experimentation, and teen suicide, grew rapidly during the Boomers' adolescence. The 30-year decline in SAT scores began with this group. The Boomer Generation introduced new fashions that involved dressing down in a unisex fashion. As the Boomers moved into their young adult years, they brought with them new fads that included exercise, food fetishes, and outdoor living. As these rising adults entered the working world, they provided the impetus for a new concept of employee: the Yuppie (young urban professional). Yuppies were noted for their strong desire for personal satisfaction, weak company loyalty, and limited commitment to altruistic institutions. Yuppies were accused of spending a great deal of time networking for their next (and better paying) job.

As the Boomers have moved into midlife, their moralistic zeal has been directed toward more socially acceptable goals. They have begun to lead the fight against smoking, drunken driving, and pollution, and for the recycling and greening of America. Their sheer numbers have already made them a powerful political force. At this writing, the Boomers, at a relatively young age, represent more than one-third of the membership of the U.S. House of Representatives, and one of their own, William Jefferson Clinton, resides in the White House.

The Boomers have outlived many labels, including "Spock children," "Beaver Cleaver children," "hippies," "bran eaters," "Yuppies," and now "neopuritans." Many of these labels would not have predicted later characterizations of this group. Yet, the common thread that winds through all of these various labels is the moral fervor that has always accompanied idealist generations. The various labels that the Boomers have carried over their lifetimes reflect the following description of idealist generations: "A dominant, inner-fixated IDEALIST GENERATION grows up as increasingly indulged youths . . . comes of age inspiring a spiritual awakening; fragments into narcissistic rising adults; cultivates principle as moralistic midlifers . . . " (Strauss & Howe, 1991, p. 74).

There have been predictions that the Boomers will show an increase in suicidal behavior as they move into old age early in the next century. This belief is based on the fact that suicide naturally increases in old age and on the fear that the large size of this cohort will create greater competition for limited resources and adversely affect the quality of life for this group. There is also some concern that because the Boomers have had relatively high rates of depression and suicide in their youth, we can expect this pattern to continue into old age. It can also be argued, however, that the most self-destruction prone members of the Boomer Generation have already died from suicide or other causes. Boomers have been very willing to seek help in a crisis. Also, Boomers have been a relatively affluent group that has achieved many of its life goals. Equally important, Boomers are an exceptionally vocal and politically powerful group, who are not likely to be shortchanged in the allocation of future government resources for the elderly.

The older half of middle-aged Americans living today are in many ways the antithesis of their younger counterparts. The Silent Generation is the smallest rather than the largest generation of Americans born in the 20th century. They are the product of a significant birth trough resulting from parents dealing with the hard times of the Depression era and the absence of husbands gone to war. Also, unlike the Boomers, the Silent Generation has been characterized as conforming rather than defiant, indifferent rather than passionate, inhibited rather than impulsive, other-directed rather than self-absorbed, and bureaucratic rather than protesting (Strauss & Howe, 1991).

The Silent Generation has been characterized as an "adaptive" generation. Strauss and Howe (1991) have characterized adaptive generations in the following less-than-flattering manner. "A recessive ADAPTIVE GENERATION grows up as overprotected and suffocated youths . . . matures into risk-aversive, conformist-rising adults; produces indecisive midlife arbitrator-leaders . . . and maintains influence (but less respect) as sensitive elders" (p. 74). The Silent Generation was indeed raised by domineering and overprotective parents and came of age during the Eisenhower years as the most conforming and least rebellious group of adolescents in recent history. The Silent teens experienced relatively few of the social ills that later generations have suffered. Teenage unemployment, pregnancy, and crime were at very low levels during the 1940s and 1950s. Especially important for the purposes of this book, the Silent Generation was the last adolescent group to have consistently low suicide rates; the precipitous growth in adolescent suicide began with the succeeding generation of Boomers.

The Silent Generation married and became parents very early and quickly added to the population of the suburbs. As young adults, they entered a friendly job market, as illustrated by a January 4, 1954, *Life* magazine article entitled, "The Luckiest Generation," which extolled the affluence of the teenagers of that time. The subtitle, "Never Before, So Much for So Few," reflected the main thesis that the birth trough of the 1930s and the good economic times of the 1950s had combined to provide large numbers of good-paying jobs for a small group of young adults. Young adult men of this generation outpaced their parents in education and achievement early on, but these opportunities were not as available to women until later in life. The Silent Generation has become an affluent generation at midlife and has achieved more of the American dream than either older or younger counterparts.

Although the Silent Generation has been characterized as conformers and followers rather than as revolutionaries and leaders, they have in their own way made substantial contributions to society. None in their group has yet been elected president; however, the Silent Generation is well represented among members of the U.S. Congress, government officials, and the courts. As adults they have adapted to social change and have supported the development of civil rights. Strauss and Howe (1991) have characterized the Silent Generation as a group that applies fairness, openness, due process, and expertise in getting things done. In many ways, they have been more effective behind the scenes in solving problems than the more flamboyant Boomers.

The Silent Generation has reaped many of the predictable benefits of living rather trouble-free lives. As a generation, they have enjoyed relatively good mental health and they have had low suicide rates relative to the Boomers at the same age. In the following section we will detail the suicide rates of today's Silent and Boomer midlifers.

THE STATISTICAL PICTURE

Suicide rates of the middle-aged are slightly higher than the rates for their younger counterparts and tend to increase from the first to the last decade of the 30-year period we have defined as the middle years. This trend can be seen in the international statistics from 13 different countries presented in Chapter 1. As shown in Table 1.2, there is an increase in the reported suicide rate for males between ages 35 to 44 and 55 to 64 in 10 of the 13 countries reporting and for females in 11 of the 13 countries reporting.

In the United States, suicide accounted for 13,132 deaths of middle-aged people in 1992. This number constituted 43% of the 30,484 total suicides that

TABLE 6.1   Suicide Rates Per 100,000 Population Among Middle-Aged Adults by Age, Sex, and Race for 1991

Age	All Groups	Males	Females	White Males	Black Males	White Females	Black Females
35–44	14.7	23.0	6.5	24.7	15.2	7.2	2.9
45–54	15.5	23.7	7.6	25.3	14.3	8.3	3.0
55–64	15.4	25.3	6.5	26.8	13.0	7.1	2.1

Source: U.S. Bureau of the Census (1994). Statistical Abstract of the United States (114th ed.): Washington, DC, p. 94.

occurred in the United States that year (National Center for Health Statistics, 1994).

Suicide rates for the three decades that constitute middle age are presented in Table 6.1 by sex and for the sexes combined. It can be seen in this table that the suicide rate for males increases throughout the middle years, but the corresponding rate for females peaks in the 45-to-54 decade and then begins to decline. These data are consistent with long-standing findings that the suicide rates for men continue to increase with age going into and throughout elderhood, while the rates for women peak around age 50.

Table 6.1 also includes middle-age suicide rates for different racial groups. It can be seen that, as with other age groups, middle-aged whites have higher suicide rates than middle-aged African Americans and males within each racial group have higher rates than females. Table 6.1 also shows that the peak in suicide rate for both black and white women occurs in the middle decade of the middle-age years. Particularly noteworthy are the reversed suicide rate trends for white and black males over the middle years. The gradually increasing white male suicide rate over the middle years is a part of this group's life-long tendency toward growing self-destructiveness that culminates in old age. African American males, in contrast, peak in vulnerability to suicide (and homicide) in the young adult years, followed by a gradual decline throughout middle age and old age.

Although the middle-aged have higher suicide rates than their younger counterparts, the trends over time are more optimistic for the older group. Suicide rates for all three decades of the middle years have declined over the past quarter century, while the rates for children, adolescents, and young adults have increased (U.S. Bureau of the Census, 1994). Interestingly, the middle-age decline has been greater for the second and third decades of the middle years than for the first. These findings may reflect the fact that the Silent Generation, a low suicide rate group, constitutes the older half of midlifers, while the Boomers, a high suicide rate group, are more heavily represented among the younger middle aged.

The changing demographics of suicide among various age groups support our belief that suicide becomes in many ways a different phenomenon as we move from one developmental level to another. In the next section we will return to the Suicide Trajectory and focus on those risk factors, warning signs, and triggering events that affect suicidal behavior in middle adulthood.

THE SUICIDE TRAJECTORY APPLIED TO MIDDLE ADULTHOOD

The risk factors, warning signs, and triggering events associated with suicidal behavior in middle adulthood are presented in Table 6.2. A review of the table shows that many of the special stresses and losses of midlife contribute to depression and suicide in this age group.

Biological Risk Factors

Two biological risk factors that may contribute to suicidal behavior during the middle years are menopause for women and the climacteric for men. These are important biological changes that affect behavior and moods and may increase suicide risk. Both menopause and the climacteric involve lower levels of hormone production and associated changes in behavior and mood.

Menopause has been labeled the "silent passage" because many women (and men) have been reluctant to talk about "the change" except in comic references to symptoms such as hot flashes (Sheehy, 1991). More recently, however, as the first wave of Boomers has moved into middle age, menopause has received feature coverage in newspapers and magazines and has been the subject of widely sold books, including *The Silent Passage* by Gail Sheehy (1991) and *The Change* by Germaine Greer (1992).

The physical symptoms and increased health risks associated with menopause vary widely. Some women have very little physical distress, while others report a plethora of symptoms including headaches, vaginal dryness, reduced sex drive, hot flashes and night sweats, mood swings, sleeplessness, increased irritability, and short-term memory loss. There is also an increased risk of osteoporosis and coronary disease during menopause. Some women have found symptom relief through estrogen-replacement theory (ERT); however, estrogen appears to be a double-edged sword that improves symptoms but also increases risk for breast and uterine cancer. These risks may be reduced by small doses of a second hormone, progesterone; however, this hormone may also increase PMS-like bloating and irritability and may reduce estrogen's protection against coronary problems.

Given their massive numbers—and that Boomers are inordinately interested in and talkative about anything that happens to them—menopause seems certain to become one of the leading women's health topics of the late 90's and the early 21st century. Janet Cawley, "Knight-Ridder," *Asheville Citizen-Times*

TABLE 6.2 The Suicide Trajectory Model Applied to Middle-Aged Suicide

Age Group	Biological Risk Factors	Psychological Risk Factors	Cognitive Risk Factors	Environmental Risk Factors	Warning Signs	Triggering Events	Suicidal Behavior
Middle Adulthood (35–64)	Menopause (W) Climacteric (M) Declining physical abilities and attractiveness	Loss of youthful dreams Increased inferiority Feelings of stagnation and self-absorption	Midlife evaluation Change in time perspective	Exit events: death, separation, divorce, Reduced interpersonal contact Early loss Negative life events Alcoholism (M)	Increased alcohol consumption	Multiple negative life events	Peak suicide rate for women

In a culture as youth oriented as ours, the physical losses of menopause, the climacteric, and aging in general may be as damaging to our self-esteem as to our bodies. A *Newsweek* cover story about menopause illustrated this point with a quotation by Anne Schleiden: "Each hot flash seemed to be blinking 'old-old'" (Seligman, 1994). The gradually declining physical abilities associated with middle age and changes in self-perceived attractiveness may increase feelings of anxiety, inferiority, and depression in many people. It is not unusual for middle-aged individuals to express significant distress over declining energy that does not allow them to work and play as hard as they did during their younger years. This group also complains about loss of physical and sexual attractiveness. One fortyish friend complained to the authors recently that he does not like to look at himself in the mirror any more because of the "old man" image that is reflected. These inevitable physical losses of midlife are especially stressful to individuals whose self-esteem is heavily invested in physical abilities and attractiveness and who cannot make the shift, as Peck (1968) recommended, from valuing physical capabilities to valuing wisdom.

Psychological Risk Factors

The loss of youthful dreams that often occurs during the middle years is a risk factor that may influence suicidal behavior in this age group. Almost all individuals face during the middle years a growing realization that they have gone about as far as they ever will and that their professional and personal accomplishments fall short of the lofty goals set forth earlier in youthful dreams. They will never be great artists or writers or company presidents. They will never attain the perfect marriage or raise perfect children. This knowledge may be accepted in stride and be reflected in the "mellowing" that is reported to occur throughout this period. However, for many middle-aged people, the realization that they will never attain these youthful goals may be regarded as further evidence of inadequacy and may serve as added fuel for personal dissatisfaction, enhanced depression, and suicidal ideation.

Increasing interiority, or Peck's (1968) concept of cathectic impoverishment, is another important psychological risk factor at midlife. Many healthy and productive middle-aged individuals, at the zenith of their careers and in the midst of mentoring colleagues and raising adolescents, may have a great deal of interpersonal contact. However, others in this age group may be withdrawing from these types of relationships. There is a natural tendency for middle adults to withdraw from interpersonal contact as they move from the early to the late middle years, when responsibilities at work and to the family of procreation may decline and fewer new people are brought into their lives. Middle-aged men and women who fail to struggle against this nature tendency toward interpersonal impoverishment may begin to slip from the generative end of Erikson's midlife stage of development toward stagnation and self-absorption (Erikson, 1980) and may thus increase their suicide risk.

Cognitive Risk Factors

Middle-aged individuals tend to evaluate their professional and personal accomplishments in order to determine whether or not they are "on schedule." For many people, this midlife evaluation of their accomplishments may result in negative attributions about themselves. From the middle-age perspective, career choices may have been the wrong ones; marriage may not have resulted in a life-time partnership; and the children may have turned out to be less than perfect adults. As discussed earlier in this chapter, several investigators have found that these major cognitive evaluations of life choices can reach such a level of intensity that the term "crisis" is appropriate (Gould, 1978; Levinson, Darrow, Klein, Levinson, & McKee, 1978; Viorst, 1986).

Many writers believe that the midlife crisis is often exacerbated when people in this age group experience changes in time perspective. Adults between the ages of 35 and 45 report that they begin to think in terms of time remaining in their lives instead of time already lived (Santrock, 1985). This seemingly small change may have dramatic implications for the life satisfaction of middle adults who are engaged in a cognitive reevaluation of important life choices and accomplishments. The person who has accomplished many of his or her life dreams and believes that most of the important decisions along the way have been the right ones is likely to enjoy significant life satisfaction during the midlife years. In contrast, the middle-aged individual who perceives himself or herself as "off schedule" in accomplishments may experience significantly less life satisfaction and, fueled by the urgent feeling that time is running out, become more susceptible to depression and suicidal ideation.

Environmental Risk Factors

In addition to the inevitable biological and psychological losses and associated cognitive factors, there are several well-documented environmental risk factors that increase the likelihood of suicide among middle-aged individuals. Table 6.2 shows that many of these environmental risk factors involve loss—especially interpersonal loss.

Slater and Depue (1981) found that exit events (death, separation, divorce) are often associated with suicidal behavior in this age group. The suicidal middle-aged adult is much more likely than others to have recently separated or divorced, lost a parent or a friend, or had a child leave home. These individuals are also much more likely than others to be functioning with a limited social support network. Studies have shown that suicidal adults are

Suicidal Ideas, Travies de DeVillers, 1800s. Lithograph. (Bettman Archive, New York.)

more likely than others to live alone or only with children and to lack a special confidante (Roy, 1982; Slater & Depue, 1981).

The losses experienced by suicidal adults are not limited to the time just before the self-destructive act. Suicidal adults are more likely than others to have experienced early losses as well as recent ones. Several studies show that suicidal adults have a higher than expected incidence of early parental loss through death, divorce, or separation (Adam, Bouckoms & Streiner, 1982; Bronisch & Hecht, 1987; Richman, 1981; Shneidman, 1971; Warren & Tomlinson-Keasey, 1987).

Extensive research by Barraclough uncovered evidence that many of the environmental risk factors listed in Table 6.2 contribute to suicidality in adults (Barraclough, 1987; Barraclough, Bunch, & Nelson, 1974). Barraclough and his associates followed up 100 suicides in southern England over a two-year period. They read coroners' reports, attended coroners' hearings, and interviewed at least one close relative of each suicide victim. They found that widowed, divorced, and single adults were overrepresented in this group of suicide victims. The suicide victims were seven times more likely to live in single-person households and to have no adult confidantes than were members of a group of depressed but nonsuicidal individuals. Also, many of the suicide victims in the study had recently experienced one or more negative life events, such as economic reversals, interpersonal conflict, and loss of job. Another study found that young and middle adult patients who had previously attempted suicide and who scored high on measures of suicide risk were significantly more likely than others to have reported interpersonal problems (Josepho & Plutchik, 1994).

It is possible that early losses coupled with later separation experiences may interact in special ways with the negative life events associated with mid-life to create vulnerability to suicide. Perhaps the sensitization created by early losses causes later losses to seem all the more unbearable, final, and devastating. The case of Beverly A. illustrates how these various factors may interact to increase suicidality.

> *Beverly A. was 43 years old when she appeared in a psychiatrist's office in March 1995. She described herself as depressed and told her psychiatrist that she was having increasing trouble resisting the urge to kill herself by crashing into a tree along the highway. "I've even picked out the tree," she confessed. "It's on a lonely strip of road between the hospital where I work and my home. The chances that anyone else would be hurt are slim, since the road is not heavily traveled and there's a long straight strip where I could pick up enough speed to be sure that the crash would be fatal."*
>
> *In taking a history, the psychiatrist discovered the following facts about Beverly: She had been adopted by a middle-class couple when she was six. Before then she had spent time in three different foster homes. She was a wife of*

21 years, a mother of two adolescent children, and a nurse with 15 years of experience at the same hospital. Her older child had gone away to college the previous fall. Beverly interpreted his leaving as "the beginning of the end of family life." Beverly had undergone two surgical procedures within the last year. The first was a dilation and curettage (D and C) to try to avert a hysterectomy. The second, performed six months after the unsuccessful D and C, was a complete hysterectomy to relieve excessive bleeding. On both occasions Beverly had been given a general anesthetic. Although she was clear that she did not want additional children, Beverly viewed the surgeries with ambivalence. As a nurse, she knew they needed to be done, but she felt sadness about losing her ability to conceive children and wondered if it somehow made her "less of a woman." Her medical background did allow her to ascribe some of the depression she was feeling to the two episodes with the anesthetics (central nervous system depressants) and to the hormonal changes she was experiencing because of surgical menopause.

Beverly described herself as the sole support for her mother. Her father had died during the previous year and her mother had developed heart trouble that necessitated bed rest. Beverly divided her time between her husband and 16-year-old daughter and her mother, who needed regular nursing care. Beverly felt both that she was "being cheated" of her daughter's last two years at home and that she was failing her mother by not being with her full-time.

Beverly's work at the hospital had suffered because of her lengthy absences following surgery and because of her depressed state. She complained that she was sleeping poorly at night as a result of worrying about her mother, her husband, her daughter, and her job. She was so exhausted during the day that she had little energy to give to her job or her home life. When asked to think of an image that would describe her life, Beverly said that she saw herself as an ant balancing the earth on her shoulders. When asked what was going to happen to the ant, she said, "She will lose her grip on the earth and will be crushed by it."

Many elements of loss and stress are evident in Beverly's story. Her foster home history revealed many interpersonal losses early in life. Her father had died within the past year. Her son's going away to school portended the loss of her role as a parent. The surgeries she had not only were insults to the integrity of her body but also resulted in the loss of procreative ability. The stress of caring for her mother, of being "the good daughter," added to her feelings of being burdened, and her job also required that she nurture others even though she was exhausted herself. Clearly, Beverly had reached a suicidal crisis in her life. She was very depressed, and her imagery revealed that she thought her life consisted of nothing but burdens—burdens that would ultimately destroy her.

There is considerable evidence that the last environmental risk factor listed in Table 6.2, alcoholism, may be more directly related to suicide among the middle-aged than any other group. Roy and Linnoila (1986) reported the results of several studies that showed the risk of suicide among alcoholics to be 58 to 85 times higher than that for nonalcoholics. The suicide rate for alcoholics has been estimated to be as high as 270 per 100,000 population (Miles, 1977).

Many more alcoholic suicide victims are men than women. The studies reviewed by Roy and Linnoila (1986) showed that 87% of the 349 alcoholic suicides studied were men. This ratio of almost 7 to 1 exceeds the relative proportions of male and female alcoholics in the United States, which has been estimated to be approximately 4 to 1. Rushing (1969) has speculated that differences in the drinking behaviors of alcoholic men and women may affect the relative suicide rates of these groups. Because more men alcoholics than women alcoholics drink in bars and other public places, men alcoholics may be more likely to experience alcohol-related interpersonal problems than women, who are inclined to drink alone at home. Also, because more men than women are employed outside the home, males are more vulnerable to alcohol-related job stress. We should also note that there are many other differences between men and women alcoholics, such as family history, developmental history, and gender-related effects of alcohol, that may impact suicidal behavior (Linnoila, Erwin, Ramm, Cleveland, & Brendle, 1980).

The typical alcoholic suicide is a middle-aged male who is currently drinking and who has been abusing alcohol for as long as 25 years (Barraclough, 1987; Roy & Linnoila, 1986). Goodwin (1973) has hypothesized that the reason alcoholic suicides are more likely to occur at midlife is that the related life problems that contribute to suicide (e.g., poor health, loss of employment, and divorce) tend to emerge only after a long history of alcoholism.

The alcoholic lifestyle creates conditions in which negative life events occur more often than in the lives of nonalcoholics. One recent study using the psychological autopsy technique found that the suicides of a group of alcoholic and/or substance-disordered individuals were significantly more likely to have been preceded within six weeks by conflicts, arguments, and attachment disruptions than the suicides of a nonalcoholic group (Duberstein, Conwell, & Caine, 1993).

The relationship between alcoholism and depression is well documented. Alcohol acts on the central nervous system as a depressant, provoking psychological changes that range from relaxation to stupor and even to death. Roy and Linnoila (1986) reviewed several studies that reported clinical depression rates of 28% to 59% among alcoholics. Whether the alcoholism causes depres-

---

She has started to drink as a way to cope that makes her less able to cop. R.D. Laing, *Knots*, 1970

sion in a direct physiological way, in a more indirect way (e.g., through the life problems and losses that a long history of alcoholism creates), or in both ways is not clear. There is strong evidence, however, that the depression associated with alcoholism is very much a part of alcoholic suicide. One study found that 78% of a group of 50 alcoholic suicides had previously been diagnosed as having affective disorder (Murphy, Armstrong, Hermele, Fisher, & Clendenin, 1979). Another study showed that the number of diagnoses of depression among a group of alcoholics who later killed themselves was significantly higher than among a group of alcoholics who did not (Berglund, 1984). Thus, when depression has been diagnosed as a correlate of alcoholism, the risk of suicide is greater.

The case of Kenneth P. illustrates the interaction between normative events of middle age, alcohol abuse, and suicidal behavior.

Kenneth P., at age 54, was brought to a hospital in an unconscious state. His wife said she had found him in his study face down on the desk with an empty bottle of Jack Daniels on the floor and a gun near his right hand. It appeared that he had been trying to write a suicide note when he passed out.

When Kenneth awakened, his major reaction was one of dismay at surviving. He lamented, "I couldn't even do that job right. I really am no good." After emergency treatment, Kenneth was admitted to the hospital for tests, because he complained of ongoing stomach pains that he feared were the beginning of the type of cancer that had killed his father. During his discussions with his doctor, the following facts emerged:

Kenneth was a successful executive with a major computer software firm. He was also the father of three children, aged 18, 22, and 25. Only the 18-year-old daughter remained at home. His wife, to whom he had been married for 26 years, was "a typical housewife." He described his home life as "very traditional." His wife had always stayed home and had taken care of his needs as well as those of the children. He credited her with his rapid rise in the company during his late 30s and 40s, because "she was so good at entertaining."

Kenneth had been a social drinker since his college days and alcohol had played a major role in entertaining at home and during "business lunches." Lately, he had found that he needed a drink to "get started" in the morning. Although he maintained that his performance on the job had not been affected, he was aware that two younger employees had been promoted over him within the last year. He confessed to his doctor that he was afraid he was being "sidelined" and would never move further up in the company. He did not tell his doctor that his boss had threatened to fire him if he continued coming to work with alcohol on his breath.

As Kenneth realized that he might have passed the zenith of his career, he began to focus more on his family, only to realize that his children no longer needed him. Under questioning, he admitted that his home life had been more

turbulent in the past year because his wife "kept harping about his drinking."
On one occasion, his wife and daughter had moved to a hotel for three days
because he had threatened to hit them if they did not leave him alone. When
asked to describe how he felt about his behavior and his future, Kenneth re-
sponded with tears in his eyes, "I'm ashamed of myself, Doc, and scared—real
scared."

Kenneth's case reflects many of the factors associated with alcohol and suicide in the middle years. A history of social drinking accelerated into alcohol dependency. Feeding into his dependency were Kenneth's growing realization that his career had already peaked and his fear of physical illness. Undoubtedly, his long history with alcohol exacerbated his physical symptoms, but in a downward spiral of dependency, the more his stomach hurt, the more he drank. Verbal and threatened physical abuse of his family was a new behavior for him, one which did not fit his self-image as a good husband and father. The guilt and shame he felt from his treatment of his wife and daughter and his growing fear that they might leave him permanently further fueled his sense of depression and hopelessness. Kenneth's case is a good example of the use of alcohol to try to escape the realities of middle age. Rather than turn to his family or to professionals for help, Kenneth's traditional value system kept him from admitting his fears about his health and his dead-ended career.

Like many middle-aged men, Kenneth began to reach out to his family for the first time as his career began to fade. But, as in the poignant song by Harry and Sandy Chapin, "Cat's in the Cradle" (1974), this source of support was no longer available to him. His children's need for their father's love had died from benign neglect.

The influence of gender socialization on suicidal behavior has already been mentioned in chapter 4 and will be discussed in detail in chapter 8; however, two prominent sex differences will be illustrated here—help seeking and striving for success. Kenneth, like many males, was reluctant to consult a physician concerning his stomach pain or to seek professional help with his drinking problem. He decided instead to deal with his problems alone in a self-destructive manner. Also typically masculine was Kenneth's strong need to be successful. Males tend to assess their self-worth in terms of ability to compete and to be successful. Kenneth's self-esteem was adversely affected by his declining status at work. Even his "failure" at taking his own life was a source of consternation.

Warning Signs, Triggering Events, and Suicidal Behavior

The warning signs and triggering events for middle-aged suicide are those that reflect the major causes of self-destructive behavior in this age group. Multiple negative life events, especially those involving interpersonal loss, usually precede a suicidal act. Also, increased alcohol consumption is often a manifestation of these problems that enhances the depression and increases the likelihood of suicide. Kenneth's case study illustrates several of these factors. His problems with health, work, and family contributed to his drinking, which in turn made all of these problems worse and enhanced his depression and suicidality in a vicious circular manner.

Finally, as we learned in the statistical portion of this chapter, the middle years mark the peak in suicide rates for white and black women. We know of no research that clearly identifies factors that make the middle years the most deadly for women. We can speculate, however, that biological factors such as menopause and role losses connected with the empty nest may interact to make this period especially stressful for some women.

In this section we have focused on risk factors, warning signs, and triggering events that relate to suicide in middle-aged people. In at least one sense, however, most middle-aged people are suicidal; that is, the majority have all considered suicide as an option at one or more periods in their adult lives. Also, it is unlikely that anyone reaches middle age without having known someone who has attempted or completed suicide. Therefore, unlike their younger counterparts, most middle-aged adults have had some experience with suicide and some associated knowledge and attitudes. In the following section we will explore what is known about adult information and attitudes concerning suicide.

ADULT INFORMATION AND ATTITUDES ABOUT SUICIDE

There have been only a few studies investigating general knowledge about suicide, and these studies have not used middle adults as subjects. Two studies investigating factual information and misinformation about suicide among college students found their knowledge to be generally poor (Leenaars, Balance, Pellarin, Aversano, Magli, & Wenckstern, 1988; McIntosh, Hubbard, & Santos, 1985).

Confronted with a dearth of information concerning what middle-aged adults know about suicide and what their attitudes are toward suicide, we decided to run our own small pilot study with subjects in this age range. We created a three-part instrument consisting of factual questions, a set of descriptors of suicidal people, and an open-ended interview protocol designed to capture people's actual words and thoughts on the topic of suicide. Participants were asked to read and respond in writing to the factual questions and the descriptors and then to respond orally to the open-ended interview questions.

A convenience sample of 40 subjects (20 males and 20 females) living in a rural area of western North Carolina was selected. The subjects in the study ranged from ages 35 to 53, with a mean age of 42. Ninety percent of the males and 50% of the females were college graduates, and most were business or professional people. Although our sample is not representative of all people in this age group, the responses of these subjects do provide a focus for examining middle-aged people's knowledge about and attitudes toward suicide.

The measures of adult information about suicide included a multiple-choice and a true-or-false test. The specific items focused on general information about suicide such as relative rates and trends for age, sex, racial groups, and geographic regions, plus characteristics of suicidal behavior. The typical subject in our study correctly answered only 45% of the multiple choice items and 74% of the true or false items. Although the scores on both tests were generally low, the specific multiple choice and true or false items that were answered correctly by 85% or more of the subjects reflect a significant fund of general information about suicide. For example, most respondents knew that national statistics underestimate the true incidence of suicides; that the greatest increase in suicide rates has occurred among the young; and that children below the age of 10 are capable of suicide. In addition, most knew that suicide attempters are more likely than others to try again and that improvement following a suicide crisis does not necessarily mean the risk is over. Most also knew that suicide is sometimes an attempt to cope with a problem and that strong religious beliefs are associated with negative attitudes toward suicide. Finally, most were aware of the tendency for males to use firearms and for females to use pills in suicide attempts.

The items that were missed by many of our respondents reflect some widespread misconceptions about suicide. The suicide myths that were supported by 85% or more of our respondents were the following:

1. The highest suicide rate occurs among the young (correct answer: the old).
2. There has been no long-term decrease in suicide among any age group (correct answer: suicide rates among the old have decreased).
3. The incidence of white male suicide peaks during the teen years (correct answer: during old age).
4. The worldwide suicide rate is highest in the Western hemisphere (correct answer: in Scandinavian countries).
5. The U.S. suicide rate is highest in the Northeast (correct answer: the West).
6. The suicide rate is highest in winter (correct answer: spring).
7. Suicide occurs most often late at night (correct answer: late afternoon).
8. The rank ordering of suicide rates from highest to lowest is as follows: (a) white females, (b) white males, (c) nonwhite males, (d) nonwhite females (correct answer: (a) white males, (b) nonwhite males, (c) white females, (d) nonwhite females).

In summary, the test scores of our middle-adult subjects were not high; however, the items answered correctly most of the time and the items frequently missed support a rather positive picture of adult knowledge about suicide. Our subjects showed broad general knowledge of important facts about suicide, and the majority of their errors occurred on items measuring more specific information of less importance.

Perhaps more important than what people do and do not know about suicide are what attributes they ascribe to suicidal people. In response to our request to select the attributes of suicidal people from a list of possible attributes, more than 85% of the subjects indicated that suicidal people are depressed, unhappy, and hopeless. More than 75% indicated that suicidal people are also upset and angry, and a remarkable 93% indicated that suicidal people are not crazy. We were impressed with the fact that the characteristics ascribed to suicidal people by our middle-aged subjects are consistent with mainstream clinical thinking. The majority of clinicians who work with suicidal people would agree that those at greatest risk are often depressed, unhappy, hopeless, upset, and angry, and that only a small minority of suicidal people are "crazy" (e.g., schizophrenics).

The third and final element of our study focused on attitudes toward suicide among our middle-aged subjects. For this portion of the study, subjects were asked the following 11 questions. Some of the questions required yes or no responses; however, all of the questions encouraged explanations from the subjects. Following each question is a summary of both the objective and open-ended responses of our subjects.

Question 1: Define the word "suicide." There was a great deal of agreement among our subjects concerning the definition of suicide. Most respondents defined suicide quite simply as "the taking of one's own life." Some respondents added qualifiers such as "deliberately" or "voluntarily."

Question 2: How do you feel in general about suicide? The responses to this question by our middle-aged subjects reflected a variety of feelings, mostly negative (e.g., "wrong," "a tragedy," "very sad," and "a waste"). Some ambivalence was also expressed; one respondent said, "it's not always bad," and another confessed, "I've contemplated it."

Question 3: Are there specific instances or situations in which you think suicide is justifiable? The majority of our respondents (60%) stated that there are circumstances that justify a self-destructive act. Conditions cited for justifiable suicide included the predictable circumstances of terminal illness and severe pain; however, other circumstances cited as meriting a suicidal response included psychological pain (e.g., "life no longer seems worth living").

Question 4: Suicide is illegal in at least two states. Do you think it should be? Why or why not? There was considerable disagreement among our subjects regarding whether suicide should be considered illegal, with approximately equal numbers of affirmative and negative responses. The most common reason given for criminalizing the act of suicide was that such a law would have a deterrent effect. The majority of those who supported legalization of suicide questioned the effectiveness of any legal deterrent. Others defended suicide as an individual's right.

Question 5: All states have laws against helping people to commit suicide. Do you think these laws should exist? Why or why not? More than 75% of our middle-aged respondents agreed with the need for laws that prohibit assisting someone with suicide. The most common reasons given for this response were the possibility of homicide under the guise of assisted suicide and the inability to properly judge the appropriateness of another person's motivation for suicide. The few respondents who disagreed with the need for laws prohibiting assisted suicide emphasized the humanitarian nature of this act in cases of terminal illness and uncontrollable pain.

Question 6: Do you approve of passive euthanasia? Active euthanasia? Why or why not? More than 75% of our subjects indicated approval of passive euthanasia. Among the reasons cited for this support were matters of individual freedom and humanitarian concerns. Endorsement of active euthanasia was much more equivocal with approximately equal numbers of subjects responding yes, no, and undecided. Those endorsing active euthanasia indicated approval only in cases of terminal illness or extreme age. People who disapproved of active euthanasia generally did so on moral grounds, stating that no person has the right to take another person's life.

Question 7: What should be done for suicide attempters? The great majority of middle-aged respondents recommended professional help for suicide attempters. Psychological evaluation, counseling, and therapy were the most frequent interventions recommended.

Question 8: If professionals know that someone is considering suicide, should they act to have him or her forcibly stopped (e.g., hospitalized)? Why or why not? The great majority of our respondents (75%) believed that a suicidal person should be stopped, primarily because a suicidal crisis is usually temporary and the person would soon again want to live. The few respondents who disagreed with forcible intervention expressed the belief that an individual has a right to self-determination.

Question 9: Do you have different feelings when you consider suicide among the following groups: women, men, young people, middle-aged people, elderly? Approximately two-thirds of our respondents expressed differential feelings about suicide among different age groups. Suicide among the young was considered to be much more tragic and perhaps more preventable than suicide among the old. Respondents cited the large number of years lost in the suicides of young people as a significant factor, plus the fact that many young people have not yet had an opportunity to develop adequate coping skills. Interestingly, our middle-aged subjects had few comments about their own age group. One respondent typified the responses of others by saying, "I don't know much about suicide in this group." Also, our subjects did not express different feelings about suicide among men as opposed to suicide among women.

Question 10: Have you ever known anyone who attempted suicide? If yes, who? How did you feel about him or her? Half of the 40 middle-aged respondents reported that they had known someone who attempted suicide. The feelings expressed by our subjects toward these suicidal people included sympathy, anger, and regret over the waste of life.

Question 11: Have you ever considered suicide? Would you ever attempt suicide? If yes, under what conditions? More than half (55%) of our subjects reported that they have considered suicide. Also, 28% indicated that they would attempt suicide under certain conditions. The conditions for suicide reported by our subjects included terminal illness, unbearable pain, loss of rationality, being a burden to family, hopelessness, and depression. Among the reasons given for not considering suicide were lack of courage, enjoyment of life, the realization that things may get better, love of family and self, and belief in God.

In reviewing our findings about attitudes of the middle-aged toward suicide, some generalizations can be made. There is a range of beliefs about suicide among this group, from the extreme that suicide is always wrong to the other extreme that the individual should have the right to take his or her own life; however, most of the people in our sample took a more moderate position. They generally believed that suicide is wrong, especially for young people. They tended to make exceptions for people who are in pain and suffering from terminal illness. They also expressed understanding of the slippery slope that runs between euthanasia and suicide. Many were willing to permit death to occur at a hopelessly suffering person's request; however, there was significant resistance to active euthanasia. Not surprisingly, a majority of our middle-aged subjects have considered suicide, and several would attempt it under special circumstances. A more detailed examination of right to die issues will be presented in chapter 10.

SUMMARY

The years of middle adulthood bring special opportunities and challenges. Middle adulthood typically marks the zenith of one's occupational career and it is a time when civic responsibilities and other burdens of preserving and promoting one's culture are greatest. Balancing these opportunities for generativity are the normative changes in middle age, most of which involve loss, that may move the middle adult toward the stagnation end of Erikson's continuum and become risk factors for suicide.

Two cohorts constitute the middle adulthood population in the United States today. The younger half of middle-aged Americans belong to the baby boom generation, and the older half are Silent Generationers. Boomers have been described as an awakening generation that has led the United States culturally and spiritually since they began to come of age in the 1960s. They are a large cohort that has witnessed the development of many social ills, including an increase in youth suicide. The Silent Generation is in many ways the antithesis of their younger counterparts. They are a small generation that has been characterized as conforming and mainstream in their values. Many of the social ills of youth that grew precipitously with the Boomers were at a low ebb when the members of the Silent Generation were teenagers. The Silent Generation was the last adolescent group to have consistently low suicide rates.

The suicide rates for the middle-aged are higher than for younger groups but their trend over time is more optimistic. Unlike younger groups, middle-aged Americans have shown a decline in their suicide rates over the past 25 years. Middle-aged whites have higher suicide rates than middle-aged blacks, and males in both groups have higher rates than females. The suicide rates for black and white women peak in the middle decade of the middle-age years. In contrast, African American men show decreasing suicide rates from the first to the third decade of the middle years, while white male suicidality increases over this period.

A number of risk factors may increase the likelihood of a self-destructive act at midlife. Biological factors include declining physical abilities and attractiveness, menopause for women, and the climacteric for men. Psychological risk factors for middle-aged suicide include the loss of youthful dreams, increased interiority, and feelings of stagnation and self-absorption. These psychological risk factors are exacerbated by the cognitive characteristics of this age group, including changes in time perspective and the tendency to reevaluate one's life choices. Many of the environmental risk factors for middle-aged suicide are exit events: deaths, separation and divorce, and the empty nest. Alcoholism enhances depression and impacts on negative life events in ways that increase the likelihood of a suicidal response, to a greater extent during the middle years than at any other time in the life cycle.

A study conducted by the authors investigated the knowledge and attitudes of middle-aged people concerning suicide. Although the respondents did not demonstrate a large fund of detailed information about suicide, they did show awareness of important facts. Also, they showed remarkable sophistication in ascribing characteristics to suicidal people, perhaps due to their life experiences. Attitudinally, we found that middle-aged individuals tend to have moderate views of suicide, stating that it is wrong in most situations, especially for young people, but not for the terminally ill who are in great pain.

7

Suicide Among the Elderly

Old age, more to be feared than death.

Juvenal, Satires XI

Elderly people have throughout history shown high suicide rates relative to other age groups. For example, Hudson Bay Eskimos pitched themselves from cliffs when they could no longer negotiate the harsh physical conditions of the long winters. Aging Crow Indians dressed themselves in their finest clothes and single-handedly attacked their enemies in suicidal fashion. Aged Samoans were buried alive at their own request. Dying of natural causes after a long, debilitating old age was considered in these cultures a major embarrassment to the individual and his or her family (Bromberg & Cassel, 1983). Although longevity is not considered an embarrassment in much of the developed world today, the suicide rate among people over 65 remains the highest of any age group.

We believe that many of the factors that influence suicide among the elderly may be inherent in this stage of life. An understanding of the normative events and changes that occur in old age may therefore be helpful in understanding the high incidence of suicidal behavior among the elderly. In the following section we will provide a profile of the developmental characteristics and the special stressors associated with this stage of development. We will then follow our profile of old age with a look at the particular cohorts that constitute the elderly in the mid 1990s.

PROFILE OF OLD AGE

One of the major realities of old age is biological change. Elderly people experience many physical changes, including loss of acuity in all the senses. Loss of hearing and eyesight are perhaps the most debilitating. Not only do these losses affect people's psychological sense of wholeness, they also isolate elderly people from normal life. In addition, poor hearing may increase the incidence of paranoia, as older people may begin to think that they are being deliberately excluded from conversations or that others are talking about them. The loss of vision prevents the elderly from having the benefit of television, which often is a friendly window to the world for those in failing health, and it makes reading, and therefore learning, more difficult. Additional normative changes in old age include the impairment of motor abilities (which affects balance), the development of brittle bones (with accompanying pain and potential for accidents), increased graying and loss of hair, and loss of teeth (which may affect the ability to eat and lead to malnutrition). These are only a few of the changes that negatively affect day-to-day functioning.

In addition, up to 86% of all elderly people develop chronic illnesses accompanied by some degree of pain and incapacitation (Sigelman & Shaffer, 1995). Elderly people go to medical doctors more often and spend more time in the hospital than younger people do. Even the healthiest older person will admit to a diminished energy level and to the need to rest more often than in younger years. Although people over 65 can do much to retain their good health throughout the early years of old age, at some time during this period they will confront physical loss.

The principle of entropy is useful in understanding this loss. This principle, established in physics, maintains that there is an inevitable, progressive disorganization that occurs in living organisms and physical systems and that leads to the collapse of the steady state system (Rifkin & Howard, 1980). There is a marked resemblance between the principle of entropy and the Freudian suggestion that a major goal of all life is death (Thanatos).

The principle of entropy was also addressed by Carl Jung, who stated,

> *Aging people should know that their lives are not mounting and expanding but that there are inexorable inner processes that enforce the contraction of life. For a young person it is almost a sin, or at least a danger, to be too preoccupied with himself; but for the aging person it is a duty and a necessity to devote serious attention to himself." (Jung, 1960, p. 96)*

Jung was the first to note a transition from concentration on external events and activities to a more internal focus. Later researchers have confirmed this psychological shift, generally referring to it as "increased interiority" (Buhler, 1961; Frenkel-Brunswik, 1963; Lowenthal, Thurnher, & Associates, 1975; Neugarten, 1968).

Two other psychological changes that seem to occur in old age are a shift in sex role perceptions and a shift in coping styles (Neugarten, 1968). Traditional sex roles, no longer needed for childbearing and child rearing, seem to disappear or even to undergo a slight reversal. Women's behavior becomes more authoritarian and less submissive, while elderly men evidence less dominance and more often engage in tasks previously labeled "women's work," perhaps out of necessity or boredom. The shift in coping styles is from active mastery to passive mastery, which is in keeping with a lowered energy level and less need to compete in the outside world.

First our pleasures die—and then our hopes, and then our fears, and when these are dead, the debt is due, dust claims dust—and we die too. Shelly, *Death*

In addition to these shifts in personality, healthy older people must maintain positive self-concepts in order to realize high levels of life satisfaction. Kalish (1975) has suggested that "if the older people have a reasonably stable recent history, an anticipated standard of living, and no strong fear of being left alone, their self-esteem rises with age" (p. 47). Thus, even in a very youth-oriented culture, it is not necessarily inevitable that aging will entail negative self-concepts or low self-esteem. Neugarten, Havighurst, and Tobin (1961) have identified six variables that they believe are important for developing a sense of life satisfaction in the elderly: zest, resoluteness, fortitude, a positive self-concept, an optimistic mood, and a strong relationship between goals and achievements.

Another important dimension in which changes occur in old age is cognitive functioning. The voluminous research on cognitive functioning in the elderly is often confusing and contradictory. Methodological problems are inherent in both cross-sectional and longitudinal measures of change in intellectual functioning over the life span. It does appear, however, that healthy elderly people do not suffer massive declines in intelligence (Schaie & Willis, 1993). In fact, one type of intelligence, *crystallized intelligence*, continues to grow until shortly before death in people who maintain an active intellectual life and who are free of organic illness. First described by Raymond Cattell (1963) and later elaborated by John Horn (1982), crystalized intelligence is the application of knowledge acquired by experience. Older adults do less well than younger people on measures of fluid intelligence, which involves thinking and reasoning applied to novel problems. Therefore, while older adults lose some ability to solve new and different problems, they maintain their general knowledge and vocabulary quite well. Perhaps the best generalization that can be made at present regarding cognitive functioning in the elderly is that although there appears to be some decline in certain aspects of learning and intellectual functioning among healthy elderly people, the decline rarely if ever interferes with their daily functioning.

One exception to this generalization is the phenomenon known as the *terminal drop in intelligence*. Noted as early as 1962, the terminal drop is the marked decline in measured intelligence that occurs shortly before death (Johansson, Zarit, & Berg, 1992; Kleemeier, 1962). The cause of the terminal drop is debatable. Perhaps it is a reflection of cardiovascular disease, depression accompanying terminal illness, or general apathy signifying a psychological withdrawal from involvement in the world's activities—similar to the depression stage in the death trajectory (Kubler-Ross, 1969). Whatever the cause, major declines in the intelligence of the elderly, especially in verbal abilities, have proven to be better predictors of mortality than has chronological age (Blum, Clark, & Jarvik, 1973; Schulz & Bewen, 1993.)

In the psychosocial dimension, Erikson (1980) described the major task of old age as the achievement of ego integrity; otherwise, one risks facing despair. As described in chapter 2, ego integrity has a great deal in common with self-actualization. It represents the highest level of adjustment in human beings, and Erikson felt it could not be attained before the age of 65. At the other end of the mental health continuum for elderly people is despair that is rooted in an awareness of an unfulfilled life and in the knowledge that time will not permit new beginnings.

Peck (1968), who expanded on Erikson's notion of a continuum between integrity and despair, suggested that there are three challenges involved in coping with this final stage of development. The first is to develop ego differentiation rather than continue to be preoccupied with past roles. Because retirement diminishes work-role opportunities, individuals must develop other meaningful activities in order to remain healthy. Activity in general declines with advancing age and it becomes harder to force oneself to learn new skills, roles, and interests; but good mental health in old age requires such a differentiated range of activities and interests.

The second challenge is to reduce preoccupation with the body and to increase body-transcendence. As the physical losses of old age accumulate, healthy individuals must find creative outlets for their energies rather than focus on their declining biological capabilities.

The third challenge is to reduce ego preoccupation and increase ego transcendence. By ego transcendence, Peck means the ability to take pride in accomplishments that will live on after one's inevitable death. Individuals who believe that their lives have accomplished little and that their imminent deaths will also be meaningless may well develop an abiding sense of despair.

In summary, the elderly period, beginning around age 65 and continuing until death, can be a period of increased life satisfaction and ego integrity, or it can be a period of dissatisfaction, despair, and disgust. Older adults who are able to stay on the positive end of Erikson's continuum may achieve wisdom during this stage. However, the principle of entropy ensures that sometime during this period individuals will experience sudden or gradual declines in health, will have to deal with the loss of friends and relatives, and will eventually face their own deaths. These parameters have defined the positive and negative limits of elderhood for many generations. There is reason to believe, however, that the dominant cohort of elders living today, the GI Generation, is perhaps better prepared and more effective in dealing with old age than any of its predecessors. In the following section we will discuss today's elderly cohorts.

TODAY'S ELDERLY COHORTS

We will once again refer to Strauss' and Howe's now-familiar book in describing the present-day generation of elderly people. According to Strauss and Howe (1991), three different cohorts constitute the elderly population of the United States in the mid 1990s. The first group, the Silent Generation, was born between 1925 and 1942 and consists of only those elders who were 70 years of age and younger in 1995. Because the Silent Generation was discussed in detail in the preceding chapter on middle-aged suicide, no further description of this group will be presented here. The great majority of elders in the United States today belong to the second generation, the GIs, a group born between 1901 and 1924, with ages that ranged from 71 to 94 in 1995. The GIs constitute all but the very youngest and oldest elderly groups in America today and therefore will be emphasized in our discussion of generational aspects of elderly suicide. The third elderly generation, one that is rapidly disappearing as we move toward the 21st century, is the Lost Generation, composed of all those Americans born between 1883 and 1900, most of whom were already centenarians in 1995.

The GIs have been described as the most positive and privileged group of older citizens in U.S. history. They are a civic generation, which as you may recall from chapter 1 is by nature strongly committed to self-sacrifice and service for the common good and optimistic about what is possible through collective action. Most of the GI generation experienced the Depression in their youth and came of age at the beginning of World War II. This is the group that witnessed the defeat of the Great Depression and won the Big War. The victorious GIs came home from the war to create and realize the American dream as no generation had before. For example, the GI Bill made them the largest and oldest college-going group of Americans in history. These older students provided the impetus for the development of on-campus, married-student housing that created new addresses with names like "Veteransville" and "Victory Village." Throughout their early and middle adult years, the GIs accumulated more personal wealth and achieved home ownership in greater numbers than any group had ever done before. According to Strauss and Howe (1991), the GIs have given more to their country and received more benefits in return than any group in history.

The GI Generation moved into elderhood at a time when this age group was beginning to be recognized as one with special needs. The first White House conference on aging focused on the GI Generation. The first age discrimination laws and the National Institute on Aging were created as this group became elderly. The GI generation brought more affluence and influence into old age than any preceding group. They were the instigators of concepts such as the "golden years" and the "Grey Panthers"; they created a market for institutions such as retirement living communities and Elderhostel; and they made the American Association of Retired Persons a significant political and economic force.

The GIs have enjoyed better health and more economic prosperity than any other elderly group in history. These factors have surely contributed to the fact that elderly suicide rates have declined in the United States over the past half century. In spite of the general decline in elderly suicide, however, the GI elderly suicide rate has remained higher than any other age group. Also, the elderly men in the GI Generation show exceptionally high suicide rates relative to same-aged women. These gender differences may be caused partly by the fact that the GI Generation has tended to endorse gender role stereotyping throughout their adult years. For example, "Rosie the Riveter" returned to homemaking as soon as the "boys" came back from overseas, and she stayed there.

The very positive image of GI elders, presented by Strauss and Howe (1991), is not shared by the Lost Generation, which now constitutes the very old-old in America. The Lost Generation, labeled a reactive generation like the 13ers discussed in chapters 4 and 5, experienced their youth around the turn of the century when parenting skills often left a great deal to be desired and child exploitation was rampant. As an illustration, Strauss and Howe (1991, p. 254) quoted the following George Burns recollection of bedtime: "My mother would stand there with the door open. When the house was full she'd close it. Sometimes I made it; sometimes I slept in the hall." Although humorous, Burns's account reflects a casual approach to parenting that is reminiscent of 13er child rearing in the 1960s and 1970s. The Lost Generation youth were the first to be labeled "adolescents" because their rowdy, streetwise, adaptive, and mercenary behavior drew special attention from adults. These flaming youth faced the horrors of trench warfare as they came of age during World War I and later returned from the war to a world controlled by their "missionary" generation elders who were determined to control their "hell-raising" ways with sanctimonious legislation such as prohibition (Strauss & Howe, 1991). As the Lost Generation moved into midlife, they became less self-destructive and more entrepreneurial, echoing the sentiment that the only revenge is living well. However, fate played a cruel trick on this group with the onset of the Great Depression, which occurred as Lost generation midlifers were gaining significant affluence. The elderly Lost Generation is dramatically different from their GI counterparts. Members of this generation are the most Republican-leaning group in history. They have regularly opposed government programs that benefit special groups, including the elderly. Compared to GI retirees, Lost Generation retirees have had less income, have received less Social Security, and have been less likely to own homes, and those remaining are more likely to live in poverty (Strauss & Howe, 1991).

The cohort differences between the GIs and the Lost may help to explain the significantly higher suicide rate among old-old (Lost Generation) men than among young-old men (GI Generation). The Lost Generation has never received nor expected much help from the government, while the GI Generation has set new standards for reciprocity between human sacrifice and government support. Equally important, however, is the fact that the Lost Gener-

TABLE 7.1   Suicide Rates per 100,000 Population Among Elderly Adults by Age, Sex, and Race for 1991

Age	All Groups	Males	Females	White Males	Black Males	White Females	Black Females
65–74	16.9	30.7	6.0	32.6	13.8	6.4	2.4
75–84	23.5	53.0	5.7	56.1	21.6	6.0	*
85+	24.0	69.7	6.3	75.1	*	6.6	*

*Base figure too small to meet statistical standards for reliability.
Source: U.S. Bureau of the Census (1994). Statistical Abstract of the United States (114th ed.): Washington, DC, p. 94.

ation has been the most suicidal cohort in American history (Strauss & Howe, 1991). The statistical dimensions of suicide among elderly GIs and Lost Generationers will be discussed in the following section.

THE STATISTICAL PICTURE

The rising suicide rate among young people has received a great deal of appropriate attention during the last two decades. The fact that young people, who during the 1950s and before were relatively immune to suicide, have now joined the adult world of self-destructive behavior is a significant problem in our society. We in no way wish to diminish the importance of this modern day epidemic which accounts for so many years of potential life lost. In this chapter, however, we will focus on the less recognized phenomenon of suicide among the elderly. In spite of the small amount of attention given to this problem, suicide among those aged 65 and beyond takes a larger proportional bite of human life than the self-destructive behavior of any other group.

Table 1.2 in Chapter 1 presents suicide rates among various age groups by sex for 13 selected countries. A review of this now-familiar table illustrates several facts about suicide among the elderly that are true for every country where data are available. For instance, elderly suicide rates are high, especially those for males. In all countries reporting, male suicide rates for those aged 65 and older are a great deal higher than those for females. The elderly male suicide rates, without exception, increase with age, making the oldest elderly (those age 75 and older) the most deadly group of all. Table 1.2 also shows, however, that in contrast to the male pattern of consistently increasing rates with age, as women move from the young-old to the old-old, their suicide rates are as likely to decline as to increase.

The demographics of elderly suicide in the United States can be seen in more detail in Table 7.1. It includes suicide rates per 100,000 population for three age groups of elderly by sex and race. The table shows that the suicide rate for all elderly groups increases from the young-old to the old-old. A closer examination of these data reveals that white males account for most of this phenomenon by becoming increasingly prone to suicide as they move through each of the three elderly age groups presented in the table. White females, in contrast, show minor suicide rate fluctuations in elderhood, and the rate changes for African American elderly are unclear because of limited data.

A second characteristic of elderly suicide that is evident in Table 7.1, as well as in the previously reported international data, is the dramatic sex difference that makes old men much more at risk than old women. In the general population, the male-to-female suicide ratio is approximately 4:1; however, the male-to-female ratio for those aged 65 to 74 is 5:1. This ratio grows to more than 9:1 for those age 75 to 84 and to slightly more than 11:1 for those over 85 years of age.

The suicide rates for whites of all ages are higher than those for African Americans. This phenomenon continues among the elderly with a ratio of approximately 2.5:1 (McIntosh, 1992). Seiden (1981) has proposed that racial differences in family arrangements may account for some of the suicide rate differences between whites and blacks. The nuclear family tends to be the predominant arrangement among whites in the United States, while the extended family with several generations living together is more prevalent among African Americans. The extended family arrangement often provides useful roles for the elderly, such as child care and domestic services, that are less available in the nuclear family. It would appear that these intergenerational roles also provide intrinsic rewards and enhance self-esteem for many older adults.

Seiden (1981) has also pointed out that the loss of financial and employment status that may occur in retirement is perhaps a more relevant motive for whites than for nonwhites. White men, especially, often lose power and influence as they grow old. Many black men, black women, and white women have long been accustomed to low status as a result of racism and sexism. Because of their former higher status, power, and income, white men have farther to fall in retirement than nonwhites and women of all races. As Dick Gregory once said about the plight of minorities, "You can't kill yourself by jumping out of the basement." Finally, nonwhite elderly appear to have higher morale than whites, perhaps because minority families often hold traditional values, including respect for age and appreciation for the wisdom of experience. Also, there may be some natural selection operating among elderly black males in that those who have made it to old age may have already shown considerable strength and adaptability in dealing with years of racism and poverty.

The elderly have the lowest suicide attempt/completion ratio of any age group. The most common estimate for the elderly is an attempt/completion ratio of 4:1, while estimates for young people run as high as 300:1 (Stenback,

1980). McIntosh (1992) has suggested several reasons for the very low ratio of suicide attempts to completions for the elderly. Foremost among them is the belief that the elderly have greater suicide intent than younger individuals, whose death wishes may be more ambivalent. Also, it is well known that old people who attempt suicide use more lethal means than the young. The elderly, for example, are more likely than younger age groups to shoot themselves (McIntosh, Hubbard, & Santos, 1981). Finally, physiological changes associated with aging may increase the likelihood of death resulting from a suicide attempt among the elderly relative to younger and perhaps hardier individuals.

The suicides of elderly people may be more underreported than any other age group, even the young. The cause of death among the elderly is often more difficult to determine. Older people are more likely to take overdoses of prescription medications, to mix drugs, to fail to take essential medicine, or to starve themselves to death (Miller, 1978b). Because of the equivocal nature of these types of deaths, it has been estimated that the actual number of elderly suicides that occur annually in the United States is at least double the official statistics (Osgood, 1985).

The old have always been overrepresented among those who kill themselves. In spite of this fact, however, the elderly suicide rate has declined significantly during the past 60 years. The annual suicide rates between 1932 and 1992 for the entire U.S. population and for those aged 65 and above are presented in Figure 7.1. The figure shows that the elderly suicide rate has been the highest of any age group throughout this 60-year period; however, the trend for this age group has been somewhat optimistic. The elderly suicide rate has dropped significantly since the Depression of the early 1930s, while the overall suicide rate has remained relatively stable.

Several hypotheses have been advanced to help explain the decline in elderly suicide (McIntosh, 1984, 1985, 1990, 1992). The first hypothesis relates to the differential longevity between the sexes that has increased by approximately seven years during this century (Stillion, 1985). In contrast to the early 1900s, when men and women were more equally represented in the elderly population, women presently constitute 60% of those over 65 years of age in the United States. Because women have lower suicide rates than men, their greater representation in this age group would naturally reduce the overall incidence.

A second hypothesis concerning the declining elderly suicide rate is that improving financial conditions during the past half century have especially impacted this age group. Two studies found significant correlations between improving economic circumstances among elderly white males and decreasing suicide rates for this group. Marshall (1978) investigated the relationship between four indices of economic well-being among the elderly and suicide rates for older white men between 1947 and 1972. The economic indicators

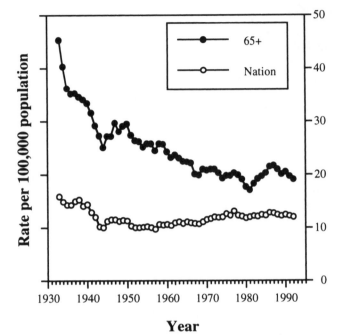

Year

FIGURE 7.1   U.S. suicide rates 1932–1992 for the nation and for those aged 65 and older.
    Source: Generated by John L. McIntosh, Ph.D., professor of psychology, Indiana University South Bend, based on annual data published by the National Center for Health Statistics.

were (1) employment rate of the aged, (2) the availability of income security for older people, (3) the portion of the labor force covered by Social Security, and (4) the average monthly husband-wife income for the elderly. The findings showed that each of these four variables were related to the suicide rate. Elderly people who were employed at least part-time, had secure incomes, had participated in Social Security, and had higher monthly incomes had lower suicide rates. In fact, these four variables collectively accounted for more than 90% of the variance in suicidal behavior among older white men during the period of the study.

The second study, by McCall (1991), found a similar relationship between improving economic circumstances for the elderly and reduced elderly white male suicide rates between 1946 and 1986. Using regression analyses and t-ratios, she found that declining suicide rates for this group were associated with (1) a reduction in elderly persons living below the poverty level, (2) improved health care availability through Medicare, and (3) increased Social Security benefits

A third widely accepted hypothesis is that the declining suicide rate reflects a cohort difference among the elderly. We have seen that the present elderly generation, the GIs, came of age and lived their young and middle adult years under significantly different circumstances than their predecessors. Because of the advantages they have experienced across their adult lifetimes, the GIs have arrived at elderhood in better physical, economic, and psychological condition than any prior generation. It should follow, therefore, that the rate of suicide among GI elderly should be lower than the suicide rate among the Lost Generation elderly.

Finally, modern-day elderly have been the recipients of significant developments in geriatric medicine. For example, depression is no longer considered to be a normal manifestation of aging but rather a condition that can and should be treated aggressively with antidepressant medications. Progress is also being made in treatment of heart disease and in rehabilitation approaches, offering hope for continued quality of life even after the onset of illness.

The declining suicide rate among the elderly over the last 60 years has been very encouraging, especially considering the fact that most of the improvement has occurred among white males, the group most at risk. There are, however, some discouraging projections that indicate that the number of suicides among the elderly may not continue to decline (Haas & Hendin, 1983; Manton, Blazer, & Woodbury, 1987). Figure 7.1 clearly shows a 60-year elderly suicide rate reduction that reached an all-time low in 1981. However, closer examination of the figure shows that the early 1980s saw a reversal of this trend and a gradual increase in the suicide rate. This reversal of fortune is difficult to explain in view of the fact that economic circumstances for older adults have continued to improve. John McIntosh (1992), a well-known researcher in the field of elderly suicide, has speculated that while the 1980s continued to bring prosperity to older adults, a decline in optimism about quality of life during the golden years may have occurred in the United States, dampening the typically cheery outlook of the GIs. In many ways, the 1980s was a period of heightened awareness of both the positive and negative aspects of the graying of America. Increasing awareness of the specter of Alzheimer's and the fact that this incurable and dreadful disease strikes a higher percentage of the elderly with each decade of advancing age has made living longer less attractive. Also, recent national forums portending financial catastrophe in elderly health care may have heightened pessimism among older citizens concerning the likelihood that they will receive quality care if they become seriously ill.

Independent of the long-range implications of the recent short-term trend in elderly suicide rates, several writers have speculated that the number of suicides among the elderly will increase significantly in the first half of the 21st century (Haas & Hendin, 1983; Manton, Blazer, & Woodbury, 1987). These writers believe that the elderly suicide rate will increase significantly between the years 2010 and 2030 as the Baby Boom Generation (those born between 1943 and 1960) moves into old age. They believe that old age will be especially stressful for this large cohort because they will overburden the social services system, which will at that time be supported by much smaller generations (the 13ers and Millenials) and thus create greater competition for limited resources. Also, as shown in chapters 5 and 6, the Baby Boom Generation began the post-1950s rise in youth suicide and have continued to show high rates of depression and suicide well into middle age (McIntosh, 1994).

In contrast to this gloomy characterization of the future generation of elders, other writers (Easterlin, Macdonald, & Macunovich, 1990; McIntosh, 1992) have speculated that the Baby Boom Generation may be psychologically stronger in old age than their predecessors. They are, for example, better educated, healthier, and more willing to seek mental health services than any preceding cohort. As middle-aged adults, the Boomers have demonstrated themselves to be a powerful social and political force and therefore may be expected to be very effective in procuring a significant portion of the nation's resources in old age. Finally, because this group showed high rates of suicide at young and early adult ages, the most vulnerable and depression-prone Boomers will perhaps have already died, thus leaving the healthiest of this generation to carry on in old age.

Although higher suicide rates for the Baby Boom Generation in old age is not a foregone conclusion, there is one inescapable demographic fact that portends higher numbers of elderly suicides in the 21st century, even if the rates continue to decline. Those over 65 constitute the fastest growing age group in the United States today. Improving lifestyles and health care for older people have resulted in this group constituting a higher percentage of the total population in the United States every year. McIntosh (1992) has projected the number of elderly suicides each decade through the year 2030 based on conservative estimates of population growth and using the relatively low elderly suicide rates of the 1980s. Based on these admittedly conservative estimates, McIntosh projects that the number of annual elderly suicides will grow from the 1990 rate of 6,280 to 6,942 in the year 2000 and then to an all-time high of 13,055 in the year 2030. It should be emphasized that these dramatic projections are based on very conservative estimates and the debatable assumption that the actual suicide rate for old people will not rise during the next 35 years as it has over the past decade. Also, these projections do not account for the possible impact of physician-assisted death on the suicide rate of this age group. The growing development of physician-assisted suicide is such a major issue that it will be detailed separately in chapter 10.

There is no doubt that elderly suicide is and will continue to be a major problem facing suicidologists. Whether the suicide rates stay the same or continue to decline, the demographics of the aging Baby Boom Generation will continue to make suicide among the elderly a growing problem that will necessitate much new research. We will now turn our attention to what research and clinical investigations have already taught us about this problem and focus on those risk factors that have been shown to be especially prominent in elderly suicide as we apply the Suicide Trajectory Model to this age group.

THE SUICIDE TRAJECTORY APPLIED TO ELDERLY SUICIDE

The Suicide Trajectory Model that was developed in chapter 1 and used in each of the preceding four chapters to consider age-specific causal factors is presented for a final time in Table 7.2. In this table we have summarized the risk factors, warning signs, and triggering events that influence suicidal behavior in the elderly.

Biological Risk Factors

In the category of biological risk factors, elderly suicidal people, like those in other age groups, often show changes in the biochemistry of the neurotransmitter system—particularly low levels of serotonin and dopamine at the synapses. One study, for example, found that levels of 5-HIAA, a serotonin metabolite, and HVA, a dopamine metabolite, in the cerebrospinal fluid of a group of elderly, depressed, suicidal individuals were lower than those of a comparable depressed, nonsuicidal group and a nondepressed, nonsuicidal group (Jones et al., 1990). Newly developing research raises significant questions concerning the possibility that aging and degenerative disease may adversely affect the serotonergic system (Rifai, Reynolds, & Mann, 1992). In other words, older people may be more at risk than younger groups for the loss of neurotransmitter function that has been shown to be related to depression and suicide. We also know that aging results in fewer postsynaptic serotonin receptors, thus making the neurotransmitters that are still present less effective (Roy, 1994). Further research on the biology of aging may enhance our understanding and treatment of depression and suicide among the elderly.

There is evidence that additional biological factors, including physical decline and organic mental decline as well as chronic illness and chronic pain, may affect suicide risk in old age (Dorpat, Anderson, & Ripley, 1968). The losses inherent in serious physical decline may cause or increase depression in the elderly; the direct relationship between loss of physical and mental capabilities and depression is well-documented. Also, physical decline has been shown to cause withdrawal from social contact—more so than retirement or change in marital status—and significant social disengagement has been shown to be associated with depression (Tallmer, 1994). Therefore, the loss of capabilities and freedom inherent in the biological changes of old age undoubtedly contributes to depression and increases suicide risk.

David Lester (1994) has pointed out that many elderly suicides are medi-

TABLE 7.2   The Suicide Trajectory Model Applied to Elderly Suicide

Age Group	Biological Risk Factors	Psychological Risk Factors	Cognitive Risk Factors	Environmental Risk Factors	Warning Signs	Triggering Events	Suicidal Behavior
Old age (65 and older)	Neurotransmitter decline Physical decline Organic mental decline Chronic illness Chronic pain	Loneliness Feelings of despair Personality traits Substance abuse	Declining fluid intelligence Acceptance of death	Permanent and cumulative losses: retirement, poverty, widowhood	Putting affairs in order Physician visits	Serious illness Highly publicized suicides	Highest rate Lowest attempt/completion ratio Largest sex difference Highest lethality Double suicides

cally ill and often are in chronic pain at the time they kill themselves. Miller (1979) found that 60% of elderly suicides visit physicians within one month prior to taking their lives. A study by Dorpat, Anderson, and Ripley (1968) found that 85% of elderly suicides were ill at the time of their deaths. Also, two studies conducted in England found that approximately 60% of a group of elderly suicides were ill at the time of their deaths (Barraclough & Hughes, 1987; Cattell, 1988).

Although many studies have shown that elderly suicides often suffer physical decline, serious illness, and chronic pain, not all suicidologists are sanguine about this relationship. David Clark, in his 1992 presidential address to the American Association of Suicidology, raised serious questions about the causal relationship between physical illness and suicidality in this age group (Clark, 1993). Clark pointed out that in his study involving community-based psychological autopsies of 73 cases of elderly suicide, relatively few of the victims were in poor health. It is important to note, however, that the "relatively few" elderly suicides in poor health constituted 37% of Clark's sample. Regardless of whether we view 37% as a large or small group, another of Clark's observations in this important paper is relevant for all primary care physicians who treat elderly patients. He pointed out that the elevated number of physician visits that frequently accompanies elderly suicide may reflect clinical depression rather than significant physical illness. Many physical complaints of the elderly (e.g., loss of sleep, loss of appetite, digestive disorders, vague and generalized symptoms) may be more an indication of depression than of physical illness.

Psychological Risk Factors

Elderly people often experience increased isolation and loneliness as spouses and friends die and adult children become heavily involved in their own complex lives. We believe that the social isolation that often occurs in old age is a major source of unhappiness for this age group and is a significant contributor to depression and suicide. Darbonne (1969) found that the suicide notes of elderly people include more references to loneliness and isolation than those of any other age group. Comparing a large group of elderly suicidal men with a nonsuicidal group, Miller (1979) found strong evidence that the presence of a confidante is very important in preventing suicide. The men in Miller's study who committed suicide were three times less likely to have a confidante or close friend than those who died of natural causes. Also, the suicidal men had fewer visits from friends and relatives and longer time intervals between visits than the nonsuicidal men.

We believe that older people who experience a significant amount of loneliness and isolation develop a strong sense of despair, the polar opposite of ego integrity (Erikson, 1980). Feelings of despair undermine both pleasure and meaning in life and contribute to depression and suicide. We do not mean to imply here that loneliness and isolation somehow affect the elderly more perniciously than the young; rather, we believe that the life circumstances of the old more often include social isolation.

Not everyone would agree that social isolation is a factor in the suicides of most older people. In Clark's (1993) American Association of Suicidology presidential address, referenced earlier in this chapter, he pointed out that 34% of the 73 elderly suicides he studied by psychological autopsy were married and 54% were living with others at the times of their deaths. It could be argued, however, that Clark's data reflect a significant amount of social isolation. By his report, two-thirds of his suicidal subjects had no spouses and 46% lived alone.

While we may not agree with Clark's deemphasis on social isolation as a causal factor in elderly suicide, it is important to note that in his address he proposed an interesting theory of the importance of personality factors and substance abuse in the self-destructive behavior of old people. He hypothesized that many elderly suicidal individuals have a long-standing personality flaw that includes an intolerance for the normal aging process. Clark described people with this flaw as being fiercely proud and independent and uncomfortable relying on others for basic needs. These individuals have life-long unfinished conflicts in Erikson's developmental stages of trust versus mistrust, autonomy versus shame and doubt, industry versus inferiority, and generativity versus stagnation. Their sense of self-worth is defined by their productivity as workers. This personality flaw begins to manifest itself as these individuals move into old age and experience the ordinary life stressors of this period. They cannot adjust to the physical decline and the increased need to rely on others for help. The interactions of these age-related stressors with the personality flaw creates a crisis of aging that Clark believes may be complicated by major depression or a substance abuse disorder and eventually lead to a suicidal crisis. Clark cited several case histories from his data that reflect an inability of these individuals to cope with some of the normal losses and stressors of aging. This is an intriguing theory that merits additional research to identify more specifically those personality traits that may chronicle special problems associated with aging.

Clark is not the only researcher to propose personality characteristics that may be idiosyncratic to elderly suicide. Conwell (1994) and his associates have reported preliminary data that show age differences in the personality characteristics of suicide completers. If these personality characteristics can be defined more specifically and measures developed to identify them early, therapeutic steps may be taken to provide some inoculation for these problems later in life.

There is growing awareness of the problem of substance abuse in the elderly and its contribution to suicide in this age group (Osgood, 1992). Many

Garden of Memories, **Charles Burchfield, 1917. Crayon and watercolor, 25¾ × 22½ in. (Collection, The Museum of Modern Art, New York. Gift of Abby Aldrich Rockefeller, by exchange.)**

people move into old age after a lifetime of increasing alcohol abuse. It is not unusual for elderly people to self-medicate with alcohol to ease their aches and pains and to elevate their spirits. Unfortunately, the depressant effects of alcohol are likely to be exacerbated in old age because of reduced metabolic processes that slow the detoxification process. The elderly also tend to experience overmedication as drugs prescribed by physicians are mixed with self-prescribed over-the-counter drugs. The sedating effects and metabolic problems associated with alcohol abuse and the interactions of the over-the-counter and prescription drugs may result in clouding of consciousness and increase the likelihood of depression and suicidal behavior in this age group (Butler & Lewis, 1982). Miller (1979) found that approximately 25% of a group of elderly male suicides were alcoholic or had significant drinking problems and that 35% of this group, whether alcoholic or not, were addicted to or heavily dependent upon drugs.

Cognitive Risk Factors

Two cognitive risk factors that may impact upon elderly suicide are listed in Table 7.2. The first is the decline in fluid intelligence. As mentioned earlier in this chapter, crystallized intelligence is the ability to apply knowledge and skills accumulated over a lifetime, and it appears to be relatively impervious to the ravages of aging. Fluid intelligence is the ability to reason and combine knowledge in novel ways; it often diminishes in later life. Older people with declining fluid intelligence may be less able than younger people to find new solutions to continuing and worsening problems and therefore may be at greater risk for depression and suicide.

The second cognitive risk factor listed in the table is perhaps more lethal than the first in its effect on elderly suicide. Many older people become more accepting of death, both intellectually and emotionally (Wass, 1977). There appears to be a natural tendency for elderly people to say (and believe), "I've lived a full life and it is time." This point of view is widely held in American culture. Our research on attitudes toward suicide has shown that elderly female suicides receive less sympathy than any other group (Stillion, White, McDowell, Edwards, 1983), and that elderly suicide is viewed as qualitatively different from suicide among younger people (Miller, 1979). Recent research has shown that suicide notes of the elderly reflect less ambivalence and a more direct wish to die than the notes of early and middle adults (Leenaars, 1992).

Environmental Risk Factors

Table 7.2 shows that the environmental risk factors in elderly suicide involve the losses that are often inherent in retirement and widowhood. The nature of loss in old age is different from that of younger ages in that most elderly losses are final. One never (or almost never) recovers the many years of meaningful work lost in retirement or a lifetime of companionship with a long-term spouse lost in widowhood.

The pattern of increasing losses that occurs in old age is usually described as *cumulative loss*. Elderly people often must cope with a rapid succession of significant losses that does not allow sufficient time for resolution of the grief and normal depression of one loss before another strikes.

I am ready to meet my Maker. Whether my Maker is prepared for the great ordeal of meeting me is another matter. Winston Churchill, *on his 75th birthday*

The following selection provides a poignant example of the cumulative losses often experienced in elderhood and the sometimes tragic results:

Today I read about a man who slashed his wrists because he lost his hat. He was old, and of course, they say he was crazy. I think not. I think he'd had all the losses he could take. He said as much. His last words were "O God, now I've lost my hat, too." I know how he felt. Every time you turn around, time—with a little help from your friends—grabs off something else. Something precious. At least to you. Hearing. Sight. Beauty. Job. House. Even the corner grocery turns into a parking lot and is lost. Finally you lose the thing you can't do without—hope (that it can get better). Dear God, when he gets to heaven, let that man find his hat on the gatepost. (Maclay, 1990, p. 69)

Retirement is an institution that may lead to cumulative loss for many elderly people. Although countless individuals deal with retirement effectively and genuinely enjoy their golden years, there is also evidence that retirement may be exceptionally stressful for some individuals and may elicit anger and depression and perhaps even suicide (Alsop, 1984).

There appears to be a general pattern of adjustment in retirement. Retirees often experience a certain amount of enthusiasm and excitement about their new status during the first year (Atchley, 1976). It is not unusual, however, for this euphoria to give way gradually to a sense of letdown during the second year as the novelty fades and as the realities of the new status become more evident. One study comparing groups of first-and second-year retirees found that second-year retirees reported significantly lower levels of satisfaction and less involvement in leisure and physical activities than first-year retirees (Ekerdt, Bosse, & Levkov, 1985). Perhaps more important, the second-year retirees showed much less optimism and future orientation than first-year retirees. The declining optimism of second-year retirees may reflect a growing realization of the losses that are inherent in retirement life. These losses include income, status, power, and prestige as well as purposeful and meaningful activity (Benson & Brodie, 1975; Breed & Huffine, 1979; Lyons, 1984; McIntosh, Hubbard, & Santos, 1981; Miller, 1978b).

Inadequate income is stressful at any age; however, poverty seems to be most traumatic in old age, especially if it occurs after a lifetime of adequate income prior to retirement. A survey of retired persons over 60 years of age found that self-perceived financial status was a stronger contributor to life satisfaction than any other factor, including functional health, age, sex, race,

---

Years following years, steal something every day; at last they steal us from ourselves away. Pope, *To a Lady,* Epistle II, Book II

marital status, or education (Useui, Keil, & Durig, 1985). The term "self-perceived" is an important one. While many individuals are in fact impoverished at the end of their working years, a larger group is poor only relative to their preretirement income. An individual's pension plus Social Security payments may provide an adequate income for basic necessities, but may seem impoverished relative to the paycheck received during the full-time employment years.

The financial impact of retirement appears to take the greatest toll on men whose preretirement income was marginal. Fillenbaum, George, and Palmore (1985) examined data from two longitudinal studies to measure the impact of retirement on the morale of men at different economic levels. They found that men at the marginal economic level were more negatively affected by retirement than those who were at the poverty level or who were financially comfortable. In addition, they found that only retirees at the marginal economic level reported reduced life satisfaction and decreased happiness in retirement. These results may occur because of the change in socioeconomic status that often accompanies retirement. Unlike those at higher socioeconomic levels, those with marginal income are unable to save for their retirement, and thus face economic reversal. Those individuals who have lived most of their lives below the poverty level may actually improve their financial status in old age through income maintenance programs for the elderly.

While financial security and independence are important employment benefits sometimes lost in retirement, other work-related factors that influence life satisfaction can also be lost simultaneously. A significant amount of status, power, and influence may be lost by those who retire from privileged positions. However, even those who have worked in less prestigious positions lose meaningful, purposeful, and social activity in retirement that can be very distressing. Retirees often complain about boredom, inactivity, and loneliness. Some individuals deal with this situation by diving into hobbies and taking on new projects. Others find the inactivity of retirement so stressful that they seek reemployment, usually in lower status jobs that often lead to the sacrifice of already-earned retirement benefits.

Men who have previously been employed in high-level positions may experience significant depression related to status and power changes associated with their retirements. They may become significantly distressed to learn that former employees show them less deference than before or that their organizations are doing well without them. The following case study illustrates some of the retirement-related (and health-related) problems faced by many elderly.

W. D. Henshaw killed himself on his 81st birthday. He carefully spread a newly purchased tarpaulin on the concrete floor of his garage, lay down on it and shot himself in the head. The terse suicide note he left said simply, "It's time."

W. D. was a self-made man. He often bragged to his children and grandchildren that he had come from a small dirt farm in the South, worked his way through college, and worked hard all his life. He had risen to a position of responsibility in an agricultural wholesale business by age 32. He had then resigned and started his own wholesale business. Working night and day, he was personally responsible for the success of his business. It was at that time in his life that he developed the habit of working from 5:30 A.M. until 7:30 P.M., a habit that lasted his entire life.

W. D. married at age 36. His wife was from a wealthy family, and her wealth provided even more security for the business. Although Mrs. Henshaw was 34 when they married, they had two children. The Henshaws appeared to have a stable if unexciting marriage. However, Mrs. Henshaw developed breast cancer at age 52 and died within six months. W. D. never remarried, devoting himself instead almost totally to his business.

W. D. bragged often about his reputation for hard work and honesty. As he grew older, his son and daughter tried to get him to slow down, to develop hobbies, to take vacations. They had little success. When W. D. turned 70, his son tried to talk him into retiring. The two men argued violently, and W. D. stayed on the job, although he did cut back his customary workday from 14 hours to 10.

In spite of his iron determination, W. D. found himself napping during the day, sometimes even in important meetings. He also complained to his daughter that he had constant indigestion and that food had lost its taste. At age 78, he agreed to have his hearing tested and was fitted with a hearing aid. In general, however, his health remained good until he began to have a series of small strokes at age 79. Between hospitalizations and as his health permitted he continued to go to the office but was aware that it was running well without him and that he could no longer remember many of the details of the business. He had a long talk with his son, admitting his growing confusion and weakness. W. D. officially resigned from the presidency of his company. He spent several months putting his affairs in order. In an uncharacteristic gesture, he invited his family and the executives of his company to a cookout on his 81st birthday. His children commented after the party that they had been impressed with W. D.'s renewed energy. His daughter had felt that it was a sure sign of physical improvement, while his son felt it was caused by removal of the stress of the job. After the party, W. D. straightened the house, piled the dishes neatly in the sink, and wrote his two-word note.

This case study reflects a number of the special losses that old people who have highly identified with their work may experience in retirement. Retirement for W. D. resulted in the loss of the high level of daily activity that

---

If you haven't yet reached your "golden years", don't let the current hype about the joys of retirement fool you. They are not the best of times. It's just that the alternative is even worse. Eli A. Rubenstein, "The Not So Golden Years," *Newsweek*, October 7, 1991.

---

was such an important part of his life for many years. He obviously gained a great deal of pride and self-esteem from his accomplishments and from his critical position in the company that were lost in retirement. The loss of physical capabilities accompanying his retirement was a significant stressor, which steadily worsened with his strokes and ultimately precipitated his suicide. Also, W. D.'s extreme self-reliance and intolerance of the physical losses of aging are reminiscent of Clark's (1993) description of lethal personality characteristics for elderly suicide, discussed earlier in this chapter. The renewed energy shown by W. D. after his suicidal decision was made is characteristic of many suicides. Once the final decision to commit suicide is made, many people experience a surge of energy, probably traceable to a decrease in ambivalence about life and the future.

Widowhood is a major source of social isolation and other significant losses among the elderly (Bock & Webber, 1972a). Included among these are the loss of a best friend and confidante and the loss of a shared history. To an elderly woman, the husband may be the only person alive who remembers her as a bride, who suffered through her pregnancies, and who takes the same pride in her children as she does. To the elderly male, his wife may be the only person who has seen him in both victory and defeat and with whom he has constantly shared his inner thoughts. In reflecting about the special pain associated with the loss of a spouse, Toynbee (1984) said, "There are two parties to the suffering that death inflicts; and in the apportionment of this suffering, the survivor takes the brunt" (p. 14).

Widowhood has been shown to increase the risk of depression and suicide, especially among elderly males during the first six months of bereavement (Benson & Brodie, 1975; Berardo, 1968; Bock & Webber, 1972b; MacMahon & Pugh, 1965; Miller, 1978a; Morgan, 1994). Those widowed by suicide have especially high suicide rates (Osterweis, Solomon, & Green, 1984). In addition, widowed people who are socially isolated are at greater risk for suicide than those who have more interpersonal contact.

Some controversy exists regarding the relative amount of stress that widowhood imposes on males and females (Glick, Parkes, & Weiss, 1975; Kart, 1981; Osterweis, Solomon, & Green, 1984; Stillion, 1984). Since males are less likely than females to have developed close personal relationships with a

---

He first deceased, she for a little tried to live without him, lik'd it not, and died. Sir Henry Wotton, *On the Death of Sir Albert Morton's Wife*

---

number of people, widowhood may be particularly stressful for them, especially during the first year or two. Females may suffer less role discontinuity when they are widowed than males do. Females are more likely to be familiar with the routines of keeping house and cooking, while males must often learn new skills in order to thrive in the role of widower. Females also tend to have a more diverse set of relationships than males do. In addition, there is evidence that females "practice widowhood" in an attempt to prepare themselves for their spouse's death and may therefore be better prepared to face the reality of the loss (Lopata, 1973). It is also true that widowhood is a normative state for most older women, since women on average live nearly a decade longer than men. In addition, since women in our culture traditionally marry men older than themselves, most can expect to live as widows for at least a dozen years or more. Consequently, females may find more support among other widowed females than men do among the fewer widowed males.

In spite of all these factors, however, it can be argued that while widowers may have more difficulty in the initial adjustment to widowhood, widows suffer more over the long term (Barrett, 1979; Stillion, 1984, 1985). Because women traditionally have invested more of their self-concepts in marriage than men, a widowed woman may actually lose a greater part of her identity with the death of her spouse. This phenomenon is best seen in widows who were the wives of rich and famous men and who vicariously profited from their husbands' status and power, but it is undoubtedly a reality at some level for most women. Women are also much more likely than men to suffer financial loss in widowhood. Many more widows than widowers live below the poverty level. Widows are less likely to remarry than are widowers (Barrett, 1979). The following case study illustrates some of the special losses of widowhood in old age.

Elena Mercado was widowed after 42 years of marriage, when she was 66 years of age. Her husband, "Merk," who had worked as a machinist for 33 years, had died of cancer after a long, expensive illness. Elena found herself facing a debt-filled widowhood. She had raised seven children. She and Merk had always taken pride in the fact that he earned enough to permit her to be a full-time wife and mother. Although Elena's seven children were concerned about their mother's financial situation, none of them was able to help very much. Elena gave up her apartment in an effort to cut down on expenses and divided her time among the children's homes. She confided to an old friend that she felt like an intruder at every home, because she always took a bed from one of the grandchildren and sometimes felt that her presence deprived the family of food as well as privacy. Elena actively investigated low-cost housing programs, but each one she examined seemed beyond her means. In addition to trying to make small payments on her husband's medical bills, Elena tried to help out with the grocery bills at whatever home she was visiting. She was never able to put aside any money.

Shortly after Elena moved in with her oldest son for the second time, she received notice that her brother was dying in New Mexico. Although she could not afford to make the trip, she sent as much money as she could to help with the funeral expenses. A week later her oldest son lost his job and told her she would have to leave his home. When Elena told her daughter she would have to move in with her sooner than expected, the daughter came to her brother's home to express her unhappiness. The resultant argument between the siblings was bitter. Not knowing what else to do, Elena began to pack. While doing so, she discovered a bottle of old barbiturates left from her husband's illness. Elena left the house, saying she was going for a walk to clear her head. She walked to a nearby park, stopping to buy a coke at a corner deli. She took all of the pills in the bottle. Her body was discovered early the next morning when the police made their routine swing through the park.

This case study illustrates some of the problems that may result from the poverty many women experience in widowhood. Attempts to deal with the unaccustomed poverty without occupational skills and experience can be humiliating and devastating for many women and can necessitate living arrangements that lead to other problems. In these and other ways widowhood often multiplies the cumulative losses of old age.

Warning Signs, Triggering Events, and Suicidal Behavior

Elderly suicidal behavior is well planned and unequivocal (Leenaars, 1992). The old neither want nor expect to be rescued. More than any other age group, old people usually put their affairs in order before attempting suicide. As stated in Table 7.2, serious illness may serve as a triggering event for elderly suicide. As we have seen, it is not unusual for a visit to a physician to precede a suicide attempt, and it may therefore serve as a subtle warning sign. There is also some evidence that mass media accounts of suicide may also trigger elderly suicide (Stack, 1991). It is interesting that the elderly, like their adolescent counterparts, may be a second group with special vulnerability to the modeling of self-destructive behavior. Table 7.2 shows that elderly suicidal behavior is highly lethal. The old have the highest suicide rate and the lowest attempt/completion ratio of any age group. Also, sex differences in suicide are the greatest among the elderly because old men have exceptionally high rates.

THE SPECIAL CASE OF DOUBLE SUICIDE

Double suicides or suicide pacts have occurred throughout history and even today they receive a great deal of media attention. A pioneer scientific investigation of double suicides in England and Wales by Cohen (1961) and subsequent work by others (Mehta, Mathew, & Mehta, 1978; Noyes, Frye, & Hartford, 1977; Rosenbaum, 1983; Young, Rich, & Fowler, 1984) have proven incorrect a number of commonly held beliefs about double suicide. We have learned, for example, that double suicides are rare. Cohen uncovered only 65 cases of double suicide in England and Wales between 1955 and 1958. Also, the stereotypical "Romeo and Juliet" syndrome of young lovers committing suicide in response to opposition to their relationship was found to be unusual. Such a scenario occurred in only 10% of Cohen's cases. Cohen's findings showed the prototypic double suicide to involve an older married couple.

Research has shown that couples who commit suicide manifest many of the characteristics associated with elderly suicide in general. At least one member is very likely to be depressed, alcoholic, or physically ill, to have a history of suicidality, and to have experienced an early loss due to suicide. Also, contrary to popular belief, elderly couples often communicate their suicide intent to others. Their suicidal ideation is not the carefully guarded "grim secret" of the commonly held stereotype about suicide pacts (Young, Rich, & Fowler, 1984).

There seems to be "special chemistry" between couples who commit suicide together. Typically, the more suicidal partner tends to be dominant and the more ambivalent partner tends to be passive in the relationship. This type of relationship has been described as "lock and key" pathology, where the interactive characteristics of the couple tend to increase the likelihood of suicide occurring (Santy, 1982).

Older couples who commit double suicide manifest other contributing characteristics. Their personalities tend to interact in ways that increase each member's depression and lower his or her self-esteem. This probably accounts at least in part for the fact that double suicide attempts are generally fatal. If one partner does survive, however, it is more likely to be the cooperating, less dominant individual (usually the female). Couples involved in double suicides tend to be interdependent and isolated from other sources of support (Mehta, Mathew, & Mehta, 1978; Young, Rich, & Fowler, 1984).

After reviewing a number of double suicide cases, Rosenbaum (1983) was impressed with the similarity between double suicides and cases of homicide/suicide. For example, the homicide/suicide perpetrator is often a depressed male with a history of suicide attempts, as is often the case in double suicides. Rosenbaum has speculated that the dominant partner in double suicides may harbor a great deal of hostility for the cooperative spouse, thus giving the suicide a homicidal flavor. Rosenbaum's work with surviving (cooperating) partners of double suicides has uncovered a rather common scenario in which the cooperating partner (usually the wife) "goes along with it" partly because of guilt over wishes that the dominant partner would die.

The End—Old Man with a Rope II, Käthe Kollwitz, 1925. Woodcut, 12 × 5 in. (National Gallery of Art, Washington, D.C., Rosenwald Collection.)

Homicide/suicide scenarios are not the exclusive domain of adult male/ female relationships. For example, recent news reports have provided extensive coverage of a university-related homicide/suicide in a dormitory in which one female student stabbed her roommate to death and then hanged herself (Rosenberg, 1995).

Not all double suicides involve intense pathology with homicidal and suicidal elements. There are examples of double suicides that are relatively rational, reflecting realistic appraisal of present and future life circumstances, as in the following news story:

> *Highland Park, Texas (The Associated Press)—after a loving 50-year marriage and successful medical careers, Don and Betty Morris couldn't bear the thought of someday being separated or finishing out their lives in a nursing home.*
>
> *So the couple, both 76, indulged in scrambled eggs with cheese, lots of bacon, ice cream and corn chips—all of which they had been forbidden to eat. They sipped their favorite sherry and drank lethal doses of a depressant, then lay down in each other's arms until the poison took effect.*
>
> *"The two of them together could function well, but not alone. If Dad had another heart attack, that would have put Mom in a nursing home. They didn't want that. They had seen too many friends who had been placed in nursing homes," said Don Morris, Jr., 49, one of the couple's three surviving children.*
>
> *The elderly Morris, a semiretired psychiatrist, and his wife, a retired psychologist, were found dead in their bedroom July 14 by police after the Southwestern Medical School in Dallas, where Morris was a faculty member, received a letter from them describing their suicide.*
>
> *A pair of suicide notes was found in the couple's bedroom, along with a menu of the couple's last meal and a list of poems reflecting on death.*
>
> *"The problem of many deteriorating old people is obviously a new one— everybody used to die too soon," Morris said in his note. "Therefore, as a society we have not learned to deal with it in a decent and respectable manner."*
>
> *The Morris's children said their parents told them they would eventually commit suicide. But in his suicide note, Morris said he regretted taking his life "surreptitiously . . . under cover of darkness"* (Asheville Citizen, *July 28, 1986, page 2*).

This news story reflects many of the characteristics shown to be associated with double suicide among the elderly. Both the husband and wife were retired and surely less occupied than during their previous professional careers. They were quite interdependent, and both feared the prospect of coping alone. The husband had suffered debilitating heart attacks and the wife was in very poor health. Also, as is often the case in double suicides, the couple had previously communicated their suicide intent to family members.

The suicide note left by the Morris's underscores the debate now beginning to gather force in this country concerning physician-assisted suicide and euthanasia, a debate we will explore fully in chapter 10.

SUMMARY

Suicide statistics for the elderly reflect the fact that this group is greatly at risk. The elderly have the highest suicide rate of any age group. More than 6,000 people over the age of 65 killed themselves during 1992. Elderly people are strongly committed to suicide once a self-destructive decision has been made. The old do not make suicidal gestures; their ratio of suicide completions to attempts is the highest of any age group.

Elderly suicide is very much a white male phenomenon. Elderly African American males and elderly females of all racial and ethnic groups have low suicide rates. Although the incidence of suicide among elderly white males has declined during the past 60 years, this group continues to have the highest rate of all. It is generally believed that the decline in elderly suicide is caused primarily by the fact that the present dominant generation of elders, the GIs, are the healthiest, wealthiest, and happiest group of retirees in history. In spite of the long-term reduction in elderly suicide, the suicide rate for this group has gradually increased since 1981. Also, even if suicide rates do not continue to climb, the huge generation of Boomers that will move into old age in the 21st century is likely to inflate the elderly suicide numbers.

Many of the risk factors for elderly suicide are related to the losses that are an inevitable part of aging. Important biological losses include physical and organic mental decline, chronic illness, and chronic pain. Also, declining neurotransmitter effectiveness in later years may enhance the depression that is naturally a part of these physical losses. Elderly people often experience loneliness, despair, and poverty within the context of retirement and widowhood. The cumulative losses of old age may be especially problematic for elderly people who engage in various forms of substance abuse or whose personality characteristics predispose them to cope less well with the problems of aging. An important cognitive risk factor for elderly suicide is an attitudinal shift that frequently occurs in this age group toward a growing acceptance of death as appropriate and timely.

Double suicides, although rare, occur more often among elderly couples than among any other group. Double suicide is more likely to occur among couples who are highly interdependent and isolated from sources of social support and when the dominant partner is physically ill, depressed, and suicidal. There is also some evidence that old people, like their adolescent counterparts, may be more susceptible to the modeling of suicide than young and middle adults.

8

Suicide Prevention and Postvention

The man, who in a fit of melancholy, kills himself today, would have wished to live had he waited a week.

Voltaire, "Cato," Philosophical Dictionary, 1764

In previous chapters, we have emphasized the complexity and interaction of risk factors feeding into suicide across the life span. This complexity, which often frustrates those who want a simple model for predicting suicide, may become an asset when considering suicide prevention since it provides multiple points that care givers can use to begin to intervene in the suicide trajectory. Some suicidologists (O'Carroll, 1993) believe that suicide prevention can best be accomplished by examining the multiple causes of suicide and finding ways to intervene and change one or more of these so as to decrease the probability of immediate suicide and increase the time available for working with suicidal people. Let us examine one example of suicide to see where suicide prevention techniques might have made a difference.

Carl N. was 46 years old when he took his life by shooting himself in the head. He was the fourth of six children born to a poor family in the Appalachian mountains. His father was one of the last of the mountaineers who bragged that he could live off the land. Carl's father raised cash for his family by making moonshine and sampled his product on a regular basis. When he was drinking, he often became verbally and physically abusive to his wife and children. Carl helped out at the still beginning at an early age and was a handy target for the abuse. He viewed his father with a mixture of admiration and contempt and was both pleased and honestly sorry when one evening his father, driving at a high rate of speed, crashed into a tree, killing himself at age 39. At the impressionable age of ten, Carl attended his father's funeral and heard friends and relatives assuring his mother that the family would be "better off" without his father and that his father was "born to die young" and "a born loser."

Carl dropped out of school in the middle of the eighth grade when he reached the age of 15. He drifted from one minimum wage job to the next and found his greatest pleasure in "hanging out" with a group of young men who prided themselves on their fast cars and their ability to drink. When he was twenty, he met and married a 15-year-old girl, Nona, from a neighboring town. Carl and Nona had three children in rapid succession and the responsibility of fatherhood inspired Carl to find work outside the geographic region. He moved his family to Washington, D.C., where he found work with a landscaping company. He was known as a hard worker and was rewarded with salary increases across a three-year period. As he made friends in the area, Carl's old drinking *habits returned. Over the next two years, his drinking increased, causing him to become less reliable on the job. After several warnings, Carl was fired. He moved his wife and family back to the mountains where his wife found steady work, becoming the primary breadwinner for the family. This left Carl free to spend most of his time drinking and hanging out with his old friends. Arguments between Carl and his wife accelerated into violent fights and Carl was arrested for spouse abuse. His wife filed for divorce and moved the children to a different house. Carl found them, broke into the house and beat his wife, and his oldest son when he tried to stop Carl from hitting his mother. Once again, the police arrested Carl and this time he was given a six-month sentence in the county jail.*

While serving his time, Carl became acquainted with three younger men who had a history of petty thievery. When he was released from jail, he became the older brother to this group, urging them on to bigger and more lucrative crimes. Inevitably, the group was caught in an armed robbery of a bank in a nearby town. They were all sentenced to prison. The younger men were released within four years for good behavior but Carl was considered to be a violent prisoner and he served a full ten-year sentence. When he was released, he spent several months tracking down Nona and his children (now nearly grown). He found that Nona had remarried and that his children now viewed her second husband as their father. None of them wanted to see him and the oldest son made it clear that he would defend the family from Carl with violence if necessary. Carl reacted characteristically. He went on a drinking spree at a local bar, where he became violent and assaulted several customers and the bartender. Before the police arrived, Carl ran from the bar. He spent the next few days hiding and thinking about his life. Fearing that he would most likely go back to jail, Carl procured a gun. He left a short suicide note, that read, "I failed at everything. Just like Pa. I won't go back to jail. Carl."

When and how could this suicide have been prevented? What if Carl's father had not been a bootlegger, drinker, and abuser? What if Carl had not been introduced to liquor in his formative years? What if Carl had found schooling more relevant and had graduated from high school, or gone on to college? What if Carl's children had not been born so close together? What if Carl had fulfilled his early promise on the job in Washington? What if, on return to the mountains, he had quit drinking and developed a career instead of relying on Nona to be the chief breadwinner? What if he had been loving instead of violent to his family? What if he had never served time in prison? What if, after meeting the young criminals, he had used his persuasive "older

---

The difficulty in life is the choice. George Moore, *The Bending of the Bough*

brother" status to develop a small business with them? What if in prison he had used his time to learn new ways of behaving and reacting? Was Carl's suicide inevitable? What could have been done at what point that might have made a difference in what appears in retrospect to be a lifelong suicide trajectory?

There are many points at which Carl's suicidal history might have been changed. Some of them, more general in nature, had to do with the poverty and violence into which he was born, the value he placed on gaining an education, his upbringing in his family, his failure experiences at work and in relationships, and the type of environment he encountered in prison. These factors form the backdrop for a suicidal career. In order to prevent suicides like Carl's in the future, the suicidogenic factors within a society must be studied.

There are three levels of suicide prevention: *primary* prevention, which involves family, school and society; *secondary* prevention, which consists of intervention and treatment of overtly suicidal individuals; and *tertiary* prevention, sometimes called *postvention*, which consists of work with individual survivors of suicide, with the family and friends of suicides, and with groups of survivors of suicide. This chapter will examine only primary prevention and postvention. Secondary prevention will be addressed in chapter 9.

Primary prevention of suicide consists of actions that can be taken to improve the cultural and/or social conditions that lead to suicide. In order to develop programs for the primary prevention of suicide, the role of society in shaping the ways in which individuals view suicidal behavior and the ways in which society might lessen suicidal risk must be understood. We will begin by reviewing what is known about how people in our society in the closing years of the 20th century view suicide.[1] Because gender differences in suicidal behavior are nearly universal, we will pay special attention to gender differences in attitudes toward suicide and suggest some ways in which socialization practices might be changed to help people view suicide in a healthier manner. We will then turn our attention to specific socializing agencies in our culture and examine what is happening in suicide prevention in families as well as in the nation's schools and colleges. In addition, we will review special task force reports and their implications for changes in the larger society that could reduce the rates of suicide. Finally, we will examine postvention, the treatment of survivors of suicide, as a special case of suicide prevention.

EXAMINING SUICIDAL ATTITUDES

There can be little doubt that suicide is an individual act embedded within a cultural reality at a given point in history; that is, while individuals

---

[1] This section is based on a presentation by the first author to the American Association of Suicidology in 1994.

take their own lives, they do not do so in a vacuum. They do so within a society that makes certain assumptions about and holds specific attitudes toward suicidal behavior. These assumptions and attitudes form the backdrop for individual suicidal behavior; therefore, the study of attitudes toward suicide among the total population as well as differences in the ways people respond by sex and by age becomes necessary before a full understanding of suicide prevention can occur.

One of the earliest findings noted in attitudes toward suicidal behavior was a difference in the way people view attempted and completed suicide. Two early studies that attempted to probe this difference were conducted by Linehan (1971, 1973). She utilized the semantic differential (Osgood, Suci, & Tannenbaum, 1969) to determine how female and male college students viewed attempted versus completed suicide. She concluded that "both males and females who commit suicide were rated as more masculine and more potent than males and females who attempt suicide" (Linehan, 1973, p. 33). This research remains an intriguing finding in the literature in that it suggests that if attempted suicide is viewed as weaker and less masculine, males would be more likely to structure any suicide attempt in such a way as to reduce the likelihood of surviving, while females would feel less stigma from surviving an attempt and might, therefore, be more likely to engage in less lethal suicidal actions. It is interesting to note that sex differences in suicidal behavior are consistent with this suggestion. Females do indeed attempt suicide four times more frequently than males, while males succeed in killing themselves four times more frequently than females.

Studies Using the Suicide Attitude Vignette Experience (SAVE) Scales

Several studies have attempted to examine gender differences in attitudes toward suicide directly. Since the early 1980s, the authors of the present volume have directed a group of researchers who have been examining responses to male and female target figures in normed sets of vignettes called the Suicide Attitude Vignette Experience-Adolescent form (SAVE-A) (Stillion, McDowell, & May, 1984; Stillion, McDowell, & Shamblin, 1984; Stillion, McDowell, Smith, & McCoy, 1986; Stillion, White, McDowell, & Edwards, 1989; White & Stillion, 1988). In these studies, high school and college students were asked to indicate their level of sympathy, empathy, and agreement with the suicidal behavior described in ten vignettes. Each vignette focused on a troubled teenager who attempted suicide because of different situational factors ranging from failure on a college entrance examination to lack of acceptance by peers to coping with terminal illness. The situations in the vignettes were based on conditions surrounding attempted suicide as described in the literature.

In the original study (Stillion, McDowell, & Shamblin, 1984), 104 males and 94 females who were enrolled in the 12th grade of a southern public high school responded to the vignette scale and several other measures. Factor analysis of the scale showed three separate factors that accounted for 91% of the variance in the responses: sympathy, empathy, and agreement. Test-retest reliability checks given approximately four weeks after the first administration yielded coefficients for each factor that were significant at the .001 level. The instrument also showed high levels of internal consistency as measured by Cronbach's alpha. The instrument seemed to have sufficient validity and reliability to be of use in research. Measures of convergent-discriminant validity included ratings of self-esteem, religiosity, depression, and suicide proneness. Students who sympathized more with suicidal actions showed more death concern, were more depressed, and had higher self-esteem than students who were less sympathetic. Students who agreed with the suicidal actions depicted in the vignettes were more depressed and tended to have lower self-esteem than those who agreed less often with suicidal behaviors. Also, students who described themselves as high in religiosity agreed significantly less with all motivations for suicide than those who had lower religiosity self-ratings.

The original study revealed that female respondents showed significantly higher levels of sympathy than males did. In addition, they sympathized, empathized, and agreed more with female target figures than they did with male target figures. The authors suggested that "it may be that females expect more sympathy and empathy than do males and, therefore, feel less restraint in attempting to end their lives. Males, on the other hand, may expect less environmental support after an attempt, thereby increasing their determination to succeed if suicide is attempted" (Stillion, McDowell, & Shamblin, 1984, p. 75).

A second study (Stillion, McDowell, & May, 1984) carried out with 386 participants was designed to examine developmental differences in attitudes toward suicide among 9th graders, 12th graders, and freshman college students. It used the SAVE-A scale with each group. The results indicated that older adolescents of both genders tended to agree less with motivations for suicide than younger adolescents did. Once again, females in all three age groups sympathized more than males with suicidal target figures. The authors interpreted the findings from a cognitive development perspective, concluding that older students, who were more practiced in formal-operations-level thinking, better understood the finality of death and were therefore less likely to romanticize suicide.

In an attempt to examine that conclusion more closely, a third study was done with academically gifted and nongifted adolescents (Stillion, McDowell, & May, 1984). Subjects were 190 ninth grade students (75 males and 115 females). Forty-eight of the participants were academically gifted students participating in a four-week summer enrichment experience on a college campus, 36 were gifted students enrolled in the public schools of a small southern town, and 106 students were nongifted students enrolled in the same schools. The results indicated once again that adolescent females sympathized more with all reasons for suicide than adolescent males did. They also showed that adolescent females who scored higher on IQ tests agreed less with all reasons for suicide than those who scored lower on IQ tests, thus partially supporting the cognitive development interpretation.

Two additional studies using the SAVE-A scale examined the relationship between mental health indicators and attitudes toward suicide and were reported in a single publication. The first compared attitudes toward suicide in a group of 15- to 24-year-olds admitted to a private psychiatric hospital during an eight-month period with the attitudes of a group of college students (Stillion, McDowell, Smith, & McCoy, 1986). Results showed that institutionalized females agreed more with all motivations for suicide portrayed in the vignettes than did noninstitutionalized females and institutionalized and noninstitutionalized males. The second study utilized two measures of positive mental health; the Personal Orientation Inventory (POI), which is based on a theory of self-actualization, and the Personal Attributes Questionnaire (PAQ), which is based on the assumption that androgynous people (i.e., those who combine the best of masculine and feminine traits) are better adjusted than those who manifest only strong stereotypic masculine or feminine traits. This study showed that students who scored higher on one measure of self-actualization (inner-directedness) sympathized, empathized, and agreed less with all reasons for suicide than did students who scored lower on the same measure. Furthermore, students who evidenced a more feminine sex-role orientation, as measured by the Personal Attributes Questionnaire, showed greater sympathy with all reasons for suicide while individuals with more masculine sex-role orientations showed less sympathy. The suggestions from these two studies were that (1) better adjusted people agree less often with suicide than those who are more disturbed, and (2) stereotypical female traits result in persons' sympathizing more with suicidal target figures.

Another study in this series was an attempt to scrutinize more closely the statistically significant difference between males and females on sympathy (White & Stillion, 1988). All earlier research using the SAVE scale had indicated that females sympathize more with suicidal figures than do males. The authors were interested in examining whether this gender difference would hold up when males and females reacted to nonsuicidal as well as suicidal target figures. Male and female college students responded to cases of troubled adolescents taken from the SAVE-A scale. The sex of the target figures was varied as usual. The new variation introduced was to delete the reference to attempted suicide on half of the vignettes. Female subjects once again gave more sympathy than did male subjects to both suicidal and nonsuicidal target figures. Also, nonsuicidal targets received more sympathy than did suicidal ones. In addition, there was a significant interaction between sex of target figure, gender of respondent, and the vignette condition (suicide attempt or no suicide attempt). Further analysis indicated that female respondents' ratings were virtually identical in all conditions; specifically, the average score for females was nearly identical in each of the four suicides by sex of adolescent conditions. A separate analysis of variance (ANOVA) for female subjects indicated that there were no significant main effects or interactions. For male respondents, however, both the main effect of suicidal condition and the interaction effect between the suicide condition and the sex of adolescents were significant. Males gave least sympathy to suicidal males and most sympathy to nonsuicidal males. On the empathy scale, again there were no significant findings for females, but males empathized most with nonsuicidal males. The authors concluded that the study had "found support for a generalized tendency on the part of women to be more sympathetic, regardless of the situation" (p. 364). However, of much more importance was the finding that males reported more sympathy and empathy with troubled males who did not attempt suicide than with females in either condition or males who attempted suicide. The low levels of sympathy and empathy given by males to males who attempted suicide seemed to support the hypothesis that males stigmatize other males who attempt suicide.

A final study in this series introduced a second form of the SAVE Scale to be used to assess attitudes toward elderly suicide (Stillion, White, McDowell, & Edwards, 1989). Called the Suicide Attitude Vignette Experience-Elderly (SAVE-L) form, this instrument contained 16 vignettes written about elderly people in specific situations who attempted suicide. The instrument was normed utilizing samples of college students and retired elderly in a rural area of North Carolina. A factor analysis of the SAVE-L scale yielded the same three factors as the SAVE-A scale: sympathy, empathy, and agreement. These three factors accounted for 55% of the variance. The internal consistency of the SAVE-L scale was .96 for sympathy, .95 for empathy, and .89 for agreement. "The most striking result was that old female target figures received less sympathy than young female target figures, who in turn received more sympathy than either young males or old ones" (p. 252). Similarly, on the empathy scales young respondents empathized least with old female targets and most with young female targets. Only elderly females empathized more with elderly female targets than they did with any other group. On the agreement scale, both young and old respondents of each gender were more likely to agree with decisions to attempt suicide when they were made by old females than when they were made by any other target figure. Young male respondents were more likely to agree with the suicide decisions of all targets than were the other three respondent groups, although the difference was not statistically significant. The authors concluded their discussion of these findings by noting that attempts to measure attitudes toward suicide are incomplete unless the age and sex of both the attempter and the respondent are taken into consideration.

As the 1990s began, Stillion and associates realized that reliance on vignettes alone to assess attitudes toward suicide was no longer enough. Vignettes can tap how respondents view suicidal people within given settings but they tell us little about other aspects of attitudes toward suicide. Attitudes are generally complex entities made up of cognitive understanding, feelings, beliefs, and behaviors. It is important, therefore, that a measuring instrument tap all of those aspects of attitudes as well as assess the way in which specific suicidal figures are viewed. Accordingly, a new instrument, the Multidimensional Suicide Attitude Scale (MSAS), was developed and normed in 1994. The scale, as conceptualized, consisted of seven subscales measuring knowledge about suicide, feelings about suicide, behaviors engaged in with reference to suicide, beliefs about suicide, and three sets of vignettes presenting suicidal target figures who differ by age (e.g., adolescent and young adult figures, middle-aged figures, and elderly figures). The scale was developed by reviewing all questions used in published research on attitudes toward suicide. The first draft of the scale was sent to more than 20 figures nationally known in the area of suicide and in clinical work with suicidal people or survivors of suicide. Their comments were incorporated into the scales that formed the final version used in the norming sample (Miller, 1994).

The MSAS was administered to 120 male and 142 female undergraduate students enrolled in introductory psychology classes at a university in North Carolina. The subjects ranged in age from 18 to 52 years ($M = 19.9$). The study found excellent reliability (ranging from the high .70s to the low .90s) for all of the MSAS subscales except one, the Knowledge scale. Because of the Knowledge subscale's low internal consistency, it was excluded from further statistical analyses. We computed factor analyses for each of the remaining six subscales. Each of the three vignette scales yielded three interpretable factors: sympathy, agreement, and probability. However, weightings of factors on the SAVE-L scale were sufficiently different to suggest that suicide among the elderly is viewed differently from suicide among younger groups (i.e., elderly suicide is seen as more rational and acceptable and as having a higher probability for respondents than are suicides in the two younger groups).

The results of the factor analyses of the three remaining subscales supported the contention that attitudes toward suicide are complex and must be studied within a multidimensional framework. The Feelings subscale consisted of four factors, indicating that when respondents think about suicide they experience (1) negative emotions such as anger, disgust, and anxiety; (2) positive emotions such as empathy, understanding, and compassion; (3) low mood states including depression, sadness, and fear; and (4) feelings of hopelessness and powerlessness. The Behavior subscale was composed of the following three factors: (1) personal, active involvement with suicide including making plans or attempts to kill oneself; (2) active but less personal involvement, including such items as taking a course or attending meetings dealing with suicide; and (3) behaviors leading to less personal, more passive understanding of suicide, such as reading about suicide or watching a TV or movie about suicide. The Beliefs subscale consisted of five interpretable factors: (1) suicide is justified under certain circumstances, (2) suicide is a sign of strength, (3) suicide is wrong, (4) suicide is a weak or selfish act, and (5) suicide carries with it a social stigma.

Several sex differences emerged in this normative study. For example, on the Feelings subscale, females expressed significantly higher levels of depression, sadness, powerlessness, hopelessness, fear, concern, and upset when they thought about suicide than did males. On the Behavior subscale, females were more likely than males to have read a book about someone's suicide and to have associated with at least one person who was suicidal while males were more likely than females to have made specific plans to kill themselves in the past. The Beliefs subscale indicated that males, more than females, believed that suicide is justified in certain circumstances. In addition, males endorsed the idea that people who attempt suicide are courageous, that physically handicapped and elderly people have the right to take their own lives, that it is honorable to kill oneself to protect one's family from disgrace, and so forth. It is clear from these findings that males, more than females, believe that suicide is a potential solution to a problem situation.

Age of the target figures in the vignettes also made a difference in the way people responded. For example, elderly target figures received more sympathy from respondents than any other age group. Suicide was also viewed as being a more rational and acceptable choice for elderly target figures. Although the statistical analyses were complicated and need to be replicated with other groups, preliminary findings from this norming study suggest that the act of suicide may be viewed by others as a qualitatively different act when carried out by elderly people than when carried out by younger people.

The authors concluded that the MSAS, with the exception of the knowledge subscale, has promise as a research tool. The entire study supported the observation that measuring attitudes toward suicide is a complex act that must take into account the age and sex of the respondents and of the suicidal target figures as well as the feelings, beliefs, and past behaviors of respondents.

Studies Using the Suicide Opinion Questionnaire (SOQ)

At the same time that the original SAVE scales were being developed in the early 1980s, an approach to assessing attitudes toward suicidal behavior was formulated by Domino and his associates. Called the Suicide Opinion

Questionnaire (SOQ), it has generated a series of studies on many aspects of attitudes toward suicide (e.g., Domino, 1990; Domino, Domino, & Berry, 1986-87; Domino, MacGregor, & Hannah, 1989; Domino, Moore, West-lake, & Gibson, 1982; Domino & Swain, 1986; Limbacher & Domino, 1985-86; Swain & Domino, 1985). The original SOQ was a 100-item questionnaire derived empirically from a set of 3,000 items written after reviewing the literature. The authors maintain that one-third of the items reflect factual knowledge of suicide while two-thirds measure attitudes toward suicide (Limbacher & Domino, 1985-86). The scale is statistically complex, resulting in as many as 15 factors, which in the original study accounted for 76.7% of the total variance (Domino, Moore, Westlake, & Gibson, 1982). However, later studies have shown different factors emerging with different populations; for example, 10 factors emerged in a study of college students (Limbacher & Domino, 1986), and 15 slightly different factors accounting for only 53.1% of the variance were identified with a sample of professionals (Swain & Domino, 1985). The researchers have also used a shortened form of the questionnaire with adolescent participants, (Domino, Domino, & Berry, 1986-87), and have used a cluster analysis technique to derive "clinical scales" (Domino, Mac-Gregor, & Hannah, 1989).

One study using the SOQ was designed to measure the responses of a large sample (N = 738) of college students who were divided into three groups: attempters, contemplators, and nonattempters (Limbacher & Domino, 1986). Using discriminant analysis, this study found that female attempters, contemplators, and nonattempters were less accepting of suicide than males in these groups. Females were also less likely than males to believe that suicide is an impulsive act and "to believe that attempters are not mentally ill" (p. 320). The authors concluded that the most noticeable difference between males and females was that males found suicide more acceptable than did females. However, if one examines the factor labeled "acceptability" in this study it appears to be made up, at least partially, of items that tap the acceptability of suicide in specific situations, such as "Suicide is an acceptable means to end an incurable illness" and "Suicide is acceptable for aged and infirm persons." Given the pressure on contemporary males to be rational problem-solvers, this gender difference may reflect a greater acceptance of suicide based on the inevitability of death in the situation described rather than a greater generalized acceptance of suicide. Therefore, the most accurate conclusion that can be drawn about gender differences in this study on the basis of the published research appears to be that males, when confronted with insoluble situations, approve of suicide as an option more often than females.

DeRose and Page (1985) used the SOQ to measure attitudes of professional and community groups toward male and female suicide. They were interested in examining whether knowledge and attitudes toward suicide differed by occupational groups, and also in discovering whether these groups had different standards or conceptions about mental health as revealed in suicidal behavior for females and males. The researchers revised the questionnaire to make 76 of the 100 items applicable either to males or to females. Their sample consisted of 168 volunteers representing psychology, social work, and nursing, and a comparison group of mixed occupations. Half of each responding group received the questionnaire with male target figures and half received the questionnaire with female target figures. When data were collapsed across occupational groups, the authors reported that significant gender differences emerged on 22 items. Among them were the following: female targets were viewed as more likely to commit suicide as a form of self-punishment, more likely to consider suicide as a response to failed relationships, less likely to be held responsible for suicide as a response to personal or professional embarrassment, less likely to undertake lethal attempts, less likely to use a gun or rifle, and less likely to attempt heroic suicide.

The authors also found support in some professional groups for the idea that females are more likely to give warning signs, to be referred to therapy, and to be recognized as potentially suicidal when the risk was high. They observed that "suicide was seen as a more frequently expected, perhaps less catastrophic option for females as an 'escape from life's problems' whereas such was less true when the item referred to a male target person" (p. 60). Suicide among males was more often tied to a nation's problems and viewed as being more puzzling since "they have everything to live for." The authors concluded that "in general, the results, in our opinion, appeared consistent with the prevalent gender role stereotype of the male as normative, i.e., as having, in essence, 'more to live for' than the female, but also as subject to relatively greater responsibilities or problems in life" (p. 60).

Studies Using Non-Normed Instruments

Other researchers have used non-normed instruments in attempts to understand attitudes toward suicide in various groups. For example, a group of investigators formulated a 51-item questionnaire to "measure participants' knowledge of facts about suicide; their attitudes toward and feelings about suicide; and their own suicide ideation, behavior, and contact with others who had attempted or completed suicide" (Wellman & Wellman, 1986, p. 363). They carried out two studies that included a total of 1157 students enrolled in an urban New England college. The authors found that females and males differed on the following dimensions: Female respondents reported a greater willingness than male subjects to talk to a suicidal person about their feelings and to make a suicide prevention effort. Male respondents reported that they would avoid discussing suicide with anyone at risk for fear that such action might precipitate suicide. Males also denied that people show warning symptoms and seemed to think, more often than females, that suicide was situational and impulsive. Male attitudes toward suicidal individuals were "more harsh" than were females' attitudes and they believed more often than females that suicidal adolescents were mostly of low socioeconomic status. Males also tended to deny the facts about suicide more than females by underestimating the incidence of suicide and by interpreting friends' suicide threats as "joking." Males, more than females, also reported beliefs that suicidal persons commit suicide after serious adverse events, and that anyone has the right to commit suicide.

In a slightly different approach, Marks (1989) asked the following six questions, most worded as statements, in a telephone survey of 491 adults in Arkansas:

A person has the right to take [his or her] own life?
A normal person would not commit suicide?
People who commit suicide are acting immorally?
Normal people do not think about committing suicide?
People who commit suicide are mentally ill?
Do you know anyone who either killed [himself or herself] or tried to kill [himself or herself]? (p. 330)

Marks found that although only 21% of his sample agreed with the statement, "A person has the right to take their own life," females were significantly less likely to agree with it than males. Females were significantly more likely than males to believe that a "normal" person would commit suicide.

Sawyer and Sobal (1987) analyzed public attitudes toward suicide by examining data from the National Opinion Research Center's (NORC) probability sample of 1982. They found that almost half (45.9%) of the respondents approved of suicide "in the case of an incurable disease" while less than 15% approved when the person was "tired of living and ready to die" and/or when the person had "dishonored his/her family" or "gone bankrupt" (p. 93). In this sample, women were more opposed than men to suicide. The study also showed geographic, socioeconomic, political, and religious differences in attitudes toward suicide. For example, nonwhites and rural residents as well as those living in central and southern states showed greater opposition to suicide than did whites, urban residents, and residents of the northeast and far west. In addition, frequent church attenders, strong Democrats, low socioeconomic respondents, and the elderly also showed higher opposition to suicide. This research lent strong support to the idea that assessing suicide attitudes is an extremely complex endeavor.

Deluty (1989) attempted to assess attitudes toward suicide using a non-normed scenario approach. He was interested in assessing attitudes as a function of the age and sex of the suicide victim, the gender of the evaluator, and the type of illness that precipitated the suicide. He used 12 scenarios, or vignettes, in which the age and gender as well as the type of illness of the victim were varied. The subjects were 780 undergraduate psychology students enrolled in the University of Maryland. Deluty divided his respondents into 12 groups of 65 subjects (40 females and 25 males). Each group received one version of a scenario that varied from other versions by gender, age (45 or 70), and type of illness (severe depression, severe physical pain, or malignant bone cancer) of the target figure. Each scenario ended with the sentence, "Jane (John) has decided to kill herself." The subjects responded to the vignette by utilizing a semantic differential technique (Osgood, Suci, & Tannenbaum, 1969) that included six bipolar adjective pairs: wise-foolish, selfish-unselfish, weak-strong, active-passive; right-wrong, and brave-cowardly. In addition, subjects were asked to indicate whether the target figure should be permitted to kill herself or himself and whether the decision to kill herself or himself was acceptable to them. Finally, subjects were asked whether they would try to convince the target figures not to kill themselves and whether they thought the targets had the right to take their own lives.

Deluty found several significant effects based on gender. Suicides by females were rated "significantly more foolish, weaker, more wrong, and less permissible than suicides by males" (Deluty, 1989, p. 320). Female respondents rated suicides as significantly more foolish and wrong and less permissible and acceptable than did male subjects. Female respondents also replied affirmatively significantly more often than male subjects to the statement that they would try to convince their friend not to commit suicide. Finally, more female evaluators (30.4%) than male evaluators (14.1%) responding to the 70-year-old suicidal target figure agreed with the statement, "The subject has no right to take her life." Over 33% of the females and almost 32% of the males responding to 45-year-old target figures denied them that right. Clearly, female respondents were less affected than male respondents by the age of the suicidal target figures, and males tended to agree more often than females that elderly target figures had the right to take their own lives.

Deluty concluded his results section by stating that "participants who were male, who judged the elderly, or who judged males tended to give more favorable evaluations of suicide" (p. 322). He also noted that "suicide by females tended to be evaluated significantly more negatively than suicide by males" and that female evaluators "tended to be significantly more unaccepting of suicide than male evaluators" (p. 324). Deluty also noted that the study found support for the idea that the stated cause of the suicide affected the respondents' ratings since those who had malignant bone cancer and decided to kill themselves were rated more favorably than those who suffered from depression or chronic pain. Deluty's research supports the growing number of studies that have found that gender of respondent and gender of target figure as well as age and disease of target figure are important variables to be considered when conducting research on suicide attitudes.

Age and education level of respondents can also be important variables in the study of attitudes toward suicide. Kalish, Reynolds, and Farberow (1974) carried out hour-long interviews with a stratified random sample of 434 people that included equal numbers of males and females as well as equal numbers of African Americans and Americans of European descent. The authors of the study divided their respondents into three groups: 20- to 39-year-olds, 40- to 59-year-olds, and those 60 and older. They found that older men tended to believe that impairment in mental or physical health was a major factor influencing suicide, while younger men were more likely to believe that love and psychological stress were the primary factors. College graduates were more likely than noncollege graduates to describe suicide as occurring in reaction to stress and less likely to describe it as the result of insanity. Most people, regardless of age or sex, viewed people who threatened to commit suicide but did not make a serious attempt as "playing a game" or "calling for help." The least educated respondents reacted with anger to chronic threateners and indicated more frequently than all the other respondents that they should either be serious or stop pretending. More-educated respondents were more likely to call for professional help for chronic threateners. Older people and the less educated tended to view clergymen as more important sources of help than did younger and more educated people. All groups viewed suicide as being less tragic than accidents, homicide, and wartime killings. The authors of the study pointed out that the attitudes people have toward suicide attempters and completers are important variables, since they undoubtedly affect the incidence and sequelae of attempted suicide.

Another study that found important generational differences in attitudes toward suicide was conducted by Boldt (1982). Utilizing a sample of Canadian students enrolled in the 12th grade and their parents, Boldt found that the younger generation was consistently less judgmental about suicide and less stigmatizing than the older generation. The 12th graders tended to view suicidal individuals as victims of societal malfunction, while their parents were more likely to attribute suicidal behavior to individual failings. The younger generation was much more likely to see suicide as the prerogative of any "competent" individual. Also, the 12th graders were less inclined than their parents to view suicide in religious-moral terms or to assume related calamitous outcomes (e.g., hellfire). This study provided some evidence that younger people are more accepting of suicide than people in older generations.

Domino and Swain (1985-86) conducted a study concerning the attitudes of health professionals toward suicide and suicide victims. A convenience sample of 128 health professionals and clergy in the Tucson, Arizona, area was asked to complete a scale designed to measure opinions about suicide and a scale designed to measure their ability to identify factors that contribute to the lethality of suicidal behavior. The study revealed that clergy differed significantly from all other helping professionals in finding suicide not acceptable. Physicians, however, found suicide significantly less acceptable than did social workers, and compared with psychologists, they were more likely to describe suicide attempts as resulting from manipulation motives. The authors of the study also found the following:

> *Professionals who are more knowledgeable about lethality of suicide are less likely to impute a self-destructive drive or mental instability to suicide attempts, . . . more likely to see suicide as a reaction to a harsh world, [to] see the elderly at greater risk, [to] have a less fatalistic outlook, and [to] see suicide attempts more as a "cry for help." (Swain & Domino, 1985, p. 446)*

Their most important conclusion was that attitudes toward suicide are complex and difficult to measure.

Conclusion from Research on Suicide Attitudes

In spite of the complexities surrounding assessment of suicide attitudes, several consistent findings that reflect gender role differences seem to be emerging. First, females seem to know more factual information about suicide than males do (Wellman & Wellman, 1986). Females may thus be in a better position than males to recognize when friends or acquaintances are considering engaging in suicidal behavior. Second, Wellman and Wellman (1986) found that females seem more willing to discuss the subject of suicide with suicidal people. This suggests that females are more likely than males to be effective both in crisis intervention and in peer counseling programs. It may also suggest that females may require less training than males to serve in those programs since both their baseline knowledge and their inclination to discuss the topic are at higher levels than those of males.

Third, Stillion and associates have repeatedly found that females report more sympathy for suicidal target figures (Stillion, McDowell, & May, 1984; Stillion, McDowell, & Shamblin, 1984; Stillion, McDowell, Smith, & McCoy, 1986; White & Stillion, 1988; Stillion, White, McDowell, & Edwards, 1989). Because they are able to express higher levels of sympathy toward individuals who are considering suicide, females may also be more supportive than males would be in real-life situations involving suicide threats, gestures, and attempts. If so, this would again argue for the use of females in peer counseling and crisis intervention situations. It may also mean that females are more likely than males to create suicidal conditions that they survive, since their expectations might be that they will receive support rather than censure.

Fourth, in spite of their greater sympathy toward those who attempt or complete suicide, females seem to disapprove of the act of suicide more often than males (Deluty, 1989; Miller, 1994). Perhaps females more than males have a general perceptual set to value life. Such a set would have species survival value since it is the female who must experience childbirth in order to give life to the next generation and who generally must play the major role in nurturing that life, at least in the early months and years. Therefore, females may have a keener appreciation for life and for the waste that death by suicide engenders. The National Center for Health Statistics has estimated that death by suicide accounted for 631,990 years of potential life lost in the year 1983, alone (Centers for Disease Control, 1986). While it is doubtful that most women respondents could cite this figure, they may have some understanding of the enormity of potential lost because of suicidal deaths. Males, conversely, may view death by suicide, especially the death of those who are old or terminally ill, as representing decisive action in the face of unchangeable fate (Limbacher & Domino, 1985-86). Therefore, rather than focusing on the waste involved in suicide, males may see it as a final problem-solving solution.

Fifth, the age of the target figure has been shown to be a direct factor that interacts with gender in determining suicide attitudes. While contradictory findings exist, it is becoming clearer that suicide by the elderly is viewed as a different kind of act than suicide among younger or middle aged people (Miller, 1994). Suicide by elderly persons is generally more accepted than suicide by younger people (Limbacher & Domino, 1986; Stillion, White, Mc-Dowell, & Edwards, 1989; Miller, 1994).

Sixth, males seem to accept suicide as an alternative in otherwise insoluble situations but they view other males who attempt suicide with less sympathy and empathy than they view the same troubled males who do not attempt suicide (White & Stillion, 1988). Attempted suicide, in general, appears to be viewed as weakness while completed suicide is viewed as strength. Perhaps this last observation sheds light on Carl's suicide. Carl, whose story was told earlier in this chapter, chose suicide in the recognition that he had failed at many things throughout his life and as a way of escaping an inevitable return to prison. While we can never be sure, it is possible that behind his choice of method was the understanding that an incomplete suicide attempt is a sign of further failure as well as of weakness while killing oneself in a violent manner is a sign of strength.

SUICIDE PREVENTION IN THE FAMILY

It is clear from suicide statistics in the United States that our society is failing to teach young people (especially young white males) how to cope in a healthy fashion with the stresses inherent in living in a complex technological society. While an in-depth discussion of general coping techniques is beyond the scope of this chapter, it is important to summarize what families can do to

Family Picture, **Max Beckman, 1920. Oil on canvas, 25⅜ × 39¾ in. (The Museum of Modern Art, New York.)**

"suicide proof" their children. Because sex differences in suicide and suicide attitudes are one of the most consistent realities in the literature about suicide, we will also examine traditional gender role socialization.

In general, parents should help their children to understand the problems involved in living and the inevitability of experiencing some failure, disappointment, and loss in life. Because caring adults want to protect children whenever possible from harsh realities, some children may come to adolescence with little expectation of encountering adversities in life and may therefore be unprepared to face such adversities. These children may overreact to failure or to conflict while children who are more adequately prepared might take such problems in stride. Conversely, some children born into turbulent homes or growing up in conditions of poverty may face severe problems before having an opportunity to learn how to cope. There is thus a need to teach healthy coping techniques to children from both extremes.

The way in which parents handle failure experiences is particularly crucial once children begin school. Parents need to help their children understand that failure should not be internalized. When children interpret failure in such a way that they denigrate themselves and weaken their own self-esteem, they are more likely to become depressed (Hafen & Frandsen, 1986). Parents who are interested in helping their children to develop positive coping techniques will teach them to view failure as a form of feedback that can lead to future success and to view disappointment as a temporary state that can, with effort and understanding, lead to greater accomplishment.

Second, parents should explore specific coping techniques with their young children. Such exploration might include an examination of the coping strategies their children use when they feel low. Children have an amazing number of coping skills that parents can help them to build upon if they know of their existence. An exercise conducted with a group of academically gifted ninth graders yielded no less than 23 coping mechanisms they employed to help themselves feel better. These mechanisms included exercising, eating, talking with friends, listening to music, writing out their feelings in diaries or in letters to friends, composing poetry, taking long walks, focusing on the pluses in their lives, and talking with parents, counselors, and other adults (Stillion, 1985b). It is important to help children understand that they already have a repertoire of coping techniques and, therefore, a base for developing stronger and more varied approaches to coping with stress.

Closely related to developing coping skills is the encouragement of humor among children. Home is the best place to learn to laugh and parents who interact with their children in play and laughter may well be providing inoculation against suicidal urges. As we have seen, suicidal ideation is deadly serious. People who can laugh at themselves and at many of life's problems can rarely sustain such negative thinking for very long. It is difficult to remain depressed if you can see humor in a situation. Young children generally appreciate humor. It is only as they grow older that they begin to lose their natural sense of laughter and play. Parents can help children greatly by setting aside some time for lighthearted play and by modeling for them an appreciation for humor.

Helping children and adolescents to set high but attainable goals for themselves is another technique that promotes coping. Historically, this technique has been shown to be associated with achievement in the classroom (Goode & Brophy, 1984). We think it is also a powerful deterrent to suicide. Long (1987) has identified variables important to a positive self-concept. The most important of these is competency, which he defines as "the development of skills and abilities which allow one to take charge" of one's life, work, relationships, and self (p. 16). Young people experience a wide gulf between who they are and who they want to become and are thus at risk for low self-esteem, self-hatred, depression, and suicidal behavior. Caring adults can encourage growing children to set short-range, realistic goals and can support them as

---

At the door of life, by the gate of breath, there are worse things waiting for men than death. Swinburne, *The Triumph of Time*

they work toward reaching these goals. Achievement enhances self-esteem and helps students appreciate their own worth and uniqueness. As students come to view themselves as increasingly competent, they will be less likely to develop on the negative end of Erikson's latency stage, with its extremes of industry versus inferiority. In this way, achievement and competence become two powerful tools of suicide prevention.

Finally, parents need to communicate to their growing children a sense of unconditional acceptance. If they do not get this at home, it is unlikely that they will ever experience it. Parents who are able to communicate a sense of cherishing each child's uniqueness give their children a powerful head start toward building a positive self-concept with high self-esteem. People who value themselves rarely kill themselves, so promotion of self-esteem may be a powerful tool in suicide proofing children (Stivers, 1991).

Other skills that can be taught to children to help them cope with stress include specific techniques such as systematic relaxation, imagery techniques, meditation, and positive self-talk. All such techniques help children attain control over stress, as well as arm them with behavioral choices other than giving in to depressed or suicidal feelings. In addition to general suicide-proofing of children, parents also need to be aware of the messages inherent in traditional gender role socialization that may impede males' and females' coping abilities.

Because sex differences are consistently found both in the rates of attempted and completed suicide and in attitudes toward suicide, we believe we should examine traditional gender role socialization to determine if there are implications for parents as they teach appropriate gender roles to their children.

GENDER ROLE IMPLICATIONS FOR FEMALES

Traditionally, the socialization of females has encouraged passivity, dependency, and inhibition of anger as well as nurturance and expressiveness (LeUnes, Nation, & Turley, 1980; Rosenthal, 1981; Stillion, 1985a; Suter, 1976; Whiting & Whiting, 1975). Of these traits, two may positively affect women's attitudes toward suicide. The first is emotional expressiveness. Because females are free to express their needs more openly than males, females can and do seek help more often than males do. For example, women are seen far more often than men by private doctors as well as in inpatient units of mental hospitals (Chesler, 1972; Gove & Tudor, 1973). The trait of emotional expressiveness may help to explain why women more often than men express sympathy toward suicidal figures. It may also have implications for the treatment of suicidal women in that they may seek help more often than men and at an earlier stage in the development of suicidal ideation. In addition, women may give themselves permission to plan less fatal suicide attempts than men do, using such attempts as another more serious form of expressing their need.

The second trait, nurturance, may also help explain the higher sympathy scores of females. Females may simply be more willing than males to reach out and nurture those who are considering suicidal behavior. The desire to nurture may also enable females to be more open than men to information about suicide and more willing to talk with those considering suicide.

Socialization toward passivity, conversely, may block troubled traditional females from exploring healthy coping skills in an active manner. Similarly, because of their socialization toward dependency, traditional females may not be able to find independent solutions to their troubled situations or to give themselves permission to leave those situations. Consequently, females may remain in problem situations, storing up their frustration and anger as they passively wait for change that does not come.

Pommereau, Delile, and Caule (1987) have endorsed this view of suicidal females by suggesting that attempted suicide in females may result from the desire to escape their life circumstances. "Many women under stress have a weaker intention to die, and their suicidal act is generally less a deliberate search for death than a desire to live another life, indicating a need to escape from a difficult situation" (p. 326). Utilizing the fairy tale of Snow White as an explanatory model, these authors suggested that suicidal females, rather than desiring to die, want to sleep through their troubles and awake to a new beginning. Their view supports the idea that females make less serious attempts than males at taking their own lives because they are less interested in dying than in calling attention to their plight in an attempt to secure help from someone outside their situation. This view of the suicidal female is widespread among practitioners who believe that females more often than males use suicidal behavior as "a cry for help" (Shneidman, Farberow, & Litman, 1961), and may account at least in part for the reason that females show greater overall sympathy with target figures who attempt suicide.

Pommereau, Delile, and Caule (1987) are among many writers who have recognized the power of fairy tales in creating expectations for girls and boys. For example, Bettelheim (1976) suggested that fairy tales influence the self-concepts of children at an early age, and followers of the therapeutic approach known as transactional analysis (TA) have suggested that fairy tales provide the scripts that many adults act out throughout their lives (Berne, 1964; Harris, 1969).

In addition to the tale of Snow White, there are other fairy tales that stress the twin themes of passivity and dependency in females. For example, the tale of Sleeping Beauty centers on a woman who sleeps for 100 years—an interesting form of simulated suicide. It is also noteworthy that both Snow

White and Sleeping Beauty are awakened not by their own efforts but by the intervention of handsome princes, who reshape Snow White's and Sleeping Beauty's lives to ensure that they "live happily ever after." Dependency on an external source for rescue is a lesson inherent in both of these popular fairy tales. Perhaps today's Snow Whites and Sleeping Beauties find their Prince Charmings in medical personnel who attempt to ensure that they have a chance at "happily ever after" by referring them for further treatment.

The socialization of females to inhibit their anger (Bardwick, 1971; Chesler, 1972) makes positive coping with frustrating life circumstances difficult if not impossible. One alternative to expressing anger is to turn it inward, courting depression and its outward manifestation, suicidal behavior. There is ample evidence that women admit being depressed more often than men do, at least until old age (Canetto, 1992; Nolen-Hoeksema, 1991; Nolen-Hoeksema, 1987, 1990). Perhaps women experiencing unresolvable anger become susceptible to depression, which in extreme cases may lead to suicidal behavior.

Compounding the tendency toward internalized anger is females' greater tendency toward rumination. Nolen-Hoeksema (1987, 1990) suggests that "women's ruminative, inactive response style amplifies and prolongs their episodes of depression" (p. 275). Female respondents to attitudinal research, some of whom may be experiencing depression and a tendency to ruminate over that depression, may project their inability to express frustration and anger as well as their depressive ruminations into the situations of the target figures, thus finding it easier to sympathize with the target figures' troubled situations or suicides.

GENDER ROLE IMPLICATIONS FOR MALES

Turning to male socialization, we see problems of a different type. Males, compared to females, show higher levels of activity and aggression very early in the first year of life and these differences persist until at least middle age. Moreover, traditional socialization of males builds upon these existing tendencies toward higher activity levels and aggression. The instructions given to small boys divert them from anything thought to be feminine ("Don't be a sissy"), encourage them to inhibit their emotions ("Big boys don't cry"); and demand that they become independent as soon as possible ("Handle it yourself"). As males develop cognitive structures, or "schemas," for masculine behavior, they begin to structure their future interactions in the world in such a way as to maintain those perceptions. Phenomenologists have long maintained that human beings attend and respond to those stimuli in the environment that agree with their concept of self as it is developing (Lecky, 1945; Rogers, 1980). In this way, males find their tendencies toward activity and higher aggression sharpened by their cognitive understanding and acceptance of the emphasis on competition and success inherent in traditional male socialization.

Especially in American culture, boys are socialized into competitive games at an early age—often learning to endure physical punishment and pain as part of "having fun" or learning to be a man (Sabo, 1994). Sabo describes it well:

> *Male supremacists are not born, they are made, and traditional athletic socialization is a fundamental contribution to this complex social-psychological and political process. Through sport, many males, indeed, learn to "take it"—that is, to internalize patriarchal values which, in turn, become part of their gender identity. (p. 160)*

In short, male socialization encourages emotional inexpressiveness and denial of feelings of pain and suffering. It also gives permission to be more aggressive and violent and to reach for success or winning at any cost—a combination that Goldberg (1977) has dubbed "a prescription for suicide".

Males are also socialized to look at life pragmatically, to be problem solvers. Research on attitudes toward suicide tends to support the proposition that males, more often than females, may see suicide as an acceptable solution to problems inherent in living. If this is so, those who are interested in preventing suicide will have to change the problem situations facing suicidal males.

In considering primary prevention of suicide, we must remember that socialization practices are subject to change. For example, Bernard (1981, p. 544) observed over a decade ago that male socialization is malleable:

> *Presented only as food for thought, and certainly not as a hypothesis, is the idea that just as the primordial fetal stuff would remain female if not prodded by the male hormone, so the "real" nature of humanity or "human nature" would probably be more like "female" human nature than like the "nature" that has to be achieved with so much effort as "male" nature is, if it were not prodded from infancy on to be aggressive, competitive, dominant.*

More recently, Lore and Schultz (1993), in a comparative analysis of aggression, maintained that although males of most mammalian species are clearly more aggressive than females, aggression is a malleable behavior that can be either expressed or inhibited depending upon the conditions and expectations dominant in the environment. These authors point to relatively simple changes that could be made to decrease violent death in our society, including adopting a national policy that discourages the expression of individual aggression, adopting more stringent gun control, and limiting "the almost continuous exposure to glorified, unrealistic violence in the entertainment media" (p. 23).

SUICIDE PREVENTION IN THE SCHOOLS

While the family is certainly the most basic ground for nurturing positive coping skills, children spend more waking time in schools as they grow older than they do at home. Schools have only recently begun to develop suicide prevention programs (See Lenaars & Wenckstern, 1991). According to Smith (1991), organized suicide prevention programs were not introduced into the public schools in the United States until the 1970s. In the early 1980s, only a few pioneering school-based suicide prevention programs existed, such as those of the Cherry Creek school system in Denver and the Fairfax County public schools in Virginia (Wiley, 1987).

By the mid 1980s, increasing awareness of the growing adolescent suicide problem and the special risk of cluster suicides among this age group led to the rapid development of many school-based programs. Community health professionals, parent groups, legislators, and educators themselves lent their voices to the growing advocacy for suicide prevention programs in the public schools. Their requests gained in salience when the parents of a boy who killed himself sued an Oregon school district over the lack of suicide prevention training for teachers. This much-publicized case was settled out of court but not before it resulted in a landmark decision which held that parents of youths who kill themselves may sue a school if the death allegedly resulted from inadequate staff training in suicide prevention (*Kelson v. City of Springfield, Oregon*, 1985). By the end of the 1980s, state legislatures had passed laws mandating the establishment of suicide prevention programs in the public school systems of California (1983), Connecticut (1987), Florida (1984), Maryland (1986), New Jersey (1985), New York (1987), North Carolina (1987), Rhode Island (1986), Texas (1989), Virginia (1987), and Wisconsin (1985) (Smith, 1991).

For the first edition of this book, we planned and carried out a study polling superintendents of public instruction in each of the 50 states of the United States. The results are still germane to our examination of suicide prevention in the schools. The brief survey we sent to these offices included questions concerning the development of materials and the availability of curriculum guidelines for teaching about suicide as well as questions about the development of policies and procedures for dealing with the response to a student suicide or suicide attempt among peers. The findings from the surveys, which were returned by 46 of the 50 state departments of public instruction, are summarized in Table 8.1.

The table shows that, although much ongoing suicide prevention activity existed in the public schools in the late 1980s, responsibility for these activities

TABLE 8.1   Suicide Prevention Activities of Statewide and Local School Systems in the United States

Prevention activities and materials	Provided by statewide education offices	Developed by individual school systems
1. Materials for teaching about suicide	17 (37%)	32 (70%)
2. Curriculum guidelines for suicide prevention	9 (20%)	35 (76%)
3. Policies and procedures for dealing with student response to a suicide crisis	5 (11%)	38 (83%)

fell heavily on individual school systems, with only limited direction from the state departments of public instruction. Only 37% of the state education offices provided individual school systems with materials for teaching about suicide, and only 20% provided curriculum guidelines for suicide prevention. The table also shows that even fewer statewide systems (11%) were involved in the development of policies and procedures for dealing with the student response to a suicide or a suicide attempt.

All state departments of public instruction were asked to include with the completed questionnaire a copy of any suicide prevention guidelines developed by their offices. We received such materials from only 15 states. Of the sets of guidelines received, 11 dealt specifically with suicide prevention and 4 contained general health curriculum guidelines. The following outline summarizes the contents of the typical suicide prevention guidelines we received.

    I.   Facts about youth suicide
       A.   National statistics
       B.   Statewide statistics
   II.   Curriculum development guidelines for teaching students
       A.   The youth suicide problem
       B.   Individual coping skills
       C.   Helping and referral skills for use with friends
  III.   In-service training guidelines for school faculty and staff
       A.   Prevention procedures
       B.   Intervention procedures
       C.   Postvention procedures
  IV.   Pupil services guidelines
       A.   Identification of suicidal students
       B.   Assessment of suicide risk
       C.   Referral procedures
       D.   Crisis response procedures

V. Appendix materials
   A. Descriptions of model programs
   B. Suicide prevention bibliography
   C. Suicide prevention media resources
   D. List of community resources
   E. Sample referral and reporting forms

Although the specific contents of these guidelines differed from state to state, most programs included guidelines for classroom instruction and for teacher and staff training workshops. The in-service training guidelines addressed issues associated with prevention, intervention, and postvention. Guidelines for pupil services were also included. The outline shows that the recommended guidelines included procedures for identification of suicidal students and risk assessment. Recommendations for risk assessment included using procedures such as the SAL (*specificity* of plan, *availability* of means, and *lethality* of method) method of inquiry with suspected suicidal youth. The guidelines also included referral procedures (e.g., keep the student with a responsible adult, inform the parents). Many guidelines included crisis response procedures to reduce the likelihood of cluster or copycat suicides (e.g., establish a crisis management team before a tragedy occurs, meet with high-risk students in small groups or individually, designate one person to talk to the press). Finally, in addition to these guidelines, the materials provided by the state departments of public instruction usually included descriptions of model programs, bibliographical material, a list of community resources, referral and reporting forms, and a list of suicide prevention resources.

As the contents of the outline show, these suicide prevention program guidelines were well prepared, complete, and very helpful for individual school systems preparing their own programs. In spite of the quality of the materials received, however, the fact that so few state departments of public instruction provide direction for individual school systems is a matter of continuing concern. Too often, individual school systems are mandated to develop comprehensive programs to deal with the youth suicide problem without adequate directions and guidelines from the state. While respect for the autonomy of individual school systems is praiseworthy, absence of direction from and lack of accountability to the state education offices result in unevenness of quality and fragmentation of efforts.

Moving from the state level to the level of individual schools, a special task force of the American Association on Suicidology conducted a survey of 158 school-related suicide programs in the United States and Canada (Smith, Eyman, Dyck, & Ryerson, 1987). The survey showed few differences between U.S. and Canadian school-based suicide programs. In fact, the only consistent difference found between programs in the two countries was one of emphasis.

The Canadian programs tended to focus on education while U.S. programs emphasized both education and crisis intervention.

Sixty percent of the 158 school-related suicide prevention programs surveyed included units about youth suicide designed for teachers to use in classroom instruction. Although some programs included curricula for all 12 grades, the majority focused on junior high school and high school students. Most curricula emphasized giving students practical information, such as facts, signs, symptoms, and referral sources, and included help in developing coping skills, such as the identification and acceptance of one's own feelings, and techniques for responding to a friend's suicidal crisis. Approximately one-third of the school-related suicide programs surveyed included an instructional component containing materials to be used with school nurses, counselors, school social workers, and parents.

One quarter of the programs surveyed included a peer support component. The "peer counseling" activities usually involved student-to-student tasks designed to identify, stabilize, or refer troubled students. These programs recommended instructing peer counselors in befriending, listening, identification, and referral skills. Approximately half of the training programs for peers were taught by school personnel and approximately half by outside mental health professionals.

Seventy-three percent of the programs surveyed included crisis intervention components for dealing with the aftermath of suicide or a suicide attempt. Most programs included a crisis management team of four to seven individuals, who were given specialized training. These teams reported that the majority of their activities in a crisis situation involved dealing with other students, especially those previously identified as being at risk.

The survey findings showed that many public school systems were heavily involved in positive suicide prevention activities. The findings also showed, however, that there were a number of weaknesses in the procedures used by many of the school-related suicide prevention programs. For example, some of the peer support programs had no provisions for monitoring the participants' behavior, and many of the peer counselors received no training in referral procedures. A number of these well-intentioned suicide prevention programs that lacked monitoring procedures were implemented in ways that made them as potentially dangerous as helpful.

Perhaps the most widespread criticism of the school-related suicide prevention programs surveyed was the absence of adequate evaluation. Very few of the 158 programs included an evaluation component. The few programs that did tended to emphasize skills learning rather than changes in the incidence of suicidal behavior. Although the procedures used in most suicide prevention programs seem likely to be helpful, their effectiveness has not been demonstrated empirically. It is possible that many of the programs designed to reduce the incidence of youth suicide may be ineffective or perhaps even harmful.

A number of writers have criticized the current "broad brush" approach to suicide prevention, in which groups apply a variety of procedures at the same time without sound theoretical bases and no measures of specific treatment-related outcomes (Berman, 1987; Garland, 1987; Streiner & Adam, 1987). The critics point out that specific outcome goals should be established for target groups. In addition, sound theories of suicide prevention must be operationalized and implemented in a manner that will allow the precise measurement of outcomes. Finally, experimental procedures such as the randomized assignment of subjects to various treatment conditions, the measurement of clinically important outcomes, long-term follow-up, and statistically significant results must be employed (Streiner & Adam, 1987).

It is important that school personnel not become overly discouraged by criticisms of current practice. As Cantor (1987) explained, we are in a crisis situation and our young people cannot wait. One report estimates that between 8 and 10% of high school students have attempted suicide at some time in their lives and reports that 29.1% of junior high school and 45% of senior high school students have known someone who took their own lives (Dyck, 1991). Progress has been made in schools in the United States and Canada, in that some help is available where none existed two decades ago. However, it is now time to refine our procedures through research, for this will lead to intervention strategies that will be more able to achieve desired outcome goals.

Parents working with the schools have been largely overlooked in the past as a potential resource for suicide prevention. Indeed, Silverman and Felner (1995) have suggested that the "needs of the child or adolescent cannot be fully or maximally addressed independent of the needs and resources of the family" (p. 102). These authors summarized approaches and assumptions that are common to effective suicide programs, including understanding that there is no single solution to a problem and that all high risk behaviors are interrelated; developing an integrated package of services and programs within each community; developing strategies focused on changing institutions such as schools and the welfare system rather than changing individuals; implementing the programs before a crisis presents itself; and maintaining the programming over a long period. Parents can also help by becoming

---

When hearing the devastating effects of a suicide on the lives of survivors—so painful that the survivors themselves become a high risk group for suicide—it is easy to conclude that one would be hard pressed to find something which would cause more pain to more people. Brodie, *Suicide with a Christian ethical context: Clarifying the question.*

educated about suicide. Survivors of Suicide (SOS) groups, many of whom
are parents, have been organized in cities across the United States. Generally,
members of these groups are willing to share their firsthand experience of
suicide with other groups. Parent-teacher association (PTA) meetings are excellent opportunities for educating both parents and teachers about the realities of suicide and the methods of coping with suicidal behavior. Such programs ideally should be done by authorities in a well-planned series rather
than in one 30- to 60-minute session; this will ensure adequate time to discuss
the complexities of child and adolescent suicide and give parents a chance to
digest material and to raise questions that occur to them between sessions.
Informed parents are invaluable as supporters of suicide education programs
in the schools and as members of crisis intervention teams.

EDUCATION FOR SUICIDE PREVENTION IN COLLEGES AND UNIVERSITIES

In late adolescence and young adulthood, a significant number of persons are involved in higher education. In recent years, the typical college
student, aged 18 to 22, has been joined by increasing numbers of adults over
30, raising the average age of college students to the late 20s on many campuses. The college experience therefore provides a final opportunity for society to offer systematic education for suicide prevention. In addition, since
colleges and universities must cope with suicide attempts and completions,
they should be in a position of leadership with respect to other segments of
society in developing models of suicide prevention, intervention, and postvention.

A study was conducted to determine how campuses respond to the issue
of suicide. Vice-presidents for student affairs from a representative sample of
different types of colleges throughout the United States were asked to respond to a two-page questionnaire (Stillion, McDowell, & May, 1989). The
survey included questions about the types and numbers of courses devoted
to suicide prevention; questions about noncredit types of suicide prevention
education; questions about procedures followed when a suicide is threatened,
attempted, or completed; and a request for an estimate of the numbers of
suicide attempts and completions that occurred on campus each year. Responses were returned from 262 (40%) of the 659 institutions contacted.

Table 8.2 shows the number of responses received for each category of
school. It is clear that the largest number of responses came from large four-
year public institutions and the smallest number from the large four-year
private institutions.

In response to the question about courses offered for credit, only 26
(10%) of the institutions offered any courses dealing with suicide prevention,
and only one institution offered a course that included the word "suicide" in

TABLE 8.2 Numbers and Types of Higher Education Institutions Responding to a Suicide Survey

Type of Institution	Number in United States	Number of institutions receiving surveys	Number of institutions returning surveys	Percentage of institutions responding
2-year private	356	109	20	6
2-year public	972	133	38	4
4-year private (small)	1,291	117	45	3
4-year public (small)	445	130	59	13
4-year private (large)	26	26	9	35
4-year public (large)	144	144	91	63
Total	2,359	659	262	11

the title. That course was "Suicide and Society" and it was offered by a large four-year public institution. It is obvious that there is little or no organized course work devoted exclusively to suicide prevention being offered at this time by our nation's institutions of higher education. Instead, where the subject of suicide is addressed at all within the curriculum it appears as a unit within more general courses addressing death and dying, crisis intervention, pastoral counseling, stress management, health, nursing, sociology, psychology, and helping relationships.

The picture looked considerably brighter regarding the question about other services on campus that deal with suicide prevention. Of those responding to this question, 111 (43.4%) offered groups through the campus counseling center and 131 (51.2%) provided groups through the local mental health center. The importance of suicide prevention for the responding institutions was reflected in the fact that 60.2% of the respondents said they sponsored in-service training for their professionals and 63.8% said they sponsored in-service training for their staff personnel. Almost 65% of the responding institutions reported using multiple community referrals in addition to campus resources in their suicide prevention services.

In summary, postsecondary institutions have an important role to play in responding to suicidal behavior exhibited by the older teenagers and young adults enrolled on their campuses. While most colleges seem to understand the importance of the topic (as evidenced by staff development programs on suicide prevention), very little suicide prevention education seems to be occurring at the postsecondary level. Given the increasing rates of suicide throughout adulthood and the fact that college represents the last organized educational opportunity for many in our culture, it would seem important to find ways to include the topic of suicide in required courses in the college curriculum. Courses in health and human behavior and introductory psychology and sociology classes would be appropriate vehicles for suicide prevention education at the postsecondary level. We also suggest developing full courses in suicide and suicide prevention for prospective care givers and educators.

SUICIDE PREVENTION IN SOCIETY

We have looked at ways in which families and schools can address the issue of suicide. At a more global level, there are many things a caring society can do to decrease the incidence of suicide. Potter, Powell, and Kachur (1995) have proposed the adoption of a public health perspective on suicide prevention. Such a perspective requires a four-step approach. First, controlled surveillance must be used to isolate patterns of suicide; second, researchers must employ epidemiological methods to identify multiple causes leading to suicide and the relationships among them; third, intervention strategies must be designed and systematically evaluated; and finally, programs consisting of proven interventions must be implemented. Potter et al. suggest eight different types of programs that might be put in place to aid in suicide prevention:

1. *School gatekeeper training,* in which staff members are trained to identify at-risk students and/or to provide crisis intervention in the case of suicidal deaths.
2. *Community gatekeeper training,* in which clergy, police, and other community members are given training to identify at-risk people.
3. *General suicide education,* following the guidelines described earlier in this chapter.
4. *Screening programs,* in which suicide prediction instruments are administered to high-risk people, preferably more than once, in order to help promote prediction of suicide and to provide intervention in a timely manner.
5. *Peer support programs,* which can be offered by schools or community organizations to promote awareness of suicide risk and to make support available to those considering suicide.
6. *Crisis centers and hotlines,* which provide telephone counseling for those in crisis and may also offer referrals to mental health services.
7. *Means restriction,* which is aimed at restricting access to handguns, drugs, and other methods for accomplishing suicide.
8. *Intervention after a suicide (postvention),* which consists of providing services to help survivors cope with the aftermath of suicide and may help deflect suicide clusters.

Several nations, including Canada, Finland, Norway, and Australia have adopted national strategies for suicide prevention. Because Canadian society is in many ways similar to that of the United States, we will examine suicide prevention in that nation in some detail.

The Canadian model conceptualizes suicide intervention as consisting of a set of responses that may occur at any point along the "river of prevention" prior to the "waterfall" that is the symbol for the suicidal action (Tanney, 1995). In 1987, the National Task Force on Suicide in Canada recognized the need to ameliorate social conditions that lead to suicide (Health and Welfare Canada, 1987). They recommended seven specific actions aimed at decreasing the suicide rate by changing social conditions. These recommendations, although designed for the Canadian culture, seem equally applicable to the United States. They are as follows:

1. Mental health professionals should consult with the media when suicide occurs to decrease the modeling effect, which has been shown to result from widely publicized suicides, and thus decrease the likelihood of cluster or copycat suicides.
2. Mental health professionals and the media should work together to decrease the stigma attached to seeking help for suicidal ideation, to inform the public of the warning signs of suicide, and to increase the use of positive coping skills.
3. In keeping with the evidence that limited accessibility to methods of committing suicide leads to decreases in the suicide rate, "measures should be taken to reduce the lethality and availability of instruments of suicide" (p. 41). Specifically, the report called for more stringent gun control and control of medications as well as limited access to attractive hazards, such as high bridges.
4. Governments should provide assistance for universities and colleges to incorporate suicide prevention programs into their curricula for health care professionals.
5. Workshops on suicide prevention should be instituted for all personnel in custodial and correctional services.
6. Additional suicide prevention training materials directed at specific groups of helping professionals (e.g., physicians, clergy, or teachers) should be developed by leaders in each group.
7. Teachers should be trained to detect and assess suicidal risk among their students and should be aware of community referral services for potential suicides.

In addition to its specific recommendations regarding prevention of suicide, the report was important because it highlighted a nation's recognition of suicide as a major social problem and focused on education as one of the most important tools for addressing that problem. Since the report was issued, several models of suicide prevention have been put in place in Canada. One such model is called the Brighter Futures program of Health Canada. It targets high risk children and engages them in broad-based activities designed to lessen the risk of suicide. A second model developed by the Correctional Service of Canada offers first-line training to care givers in the area of suicide prevention. The province of Alberta has developed an information flow model based on data that emphasizes early intervention, changing the environment, and education and training for care givers. In addition to national and provincial initiatives, some nongovernmental organizations have begun to be influential in suicide prevention in Canada (Tanney, 1995). Among these are the Quebec Association of Suicidology and the Canadian Association for Suicide Prevention. Both of these groups consist of individual members who are committed to preventing suicide by supporting educational and clinical initiatives.

In the United States, voices have also been raised suggesting that a new commitment to suicide prevention should be made. Selkin (1983) pointed out that since the suicidology branch of the National Institute of Mental Health was closed in 1973, the federal government has made only minimal contributions to suicide prevention. He maintained that the U.S. government has endorsed and continues to endorse a number of public policies that promote suicide, including "free and easy access to handguns, lack of vocational and educational opportunity for youth, racial discrimination and divisiveness, moral condemnation of welfare benefits, and a philosophy of punishment for those convicted of crimes without accompanying concern for their human needs" (p. 10). Selkin recommended that a computer-based model of suicide prevention be developed that would include software that could be placed in every school and suicide prevention center to help diagnose, project a lethality rating, and recommend a follow-up schedule for suspected suicides.

Hudgins (1983), echoing some of Selkin's suggestions, called for more social changes to prevent suicide. He pointed out that the rise in suicide in the last three decades can be accounted for almost entirely by the rise in deaths caused by handguns. Explaining that suicide rates are lower in states that have strict handgun laws, Hudgins called for practical measures to decrease suicide, including adopting tighter gun control laws, limiting the number of prescription drugs given at one time, fencing dangerous high places, and in general making suicide less convenient. In a study of 565 suicides that occurred in the home of the victim, a group of researchers found that 58% (326) of them were suicide by gunshot (Kellermann et al., 1992). After controlling for such contributing factors as alcohol, use of drugs, and lack of education, these researchers found that the presence of one or more guns in the home was associated with an increased risk of suicide. The researchers concluded, "People who own firearms should carefully weigh their reasons for keeping a gun in the home against the possibility that it may someday be used in a suicide" (p. 472).

POSTVENTION

The final topic to be discussed in this chapter is postvention. Shneidman (1984) has defined postvention as consisting of "activities that reduce the aftereffects of a traumatic event in the lives of the survivors. Its purpose is to help survivors live longer, more productively, and less stressfully than they are likely to do otherwise" (p. 413). The term postvention is used in the literature to refer to two different types of actions taken after death by suicide: diagnostic and therapeutic.

The diagnostic type of postvention is the less well-known type; it is intended to determine that the cause of death was suicide. At its best, this type of postvention involves securing the services of a suicide team that will investigate the circumstances around an equivocal death to determine if suicide has occurred. The suicide team conducts a psychological autopsy by interviewing people who knew the deceased in an attempt to reconstruct his or her state of mind in the days preceding the death. The team examines in particular information about earlier suicide attempts, symptoms of depression, morbid communications, behavior indicating low self-esteem or self-hatred, and other evidence that may indicate an intention to commit suicide.

The results of such an investigation can have a major impact on the survivors. As Curphey (1961) has noted, "The statement 'your father committed suicide' made to a child may cause genuine anguish and even severe trauma for years to come" (p. 114). If there is even a small chance than an equivocal death might not be a suicide, such an investigation is worthwhile. However, even when the death is deemed a suicide, the process of conducting a psychological autopsy may be helpful to the survivors. The investigation may help the survivors to understand better the "why" behind the suicide. In addition, survivors have acknowledged that the interviews themselves have been therapeutic (Curphey, 1961). Many survivors of suicide do not routinely have caring professionals with whom to discuss the death of a loved one. Merely venting anger, sorrow, guilt, and anxiety to a trained member of a suicide team may promote adjustment.

The National Task Force on Suicide in Canada (Health and Welfare Canada, 1987) reported that "the procedures for performing a psychological autopsy are much less threatening than the quasi-judicial procedures of an inquest, which have been shown to only aggravate the distress of the bereaved." The task force recommended that psychological autopsies be performed in

---

Survivor-victims of such deaths (suicides) are invaded by an unhealthy complex of disturbing emotions: shame, guilt, hatred, perplexity. They are obsessed with thoughts about the death, seeking reasons, casting blame, and often punishing themselves. Shneidman, Postvention and the survivor-victim.

TABLE 8.3   Contents of the Psychological Autopsy

Categories	Descriptions
Identification	Name, age, sex, marital status, residence, religious practices employment status
Details of death	Cause, method, time, place, rating of lethality
Personal history	Medical history, psychiatric history, family history (medical illnesses, psychiatric illnesses, death, other suicides)
Personality and behavioral profile	Personality, lifestyle, typical reaction to stress, nature of interpersonal relationships, attitudes toward death (accidents, suicide, and homicide), extent of use of drugs and alcohol and their possible role in the death
Precipitating events	Circumstances immediately preceding death, changes in routine prior to death (habits, hobbies, sexual behavior, eating, work, etc.), incidence of positive influences in life (e.g., success, satisfaction, enjoyment, plans for the future), crises during past 5 years
Assessment of intentionality	
Reaction of informant to the death	
Comments	

"all cases of equivocal or causally undetermined deaths, as well as in suspected cases of suicide in psychiatric and general hospitals, prisons, community clinics, and probation services" (p. 50). Table 8.3 presents the categories that the task force suggested should be included in the psychological autopsy. It is obvious from the breadth and depth of the information requested that psychological autopsies carried out according to these standards will yield a rich base of new information for understanding both the dynamics of suicide and its effects on survivors.

The second and more common type of suicide postvention, the therapeutic type, is systematic involvement with the survivors over several months in order to help them work through their special kind of grief. The death of a loved one is always a traumatic event that engenders a grief reaction. Evidence is accumulating that grief can cause physiological changes that may endanger the health of bereaved people (Berardo, 1988; Parkes, 1972; Rando, 1985; Raphael, 1983). When the cause of death is suicide, the trauma experienced may be greatly increased.

Numerous studies have shown that bereavement following suicide differs from bereavement following death by natural causes (Dunn & Morrish-Vidners, 1987; Sheskin & Wallace, 1976; Wrobleski, 1984). Although not all studies agree, there is evidence that the grief of survivors of a suicide seems to differ both in kind and in intensity from the grief following a death by natural causes. Besides the feelings of sorrow and loneliness common to grief, the suicide survivor characteristically feels higher levels of guilt, shame, abandonment, and anger toward the deceased. In addition, Cain (1972) observed the following reactions among survivors of suicide: reality distortion, problems with object relations, disturbed self-concept, identification with the suicide, self-destructiveness, search for meaning, and incomplete mourning. Dunn and Morris-Vidners (1987) documented the following responses among a group of 24 suicide survivors: initial reactions included the shock and disbelief common to survivors of many types of death; in addition, however, these survivors reported feelings of fear and anger and a great need to talk to people about the death, a need that was difficult to meet because so many potential listeners were uncomfortable with the subject of suicide. Moreover, the authors suggested that the presence of several interrelated psychological reactions might account for the intensity of grieving among suicide survivors, including feelings of utter powerlessness; feelings of deep rejection and punishment as a result of willful abandonment by the suicide victim; feelings of responsibility, self-blame, and guilt; and uncertainty as to the cause of the death.

Rudestam (1977) conducted a study with 39 families of suicides. He found that the survivors continued to experience physical and psychological symptoms six months after the death of the loved one. It is interesting to note that Rudestam did find some families whose relationships had actually been strengthened as a result of working together to understand the suicide and its meaning in their lives. Other studies have not shown such positive findings. A study by Cain and Fast (1972) showed that children of parents who have committed suicide have shown increased incidence of emotional problems. Osterweis, Solomon, & Green (1984) reviewed the literature on the impact of suicide on survivors. They pointed out that studies of children who experience the suicide of a parent show evidence of a wide range of psychological problems, including "psychosomatic disorders, obesity, running away, delinquency, fetishism, lack of bowel control, character problems and neurosis" (p. 126).

Problems seem to be more severe in children who survive a parental suicide than in children whose parents die from other causes. In addition, guilt, depression, and self-destructive behavior seem to last a long time. For adult survivors, the effects of suicide may be less devastating, but they still present special problems. In addition to feelings of rejection, guilt, and anger at the deceased person, adult suicide survivors often feel some degree of responsibility for the suicide and some degree of social stigmatization (Osterweis, Solomon, & Green, 1984). Even if we agreed that individuals have the right to take their own lives, we would champion suicide prevention and postvention techniques in order to avoid the high price the survivors of suicide pay in emotional pain and prolonged suffering. In short, suicide is an event dangerous to the mental and physical health of surviving loved ones, and it therefore requires special awareness and sensitivity from helping professionals.

In 1972, Shneidman, in the foreword to Albert Cain's landmark book, *Survivors of Suicide*, estimated that there were six survivors who are affected by every suicide (Cain, 1972). More recently Shneidman pointed out that the largest public health problem in dealing with suicide is the need to provide postvention efforts for survivors of suicide "whose lives are forever changed and who, over a period of years, number in the millions" (Shneidman, 1984). Postvention efforts need to be mobilized both to deal with the needs of individual survivors and to change the conditions in society that exacerbate their grief. In addition to individual and group therapy approaches, survivors can be helped by breaking down the stigma attached to suicide. This can only be done by education. Other authors have suggested that educational efforts should be directed at helping people understand the destructive effects that suicide has on survivors and on their ability to interact positively with others (Dunn & Morrish-Vidners, 1987). Education programs that discuss suicide without moralizing are also needed if the social stigma is to be removed from suicide survivors. Such programs need to stress the complexity of any suicidal action and to publicize the growing literature that illuminates the biological-social-psychological-cognitive bases of suicide.

Postvention efforts often merge into prevention efforts. As we have seen, many school districts are developing or already have in place suicide prevention programs. Many individual schools are also adopting a policy on postvention. When a suicide occurs in a school, a crisis team responds, mobilizing the combined energies of teachers and informed students and even reaching out to parents in an attempt to involve them as partners in suicide prevention. Wenckstern and Leenaars (1991) have suggested that postvention work in the schools has much in common with work with posttraumatic stress victims. They proposed the following eight principles of postvention:

1. Begin as soon as possible after the tragedy.
2. Expect resistance from some but not all survivors.
3. Be willing to explore negative emotions toward the victim when the time is right.
4. Provide ongoing reality testing for the survivors.
5. Be ready to refer when necessary.
6. Avoid cliché and banal optimism.
7. Be prepared to spend significant amounts of time (generally several months) in one school.
8. Develop the postvention program within a comprehensive health care setting that also includes prevention and intervention.

Every school must adapt those principles to its own setting. Keeping parents informed about what is being done is an important consideration. One Wisconsin school sends out the following letter to all parents after a suicide occurs among the student body:[2]

_____

[2] Jeanne M. Harper, M.P.S., Alpha-Omega Venture, P.O. Box 735, Marienette, WI 54143-0735.

Dear Parents:

On [date], one of our [name of school] students committed suicide. Student reaction has been filled with both confusion and grief.

A crisis center has been established in the high school guidance office to assist students in their struggle to cope with this tragedy. Counselors from [name of city] Mental Health and [name of specialist], a local specialist on issues of death and dying, have been assisting our school counselors in working with students all day today, and will continue to be available in the days to come.

This is a tragedy that has affected our entire school community, and the administration and staff are very concerned about the continued effects it could have on the student body.

Please encourage your [children] to talk with you about this incident. Encourage them to share their feelings. If you notice any change in what you could consider their normal behavior or habits, i.e., sleeplessness, loss of appetite, moodiness, please notify their school counselor immediately. The crisis center and counselors will continue to provide assistance to students and their families as long as the need exists.

As of this writing, the school has been informed that funeral services for the student will be held [date, time, and place]. Students wishing to attend these services are encouraged to travel as a group on a school bus. Parental permission slips will be needed for students who wish to go on the bus.

The school staff will continue to monitor student reaction on a daily basis, and adjustments will be made as needs arise. If we can be of any further assistance to you or your child please contact us.

Sincerely,
[School Official]

Proponents of this school-based postvention effort maintain that such open communication reassures parents that school personnel care, provides opportunities for dialogue about suicide with parents and between parents and their children, and sets the stage for more complete suicide prevention programs.

However, in order to be able to respond effectively to a suicidal crisis, schools must be mobilized for action long before the crisis emerges. Siehl (1990) has suggested that a special suicide task force should be set up composed of volunteers and including counselors, area resource persons, volunteer teachers with special training, and school psychologists. He has further recommended that in-service programs presenting the causes and warning signs of suicide as well as sources of help be included in every school. Carter and Brooks (1990) have pointed out that an individualized approach for each specific school is essential and that group techniques can be especially helpful when working with adolescents.

Colleges and universities also routinely engage in postvention following suicides. One study showed that most reporting institutions indicated that postvention procedures were in place for responding to a completed suicide (Stillion, McDowell, & May, 1989). Almost 57% of the institutions reported that they had an organized procedure for dealing with the victim's family, 56% had a procedure for the victim's close friends, 50% had a procedure for acquaintances, and 31% had a procedure for the student body as a whole. As expected, smaller schools more often reported a campuswide response, such as a memorial service. Other responses included attendance at the funeral by university officials, sending flowers, holding memorial services, writing to families, offering support groups, and using outreach services (e.g., brochures, educational programs, newspaper articles, hall meetings). The majority of institutions reporting seemed to understand the need for addressing the topic of suicide with those groups most at risk (e.g., close friends and those sharing the same housing facilities) and seemed to be willing to use campus resources in working with these groups. Some respondents indicated awareness of "cluster suicides," while others spoke of the need to lessen the modeling effect on other at-risk students.

Selkin (1983) has suggested that the time has come for us to develop and test computer-based models of suicide prevention. Software that contains a description of suicide prevention programs and principles could be placed in mental health clinics, hospitals, and medical schools. In addition, suicide prevention centers could provide on-line consulting services to school personnel.

We have come full circle in this chapter. In discussing postvention, we find that we are once again discussing the need for education about suicide. Indeed, as Shneidman (1984) has said, "Postvention can be viewed as prevention for the next decade or for the next generation; . . . and a comprehensive total health program in any enlightened community will include all three elements of care: prevention, intervention and postvention" (p. 419).

SUMMARY

The important topics of suicide prevention and postvention were discussed in this chapter. Several different levels of suicide prevention were examined. At the most general level, society influences people's attitudes toward suicide. A review of current attitudes shows that there are gender differences in the way people respond to suicidal target figures presented in vignettes or scenarios. Females, more than males, seem to know more factual information about suicide, are more willing to discuss suicide with others and with suicidal people, and report more sympathy with suicidal figures. At the same time, females tend more often than males to disapprove of suicide.

Age also seems to be an important factor in determining attitudes toward suicide. Although much more research needs to be done, an accumulating body of evidence suggests that suicide among elderly people is viewed as qualitatively different from and more acceptable than suicide among other age groups. Whether this is an example of ageism or whether it is a universal remains to be seen.

Suicide prevention can be carried out by many institutions within society. For example, families can examine traditional gender role socialization with an eye toward implications for suicidal behavior. They can also explicitly teach their children coping skills such as interpreting failure experiences as feedback on which to grow, encouraging humor, setting high but achievable goals, and creating conditions of unconditional acceptance. Schools can and should plan and offer suicide prevention programs at the middle school, high school, and college level. We reviewed suicide prevention guidelines as revealed by a study of public schools and reported on what colleges are doing to help prevent young adult suicide. We also described eight types of programs that might decrease the incidence of suicide and reviewed and endorsed the recommendations of the National Task Force on Suicide in Canada. In addition, we pointed out that the single step of restricting access to handguns would decrease the suicide rate.

Two types of postvention were described in this chapter. The psychological autopsy was explored as a technique to establish the cause of death and the state of mind of the deceased. We suggested that the help the psychological autopsy gives to survivors of suicide in answering their questions about the suicidal act may provide comfort and relieve guilt and/or anxiety, thus beginning the process of postvention. The importance of working with suicide survivors was also emphasized. Finally, we suggested that good postvention is actually equivalent to prevention and that many of the educational techniques reviewed in the prevention section are equally applicable in postvention efforts.

Approaches for Treating Suicidal People

"For those who have dwelled in depression's dark wood—whoever has been restored to health has almost always been restored to the capacity for serenity and joy . . . for having endured the despair beyond despair."

William Styron

In this chapter we will review multiple approaches for working with suicidal people. There are some commonalities in responding to suicidal people regardless of the clinical approach favored by a therapist. We will review those commonalities in the first section of this chapter.

After the immediate threat of suicide has passed, therapists use many different approaches in working with suicidal clients. Most therapists are eclectic practitioners; that is, over the years they develop their own personal therapeutic style, incorporating elements of different approaches that seem to fit the needs of clients as well as the therapists individual strengths. Such styles are based on each therapist's belief system and utilize his personal strengths. In a text for prospective counselors, Corey (1991) endorses the eclectic view when he states,

> *I see it as a mistake to equate counselor effectiveness simply with proficiency in a single technique or even a set of techniques. It is possible to learn that effective counseling involves proficiency in a combination of* cognitive, affective, and behavioral *techniques. Such a combination is necessary to help clients* think about their beliefs and assumptions, experience on a feeling *level their conflicts and struggles, and actually translate their insights into* action *programs by behaving in new ways in day-to-day living* [emphasis in the original]. (*p. 439*)

In this chapter, we will provide an overview of selected approaches to counseling with suicidal people, following the traditional schools of psychology reviewed in chapter 2. We will also review what is known about biological treatment of suicidal people. Finally, in keeping with the theme of the book, we will suggest some approaches and issues that therapists should bear in mind as they counsel suicidal people of different ages and in different life stages.

Therapeutic change is an enormously complex process—that occurs through an intricate interplay of various guided human experiences. Yalom, *The theory and practice of group psychotherapy.*

SUICIDE INTERVENTION

One of the guiding principles of this book is that suicide is an act that should be prevented whenever possible. This principle is based on the premises that human life is valuable and should not be taken prematurely and that suicide is not a desirable solution to problems of any kind with the possible exception of terminal illness accompanied by intractable pain. As we have seen, suicide is generally a highly ambivalent act committed by an individual who is reacting desperately to both external and internal circumstances in an attempt to avoid emotional pain. Because the individual feels drawn toward life as well as to death, there is often room for knowledgeable people to intervene on the side of life.

Shneidman (1984, 1985), often regarded as the father of suicidology in the United States, has described four general psychological features that shed light on the state of mind of many suicidal people. Most of them experience (1) an intensification of their generally troubled state, which Shneidman termed *acute perturbation;* (2) an increase in negative emotions such as self-hatred, guilt, shame, and so forth, which Shneidman called *heightened inimitability;* (3) a sharp, sudden constriction of the thinking processes marked by rigidity and the inability to consider multiple options; and (4) the continuing presence of the idea of cessation as the way to end emotional pain. What Shneidman described in four parts, psychoanalytically inclined thinkers might more simply describe as an imbalance between Thanatos and Eros in which Thanatos has the upper hand. Such an imbalance is temporary, however, and if suicidal action can be delayed until one or more of those four conditions abate, death need not occur.

The belief that suicidal action is generally the product of a temporary, reversible, ambivalent state of mind is the basic tenet of crisis intervention programs worldwide. Kiev (1984) highlighted this statement when he wrote:

> *There is considerable evidence in the biological and neurophysiological work now going on at the National Institutes of Health and elsewhere that fundamentally we are dealing with a stress-related phenomenon which has a biological basis. What one needs is time, a reduction of stress, or major antidepressant medications. (p. 28)*

The most common way of buying that time is to intervene in the suicide trajectory as soon as it becomes evident.

Advice for Untrained Individuals

The success of suicide intervention techniques frequently depends on the skill and commitment of caring adults. Often, suicidal people will make their intentions known to friends or relatives who are untrained in crisis intervention. In such cases, the untrained individual may be overwhelmed with the responsibility inherent in serving as a confidant. The following general principles are recommended by a variety of sources and designed to help untrained individuals respond to a person who may be suicidal (Berger, 1984; McBrien, 1983; Shaughnessy & Nystul, 1985).

At the outset, it is important to determine the seriousness of the suicide intent (Kral & Sakinofsky, 1994). Direct questioning is generally the quickest method to ascertain this. A thoughtful confidant will recognize the distress of the individual and build on this recognition by, for example, making comments such as: "I can see that you're very upset. How bad are you feeling? Bad enough to consider harming yourself?"

A positive response to the last question should lead the confidant to ask for specifics (e.g., "Have you considered how you would do it? When you might do it? Where?") Obviously, the suicidal girl who has secured a gun and keeps it under her pillow or the man who has accumulated 100 barbiturates and is planning to take them before his 60th birthday next month is at higher risk than the young person who expresses a death wish but has no clear plans for suicide. This process of assessing the current level of danger, sometimes called the *level of lethality*, is important in preventing suicide.

Having ascertained the immediate danger level, the untrained helper should ensure that the suicidal person is not left alone. Especially in cases of emotional upset, when impulsive action is likely, individuals should not be left alone even for brief periods until help can arrive. Victoroff (1983) gave an example of a woman hospitalized for physical and emotional problems who was left alone in a hospital room for the time it took the attending physician to write the orders for transfer to a psychiatric wing. The woman jumped out the window to her death while the physician was standing just outside the room. It is impossible to overstate the importance of continuous surveillance and support in the face of an obvious suicidal crisis.

A final principle for untrained people dealing with potential suicides is to secure qualified help as soon as possible. Confidants should try to determine who would be most acceptable to their suicidal friend. The types of referrals that can easily be made include referrals to medical doctors, psychologists, counselors, pastors, social service agencies, police and fire departments, and crisis intervention centers. The important thing is to contact some agency that can give support to the confidant and share the responsibility of staying with the suicidal person until ongoing professional help can be secured.

Formal Crisis Intervention

One of the most helpful referrals that can be made is to a crisis intervention center (Frankish, 1994). Such centers are staffed 24 hours a day and have volunteers specifically trained in suicide prevention techniques. Many centers

Despair, Robert Godfrey, 1984. Oil on linen, 84 × 43 in. (Courtesy of Blue Mountain Gallery, New York, New York and Art Gallery, Ltd., New Bern, North Carolina. Photograph by Cathryn Griffin.)

are patterned on the model pioneered in Britain in 1953 by the Samaritans and established in the United States in 1958 by Shneidman and others.

The Samaritan organization, now part of a worldwide movement entitled *The Befrienders*, was begun by a group of volunteers in central London. It started as a 24-hour hotline and center based on the principle of "one-to-one befriending." From the beginning, the principle of anonymity was respected, but individuals were free to drop into the center to talk without "being preached at, counseled or therapeutized" (Fox, 1984, p. 46). The Samaritan center adopted the principle of offering unconditional friendship without regard to race, class, or creed. As the idea took root, many other cities set up such centers. Currently, volunteers are still taught during seven nights of preparation classes to be unshockable and nonjudgmental. The centers have a consultant available in both family medicine and psychiatry. Interestingly, the growth of the Samaritan centers in England coincided with a dramatic decrease in suicide. However, careful analysis of suicide rates in towns with Samaritan groups and towns that did not have such groups has revealed no significant differences in the incidence of suicide (Jennings, Barraclough, & Moss, 1978). Some authorities (e.g., Lester, 1987) have suggested that the overall decline in British suicide rates was caused by the detoxification of household gas, which occurred at the same time that the Samaritan centers began to spread. Whatever the reason, the decrease in the suicide rate promoted acceptance of the crisis intervention model in many developed countries.

The American version of the crisis intervention center, as we saw in Chapter 1, emphasizes research and community service as well as individual intervention. Indeed, much that we know about suicide, as well as many of our theories about it, has come from the seminal work begun at the Los Angeles Suicide Prevention Center. To date, figures in the United States do not show a clear pattern of suicide reduction in cities with suicide centers (Lester, 1971). Nevertheless, the availability of caring, trained volunteers who are willing to respond to suicidal people is a mark of a humane society.

Berger (1984) has well described the work of a staff member in a crisis intervention center:

> *The first task confronting the therapist in the phone contact situation is to keep the patient talking and then assess the lethality of the situation. The second task is to obtain some idea of the particular state of mind or of the diagnostic picture. The task is much different in dealing with one who is severely depressed than in dealing with a schizophrenic or an individual in a state of high panic. All of these will commit suicide, but each will respond differently to the kinds of communications that the therapist is likely to deliver. (p. 69)*

In addition to determining the state of mind of a potential suicide, it is important to identify as soon as possible the sex, family constellation, available support systems, level of religious commitment, recent loss history, and adequacy of past coping behaviors. From the point of view of this book, one of the most salient factors in determining how to work with a suicidal person is his or her age-related developmental level.

Crisis intervention is not equivalent to suicide prevention. It at best buys time for the suicidal patient. Its goal is to defuse the current situation, ensuring time for subsequent ongoing therapy. Schoonover (1982), the director of an inpatient psychiatric unit, recommended that in order to move from crisis intervention to therapy, the therapist should take an active and directive stance. He further recommended that therapists of suicidal people remain maximally available to them by, for example, making home visits to nonhospitalized clients or providing 24-hour telephone access, and by increasing availability for therapy sessions, especially during the acute crisis. Encouragement of client responsibility, mutual setting of time limits, and explicit setting of therapeutic goals are also recommended techniques for dealing with people in suicidal crisis. Schoonover further suggested that specific techniques such as "correction of cognitive distortions and ventilation and labeling of feelings" are necessary for the treatment of many suicidal people (p. 54). He summarized the crisis approach to suicidal behavior as one that "refocuses the patient from intrapsychic issues to his actual roles and relationships in the world" (p. 55). While these general guidelines may serve as useful background, it may be helpful to describe highlights of several general approaches to therapy before focusing on treatment approaches for suicidal people in different age groups and to note the special circumstances and techniques that may affect the course of intervention.

It is clear that at the very least therapists must protect suicidal clients from the clients themselves. Corey (1991) has pointed out that therapists who sense that a threat of suicide may exist must investigate it directly and must take "appropriate and responsible intervention" (p. 76). Legal liability as well as ethical questions may result from ignoring or minimizing a suicidal threat. Actions available to therapists include keeping detailed notes of threats, asking patients to sign contracts that they will take no destructive action without notifying the therapists, consulting with family members, and even taking steps to hospitalize or institutionalize the patient (a process that differs from state to state).

Training and Support for Therapists Working with Suicidal Clients

In spite of the fact that dealing with suicidal clients is threatening to most therapists, very little training in coping with the suicidal death of a client is included in graduate programs for therapists. In a recent panel discussion on the impact of suicide on the professional in training, participants suggested that training on suicide might be omitted because it is considered inconvenient, because it might result in students leaving the programs, because of magical thinking (i.e., "out-of-sight, out-of-mind"), or because the incidence of completed suicide by patients undergoing therapy is low (Lavin, Roy, Dunne-Maxim, & Slaby, 1994).

In addition to the issue of possible legal liability, attempted or completed suicide of a client prompts therapists to question their competence, triggers a grief reaction, and may even lead to reexamination of one's commitment to the profession. While there is little research on the impact of suicides on therapists, Dunne-Maxim (1994) has suggested that therapists who have clients who take their own lives should be debriefed and offered support either in group or individual therapy sessions. She has pointed out that some therapists have an exaggerated sense of responsibility and are therefore likely to blame themselves for the death. She maintains that in following up the death of a client, professionals must create a "delicate balance between the witch hunt and the white wash" (Lavin, Roy, Dunne-Maxim, & Slaby, 1994).

Most therapists can cope with the threat of suicide relatively well when it is out in the open. However, once the possibility of suicide in a client has been identified and immediate steps have been taken to hospitalize the client, to safeguard his or her surroundings by removing weapons, and/or by securing the client's promise to call before taking any hurtful action, the therapist must begin to plan day-to-day treatment of the client. The beliefs, attitudes, and therapeutic background of each therapist will determine the way in which he or she proceeds with ongoing therapy of a suicidal client. Using the theoretical perspectives discussed in chapter 2, we will now examine how therapists with different backgrounds might begin to carry out therapy with a suicidal client.

PRINCIPLES OF THERAPY FROM SEVERAL PERSPECTIVES

The Psychoanalytic Approach

In chapter 2, we reviewed briefly the principles of psychoanalytic theory. Here we will mention only some of the hallmarks of a psychoanalytic approach to treating suicidal clients. The psychoanalytic approach stresses the role of intrapsychic forces within the suicidal personality and views suicidal people as having such characteristics as "low self-esteem, excessive guilt or shame, anomic feelings such as isolation, powerlessness, hopelessness, and meaninglessness, sense of failure or incompetence" (Barry, 1989, p. 185). The goals of Freudian-oriented psychotherapy are "to make the unconscious conscious and to strengthen the ego so that behavior is based more on reality and less on instinctual cravings" (Corey, 1991, p. 114). In order to accomplish this, therapists attempt to help clients gain insight into their behaviors by reexperiencing and restructuring unconscious material. Unconscious material can be revealed by the use of free association techniques (i.e., asking clients to "let their minds roam freely among the images and thoughts associated with problematic behaviors" [Cottone, 1992, p. 106] and reveal these without censoring them to the therapist).

Dreams are another way in which the unconscious can be revealed and Freudian therapists often make dream interpretation a centerpoint of their therapeutic approaches. Heavy emphasis is also placed on the process of transference between the therapist and client, in which the client projects onto the thereapist repressed feelings from earlier situations. In addition, therapists often analyze the transference material with the help of their clients, helping to make what was unconscious become conscious. Such analysis can lead to insight for the client and help him or her to reach new levels of understanding and adjustment. Analysis of resistance is also a tool used by psychoanalytic therapists. When clients show an aversion to following a particular avenue of thinking, therapists will point this out and examine the meaning of the resistance itself.

Another approach that psychotherapists from the Freudian tradition might use is to focus on the balance between Eros and Thanatos—the essential ambivalence of the suicidal act. Gentle probing concerning what might be done to make life more bearable, followed by action to improve the circumstances of the individual even marginally, might swing the balance toward Eros (life) and away from Thanatos (death) (Shneidman, 1993).

Finally, psychoanalytically oriented therapists often endorse the concept of ego strength. They see the ego as the arbiter between the demands for pleasure made by the id and the demands for perfection made by the superego. Because the ego is the part of the personality that relates to the real world, therapists may attempt to develop more ego strength within suicidal individuals. Increasing ego strength may enable individuals to consider their situations from a more realistic and adult viewpoint.

Freudian-oriented psychotherapy demands much from the therapist's ability to understand and interpret the internal framework of the client. No doubt that is why people experiencing such psychotherapy often refer to it as being "in analysis." This type of therapy traditionally takes years and for this reason may not be very effective in working with clients who are experiencing a suicidal crisis. Because it represents an approach that plumbs the unconscious, it can be conceptualized as "depth" therapy and is perhaps better suited to situations in which clients have adequate resources of time, money, and energy to spend gaining fuller insight into themselves and their problems.

The Behavioral Approach

Behavioral approaches are based on the belief that faulty learning is behind suicidal behavior and that what has been learned can be unlearned and replaced with healthier tools for living. Behaviorally inclined therapists focus on the problems of the present and specify goals for treatment that are as objective and measurable as possible. Some therapists view behavioral approaches as essentially educational in nature and emphasize teaching of self-management skills (Corey, 1991). In this way, these approaches resemble some of the techniques described under cognitive approaches.

Specific techniques that behavioral therapists might use include *relaxation training,* which is aimed at enabling the client to enter a state in which new learnings are easier to acquire; *systematic desensitization,* which consists of eliminating anxiety over a specific situation by exposure to the situation in steps; and *modeling* appropriate behaviors to replace faulty ones learned previously. Therapists using this approach focus on their client's current problems, not on the history of those problems. They specify therapeutic goals in concrete terms and use overt teaching methods, including homework assignments, to promote learning of new behaviors. Therapists often model new or more positive behaviors for their clients.

Behaviorally oriented therapists share in common an understanding of experimentally derived principles of learning and a focus on gathering data to document change. They are likely to combine therapy with research and to develop models such as the learned helplessness model, introduced in chapter 2, which served as an animal paradigm for human depression. Once they have developed the models, they often turn their attention to developing a specific approach to counteract the model. For example, self-efficacy approaches that specifically teach depressed individuals new ways of behaving and taking control of situations may result in breaking down all but the most resistant cases of learned helplessness.

A common observation concerning behaviorist approaches is that they are probably most effective in addressing simple, concrete maladaptive behaviors. Complex behaviors, such as suicide attempts, rooted as they are in a combination of biological, psychological, cognitive, and environmental causes, may be less likely to profit from strictly behavioral approaches. Nevertheless, behavioristic models such as learned helplessness have been most productive in furthering our understanding of depression and suicide. Also, techniques such as systematic desensitization and training in self-efficacy have found a place in almost all therapeutic approaches.

The Humanistic/Existential Approach

Called the "third force" in psychology to distinguish it from the psychoanalytic and behavioral approaches commonly used throughout the first half of the 20th century, humanistic/existential approaches focus on both the freedom and the responsibility of individuals. The existential approaches also focus on meaning in life. They view life as essentially anxiety producing and attempt to help people find meaning in their own existence rather than to seek some external and universal truth. They also tend to view death as "a positive force, not a morbid prospect to fear, for death gives life its meaning. The existentialists have contributed a new understanding of anxiety, guilt, frustration, loneliness, and alienation" (Corey, 1991, p. 195). Existential therapists therefore have much to offer depressed and suicidal people.

Existential counselors use a variety of techniques but they share in common an emphasis on the quality of the therapeutic relationship and an attempt to focus on what choices and avenues are available to the individual. These core values coupled with an emphasis on defining individual meaning and taking responsibility for one's own growth and life choices are hallmarks of the existential approach to counseling. This approach can be used in either individual or group therapy. In fact, Yalom (1980), a pioneer in group therapy, has endorsed this approach by stating that it is a "valuable, effective psychotherapeutic paradigm, as rational, as coherent, and as systematic as any other" (p. 5).

Humanistic approaches share much in common with existential therapy. Perhaps the best known and most well developed humanistic approach is that developed by Carl Rogers. Called *person-centered therapy*, it is grounded in the belief that every person has the ability to actualize his or her potential and that meaning in life is found as we strive to reach that potential across our lifetimes. Person-centered therapists believe that they must create three conditions in order for change to occur: Counselors must be genuine or congruent throughout their relationships with their clients, they must show unconditional acceptance of and caring toward their clients, and they must be able to empathize with them, that is, to understand the subjective world of another person. Thus, person-centered therapy requires specific attitudes and skills on the part of therapists. The goals of therapy are to help clients find more independence and integration. Therapists also strive to help clients become more open to experience, to develop more internal sources of evaluation, to increase trust in themselves, and to develop a more positive attitude toward their own growth; in short, to become more self-actualized (Corey, 1991). Person-centered therapists also work to help clients enhance their self-concept and increase their self-esteem, always important issues for depressed and suicidal individuals. This therapeutic approach, more than any other, follows the lead of the client because person-centered therapists believe that if conditions are positive, clients will begin to grow in positive ways. Like existential therapy, this approach may be used with individuals and in groups.

The Cognitive Approach

The cognitive approach to therapy with suicidal people has gained much attention and approval in recent years. One of the forerunners of applied cognitive psychology was Albert Ellis. Although he was trained in traditional psychoanalytic thought, Ellis began very early to develop his own therapeutic approach to dealing with mental illness. He called it *rational-emotive therapy* (RET) and in a series of books he pointed out how we contribute to our own psychological problems by continuously repeating messages that reinforce "neurotic" behavior that causes us pain (Ellis, 1962). Ellis characterized neurotic behavior as "stupid behavior." He spelled out what he called the ABCs of stupid behavior, where A refers to the *activating event*, B to the *belief systems* of the individual, and C to the *consequences* of the activating event. To Ellis, aberrant behavior was not so much a result of the conditions in life as of the belief system of the individual who assigned personal meaning to those conditions. For example, Ellis believed that neurotic people often made themselves unhappy by believing that they must be loved or approved of by everyone for everything they do; that they must excel in everything in order to be worthwhile; or that it is terrible, horrible, and catastrophic when things are not the way we would like them to be (Ellis, 1974). Such beliefs, repeated over and over again, often reinforce an individual's basic unhappiness with life events.

In working with suicidal clients, Ellis would try to teach them ways of dispelling their neurotic belief systems; thus adding a D, for *disputing*, to his ABCs. People can learn to attack their negative belief systems by identifying the beliefs that they have; debating those beliefs in a logical fashion, and discriminating between irrational and rational beliefs (Ellis & Bernard, 1986). Therapists practicing RET often begin by pointing out the irrational "shoulds, musts, and oughts" that clients use to maintain negative feelings. They then teach clients to dispute such beliefs and to replace them with more rational beliefs and attitudes. The goal of therapy is to help clients internalize a more rational philosophy and to give them tools based on the scientific method to help them take control over their internal "self-talk" and make it more positive and adaptive.

In recent years, Aaron Beck has become known for his cognitive approach to therapy. In fact, Beck's work was recently reviewed, along with 15 other theories of suicide, and judged to be most applicable to suicidal lives (Lester, 1994). Beck's approach shares much in common with RET in that it maintains that people's beliefs and behaviors are based on their own internal structuring of their experience. Therapy attempts to change dysfunctional thinking and to help people correct faulty concepts of self. Beck more than many other therapists illuminates the characteristic rigid and constricted

---

My mother does not love me, I feel bad, I feel bad because she does not love me, I am bad because I feel bad, I feel bad because I am bad, I am bad because she does not love me, she does not love me because I am bad. R. D. Laing, *Knots*, 1970

thinking of suicidal people and exposes their characteristically negative self-talk. In contrast to Ellis, however, Beck places an emphasis on the therapeutic relationship and stresses some of the same principles emphasized in humanistic therapeutic approaches. For example, Beck believes that therapists should display genuine warmth and accurate empathy, and should not judge their clients (Beck, 1987). He specifically addresses three parts of suicidal people's worldviews. First, he addresses their negative view of themselves; second, their negative interpretation of their life experiences; and third, their gloomy projections about the future.

Accepting the work of Beck, Martin Seligman, the one-time behavioral researcher who established learned helplessness as a model for human depression (see chapter 2), has taken cognitive approaches one step further (Seligman, 1990). He maintains that as children we all learn an *explanatory style,* that is, a way of accounting for events when we experience setbacks or reversals. That explanatory style can lead to either an optimistic or pessimistic way of being in the world. For example, a student who fails a test may interpret that failure as evidence that she is "stupid" or a "real loser," or she may choose to interpret the failure as evidence that she did not study hard enough and needs to seek help in understanding the material. The first interpretation is a pessimistic one that sets her up for negative self-talk and supports a depressed mood. The second interpretation, in contrast, permits her to avoid permanent negative internalizing of the failure, allows her to assume responsibility for her performance without condemning herself, and even suggests future actions that may help her avoid the same painful situation in the future. In his wide-ranging review of the literature, Seligman (1990) shows that an optimistic explanatory style can lead to greater success, better health, and higher levels of happiness.

Seligman also pointed to specific tools that individuals can use to become more optimistic in their thinking. For example, he suggested that when you find yourself going over and over events in a negative way, you simply order yourself to stop or shift your thinking to something positive or make a deal with yourself that you will set aside time later to think about the situation, or you take a minute then to write out your troublesome thoughts and put them away for later consideration. In addition, Seligman suggested ways that you can dispute negative beliefs, including by examining evidence for your beliefs, considering possible alternative explanations, exploring the implications your negative beliefs have for you currently and in the future, and investigating what use your current beliefs are serving in your life for better or for worse. In short, Seligman maintains that just as learned helplessness is a model for depression and a pessimistic lifestyle, learning to be optimistic can function as an antidote to depression. Because it offers control to individuals through changing their customary ways of thinking, Seligman's learned optimism is a positive addition to cognitive therapies (Seligman, 1991).

The Biological Approach

Chapter 2 discussed some of the evidence that supports the idea that there is a biological component to suicidal depression. While medical doctors and psychiatrists are the professionals best equipped to explore the biological component of suicide, therapists in every perspective needs to be aware of the interplay of biology and psychology. They need to understand the developing research into the role that drug therapy can play in helping suicidal clients, and they need to be willing to refer their clients to medical doctors as well as to work as part of a supportive team in dealing with suicidal individuals.

The biological or medical approach to treating people assumes that there is an organic cause behind suicidal depression and that the cause often can be addressed by prescribing chemical substances or by prescribing treatments that affect the body's chemistry in some other way (e.g., electroconvulsive therapy) (Cory, 1991). As discussed in Chapter 2 and reviewed in this book's developmental chapters, there are biological correlates to depression. Whether an event such as the death of a loved one triggers a depressive episode or whether the effect is something less visible but more constant, like a pessimistic worldview, evidence is beginning to accumulate that the mind and body are inextricably connected (Stillion, 1986b). When someone is feeling suicidal, there are physical changes in every system of the body. Digestion is upset; the sleep-wake cycle is affected; even the individual's appearance and rate of movement are affected. However, the most basic level at which biological change occurs is in the brain. Seligman (1990) described these changes as follows:

> *Depression produces catecholamine depletion and increases in endorphin secretion. Endorphin increases can lower the activity of the immune system. Each link of the loss—pessimism—depression—catecholamine depletion—endorphin secretion depletion—immune suppression—disease chain is testable, and for each we already have evidence of its operation. This chain of events involves no spirits and no mysterious, unmeasurable processes. What's more, if this is actually the chain, therapy and prevention can work at each link. (p. 182)*

What Seligman is describing is biological change that begins at the cellular level and can lead to physical illnesses such as heart disease and cancer. It can also lead to psychological illnesses, including depression and suicide.

We have seen that neurotransmitters at the synapses of the cells within

---

Mind and body are intimately linked, so in one sense everything we think, remember, feel, or do reflects activity in the central nervous system. This basic fact has led some researchers to conclude that all psychological disorders ultimately stem from, or at least involve, biological causes. R. A. Baron, Psychology, Third Edition.

the brain appear to be different in depressed people than in nondepressed people and even more different among those who are extremely depressed and overtly suicidal. Four such substances have been identified: acetylcholine, norepinephrine, dopamine, and serotonin (Stillion, 1986b). Of these, decreased serotonin levels have been most consistently correlated with suicidal behavior (Asberg, Traskman, & Thoren, 1976; Teuting, Koslow & Hirschfeld, 1981). Drug treatment that is able to increase the levels of serotonin within the brain been shown to help relieve suicidal depression in many people. Some drugs that have shown promise in working with suicidal people include MAO inhibitors, tricyclics, serotonin reuptake inhibitors, and, for people suffering from bipolar (manic-depressive) episodes, lithium. Drug treatment rarely occurs without some type of conversation between the doctor who prescribes the treatment and the depressed patient. In a strict biological approach, the accompanying conversation is generally educational in nature. The patient is informed about the nature of his or her disorder, the limits that the disorder may place on everyday functioning, and the types of side effects that may develop as a result of the proposed treatment. The individual is then monitored at successive follow-up periods. Treatments are considered successful in this paradigm if the client experiences a lessening of symptoms and if the client can conduct his or her affairs in a purposeful and productive manner.

As with many things in life, it is not necessary to take an either-or approach to treating suicidal people. Drug therapy combined with one or more of the approaches mentioned above and/or those that follow may well be the strongest approach to reaching suicidally depressed people.

New Approaches

Recently, some imaginative new approaches that attempt to address both body and mind have been proffered. For example, vitamin and mineral treatments as well as exercise have experienced a renaissance among some biologically oriented therapists since these are viewed as less intrusive ways to affect the balance of the organism. In addition, approaches like clinical imagery are being championed by some medical doctors in conjunction with psychologists. Rossman, a physician, and Bresler, a psychologist, have developed a system of clinical imagery that they claim can be used as an access system to allow a "360-degree view of our inner landscape" (Rossman, 1984). Such an approach combines relaxation techniques and guided imagery exercises to help clients gain access to self-knowledge that may prove curative in nature. Therapists using this technique then discuss results of the guided imagery as a part of their therapeutic approach. One review of the literature found six studies that used imagery to alleviate depression. The author concluded that there was clear evidence that *various types of directed imagery procedures, either alone or in combination with other cognitive and behavioral approaches, can reduce both self-report and behavioral indices of depression for mild to moderately depressed college undergraduate students, mental health center patients whose symptoms included depression, and moderately to severely depressed psychiatric patients.* (Schultz, 1984, p. 142)

Up to this point, we have discussed general approaches for dealing with suicidal people. It is becoming clear, however, that many of the techniques developed within specific theoretical frameworks are complementary. This observation provides support for the development of an eclectic approach to working with suicidal people. A brief description of the way an eclectic counselor might use elements from each of these approaches in responding to a specific situation might be useful.

A CASE STUDY

Lisa M. was 25 years old. She was the only child of a physician who taught at a university medical school and his upper middle class wife. Although the family seemed stable, Lisa had borne the brunt of internal strife since she was a toddler. Both parents spoiled her throughout her childhood as they sought her approval and attempted to get her to take their side in every little dispute.

When she turned 18, Lisa went to a private college far from home. Within a few weeks, however, she realized that she had made a mistake since the students seemed unfriendly to her and the professors did not seem to care about her views or her ambitions. She left school before the fall break, returned home and enrolled in the local university. Although she had always made straight A's in high school, she found in college that she only made good grades in the subjects that she liked and in which her professors took a personal interest in her. She changed her major several times a year, which resulted in her taking six years to complete her undergraduate degree. Not knowing what else to do, she enrolled in graduate school at the same university to study art, a subject that she had come to love during her last three semesters of undergraduate school. She became deeply involved with another graduate student, Brad, who had taught several of the art labs she took as an undergraduate. Over her parents' objections, she moved in with him and began to adopt his lifestyle. She neglected her physical appearance and began using cocaine. Each time her parents urged her to return home, a bitter fight ensued, and Lisa generally ended the quarrel by leaving town for a few days, during which she would go on a drug and alcohol binge.

In April following her 25th birthday, Lisa found out that she was three months pregnant. Although she and Brad had talked about having children, Lisa realized that this child would probably be born addicted. Moreover, she realized that she could not have an abortion locally because her father would doubtless find out about it as the medical community was relatively small. After much thought, she came to believe that she could never live with the guilt of having aborted a child, but she also felt that she could not be responsible for bringing an addicted child into the world. She decided that the only solution was to take both her life and that of her unborn child.

In Lisa's case, the first necessity is to react to the suicidal crisis. The therapist handling this case will want to assure himself or herself that Lisa will not take any precipitous action. Clearly, biological considerations become primary in this case. While it may not be possible for Lisa to consider the usual antidepressant approaches because of the pregnancy, she will certainly need to be under a medical doctor's supervision in order to establish adequate prenatal care. Medical personnel might also be able to ascertain whether extensive damage had already occurred to the fetus. Issues of proper nutrition and exercise also become paramount in this case, especially if the pregnancy is to be continued.

Elements of a humanistic/existential approach might have particular appeal in this case since these approaches are essentially hopeful in nature. They stress the notion that no matter what mistakes have been made to date, it is possible to fulfill your unique potential. In addition, they communicate respect for the inherent worth and value of the individual regardless of past behaviors, a communication that Lisa may need to begin the process of self-forgiveness.

Techniques coming from a cognitive approach might include trying to uncover what messages Lisa is giving herself about who she is and what she has experienced in her life. Because Lisa may have internalized rigid, perfectionistic goals for herself, the therapist might want to explore what self-talk she is carrying on about her future. The therapist might also want to take an active role in pointing out to Lisa that different interpretations are possible for her past, present, and future behaviors. In this way she might come to see that although she has indeed made some mistakes, it does not mean that she is lost, a loser, or totally worthless. She might also come to see that she has several alternatives in the present, none of which may be ideal but all of which stop short of suicide. For example, she could abort the baby; she could have the baby and put it up for adoption; or she could have the baby and determine that she will cope with whatever problems the baby has and raise it as best she can. Through a combination of didactic teaching and challenging of beliefs and thought patterns, while supporting the individual as well as actively exploring alternatives, the cognitive approach might help Lisa begin to restructure her current situation and cope with it more realistically.

One of the behavioral techniques that the therapist might want to bring to Lisa is the use of relaxation techniques that might help her handle the stress of her pregnancy and prepare her to use Lamaze techniques for the childbirth phase if the pregnancy is continued. In Lisa's case, with a critical decision imminent with regard to her pregnancy, the psychoanalytic approach seems to offer little of value, although it might well be an option after the crisis is resolved, providing Lisa wanted to explore the hidden foundations of her personality that may be contributing to her self-destructive behaviors.

We have introduced a limited number of approaches to dealing with a depressed and suicidal person and have attempted to show how an eclectic therapist might approach a suicidal client using techniques from several different perspectives. Many other approaches exist, including Gestalt therapy, reality therapy and transactional analysis, and family systems therapy, to name just a few. Most of these approaches are grounded in one or a combination of the theoretical approaches presented in chapter 2. Consequently, therapists in training are generally required to study both theories of personality and theories of abnormal behavior prior to beginning to study individual therapeutic approaches. Most therapists read widely and develop their own eclectic approaches to working with suicidal clients. However, regardless of the therapeutic approach favored, therapists must also bear in mind the age and developmental stage of the people with whom they work. In the next section, we will examine developmental issues that therapists should keep in mind when working with suicidal people of different ages.

DEVELOPMENTAL ISSUES IN WORKING WITH SUICIDAL PEOPLE

Special Issues in Helping Suicidal Children

As discussed in chapter 3, suicide and suicide attempts have increased among children since the mid 1960s. Pfeffer (1984a) has pointed out that in spite of this documented increase the statistics underestimate the extent of the problem for several reasons. First, many adults deny that children are capable of attempting suicide. Such denial may stem from the belief that children under age 10 cannot understand the finality of death and therefore cannot really knowingly attempt suicide, or it may stem from the same general social pressures that result in underreporting of suicide at all ages, exacerbated by family pressures to withhold the real cause of death. The basic parental imperative is to keep children safe. Parents whose children commit suicide may feel doubly guilty. Not only have they failed to keep their children safe, they have also failed to see the signs leading up to suicide and may even have knowingly or unknowingly contributed to conditions that often are associated with it. For these reasons, it is important that helping professionals be alert to the conditions associated with child suicide and be willing to help parents see that their children may be at risk.

Until the early 1980s, most adults doubted that children could experience depression. It is now clear, however, as shown in chapter 3, that children can and do become depressed and suicidal. Caring adults should be aware that depression in children may be expressed differently than the classical adult symptoms, which include appetite and sleep disturbances, sexual dysfunction, self-reproach, feelings of despair, and loss of pleasure in life. Although suicidal children may show many of the adult symptoms, they may also act out more, refuse to go to school, make failing grades in school, and become disobedient, self-mutilating, and aggressive toward others. These reactions represent unsuccessful attempts to cope with painful feelings of worthlessness, hopelessness, and helplessness. The use, however, of these inappropriate coping techniques only increases the painful feelings, thus feeding into a downward spiral of emotions that may end in a suicide attempt. Therapists working with suicidal children should be aware of these negative coping mechanisms and recognize that they are part of the symptom picture in this age group.

Chapter 3 noted that the family situations of suicidal children are often turbulent and that depression is a frequent concomitant. Separation, divorce, death, parental psychopathology, and family violence, including physical and psychological child abuse, are all correlates of suicidal behavior in children (Pfeffer, 1984a). Parental depression and suicidal thoughts or attempts are also associated with an increased risk of suicide among children, as is childhood depression. Therefore, intervention programs with suicidal children must focus on the family as well as the child.

Because so much of a child's world is dependent upon the family structure and strengths, a systems approach to family therapy is often helpful (Bowen, 1978; Satir, 1967; Mclean & Taylor, 1994). At the core of this approach is the understanding that the family is a balanced system. If you succeed in helping one member of the family to perceive himself or herself differently, he or she will play a different role within the family than he or she did as a less healthy person. This will throw the system out of balance. Often, great pressure will be put on the child to reassume the unhealthy role he or she was playing in order to restore balance. By seeing each member of the family privately and by having some whole family sessions, family therapists are often able to move the entire family structure to a higher plane of adjustment.

Compounding the problem of treating suicidal children is the issue of children's understanding of death. As shown in chapter 3, the bulk of developmental literature across the last 50 years shows that young children (under age 10) do not have a clear understanding of the finality of death. Consequently, children may fantasize that suicide will replace the pain and depression they are experiencing with a more pleasurable state. Pfeffer (1984b) illustrated this kind of immature cognitive state in a discussion of the case of an eight-year-old boy who was hospitalized because of suicidal tendencies. When the boy was questioned closely, it became clear that he believed he would be reunited with his loving grandfather, who had recently died, if he committed suicide. Furthermore, he thought suicide would provide escape from an extremely stressful family situation. Such incentives are often a part of children's fantasies about suicide. Adults working with at-risk children should explicitly determine what children think death is and what their expectations are for existence after death.

Another common fantasy that children have about suicide is that suicide (like running away from home) will punish the parents. While this fantasy is undoubtedly true in most cases, the unspoken expectation among children is that, like Tom Sawyer, they will be around to witness the grief and remorse of the survivors. Once again, an incomplete understanding of the finality of death might make suicide seem more tempting.

Young children also frequently have trouble expressing their emotions in words. Although they may be experiencing sadness, helplessness, and anxiety, they may be unable or unwilling to verbalize their feelings. Complicating their lack of verbal ability is the fact that many children, especially those from troubled homes, may feel insecure about exposing their home life. Therefore, adults who work with suicidal children may wish to become familiar with several therapeutic approaches designed especially for children. *Traditional play therapy* (Axline, 1947) has a distinguished history, especially when used with younger children. *Art therapy* helps many children to express strong emotions like hopelessness and despair that they might not be able to express in words (Alshuler & Hattwick, 1947).

Dream work with children is also an effective therapeutic approach. Rosenn (1982) reported the dream of a depressed and suicidal child as follows: "An 8 1/2-year-old reported dreaming that the floor of his bedroom suddenly sank, leaving him hanging on an overhead lamp. He received an electrical shock and fell, leaving part of his arm attached to the light" (p. 204). Rosenn pointed out that the sinking floor could be interpreted as the "child's feeling of lack of support and groundedness in his family" and the loss of the arm might symbolize "the painful absence of a sustaining and anchoring relationship" (p. 205). Common themes appearing in dreams of depressed children include abandonment, emptiness, fragmentation, and loss, as well as generalized anxiety, physical punishment, and aggression.

Generally, dream therapy, art therapy, and play therapy are based on psychoanalytic theory. A major assumption underlying each of these types of therapy is that a child knows more than he or she can express and that expression of such knowledge not only helps the therapist understand the child's world but is curative in itself, because of the catharsis it brings. In order to become skilled in such therapeutic approaches, graduate study is required. However, unskilled, caring adults can often help a child to experience some relief from painful emotions simply by encouraging the child to express his or her emotions in play or in artwork.

A final approach to working with suicidal children is closely related to cognitive theory (discussed in chapter 2)—namely, *explicit teaching*. Children are natural learners if emotional blocks can be removed. Indeed, many trained therapists describe their work as one-on-one teaching. Adults need to teach children coping techniques such as those mentioned earlier in this chapter. Such techniques, taken together, constitute what Jaco (1987) has called *education for social functioning*. In a thoughtful article on suicide-proofing youths, Jaco emphasized the need to teach children to communicate effectively, to develop self-awareness of emotional states, and to increase their relationship skills, including such specifics as the ability to empathize and to analyze the effect of one's own behavior on others. Other elements of education for social functioning include the ability to solve problems, to see the connections between means and ends, to do realistic planning, to make decisions, and to take responsibility for one's own behavior. Each of these abilities will help children to cope more effectively and will decrease the likelihood of attempted suicide.

In summary, although suicidal behavior in childhood may appear to be impulsive, it is generally grounded in family conditions of turbulence, loss, and psychological or physical abuse. It is especially important in working with suicidal children to understand their developmental level (paying particular attention to their knowledge about death), to attend to family constellation and functioning, to help children find multiple ways for communicating their concerns and feelings, and to inventory children's coping skills. Specific techniques well-suited for working with children include play therapy, art therapy, family therapy, dream analysis, and the specific teaching of positive coping skills.

Issues in Helping Suicidal Adolescents

Adolescence has long been recognized as a period of *sturm und drang* (storm and stress) (Hall, 1904). The statistics about adolescent suicide and suicide attempts reviewed in chapter 4 reinforce this view and suggest that the stress associated with this period seems to be increasing rather than decreasing in today's society. People confronted by suicidal adolescents should

---

Curative factors in therapy include instilling hope, promoting feelings of universality, imparting information, modeling altruism, reproducing healthy versions of the primary family group, developing socializing techniques, providing models for imitative behavior, promoting interpersonal learning, nurturing group cohesiveness, accepting catharsis and exploring existential factors. Yalom, *The theory and practice of group psychotherapy.*

remember that adolescence is a bewildering time during which every aspect of the young person is undergoing radical change.

In addition to the many physical and cognitive changes discussed in chapter 4, there is pressure on many adolescents to become independent of their families—to choose careers, to excel in school, athletics, and so on. This pressure and the attendant stresses are not new to today's adolescent. What is new is that they are occurring against a background of loss and lack of support that is unprecedented in modern history.

Today's young people are not strangers to loss and the insecurity it causes. Many have experienced divorce and the accompanying loss of one full-time parent. In addition, many have moved several times during childhood, losing friends as well as familiar places and routines with each move. Another area of concern is the knowledge possessed by young people about nuclear issues. Research shows that American youngsters, like their European counterparts, know much about nuclear threat by the time they are ten years old (Blackwell & Gessner, 1983; Stillion, 1986; Stillion et al., 1988). While this knowledge may be less salient than it was during the cold war era, it still helps to shatter their illusion of safety and adds to the insecurities inherent in the adolescent period. All of these factors need to be kept in mind when working with suicidal adolescents.

Many of the therapeutic techniques used with children, such as art therapy and family therapy, also work well with adolescents. The evidence suggests that adolescent suicide often occurs within the context of a dysfunctional family. Therefore, a reexamination of family structure and function, an inherent part of the family systems therapy approach, is particularly helpful.

Many adolescents experience real relief from stress and depression by expressing themselves in writing. Keeping journals or sharing poetry are often helpful adjuncts to therapy. Psychodrama is also a natural therapeutic approach at this time, since teenagers almost universally experience a heightening of egocentrism (Elkind, 1967; Inhelder & Piaget, 1958). One result of this increase in egocentrism is the creation of an imaginary audience, which makes adolescents feel highly self-conscious. They themselves are on center stage and think that everyone watches and judges their appearance, behavior, and achievements. Research has shown that such self-consciousness peaks around age 13 for girls and age 15 for boys (Elkind & Bowen, 1979; Gray & Hudson, 1984). Because adolescents are used to performing for an imaginary audience, most will understand and accept the principles involved in psychodrama.

Adults working with at-risk adolescents may also want to avail themselves of the power of the peer group. One of the ironies of adolescence is that, as young people try to become independent of their families, they become increasingly dependent on their peer group for understanding and support. This interdependence strengthens the power of the group as a technique for reaching adolescents. Elkind (1967) has suggested that many adolescents create for themselves a "personal fable," a script in which they feel unique and misunderstood, and at the same time, indestructible. Group work helps to counteract the intensive feelings of separateness, uniqueness, and aloneness that adolescents often experience, because one of the key healing elements in group therapy is experiencing universality (Yalom, 1975). Adolescents in a group cannot avoid the realization that many others in the group share their feelings and concerns. This insight, coupled with the support, warmth, respect, concern, and positive interactions that occur in well-run groups, may bring about more positive change in less time than many other therapeutic techniques used with adolescents.

Issues in Working with Suicidal Young Adults

For most young adults, the period between ages 25 and 34 is marked by major life decisions. Commitments to work, to a spouse and family, and to a lifestyle are all initially made and often reevaluated at least once during these years. Sheehy (1976) called the common reevaluation that occurs around age 30 "catch 30," and she suggested that many young adults use this period to reflect on their accomplishments to date and to chart a new course or recommit to their earlier decisions.

There are four special issues that helping professionals should recognize when working with suicidal young adults. The first is the continuing need for young adults to prove their independence and competence to the world. This need may inhibit them from seeking required help, and it may even add to the suicide statistics of that age group, especially in the case of males, since it will motivate attempters to make sure their suicide attempts are successful. In current U.S. culture, competence tends to be judged by the person's position at work and by the amount of money earned. Therefore, young adults, especially males, may experience increased stress levels as they accept external definitions of their worth in terms of salary and job titles. In pursuing success as defined for them, they may become workaholics or compulsive spenders. Debt incurred during the early adult years in an effort to authenticate success often merely adds to the stress of that period. As one 26-year-old told his therapist, "It seems I work to pay for things that I don't have time to use. I look around my apartment and it's filled with *things,* nice things, but they don't make me happy. I hate my job. I have no time to make friends, and until I decided to see you, I had no one to talk to. I don't understand it. I've got what everyone says is a good job. I've got money and lots of things,

---

"Why has Thou done all this? Why hast Thou brought me here? Why, why dost Thou torment me so terribly?" He did not expect an answer and yet wept because there was no answer and could be none. Tolstoy, *The Death of Ivan Ilych*

The Voyage of Life: Manhood, **Thomas Cole. Oil on Canvas, 52 × 78 in. (Collection of Munson-Williams-Proctor Institute, Utica, New York.)**

but none of it seems to really matter. If this is all there is to life, why bother?" People in the helping professions may have to be extremely sensitive in order to detect suicidal predispositions in young adults and to get them to discuss their problems openly.

Second, sexuality issues may impede therapy, especially group therapy, during this period. Because interest in the opposite sex is at a peak during young adulthood, and because young adults typically review life choices (e.g., their choice of a spouse), group therapy for suicidal young adults may be more difficult than for adolescents and older adults. Young adults may not be willing to expose suicidal weaknesses to those whom they might regard as potential mates. In addition, young adults often need more privacy than adolescents do. For these reasons, helping professionals may want to discuss the relative merits of group and individual therapy with young adults before deciding on the type of referral (See Canetto, 1994, for a more complete discussion of gender issues in the treatment of suicide).

The third major issue to be considered in working with suicidal young adults is the issue of parenting. The years between 20 and 34 have traditionally been the peak parenting years in the United States. While the trend in recent years has been toward having babies at a later age, parenting concerns remain major sources of anxiety during the young adult years. For some couples, the anxiety stems from wanting children and being unable to conceive, with accompanying feelings of inadequacy and loss. For others, anxiety and division may occur when one mate wants children and the other does not. Still others may experience disruption at the birth of a child, especially if the mother experiences postpartum depression. Some couples may adjust to the addition of an infant easily only to find their lives increasingly strained as the child matures and arguments ensue over child-rearing practices. As discussed in chapter 5, single mothers with several preschool children are at special risk for suicidal depression. All of these conditions related to parenting require special consideration from helping professionals. Couples therapy or family therapy are referral alternatives when a suicidal young adult identifies parenting as a major source feeding into his or her suicidal ideations. Suicidal young adults also need to consider the negative effects that completed suicide has on loved ones.

Finally, the issue of AIDS presents special threats to young adults. We have seen that the greatest danger of suicide may occur with people who have been diagnosed as HIV positive and before major symptoms have set in. We believe that this is true because HIV positive young people are experiencing a severe anticipatory grief response. The term "anticipatory grief" was coined by Lindeman (1944). It originally referred to people who were living with a dying person and who were able to work through much of their grief reactions prior to the death of that person, leaving them with less grieving to do after the death. However, more recently the meaning has been expanded to include those people who are dying from illnesses in which the dying trajectory is so prolonged that there is time for mourning one's own passing. AIDS is just such a disease. Clinicians working with AIDS patients might do well to review the literature on helping people cope with bereavement and grief resolution.

One of the foremost writers in the area of grief therapy, J. William Worden (1991), has pointed out that counselors must help clients experiencing anticipatory grief in order to accept the fact of their eventual death and to cope with the existential anxiety that facing death entails. Worden suggested that there are four tasks that mourners must perform in order to move successfully through to resolution of their grief. With a little adaptation, two of these also pertain to people grieving their own imminent deaths.

The first task is accepting the reality of death. For those who are dying from a prolonged disease such as AIDS, this means facing the loss of everything and everyone that they have ever loved as well as the loss of their entire being, future, and possible growth. Facing such total loss requires a great deal of courage, continuous effort, and ongoing support from care givers. Finding meaning for one's life when faced with such total loss seems a Herculean task, but one that young AIDS patients must struggle with every day.

Worden's second task is to experience and work through the pain of grieving. As Bowlby, one of the pioneers in studying grief, has noted, "Sooner or later, some of those who avoid all conscious grieving, break down—usually with some form of depression" (Bowlby, 1980, p. 158). Kubler-Ross (1969) also illuminated the state of mind of dying patients by introducing her now-famous, and much criticized, stages of grieving: denial, anger, bargaining, depression, and acceptance. Although most critics agree that these emotions are not stages, they do accept that dying people feel all of these emotions as they work through the pain of grieving. Caring professionals need to be sensitive to the emotional turbulence that dying people are experiencing. Appropriate strategies for helping people cope include active listening; helping individuals to identify, clarify, and express feelings; pointing out alternatives where they exist; supporting choices whenever possible; and reassuring dying individuals that they will not be left alone. Accepting the existential despair that individuals are feeling and helping them find ways to express it actively are also important techniques. Finally, it is important to remember that depression can be treated as a symptom in itself. Antidepressant medication can be administered to at least some clinically depressed AIDS patients and should not be overlooked as a tool that may help them live their lives as fully as possible for as long as possible.

Issues in Working with Suicidal Middle-Aged Adults

As shown in Chapter 6, there are many issues adults must struggle with between the ages of 35 and 64. These include redefining their identities, finding ways to be nurturant and creative, and developing a positive philosophy of life. However, the central issue for this age group, beginning as a whisper in the busy years of young adulthood but gradually increasing to a roar in middle age, is that of continuing to be generative in the face of mounting losses.

Losses are frequent throughout the middle adult years. Primary losses (those that cannot be avoided) include the loss of one's youthful appearance (as a result of getting wrinkles, gray hair, etc.), the weakening of muscles, and the development of problems with sight and hearing. Many people develop chronic illnesses, which cause pain and a further loss of physical functioning. Such chronic illnesses may necessitate medications, which sometimes have side effects that increase anxiety or depression. Physical losses are paralleled by others, such as the loss of the young dreams of high achievement, the loss of the parenting role, divorce, and the deaths of parents, siblings, and friends. Yet another loss of midlife is the loss of time remaining. Research indicates that a central factor in midlife crises is a sense of time running out. Erica Jong (1994) underlines this factor when she suggests that fifty is the time when time itself begins to seem short. She points out that men and women who are over fifty need to prepare for death, to see themselves as part of the flow of creation, and to reflect on meaning and the nature of the spirit.

Helping professionals who work with suicidal adults should consider taking a loss history. Such a history generally includes a listing of all losses that an individual has experienced, the age at which the loss occurred, the effect the loss had on the individual, and the methods and resources the individual used to cope with the loss. Loss histories help not only in assessing the burden of cumulative loss suffered by the suicidal adult but also in pinpointing past coping skills and available resources.

Since middle age is also the time of menopause, suicidal females may respond well to drugs, including estrogen replacement therapy. It is therefore essential for helping professionals working with middle-aged adults to be aware of the drugs being used by their clients and to work in close communication with their clients' medical doctors.

Helping professionals should also attend to the middle-aged person's level of sociability. Many middle-aged people have difficulty beginning new relationships. During their early adult years, they may have been so busy with their careers and families that little time was available for investing in friendships. Many find themselves lonely at age 50—with their children grown and friends from their youth dead or living elsewhere. For these individuals, group therapy may prove very effective, since groups provide opportunities for practicing rusty interpersonal skills in addition to providing specific therapeutic benefits. However, helping professionals should expect to find initial resistance to the idea of working within a group setting.

As shown in chapter 6, alcohol abuse is often associated with suicide among middle-aged adults. Alcoholism and its related problems tend to exacerbate the losses of this stage of development, particularly those losses associated with health, occupation, and family. Alcoholics Anonymous, a worldwide organization, has experienced a great deal of success in helping alcoholics to stop drinking. It is also likely that the group support and social interaction provided by the weekly meetings and the 24-hour emergency services of this organization significantly reduce suicide among alcoholics.

Helping professionals who work with middle-aged adults are also more likely than those who customarily work with younger people to encounter patients who are considering suicide because of life circumstances that are not realistically changeable. By the time adults have reached the middle years, many have developed chronically painful, life-threatening conditions, have experienced overwhelming failure, or are facing imminent death. Adults who are terminally ill present special challenges to helping professionals. Consequently, it is doubly important that helping professionals be very clear about their own attitudes toward suicide.

Barry (1984) has suggested that all helping professionals need to be aware of the "cultural, personal, and professional *baggage* we bring into suicide-related situations" (p. 17). He described eight different positions that helping professionals may take with regard to suicide, including viewing suicide as a cry for help or as heresy, sin, tragedy, duty, an act of cowardice or heroism, a threat to one's own professional reputation and feelings of competence, or a rational solution to an otherwise insoluble problem. We would agree with Barry that helping professionals, particularly those working with suicidal middle-aged and elderly adults, need to be clear about their own views of suicide and honest about these views with the people with whom they work. Without such honesty, the helping relationship may easily become colored by the biases of the therapist and may actually result in clashing values obstructing the therapeutic process. Alternatively, the therapist may accept the reasoning of the client and overtly or covertly support suicidal ideation and behavior.

Although not specifically addressing suicide, Weisman (1972) introduced the concept of appropriate death as a goal to be achieved whenever possible. Appropriate death was defined as death that is consistent with the way in which someone has lived, the kind of death that the individual would choose if in control of the conditions of his or her death. Obviously, such a definition includes the possibility of suicide, especially for those who are painfully and terminally ill. Nelson (1984) has suggested that there might be "circumstances under which mental health professionals might consider the option of death as appropriate to the individual who wishes to die and, having done so, neutrally stand aside or not actively intervene in the termination of that person's life" (p. 177). While such a position is likely to be viewed as extreme by most of the mental health community, Nelson maintains that for some people suicide may be a realistic choice. For helping professionals working with middle-aged clients whose lives may appear to be barren of satisfaction and full of pain, whose coping skills may be negligible or totally exhausted, and for whom the future may in reality be limited and bleak, the question of the morality of suicide becomes salient.

Another problem facing professionals working with middle-aged adults is related to the change in time perspective that was discussed in chapter 6. Many middle-aged individuals believe that they do not have much time remaining. They also feel that because their present problems are the result of many years of ineffective coping, the time remaining is not adequate to improve their life situation substantially. In addition, many middle-aged adults experience a decrease in energy levels. As one wag put it, "Middle age is the time when a man is always thinking that in a week or two he will feel as good as ever." More seriously, perceptions of middle-aged people that their accumulated problems cannot be resolved within the remaining time and with their energy levels are significant factors that must be addressed by any helping professional working with suicidal individuals in this age group.

Finally, in this age group as with the elderly, it is often helpful to explore issues surrounding personal meaning in life. From middle age onward, many people find themselves becoming more introspective as well as raising questions about the true meaning of their individual lives. For this reason, existential and humanistic approaches to working with depressed and suicidal persons are often effective with middle aged and elderly adults.

Issues in Working with the Suicidal Elderly

Of all suicidal patients, those over 65 may be the most difficult to work with, for various reasons. As discussed in chapter 7, elderly people tend to be devalued in our culture. The suicide of a 70-year-old seems infinitely less sad to many than the suicide of a 17-year-old. Conventional wisdom holds that the 70-year-old had a chance at life while the 17-year-old never really did. Such "commonsense" assumptions undoubtedly affect the way elderly people view their own suicides and, perhaps as important, the way care givers react or fail to react to suicidal signs among the elderly. Osgood, Brant, and Lipman (1988–1989) documented that suicide among elderly people living in nursing homes was more than four times the rate reported among elderly people living independently. Such a finding highlights the need for increased awareness of the following special issues relating to suicide among the elderly.

The first issue concerns case-finding procedures. The elderly are over-represented among suicides but underrepresented among the clientele of suicide prevention centers (Farberow & Moriwaki, 1975; McIntosh, Hubbard, & Santos, 1981; Rachlis, 1970; Resnik & Cantor, 1970). Because the elderly do not use crisis hotlines and other conventional services, a number of writers have recommended establishing special suicide intervention centers for the elderly that would be staffed with older counselors and be in locations frequented by the elderly (Farberow & Moriwaki, 1975; McIntosh, Hubbard, & Santos, 1981; Rachlis, 1970, Renik & Cantor, 1970). Also, new case-finding methods are needed with outreach programs in order to provide services before tragedies occur (Butler & Lewis, 1977; McIntosh, Hubbard, & Santos, 1981).

The second issue concerns depression, easily the most prevalent mental illness among elderly people (Butler & Lewis, 1982). It is more likely to go untreated in this age group, however, primarily because depressive symptoms are confused with those of normal aging but also sometimes because of fear that the treatment may interact with other drugs the elderly person is taking. Nevertheless, the relationship between depression and suicide documented in other age groups is just as real for the elderly, and it undoubtedly contributes to the very high suicide rates among people over age 65. Helping professionals working with this age group must work in close cooperation with physicians to ensure that underlying symptoms of chronic depression are treated.

A third issue that should be recognized when working with the elderly concerns cumulative loss. Chapter 7 reviewed the normative losses elderly people endure, including physiological losses, losses of interpersonal relationships, the loss of meaningful activity, the loss of roles in life, and the loss of status. While losses may occur at any time during the life span, they are the rule rather than the exception in old age. The elderly therefore find themselves dealing with cumulative losses. They often do not have time to work their way through grief over one loss before they are confronted with another. In addition, loss may breed loss. A woman whose husband dies may give up her home to move in with her daughter. In giving up her home, she loses her independence, the security of a well-known routine, her neighbors, and her roles as home owner and hostess. As with middle-aged clients, thoughtful helping professionals working with suicidal elderly people should take a loss history. Such a history will show the extent of loss a person has suffered and the timing of the losses. It will also, in the hands of a sensitive professional, help the elderly person to understand why he or she may be feeling depressed and to identify (and perhaps mobilize) coping techniques used in the past.

Sensory deficits have also been shown to be related to depression among elderly people. Butler and Lewis (1982) have pointed out that failing eyesight and hearing add further to the social isolation elderly people experience. Even in the midst of a warm, supportive family, a person who cannot see or hear is not a part of the scene. Loss of taste is another normative change among elderly people. Since the loss of taste makes eating less pleasant, elderly people may eat less or may eat only certain types of food. Helping professionals should observe the eating habits of elderly persons, since preliminary evidence suggests that nutritional status may be related to depression.

Elderly people also often suffer from a lack of touching. Living alone or in impersonal nursing homes, many elderly people go for weeks or months without the loving touch of a caring human being. In recent years, a variety of programs have been started to address the essential loneliness of the elderly. Some of these programs match young children with elderly in nursing homes. Young children tend to be spontaneous in touching as well as naturally social and curious. Such programs can be mutually beneficial, since they help children understand and accept the aging process and at the same time decrease the isolation and loneliness of the elderly.

There are many other examples of intergenerational programs designed to build social ties between the elderly and other segments of society and thus combat loneliness in elderly people. For example, the Elder Neighbor program in western North Carolina promotes healthy interaction by assigning volunteers to call or visit elders at specific times each day. The national Meals on Wheels program provides both nutrition and social contact for homebound elders. A program called "Age-Link" attempts to match healthy elders with school-age children during after-school hours in order to meet the needs of both groups for positive social interaction. Other programs, like Daniel Levitan's exercise program at the University of Maryland, promote intergenerational socializing while developing health habits of exercise and nutrition. One San Francisco-based program designed specifically to prevent elderly suicide has created a "Friendship Line" for the elderly, which is staffed by volunteers on a 24-hour basis. These volunteers take calls from and place calls to elders, and they also disseminate information about elderly suicide to a wide range of professional groups. Most communities have programs like these available. Anyone working with suicidal elderly should examine community resources and make appropriate referrals. Perhaps the most important question an older suicidal person can be asked is, "What differences would have to occur in your life to make you feel that life is worthwhile again?"

Finally, helping professionals who work with suicidal elderly persons should be aware of what Erikson called the task of developing ego integrity instead of despair and disgust. Elderly suicidal people frequently are on the negative end of this bipolar continuum. They have lived most of the years they can expect to live and now, as they review them, they find little meaning or value. Butler and Lewis (1982) have described an approach called *reminiscence therapy*, which provides an opportunity for elderly people to search for themes that once gave meaning to their lives. Done individually or in groups, reminiscence therapy involves evoking memories about specific events in younger years; these memories help elderly people to focus on times when their self-esteem was higher and their self-concepts were more positive than they currently are. Reminiscence therapy can also help elderly people to validate their existence by highlighting their past ability to cope and their survivorship. In addition, if the suicidal elderly can be helped through reminiscence to discuss critical events in their lives and the meanings of those events, they may be helped to see patterns of values in their lives. Finally, reminiscence therapy may help alleviate some of the hopelessness suicidal elderly experience by helping them to take pride in past accomplishments. Although called reminiscence therapy, this approach is more a technique than a full-blown therapy, and it can be used by caring individuals without intensive training. The power of the technique can be seen in the following story, which was told to the authors by the social worker involved.

> *Ms. Benson was a social worker who often led groups of elderly people in reminiscence therapy. She was asked to include in a new group an elderly widow, Mrs. Langley, who had become depressed and almost totally nonresponsive to people in her nursing home. Ms. Benson formed a group of eight elderly widowed women that met in the "parlor" of the nursing home twice a week. Ms. Benson started each session by playing music from earlier times. She encouraged the women to share their memories of those times. In one session she suggested they talk about their wedding days. In other sessions she suggested they discuss the birth of their firstborns, the ways in which they coped during the*

Depression, the day World War II ended, and so on. Mrs. Langley tended to sit passively through the sessions, sometimes weeping quietly. When Ms. Benson played the song "Don't sit under the apple tree with anyone else but me" to begin the session on memories of World War II, Mrs. Langley began to cry and then to talk about her life during the war, her marriage to a naval officer, and her work with the U.S.O. From that time on, she participated actively in the sessions.

When all the sessions were over, the social worker talked to Mrs. Langley in private. She said, "I envy you. Here I am at 30, just starting out. I don't know if I'll accomplish anything in the next 50 years or if I'll stick to my principles and live a productive life. There you are, almost 80 years of age. You've raised four children, been active in your church and community, accomplished so many good things, were a part of so much history, and you did it all with such patience and caring."

Mrs. Langley just smiled.

A major element of success in working with the suicidal elderly is respect. All caregivers must sincerely respect the life experiences of elderly persons and help them retain or develop respect for their own life histories. As Erikson defined it, ego integrity, the last stage in positive mental health, consists of the elderly realizing that they had only one life to live and that, considering their opportunities, they lived it pretty well. Anyone who comes to that realization is unlikely to commit suicide. On the other hand, people who reach old age deprecating themselves and finding little meaning in their lives are prime candidates for suicide. Despair and hopelessness undoubtedly contribute to the elderly suicide statistics.

Care givers would do well to remember that when elderly people attempt suicide, they are much more likely to complete it than are younger people. In addition, care givers may have less warning about elderly suicides. Elderly people who choose suicide generally do so without fanfare. Because they do not make as many suicidal gestures and because they exhibit less ambivalence about ending their lives than do many people in younger groups, any suicide threat by an elderly person must be taken very seriously. Elderly males in particular are at higher risk for suicide than females and care givers must be especially sensitive to males who exhibit signs of depression.

Care givers who work with elderly people must also be positive forces in promoting a sense of ego integrity and combating a sense of despair and disgust if the elderly suicide statistics are to decrease in the future. The promotion of integrity among the elderly necessitates more and better public education. As a society, we need to foster greater awareness of the special stresses experienced by the elderly and their special vulnerability to suicide. Perhaps even more important, we need to encourage among all age groups cultural attitudes toward the elderly that are more positive.

SUMMARY

The important topics of suicide intervention and ongoing treatment were discussed in this chapter. Intervention was described as a responsible and moral process that is necessary because almost all people who take their lives do so in an ambivalent state. Therefore, intervention may shift the balance toward life and away from death. Shneidman's four psychological features of suicidal people (acute perturbation, heightened inimicability, constriction of the thinking processes, and cessation as the way to end emotional pain) were discussed. Advice for untrained professionals confronting a person in a suicidal crisis included a discussion of the questions that should be asked of such a person and the injunction to stay with a suicidal person until professional help can be obtained.

Formal crisis intervention programs discussed included the Samaritan program and the American model of crisis intervention. Legal liability of therapists was introduced as a reason for taking a proactive stance, even to the point of initiating mandatory hospitalization procedures. The impact of the death by suicide of a client on a therapist was briefly explored and the suggestion was made that therapists should have support following such a death to prevent guilt reactions and possible burnout.

Ongoing therapeutic approaches were explored from the perspectives of the psychoanalytic approach, the behavioral approach, the humanistic/existential approach, and the cognitive approach. Other approaches, including Bresler and Rossman's clinical imagery and a family systems approach, were briefly introduced. A case study was shared, with suggestions for utilizing aspects of each approach in an eclectic orientation to ongoing therapy.

Special issues that might impact on suicidal persons of different ages were presented. Play therapy, art therapy, dream work, and family therapy were suggested as approaches for helping suicidal children. The use of journals, psychodrama, and group therapy as well as family therapy were recommended as approaches for working with adolescents. Issues of reviewing past choices and making life changes surfaced in the discussion of young adulthood. Problems in using group therapy were mentioned. Special attention was given to issues associated with AIDS in working with young adults. The addition of a loss history was suggested when working with middle-aged suicidal persons as well as group therapy for those who find loneliness feeding their depression. Use of such well-established programs as Alcoholics Anonymous in cases where alcohol is a problem was also recommended. In working with both the middle aged and the elderly, existential/humanistic approaches that help individuals focus on the meaning of their individual lives were suggested. Finally, reminiscence therapy was emphasized as an approach that might help elderly people grow toward ego integrity and satisfaction with their accomplishments.

Contemporary Issues in Suicide

Canadian Medical Association members should specifically exclude participation in euthanasia and assisted suicide.

CMA Policy Summary, *Physician Assisted Death*, 1995, p. 248A

I think it inevitable that the practice of physician-assisted suicide will become more widespread, whether technically legal or not—

Margaret Battin, *Physician-Assisted Suicide*, 1995, p. 223

No book on suicide would be complete without an examination of the ethical and legal issues surrounding suicide. Because it would be an impossible task to review all of the burgeoning literature in this area in one chapter, we will review only selected literature concerning the case for and against rational suicide. For interested readers, however, we have provided a list of suggested readings that we believe will be helpful in attaining a more complete understanding. We will also explore in some detail the recent history and future outlook of right-to-die legislation, often discussed in conjunction with physician-assisted suicide and/or euthanasia. We will then provide arguments both for and against physician-assisted suicide and euthanasia. Finally, we will provide a reprise of the major points of this book in order to underline their importance as you complete your study of suicide.

RATIONAL SUICIDE

We should begin our discussion by pointing out once again that suicide is a controversial issue. There have been voices in every age that have spoken in favor of a universal human right to suicide. In chapter 1 we presented the views of the ancient stoics on this matter. Such voices are still heard as we approach the threshold of the 21st century. For example, Lester (1987), has argued that "completed suicide may be a desirable act for a person, given his [sic] life circumstances and expectations for the future. Furthermore, we all have to die, and it is important to consider what would constitute an appropriate death for a person" (p. 69).

The issue of the right to suicide has become more salient in recent years both because our society has become less religious and therefore less likely to follow religious proscriptions blindly and because technology has reached the point where people may be kept alive long after their lives are productive or even comfortable. There is growing evidence that the general public is supporting the right of terminally ill people to take their own lives (e.g., Deluty, 1988, 1989; Droogas, Siiter, & O'Connell, 1982; Malcolm, 1990; Minear & Brush, 1981). Even among therapists there seems to be growing acknowledgment of suicide as an acceptable response in certain situations, especially those involving terminal illness accompanied by great pain and suffering (Werth, 1996).

Battin (1984), a philosopher, has made a thoughtful case for rational suicide in four different situations. First, she noted that suicide may be considered rational when it meets the expectations of the society in which the individual lives. The ancient Scandinavians, for example, practiced suicide because of their belief that it assured them of a place in Valhalla (which according to Norse mythology is where the souls of heroes slain in battle are received). This belief seems to be echoed in modern times by some in the Moslem faith who view dying for a cause as noble. A second basis for rational suicide, according to Battin, is avoidance of harm, such as the pain that attends certain terminal illnesses. A third basis was characterized by Battin as "in accordance with fundamental interests." People who commit suicide based on a belief or who allow themselves to die for a cause provide examples of this type of rational suicide. The mass suicide of Jews at Masada is an example of this type of suicide. Finally, Battin delineated what she called "expressive suicide," in which individuals kill themselves to express an emotion, such as remorse for some action they have taken that they now find reprehensible. The suicide of Judas Iscariot illustrates this type of suicide.

Siegel (1986) has also spelled out characteristics of rational suicide. According to him, persons considering suicide must understand their situation realistically and must be in such a situation that their desire to kill themselves would be understandable to most objective observers. In addition, they must be unimpaired by psychological illness and/or grave emotional distress.

Werth (1996) has challenged the traditional view that the act of suicide is evidence of instability. In an in-depth analysis of rational suicide, he suggests not only that suicide is rational in certain situations, but also that counselors have an obligation to understand, evaluate, and treat their clients from a perspective that includes the possibility of rational suicide.

Szasz (1976, 1986) an original thinker in the field of psychology, has argued against suicide prevention in most situations for two reasons. First, suicide prevention often requires stripping people of their individual rights and compelling them against their will to remain alive. Second, it requires professionals to engage in "therapeutic paternalism," which violates the maxim that people are responsible for their own behavior. Szasz warned that therapists who are willing to take the responsibility for preventing suicide are open to lawsuits in cases where therapy fails and suicide occurs. He pointed out that

> because, in fact, it is virtually impossible to prevent the suicide of a person determined on killing himself or herself, and because forcibly imposed interventions to prevent suicide deprive the patient of liberty and dignity, the use of psychiatric coercion to prevent suicide is at once impractical and immoral. (1986, p. 809)

Szasz noted that because children typically are subject to paternalistic and coercive techniques, they should be exempted from this generally permissive policy. He did not, however, exempt people who might be psychotic, depressed, or otherwise mentally ill. Instead, he reminded his readers that people in the United States are considered sane until proven insane and therefore should be free to take their own lives unless they voluntarily seek treatment. He advocated that suicide should be given the "status of a basic human right" and that "power of the state should not be legitimately invoked or deployed to prohibit or prevent persons from killing themselves" (1986, p. 811).

While most helping professionals do not endorse all of Szasz's broad views for treating suicidal people, it seems that many do accept the argument that a decision to die can be rational. Werth and Liddle (1994) carried out a study with members of the American Psychological Association's Division of Psychotherapy. They used vignettes describing suicidal people who were suffering from terminal illness, who had chronic physical pain, who were experiencing psychological pain, or who had experienced bankruptcy. They found that 81% of those responding reported that they believed in rational suicide. What is more, their respondents were most likely to accept the idea of suicide in people who were terminally ill and least likely to accept it in the situation of bankruptcy.

Recently, as technology has increased the number of people who can expect to spend months or even years in terminal pain and suffering, many more voices have entered the debate about the right of an individual to take his or her own life, asserting that people do indeed have a right to die. Because the issue is intimately connected in the public mind with suicide, we believe we must address it as clearly as possible, for whatever it is called, it promises to be as controversial an issue as abortion has been across the past few decades in American society. Because we believe that students of suicide need to have a clear understanding of this issue, we will provide some definitions that may help clarify the differences between right to die, physician-assisted suicide, and euthanasia. We will then review the past 20 years of the public dialogue on this issue.

The phrase "the right to die" is the most general of terms used to discuss this issue. It is generally taken to include a person's right to self-determination and may include such things as advance directives, including a living will and specific directions to doctors and relatives regarding the conditions under which a person would not want to continue living, as well as the request for withholding or withdrawing life-sustaining treatment.

Is it Sin? To rush into the secret house of death ere death doth come to us? Shakespeare, *Anthony and Cleopatra*

The term "physician-assisted suicide" usually refers to the idea that a physician will supply but may not administer a lethal dose of a substance. It is important to understand the limits that people have in mind in discussing physician-assisted suicide. One person may mean only being given access to an appropriate amount of medicine to bring about death. A second person may understand the term to mean that a physician will be present at the time of death to see that no adverse reaction occurs from the medication and to give comfort and support to the dying person.

The term euthanasia goes one step further and assumes that the physician or some other interested party will administer a lethal dose of poison or use another active form to bring about a person's death. An older differentiation distinguished between two types of euthanasia: passive and active. Passive euthanasia generally referred to allowing an individual to die by withholding medication or treatment, while active euthanasia meant taking steps to help end a life. The usefulness of this dichotomy has decreased as technology and drug therapies have expanded to the point where the line between life and death has become blurred.

A RECENT HISTORY OF EUTHANASIA IN THE UNITED STATES

Throughout most of human history, people died from disease—generally, rather abrupt deaths and at early ages relative to present times.[1] Within the 20th century we have witnessed nearly a 60% increase in the average life expectancy: People in 1900 lived about 47 years; in 1995, they can expect to live to be more than 75 years of age. At the same time that modern science was developing enhanced understanding of germ theory, nutrition, and sanitation, which lengthened life, medicine was using new technologies and understanding to become specialized and to prolong life long beyond its ability to be useful or even cognizant. A second outcome of this technology has been the development of the ability to predict imminent death well in advance and to extend the dying process over weeks, months, or even years. Death also became specialized, moving from an event that occurred in the home to one that now occurs in a hospital 85% of the time. Hospitalized death is often synonymous with technological death. Tubes may be inserted in every imaginable orifice. People may be kept alive by respirators breathing for them and/or by artificial hydration and feeding. As more people have seen these types of death, they have begun to consider alternatives that they would prefer to technological death. Twenty years ago the discussion concerning euthanasia was fairly theoretical. Today it has become highly practical. Let us examine some of the high points of the discussion of the last two decades.

[1] This history was primarily taken from an address by Howard Brody on physician-assisted suicide before the National Health Forum sponsored by the University of Florida, March 1995.

In 1975, James Rachels argued in an article published in the *New England Journal of Medicine* that there was no moral difference between active and passive euthanasia. His article was so influential in establishing the tone for the ensuing debate that it is still widely used in medical ethics classes. However, the article was regarded at the time mainly as an intellectual discussion rather than as an applied issue.

The next major milestone in the debate was the Karen Quinlan case, which stands as the first national right-to-die case. Karen, aged 21, collapsed in April of 1975 after taking a mixture of tranquilizers and alcohol (Worsnop, 1992). As her condition deteriorated into a "persistent vegetative state," her parents requested removal of the respirator that was breathing for her, asking that their daughter be allowed to die "with grace and dignity." This request was denied by a judge. On appeal, however, the New Jersey Supreme Court reversed the lower court's ruling. The legal importance of this case was that the court held that the state generally has an interest in preserving life but that when the state's interest declines (as it does in the case of irreversible coma) then the right of privacy may take over. Since Karen was not able to exercise her constitutional right to privacy, the judge ruled that Karen's parents could decide "whether she would exercise it in these circumstances" (Worsnop, 1992, p. 155). It is worthwhile noting that once the respirator was removed, Karen lived another 9 years being fed and hydrated with tubes because her parents did not request their removal. The important legal outcome of this case was to establish the patient's right (and by extension the parents' or guardians' right) to refuse treatment.

In 1977, another case received national publicity. Joseph Saikewicz, a mentally retarded 67-year-old man who had a mental age of 3, developed leukemia. Although the disease was terminal, with aggressive treatment he might be expected to live for a longer period. The dilemma was that this man, who had no memory of living anywhere else but in a total-care institution, would have to be moved from his familiar environment and treated aggressively with painful and perhaps scarring technologies in order to extend his life for a relatively brief period. The Massachusetts court that heard this case agreed that competent adults could refuse treatment for those who are not competent if the competent adult could put himself or herself in the place of the incompetent person. Mr. Sakiewicz was not forced to receive the life-prolonging treatment. This case highlighted the importance of both competency and quality-of-life issues.

Another milestone in recent history was the case of Paul Brophy, which

---

If, as it has been said, war is too important to be left to generals, then is a life too precious (or too miserable) to be left to the judgment of doctors? E. S. Shneidman, *Death: Current Perspectives,* Fourth edition

was settled in 1986. Brophy, like Karen Quinlan, was in a persistent vegetative state. The case was brought to court in an attempt to have the feeding tube, which was keeping him alive, removed. The lower court decided that the feeding tube must stay. The Supreme Court said the right to refuse medical treatment established in the Karen Quinlan case applies to all medical treatment including feeding and hydrating treatments. In this way, the case expanded the legal definition of the right to die as applying to the right to withdraw sustenance as well as medical treatments.

Brody (1995) reported that a most important milestone in the history of euthanasia occurred when the *Journal of the American Medical Association* published an article entitled, "It's Over, Debbie." In this article a resident physician confessed to administering a large dose of morphine in the middle of the night to a woman patient who asked for death but with whom he had had no prior interaction. This case was virtually unanimously condemned by all who were involved in the debate for a number of reasons: The physician did not have an on-going relationship with the patient; the request was not made across a period of time; no one had examined the patient's state of mind; and the action happened secretly in the middle of the night. Nevertheless, this short communication served to increase the level of the discussion within the medical community and led to the emergence of some consensus regarding improper physician roles in euthanasia.

Yet another milestone in this history was the case of Nancy Cruzan, a 23-year-old woman who was in a persistent vegetative state that required the use of a feeding tube. The Missouri Supreme Court reviewed 50 previous state court decisions and in 1988 decided that they were all wrong. This court maintained that the state's interests in maintaining life were supreme in cases like this and that feeding is not a medical treatment. The ruling maintained that Cruzan's parents could no more exercise her right to discontinue treatment than they could exercise her right to vote. The ruling in this case underscored the tension between supporting biological life as contrasted with biographical life; that is, the court did not recognize that when an individual's conscious personal history (biographical life) is over, biological life may have little or no meaning. In 1990, however, the Supreme Court decided that adults' rights to refuse treatment are guaranteed by the 14th amendment and that artificial feeding cannot be distinguished from other forms of medical treatment. The Supreme Court's ruling supported the contention that biographical life is more important than biological life.

In 1988, a group of physicians published an article in the *New England Journal of Medicine* that inadvertently furthered the debate concerning assisted suicide (Ruark, Raffin and the Stanford Medical Center Committee on Ethics, 1988). These doctors reviewed standards of care for hospitalized dying patients and made a plea for emphasizing pain control in the treatment of terminally ill patients. In the first published reference to physician-assisted suicide, they agreed that there is a big difference between allowing patients to die and performing active euthanasia. Ten of the doctors thought that in some cases physician-assisted suicide was appropriate; two thought it never was. Although the main thrust of this article was a plea for better pain control for dying patients, the press seized on the article as an example of doctor disagreement about right-to-die issues.

In 1990, Dr. Kevorkian burst onto the national scene and increased the salience of the right to die debate by helping Janet Adkins, a patient who had been diagnosed as being in the early stages of Alzheimer's Disease, take her own life. This began a series of cases in which Dr. Kevorkian used a machine capable of administering a lethal dose of drugs to patients who wanted help in terminating their lives. At the time of this writing, Dr. Kevorkian has been present at the death of 24 patients and many related court battles still have not been settled. Public opinion ranges from believing that he is a hero to believing that he is a murderer.

In 1991, Dr. Timothy Quill published an article in the *New England Journal of Medicine* describing the relationship he had with a patient named Diane who had a chronic terminal illness. In the article he described his behavior in writing a prescription for a lethal dose of drugs (Quill, 1991). In arguing his case, Quill maintained that there is a difference between extending life and extending the dying process. Quill has also joined with other doctors in a case that at this writing is pending hearing by the Supreme Court. He has also written a thoughtful book, dedicated to Diane, in which he explores deeply the moral, ethical, and economic issues surrounding assisted suicide (Quill, 1993). In this book, Quill squarely faces the reality that medicine is not yet able to keep all terminally ill people comfortable while they are dying. Quill states:

> *While I am an enthusiastic advocate of comfort care, I am deeply troubled by our profession's unwillingness openly to acknowledge our limitations. If we don't admit to the possibility of intolerable end-of-life suffering, how are we ever going to explore alternatives that will respond to the real needs of patients who have only death to look forward to? This borders on abandoning those whose need is greatest, and it violates fundamental principles of comfort care for the dying. (Quill, 1993, p. 24)*

This brings us to the present. It is clear that the United States is a nation that is exploring the issue of physician-assisted suicide in great detail and that a transition is occurring. It is also clear that the subject is an emotional one and promises to arouse the same kinds of feelings, debate, and action we have seen surrounding the abortion issue in our country.

THE LAW AND ASSISTED SUICIDE

Many states are currently considering legislation in the broad area of right to die. Much of the discussion around each of these legislative bills is based on guidelines for carrying out euthanasia that were suggested in the Netherlands in 1984 and supported by the Dutch government in 1985. These guidelines specify the conditions under which persons may request help in dying from physicians. First, the patient must be incurably ill and must be suffering intolerably. Second, the patient must initiate the request without coercion and the request must be repeated over a period of time. Third, the patient must be informed about his or her illness, including possible treatments and the prognosis. Finally, physicians may not perform euthanasia until a second physician has verified that the first three criteria have been met. Although these guidelines have been in place in the Netherlands for ten years, there is little evidence that physician-assisted suicide is carried out widely. One study conducted by the government of the Netherlands recently found that only 1.8% of deaths reported by a group of 405 Dutch physicians could be attributed to active euthanasia (Quill, 1993).

Although these early findings seem to indicate that having access to euthanasia will not lead to abuse, much more research is needed to determine the effects on the general public of legalizing euthanasia. For example, will the general public come to view doctors differently and more negatively if they know that they have a dual role—to cure or to help die? Will euthanasia, as it becomes accepted into the fabric of society, begin to be used by many people as an easy way out? Will the elderly and the terminally ill in a society that recognizes euthanasia and physician-assisted suicide come to be expected to seek these services rather than be a financial or physical burden on relatives? Will poor people, more often than those who are well-off, find themselves with no other alternative than to request euthanasia even when they may not be ready to die? These and many other issues form the backdrop against which other countries and states within the United States are considering legislation.

Within the last five years, the citizens of three states have voted on issues related to assisted suicide and more than a dozen other states are considering such legislation. In California, an initiative to legalize euthanasia was proposed in 1988. The legislation specified that a person must be terminally ill and have only six months to live. It further specified that an individual could have an advance directive requesting euthanasia. This initiative did not get enough signatures to get on the ballot; however, in 1992, a similar initiative combining active voluntary euthanasia and assisted suicide was voted on and defeated in California.

In the state of Washington, legislation called the Natural Death Act was narrowly defeated in 1991. This legislation, titled Initiative 119, had the support of many groups including ill patients, clergy, lawyers, and physicians and consisted of three components. First, it specifically defined "persistent vegetative state" as a fatal condition, thereby permitting it to be treated like any other fatal illness. Second, it specified that feeding tubes could be removed from unconscious patients who had made their wishes known in advance. Finally, and most controversially, it specified that terminally ill patients would be allowed to receive "aid in dying" from their physicians. Such aid could include both voluntary euthanasia or assisted suicide. Like the California measures, this legislation specified that such aid could only be given to patients who had been diagnosed as terminally ill and whose death was expected within six months. Moreover, those patients requesting such aid must be deemed to be competent and not depressed and they must request the aid voluntarily, rather than under duress from family. This legislation was defeated by a 54 to 46% margin.

In 1994, the state of Oregon passed death-with-dignity legislation by a vote of 51% in favor to 49% against. The Oregon law requires that a request for physician-assisted suicide may only be made by competent adult patients who can administer their own medication. It also provided that the physician must seek a second opinion before agreeing and that the patient must be terminally ill and must not be regarded as suffering from clinical depression. Care givers from other disciplines may also be consulted if needed, in order for the attending physician to be sure that all positive steps have been taken to assure continued life with quality. As soon as this law was passed, opponents sought and gained a preliminary injunction against it, stating that "the public interest in protecting vulnerable citizens from the irreparable harm of death is greater than the hardship that will be endured by terminally ill people who must continue to live with the status quo" (Judd, 1995). At the time of this writing, the Oregon law is pending review by the Supreme Court.

REACTIONS OF PROFESSIONALS
TO PROPOSED LEGISLATION

It should be noted that many health professionals have raised questions about all types of right-to-die legislation. For example, the American Nurses Association has adopted a strong statement that asserts that nurses should not participate in assisted suicide and that such acts are in violation of the "Code for Nurses with Interpretive Statements and the ethical tradition of the profession" (American Nurses Association, 1992). Pharmacists likewise have raised concerns about unknowingly supplying drugs prescribed for the express purpose of ending a person's life, and some are suggesting that pharmacists should be informed in such situations and should have the right to refuse to fill such prescriptions (Rupp, 1995).

Many physicians also raise objections to physician-assisted suicide. The Canadian Medical Association, for example, has adopted the following statement: "Canadian Medical Association members should specifically exclude participation in euthanasia and assisted suicide" (Canadian Medical Association, 1995). In the United States, the National Hospice Organization, which includes large numbers of medical doctors, approved a resolution in 1990 that specifically addressed the issue of assisted suicide. In this resolution they suggest that hospice care is an alternative to voluntary euthanasia and assisted suicide and they reaffirm the basic philosophy that hospice care neither hastens nor postpones death" (National Hospice Organization, 1990). They go on to specifically reject the practice of voluntary euthanasia and assisted suicide in the care of the terminally ill.

In a more detailed statement, representatives of the National Hospice Organization have raised concerns about physician-assisted suicide on ethical grounds. Citing the usual dimensions of medical ethics including autonomy, beneficence, justice, and integrity of the health care professional, this statement suggests that euthanasia fails all of these tests. With regard to autonomy, the statement questions whether a decision concerning euthanasia can ever be a fully informed or truly voluntary choice. The authors point out that "the choice between euthanasia and a painful, suffering death presented by euthanasia proponents is far different from the choice between ethane and peaceful, comfortable death supported by appropriate hospice care" (p. 3). Furthermore, family members, health care providers, and others in society may begin to exert subtle or overt pressure on terminally ill relatives to request euthanasia, thereby affecting the principle of autonomy.

The statement further suggests that by definition euthanasia causes the most grievous kind of medical harm—death—and therefore fails the test of beneficence. In addition, it forecloses on the time a dying patient and his or her family might have to finish unfinished business or to realize new understandings.

On the issue of justice, the statement suggests that equal access to alternatives to euthanasia and assisted suicide are not yet available in our country. Poor people and people living in rural areas, for example, often do not have the advantages of readily available aggressive medical treatment and hospice care for pain control. Therefore, they are more likely to become candidates for euthanasia. Moreover, the statement suggests that if euthanasia and assisted suicide become law, we can expect to see them extended to incompetent adults through advanced directives, and beyond them, perhaps, to other populations such as the disabled, frail, and elderly, who may have a questionable quality of life. This "slippery slope" argument is one of the most often heard arguments against the right to die. It suggests that passing a law that makes the killing of another person legal, even if proper precautions existed, would be the first step in devaluing life and that that first step may start our society on a long slide down a slippery slope to a climate where only those who are young, in excellent health, and have no impairments might be considered worthy of life.

The final medical ethics principle of integrity of the health professional may be violated by requiring physicians to assist in the death, rather than in the care, of terminally ill patients. Even if doctors are permitted to opt out of physician-assisted suicide and euthanasia, they may have to be involved indirectly by giving terminal prognoses to patients.

Some philosophers and ethicists also are uneasy with the legal and ethical levels of current discussion. For example, Daniel Callahan of the Hastings Center has raised concerns about the challenge euthanasia and physician-assisted suicide present to our accepted definition of the conditions under which one person can kill another, as well as the kinds of claims people can make on medical doctors (Callahan, 1992). Callahan suggests that people do not have the right to consent to be killed, although they may choose to forego life-sustaining treatment. Furthermore, he warns that we should not confuse ethics and medicine, placing physicians in situations where they must make judgments about mortality that have ethical and spiritual dimensions for which they may have little or no formal educational preparation. He is also concerned with terminology in legislation that would permit physician-assisted suicide, raising questions about who determines what is meant by "unbearable suffering" or "terminal illness." Courtney Campbell, a philosophy professor at Oregon State University, echoed some of Callahan's reservations when he noted that "what began as a right to die can, through economic influences, be transformed into a duty to die" (Campbell, 1995, p. S-9). He pointed out that Oregon is now the only state that both legalizes assisted suicide (pending Supreme Court action) and has a specific program that rations health care to the poor. It is telling that the current Oregon health plan will provide insurance coverage for assistance in suicide, although it rations other types of health care. According to Campbell, economists studying the Oregon measure have estimated that if only 20% of the terminally ill population of the state took advantage of their rights under this act, approximately $700,000 annually would be saved in state and federal health care funds. Such savings might prove a powerful incentive to coerce people already weakened by illness to choose a premature death.

In contrast to these concerns expressed by members of the helping professions, the National Association of Social Workers has issued a policy concerning end-of-life decisions. It states:

> Social workers should be free to participate or not participate in assisted suicide matters or other discussions concerning end-of-life decisions depending on their own beliefs, attitudes, and value systems. If a social worker is unable to help with decisions about assisted suicide or other end-of-life choices, he or she has a professional obligation to refer [clients] and their families to competent professionals who are available to address end-of-life issues. (1994, p. 60)

The policy goes on to specify that social workers should work with terminally ill clients to help them express their thoughts and feelings as well as to give information, explore alternatives, provide liaisons with other health care professionals, and help clients and their families deal with loss and grief issues.

This statement by a professional organization clearly reflects the pendulum swing toward accepting individual autonomy and the right to die. It also raises another issue to be debated in the coming dialogue: Why should we be discussing *physician*-assisted suicide? Perhaps we should be considering a whole new kind of care giver whose central role would be neither curing nor caring for dying patients but rather accompanying them through the dying process. Such a group of professionals would definitely need appropriate education and training and would be held to a rigid code of ethics. They would step in only when doctors have agreed that the condition of the patient is terminal and when depression and economic factors have been ruled out. They might form an interface between dying persons and the final demands of the world, helping them to resolve unfinished interpersonal business, plan their funeral or memorial services, and become aware of and cope with legal and financial affairs. They would then be present to give psychological support in most cases and to actively assist in some cases after legal and medical conditions had been satisfied. Others have suggested that such a cadre of professionals should be developed. Dr. Jack Kevorkian even gave them a title—*obidiatrist*—in one of his interviews. Whether one chooses to coin a new term for this profession or to attach it to already-recognized professions as a subspecialty (e.g., thanatologist-social worker or nurse-thanatologist), if we developed a group of professionals to guide people through the dying experience, we would avoid the demands on all medical doctors to practice physician-assisted suicide and avoid assigning them the contradictory role of healer and killer. An added side benefit of creating a new professional group to provide these services would be cost containment. If educated properly, the new professionals would view their role as acting for the dying person and serving as an intermediary between that person and worldly institutions such as medicine, law, and the family. There would be no need for expensive medical or legal training.

Whatever the future might hold with regard to training a new type of professional, people in the present clearly are considering assigning this task to the medical profession. Recognizing the shift in public awareness of and opinion about assisted suicide, Margaret Battin, in her book *Ethical Issues in Suicide,* predicts that the "practice of physician-assisted suicide will become more widespread, whether technically legal or not" (Battin, 1995a, p. 123). She suggests that therefore there are specific issues that must be addressed in the immediate future to provide protection for all concerned when physician-

---

To wish for death is a coward's part. Ovid, *Metamorphoses,* 4.1.115

assisted suicide is a reality. The first issue is the necessity for available, nondirective, and nonpaternalistic counseling designed to help patients explore alternatives and consider the impact of their suicide on others, and to rule out any chance that the choice for suicide is being made under coercion. The second issue is to establish methods of regulating the practice of physician-assisted suicide and guarding against abuse. Battin suggests that among the safeguards to be considered are waiting periods to assure that the patient will not change his or her mind, reporting requirements, prohibitions against charging fees for assisting in suicide, psychiatric consultations, close auditing of the practice, and development of specific indicators of abuse that could be used to assure proper treatment. She also suggests that the education of physicians in the future will have to include specific instruction on providing comfort care to dying patients, instruction in nondirective counseling techniques to use in helping patients choose suicide, and training in the pharmacology of assisting in suicide and personal preparation for ending patients' lives.

Werth (1996) has suggested a set of criteria that professionals may use to determine if a suicide is rational. The first criterion is that the situation must be hopeless. Clearly, if there is hope that the situation can be changed for the better, suicide would not appear to be a rational choice. The second criterion is that there must be a lack of coercion. People considering suicide must be free from outside pressure to take their lives. The third criterion calls for a sound decision making process, including an assessment of mental competence by a mental health professional, an exploration of possible alternatives, an attempt to be sure that the suicidal decision is in keeping with the individual's values, a consideration of the impact on others, and consultation both with objective people and with the significant others of the person considering suicide. As we have already discussed, attempts to pass legislation permitting assisted suicide have incorporated most of these points.

EXAMINING THE ARGUMENTS AGAINST PHYSICIAN-ASSISTED SUICIDE

Some of the arguments for and against physician-assisted suicide are inherent in the preceding sections. These arguments may have different meanings when applied to real cases. Let us look at just two situations in which people have made it known that they would like to participate in physician-assisted suicide in the near future. The first case involves a young professional woman suffering from multiple sclerosis (MS).

When even despair ceases to serve any creative purpose, then surely we are justified in suicide.
Cyril Connolly, *The Unquiet Grave*

Madge R. is a single 40-year-old former attorney who was diagnosed with MS in her early thirties. Since diagnosis, she has suffered a loss of balance that has lessened her ability to live independently; her vision has declined, rendering her legally blind and leading to her driver's license being taken away; she has lost her highly paid job as a corporate attorney, causing her to declare bankruptcy; and she has experienced multiple bouts of depression as her illness has taken its downward course.

Madge has come to understand that she can live a long time with this disease. She often says that she does not expect to die of MS. However, she publicly maintains that when the conditions imposed by the disease become so negative that she is unwilling to endure them, she not only should have the right to die but also should have the help of a knowledgeable physician to provide support and to ease her suffering. Madge has read extensively in the literature, particularly in the legal area. She is familiar with all of the cases in which people have been kept alive against their will, as well as those cases in which individuals made "botched" suicide attempts and ended up even more incapacitated and in even more pain than they were prior to the attempt. Madge is using her legal education to try to get laws changed in her state, but her failing energy level makes her doubtful that anything can be accomplished in time to be of use in her own situation.

The second case involves a young man who is HIV positive:

Josh L. is a large, unusually handsome man of 33. He dropped out of a medical residency program four years ago when he was diagnosed with HIV. He has spent the last four years as a volunteer, helping other victims try to live with AIDS. He also admits to helping several AIDS patients die. Although his disease has not yet progressed to the active stage of AIDS, he is very clear that when it does he wants to be able to decide when, where, and under what circumstances he will die. Like Madge, he believes that in a caring society that recognizes individual rights, people should be able to control their deaths and should be accorded respect and support as they do so.

Both of these people would seem to meet many of the usual conditions that are expected for individuals to qualify for physician-assisted suicide and/ or for euthanasia. Both have life-threatening illnesses that will negatively affect the quality of their lives. Both have experienced and will continue to experience physical pain and psychological suffering. Both seem rational and have repeated often and put in writing their desire to be assisted in dying when they decide the time is right. Are there any arguments that should be considered before their requests are granted?

Many would say yes. At the most fundamental level, there are people who maintain that life is a gift that comes from a divine source and does not belong to the person to whom it has been given. The most concise way of putting this argument is found in the statement made at many funerals: "The Lord giveth and the Lord taketh away." According to this way of thinking, humans do not and should not have the right to destroy themselves, no matter what the situation.

Closely related to this stance is the widely accepted idea, "Where there's life, there's hope." People who adhere to this idea believe that no one should ever give up on life, that it is never too late to hope for a drug that will ease the situation or even for a spontaneous remission or "a miracle." These people point out that those who control their own deaths may be cutting themselves off from treatment prematurely and that those who help them may indeed be guilty of murder.

A third argument made by many who consider physician-assisted suicide incorporates some of both of the previous arguments but goes beyond them. It maintains that life in and of itself is a valuable commodity, perhaps *the* most valuable commodity in an infinite and seemingly empty universe. Because this is so, life deserves to be treated with reverence and sustained as long as possible.

A fourth argument is the now-familiar "slippery slope" argument. In these situations, it would be elaborated in the following way: If Madge and Josh are allowed to dictate the situations and times of their death, why shouldn't everyone have the same privilege? And if all do, what is to stop a young adult who is suffering from what appears to be a hopeless drug addiction from demanding help in taking his own life? Or a grieving middle-aged widow who believes that the quality of her life without her husband will be unacceptable? Indeed, in a review of suicide in the Netherlands, Hendin (1995, p. 194) has documented a type of slide down a slippery slope in regard to physician-assisted suicide in that country. He stated: Over the past 20 years practice in the Netherlands has moved from assisted suicide to euthanasia, from euthanasia for the terminally ill to euthanasia for patients who are chronically ill, from physical suffering to mental suffering, from voluntary euthanasia to involuntary euthanasia (called "termination of the patient without explicit request").

Hendin explained that the extension of the right to die with assistance to the chronically ill and those suffering psychic pain was made based on the argument that these groups of people will have to suffer longer than terminally ill people and should not be discriminated against in this way. Ending the lives of people who have not requested it has been defended as necessary for patients who are not competent to choose for themselves. Hendin concludes his article by arguing the following: "Normalizing" suicide as a medical option along with accepting or refusing treatment, inevitably lays the ground-

Blind Botanist, **Ben Shahn, 1963. Lithograph in colors, 26¾ × 20½ in. (New Jersey State Museum Collection, Trenton. Purchase. Photograph by Geoffrey Clements. Used by permission of Mrs. Ben Shahn.)**

work for a culture that will not only turn euthanasia into a "cure" for depression but may prove to exert a coercion to die on patients when they are most vulnerable. (p. 203)

A fifth type of argument must also be noted. If physician-assisted suicide is legalized, it effectively lessens the need for active research into better methods of care for the dying. The Hospice movement has been very active in most developed countries across since the mid 1960s. Hospices exist to provide compassionate care to dying people and to make it possible for many dying people to realize growth during that phase of their lives. It is at least partially on these grounds that the National Hospice Organization rejected the practice of assisted suicide as well as voluntary euthanasia in the care of the terminally ill.

The sixth point often raised is more a series of questions than an objection: Who will decide? Should physicians be placed in the role of arbiter of life and death? How do they know when an individual has reached his or her limits in dealing with pain and suffering? Should such decisions be made by an interdisciplinary team, including perhaps a physician, a psychologist, a social worker, and a nurse? Although that may seem safer, can any society afford such a team approach? The reality of the situation is that all humans will die, and most will die after a period of declining health that may involve suffering. Can any health system afford to have a staff conference for each person dying in their community who requests it?

That brings us to the final issue that critics of euthanasia and assisted suicide often address: the total economic impact of legalizing assisted suicide. Caring for dying people and people in psychological pain is expensive. Assisted suicide, whether carried out by physicians or by other care givers, has the potential to provide a cheaper option for coping with these people. If efficient decision guidelines could be developed, it might even be possible for computers to handle most of the decision making involved in right-to-die cases using a cost/benefit analysis type formula. In a society like the United States, where health care is delivered by specialists who often do not know their patients well, it may be convenient to acquiesce to patients' requests for assisted suicide, rather than spend the time and resources to explore all other alternatives. This might be particularly true when doctors are confronted with suffering patients who do not have the resources and/or education to demand ongoing expensive treatments. The question of access and equality in treating people of all walks of life must be considered in making decisions to legalize assisted suicide.

Callahan (1992) places the arguments against the right to suicide in perspective by claiming that the outcome of this debate will determine the future course of Western society in three major areas of thought. First, the outcome will determine whether we will make further encroachments on the circumstances in which one person can lawfully take the life of another. Except in the instances of war and capital punishment, Western culture has been remarkably stable in attempting to limit those circumstances. Legalizing euthanasia would reverse those long-standing limits. Second, accepting assisted suicide would strengthen the individual's right to self-determination even at the risk of inflicting harm on others and on society. Third, if euthanasia and/or assisted suicide were legalized, the limits of medicine would have to be redefined. Doctors would no longer be expected only to fight disease and prolong health. They would also be expected to actively end suffering of patients who request it.

Having explored arguments against assisted suicide, we now return to the pressing needs of Madge and Josh. Their rights to self-determination and to the pursuit of happiness may well be violated by the lack of laws permitting assisted suicide. To some extent, their situations reflect the tension that has always existed between the rights of the individual and the rights of the community. If in passing laws that permit them to have help in ending their lives we create a situation in which others may experience inferior care or even be urged to end their lives prematurely, have we really gained as a society? Conversely, who has the right to tell these two suffering human beings that they must continue in their personal pain indefinitely in order that others yet unidentified may benefit from better care or experience less pressure for early death? This kind of question will require the attention of the best legal, ethical, and medical minds of our society.

AGE CONSIDERATIONS IN THE RIGHT-TO-DIE DEBATE

In keeping with the focus of this book, let us now consider the effect that such laws might have on people of different ages. All of the material reviewed for this chapter explicitly states that assisted suicide may only be considered by rational, competent adults. Therefore, at least in theory, children and adolescents are exempt from any laws permitting or encouraging assisted suicide. In reality, however, it is very likely that parents or guardians will be asked to make decisions regarding assisted suicide for their terminally ill children and adolescents. Depending on the relationships that exist between the parent or guardian and the child or adolescent, youth who desire to have support and help in dying may be able to influence the process by being open and assertive with their parents and caretakers. Therefore, these age groups are likely to be affected by whatever shape the laws may take, although their wishes will have to be expressed by competent adults.

Beginning with young adults, however, and continuing throughout the life span, everybody but the mentally ill and the intellectually incompetent will be affected by the legal developments discussed in this chapter. Involvement in young adulthood is made more salient with the appearance of AIDS, which as we have seen is now the number one killer of Americans between the ages of 24 and 44. Just as Josh is struggling with issues of control over his dying trajectory, so are thousands of other young adults. Since a central task of young adulthood is to assume control over one's own life, it would follow that in the near future people in this age group may become the most insistent voices in favor of assisted suicide.

Middle-aged people, as reviewed in chapter 6, begin to experience time differently and also begin to see their peers die from wasting diseases such as cancer and multiple sclerosis. Like Madge, many middle-aged people cannot avoid confronting the probable conditions of their death. While middle-aged people may be experiencing some "mellowing" as they come to grips with their own mortal nature, they also have lived long enough to appreciate being in control of situations as much as possible. The popularity of the living will and the astounding commercial success of the book *Final Exits* (Humphrey, 1988) attest to the salience of this issue for the large cohort of middle-aged Boomers. This is the age group and the cohort that is likely to exert the most political influence in drafting new laws and in addressing the medical, psychological, and economic issues surrounding assisted suicide as they move through the middle years and into elderhood.

Among the elderly, the issue of assisted suicide is very personal and very timely. However, the three cohorts comprising today's elderly population are unlikely to exert much leadership in the debate, for very different reasons. The eldest of them, members of the Lost Generation, have little use for the system. They are far more likely to go outside of the system than to spend precious energy attempting to change it. Moreover, their advanced age almost guarantees that this generation does not have enough time left to be a major factor in changing the status quo.

In contrast, members of the GI Generation have always been involved in and profited from the system. GIs are also an optimistic cohort, deeply involved in the process of living. While this group is likely to insist on the best technology and the best type of medical care as they enter the final stage of their lives, they are not too likely to lead the demand for legalization of assisted suicide. Their motto from World War II, "Never say die," as well as the memory of many of their peers who died at an early age, is likely to keep them appreciating the value of their lives and fighting to stay alive until resistance is impossible.

Members of the Silent Generation, like the authors of this book, are likely to see both sides of the issue. Interested in fairness and equality of opportunity and concerned about the philosophical cost to society of beginning a ride on the slippery slope, they most probably will mute their requests for individual help in dying. They are very likely, in this debate as in most other issues occurring in their lifetimes, to raise the right questions, insist on reason and civility in the debate, and remain true to their group name—the Silent Generation.

SUMMARY

Having completed our look forward at physician-assisted suicide, the most emergent issue in the field of suicidology today, we will complete this chapter by summarizing a dozen conclusions that we believe are important generalizations to carry away from your study of suicide. While students of suicide need to know specific information that we have provided in the preceding chapters, it is just as important to generalize this material into some basic conclusions that may guide your behavior as you deal with suicidal people or instruct others about the suicidal condition. We offer these generalizations as answers to the question concerning the relevance and usefulness of the material you have studied.

The first conclusion is that *suicide means different things to different people at different times in history*. As we have shown, suicide has been characterized in various ways throughout history: as a mortal sin, as a reflection of deep religious faith, as the right of no human being, as everyone's right, and even as an issue of importance to the judicial and legislative systems. The relevance of this generalization is that it is cautionary; that is, the meaning of suicide must always be interpreted within the cultural context of its occurrence and we must never presume that our definition of suicide is shared by all people everywhere. People working in the field of suicide would thus do well to compare definitions and understandings with co-workers, students, and clients before proceeding to address the topic of suicide.

The second generalization is that *suicide is a multifaceted problem that must be addressed by many disciplines and theoretical perspectives*. Our Suicide Trajectory Model classifies the risk factors that influence suicide into biological, psychological, cognitive, and environmental components that both act independently and interact with one another. The relevance of this insight to those interested in the topic of suicide is clear: We need practitioners from many fields, including sociology, psychology, medicine and the other health sciences, as well as philosophers, demographers, social workers, and many others, to conduct research on suicide and to provide clinical services to those who are considering taking their lives. In other words, we are in this together. No one discipline or approach holds all the answers to the tragedy that suicide represents. In addition, if we want to remain informed about suicide, we must read interdisciplinary materials from all of the fields just mentioned.

Third, and central to the theme of this book, is the fact that *the specific risk factors that contribute to the probability of a suicidal act differ among age groups*. Suicide is in many ways a different phenomenon when considered by people at different developmental levels. Helping professionals must therefore consider the age and developmental level of each client and all of the associated pertinent information when providing care for suicidal people. Moreover, it is important to note that suicide vulnerability generally increases across the life span and that it fluctuates within individual developmental periods. The danger of suicide is usually greater when individuals begin to address the challenges of a new developmental stage than after they have settled into a particular period of life. Helping professionals should therefore be alert to the special stresses of people engaged in transitions to adolescence, young adulthood, middle adulthood, or old age.

Fourth, *the young and the old are especially vulnerable to cluster and copycat suicides*. The suicide of a peer or a famous person often serves a modeling or permission-giving function for at-risk youth. At the other end of the life span, elderly people who are considering ending their lives may also be freed to act on their ideation by reading about the suicide of someone within their age group. Suicide prevention programs must therefore include procedures for recognizing and dealing with situations that may initiate the contagion effect in at-risk individuals. Implications for those working in the area of suicidology include the need to create crisis intervention teams that provide intervention and postvention services to schools and communities. In addition, support and care for the survivors of suicide is often necessary to prevent additional suicides by those most adversely affected by the initial act of self-destruction. Therefore, as we work with schools and communities to establish suicide prevention programs, we need to be mindful to incorporate postvention approaches within each program.

Fifth, beginning in middle age and continuing through elderhood, *loss becomes increasingly normative in the lives of men and women*. Loss of abilities, relationships, valued roles, youthful dreams, purposeful activities, and so on begin to parade slowly through people's lives during the middle years. These losses gradually but steadily accumulate as people move into elderhood, and they increase vulnerability to suicide. It is often helpful, therefore, to collect a loss history when working with suicidal people who are middle-aged or older. Using such a loss history to help people recognize past coping behaviors and identify support systems can be a helpful adjunct to any therapeutic approach.

Sixth, *the old have always been the most self-destructive of any age group*. Their suicidal decisions tend to be unequivocal, their plans exceptionally complete, and their methods highly lethal. Helping professionals should therefore probe for suicidal intent with at-risk elderly and must take very seriously any suicide threat by an elderly individual. Moreover, each of us can take action every day to lessen the suicide rate among the elderly. If we recognize the ageist bias in our society and commit ourselves to change existing negative attitudes toward the aging process, we can make a positive difference in the general climate for elderly in our culture. With increasing respect, elderly people are more likely to maintain the high levels of self-esteem that help prevent the depression and self-hatred associated with suicide.

Seventh, we want to emphasize *cohort effects on suicidal behavior*. Special life circumstances that profoundly affect people's lives are associated with coming of age in a particular culture at a specific time in history. Every generation has resulting idiosyncratic characteristics, called the peer personality, that influence their behaviors, beliefs, and attitudes—including their attitudes toward suicide. The cohort membership of every suicidal individual is therefore an important consideration when providing care. Those working with suicidal people would do well to consider their generational membership and to acquaint themselves with the specific peer personality of that generation as a kind of shorthand entree into establishing rapport with each individual.

Eighth, *males and females differ greatly in their suicidal behavior.* They have dramatically different suicide attempt and completion rates, attitudes, and propensities to seek help in a crisis that are deeply embedded in gender-related socialization practices. Helping professionals must therefore tailor their approaches to working with males and females based on a knowledge and understanding of the sex and gender differences in suicide.

Ninth, *everyone is a unique individual with a genetic blueprint and an environmental history unlike any other.* Although common risk factors may be involved in the suicidal circumstances of many people, these interact idiosyncratically with each suicidal individual's unique personality. Therefore, while care givers can and should consider general background information, it is extremely important to recognize and respect the uniqueness of each individual.

Tenth, *the suicide statistics provide a numerical accounting of the prevalence of unhappiness in the world today.* However, these numbers represent only the tip of the iceberg of misery in our society, much of it caused by what we teach and do not teach our children. Therefore, we must do a better job of raising and educating our children to cope more effectively with life's challenges and inevitable failures; in so doing, we will be engaged in the primary prevention of suicide. Moreover, we must recognize that suicidal ideation is far more prevalent than suicidal behavior and we must work to bring such ideas into the open with our clients and students so that it can be recognized and addressed.

Eleventh, *almost all suicides are highly ambivalent acts with a number of positive and negative factors lending weight to the final decision at a particular point in time.* Most suicidal decisions could be postponed with some minor or major changes in circumstances. Helping professionals dealing with a suicidal crisis must therefore seek out the ambivalence in the victim's motives and find ways to shift the balance in the direction of life. Care givers and others need to recognize that suicide is almost always a premature exit from the stage of life, a cutting short of a human being's precious few years. Therefore, suicide should be prevented in almost every circumstance.

Twelfth, *the many considerations pertaining to euthanasia and physician-assisted suicide have become central issues in most developed countries in recent years.* These complex and highly emotional issues demand the most intelligent decision making our society can provide. We must therefore call upon the very best legal, ethical, and moral thinking possible in order to properly address the issues surrounding the right to die, and we should be prepared to raise our informed voices to help further this debate.

We hope that these concluding principles and other information you have learned from reading this book will be helpful in dealing with suicide wherever you encounter it. Although we have shared a great deal with you over these 10 chapters, there is much more to be learned in order to prepare you fully for work with people at risk for suicide. One important aspect of suicide that we have not addressed in this book is the affective element. We have not told you just how incredibly bad it feels to be clinically depressed, so depressed that suicide seems to be the only way to end the intolerable suffering. In the following brief afterword we will end this book on a more personal note by giving you an inside-looking-out view of suicidal depression, and we will provide several recommendations for help in avoiding or coping with the "despair beyond despair."

SUGGESTED ADDITIONAL READINGS

Active euthanasia: Should it be legalized? (1993, April). *American Bar Association Journal, 79,* 42.

Boethicists' statement on the U.S. Supreme Court's Cruzan decision. *New England Journal of Medicine 323,* 686.

Battin, M. P. (1994). *The least worth death: Essays in bioethics on the end of life.* New York: Oxford University Press.

Battin, M. P. (1995). *Ethical issues in suicide.* Englewood Cliffs, NJ: Prentice-Hall.

Brody, H. (1992). Assisted death: A compassionate response to a medical failure. *New England Journal of Medicine, 327,* 1384–88.

Callahan, D. (1992). "When self-determination runs amok." *Hasting Center Report, 22*(2), 52–55.

Celocruz, M. T. (1992). Aid-in-dying: Should we decriminalize physician-assisted suicide and physician-committed euthanasia? *American Journal of Law and Medicine, 18,* 369.

Cohen, J. S. et al. (1994). Attitudes towards assisted suicide and euthanasia among physicians in Washington State. *New England Journal of Medicine, 331,* 89.

Cox, D. W. (1993). *Hemlock's Cup.* Buffalo, NY: Prometheus Books.

Dickey, N. W. (1993). Euthanasia: A concept whose time has come. *Issues in Law and Medicine, 8,* 521.

Gifford, E. A. (1993). Artes Moriendi: Active euthanasia and the art of dying. *UCLA Law Review, 40,* 1545.

Girsh, F. J. (1992). Physician aid in dying: A proposed law for California. *Criminal Justice, 14,* 33.

Gostin, L. O. (1992). Drawing the line between killing and letting die: The law, and law reform, on medically assisted dying. *Journal of Law, Medicine and Ethics, 21,* 94.

Humphrey, D. (1993). *Lawful exit: The limits of freedom for help in dying.* Junction City, OR: Norris Lane Press.

McCord, W. (1993). Death with dignity. *The Humanist, 53,* 26.

Messinger, T. J. (1993). A gentle and easy death: From ancient Greece to beyond Cruzan toward a reasoned legal response to the societal dilemma of euthanasia. *Denver University Law Review, 71,* 175.

Mott-Busby, S. (1993). The trend towards enlightenment: Healthcare decision making in Lawrence and Doe. *Connecticut Law Review, 25,* 1159.

Persels, J. (1993). Forcing the issue of physician-assisted suicide. *Journal of Legal Medicine, 14,* 93.

Pugliese, J. (1993). Don't ask, don't tell: The secret practice of physician-assisted suicide. *Hasting Law Journal, 44,* 291.

Quill, T. E., Cassel, C. K., & Meier, D. E. (1992). Care of the hopefully ill: Proposed clinical criteria for physician-assisted suicide. *New England Journal of Medicine, 327,* 1380.

Quill, T. E. (1991). Death and dignity: A case for individualized decision making. *New England Journal of Medicine, 324,* 691.

Quill, T. E. (1993). *Death and dignity.* New York: W. W. Norton.

Smith, C. (1993). What about legalized assisted suicide? *Issues in Law and Medicine, 8,* 503.

Worsnop, R. L. (1992). Assisted Suicide, *CQ Researcher, 2*(7), 145–168.

Afterword

All our past efforts to relate to or to correlate suicide with simplistic nonpsychological variables, such as sex, age, race, socioeconomic level, case history items (no matter how dire), psychiatric categories (including depression), etc., were (and are) doomed to miss the mark precisely because they ignore the one variable that centrally relates to suicide, namely, intolerable psychological pain; in a word, psychache."

Shneidman, 1993

As we neared completion of the second edition of this text, we realized that an important dimension of understanding suicide had been omitted. Good students, reading and digesting everything that was in this book, could still go away without a fundamental understanding of the nature of the suicidal state of mind and without insight into how to avoid or help others to avoid becoming suicidal. We decided, therefore, to include this brief afterword. We intend it to be an exercise in empathy; that is, we hope you will enter into the mind-set of suicidal people in an attempt to understand the range of emotions they feel. Then we trust you will explore the suggestions we make for avoiding and helping others to avoid the suicidal state of mind. Finally, we expect that you will have additional ideas for healthy living. We hope you will take time to record your reactions to the suicidal state of mind as well as to the suggestions for healthy living so that you will create your own record of understanding and tools for helping suicidal people. Let us turn first to the full range of emotions experienced by suicidal people.

Beginning helping professionals often believe that the suicidal state of mind is a unity; that is, that people who are suicidal are single-minded. When we examine it closely, however, suicidal depression is not a unity. Instead, it is like an emotional alphabet soup consisting of multiple emotions that can be viewed separately, but taken together they add their individual dimensions to produce that painful psychological state we call suicidal depression. Since the first step in helping suicidal people is to try to understand what they are feeling, let us now examine that soup. As you read the next few paragraphs, try to feel each of the emotions described. To the extent that you succeed, you will understand more fully the affective or feeling part of depression.

EXPLORING THE SUICIDAL STATE OF MIND: AN EXERCISE IN EMPATHY

One major emotion felt by suicidal people is anxiety—that formless, free-floating unease that warns you even in the midst of family, of pleasure, that all is not well. Anxiety—which causes you to feel tense and to be mobilized to fight

293

or flee at all times. Anxiety—which makes you want to scream at fate: "Enough! Enough!"

Another A in the alphabet soup is anger. You feel anger at everything, and at nothing. The anger seems to be always present. It wakes you in the middle of the night and will not let you go back to sleep; it tugs at your consciousness throughout the day. You try to find reasons for being so angry and you can always identify some. No one lives a life without some frustration, and frustration breeds anger. But such violent anger? Such all-encompassing anger? You literally become trapped in it and find yourself raging against your own existence.

As your anxiety and anger increase, you become egocentric. Your emotional pain is so threatening to you and so overwhelming that it takes all of your energy to withstand it. You have no energy to use in reaching out to others and the world. Your world narrows until there is nothing but you in it. Even when you are with others, you are alone. Every waking moment is spent thinking about your pain, your problems, your miserable existence.

Exhaustion is another emotion you feel. You cannot sleep, do not eat well, and have no peace from the negative emotions that nag at you constantly. No wonder you feel so tired. Every chore seems to demand too much from you. Exhaustion follows, further weakening your ability to cope with life. You are just too tired—too tired to live.

Guilt and its twin, regret, are also there, waiting their turn for your attention. You compulsively recite all of your failings and failures while overlooking your strengths and successes. You feel guilt for the things you did and the things you failed to do. You regret the roads not taken and you hear, like an unwelcome song going round and round in your brain, the phrase, "Of all sad words of tongue and pen, the saddest are these: It might have been."

Adding to the guilt and regret is the feeling of helplessness you experience. You are not in control. You cannot change your life circumstances. You are stuck in emotional quicksand and there is nowhere to go but down.

And when the strength of the feeling of helplessness reaches its apex, you know without a doubt that it is hopeless; that tomorrow will not be better—that tomorrow is a bad joke. You lose your sense of the future—your ability to plan, to anticipate, to build toward something yet to come. Time collapses in on you and there is nothing but the here and now and the blackness of your depression—and there will never be anything else.

With the ascent of hopelessness comes the inability to feel. Things keep happening in the real world out there. Babies get born, people die, celebrations occur, holidays come and go, but they do not touch you. It is as though you are cut off from human experience emotionally. You know what you should feel, and sometimes you can feel the faint echo of an emotion, but generally you are dead inside. Perhaps most troubling is the sense of joylessness you experience, an overwhelming lack of pleasure in anything. This inability to feel anything

Woman Meditating II, Käthe Kollwitz, 1920. Lithograph, 21¼ × 14¾ in. (National Gallery of Art, Washington, Rosenwald Collection.)

positive adds pain to pain until attempting death may be the only way to feel anything again.

And then there is indecision. You, who used to handle a myriad of decisions easily, fluently, without hesitation, find on bad days that you can barely decide to get out of bed. What to wear or eat becomes a major struggle. And why should you bother? What does it matter what you wear or what you eat, when nothing matters anymore? When nothing counts?

More threatening than any of these is the loneliness, the isolation you feel. You remember the old cliché "Laugh and the world laughs with you, weep and you weep alone." You look around at those people in the distance, all of whom seem connected to each other and to the world, and you see yourself as alone, unloved, and unlovable. What is more, you know you deserve it, that this is the way it was supposed to be, the way it is, and the way it will be until death claims you. You are separated from your fellow human beings and cannot make contact.

With sudden clarity, you know all of life for what it is: some cosmic joke played by a vicious, impersonal universe. There is no meaning, you realize. Try as you might throughout your little life—there is no meaning. All of human action is folly and vanity. You are a silly, posturing creature, trying to invent meaning by structuring time, by accumulating things, by staying busy. But in the end, it is all meaningless and you are dead.

You writhe in the pain of that realization; pain that cannot be understood by others because there is no blood, no broken bones—just suffering of the psyche, huge and ongoing, with no chance of reprieve. You experience pain that is so real for all of its invisibility that you feel like crying out, like howling in anguish, but that would not be appropriate, and it would do no good.

You look around you at the pleasant, calm people going about their lives with satisfaction, even happiness, and you pity them because you know they are living an illusion. But then you see yourself, unable to share that illusion, weak, contemptible in your little womb of misery, and you are filled with self-hatred. As you review those things you could have done and should have done, the people you should have reached out to, the person you should have become, the self-hatred grows until there seems to be only one solution—eliminate the object of your hatred. Turn the anger inward. End the psyche's suffering.

To bring it all into focus, to sum it all up, suicidal people are generally experiencing extreme grief reactions. They are mourning multiple losses in their lives. They may be specific losses caused by the death of loved ones or the break up of relationships or the loss of jobs and material goods, or they may be more general losses including loss of peace of mind, of meaning in life, or of the capacity to love. Whatever the types or degrees of loss, the effect is the same in suicidal people. They feel depressed, overwhelmed, and unable to deal with life. Caring people who understand the complexity of the emotions contained within the suicidal state are well advised to consider multiple tools for helping those who are experiencing it.

Faced with such a complexity of emotions, how can we reach out to suicidal individuals to decrease the likelihood of their taking their lives? Some answers pop into mind right away—and they do not necessarily cost anything or require a graduate degree in the helping professions. What they do require is the ability to give of your time and understanding to someone who is considering making a premature exit from life. We believe there are at least a dozen accessible tools or approaches that can be utilized by caring individuals against the waste of suicide. They are not mysterious, and most of us would not think of them as healing tools, and yet they can make a major difference in anyone's quality of life, helping him or her to experience the best of what it means to be human. As you review our list, answer the following three questions: First, how many of these tools do you use in your own daily life? Second, how many of these would you be willing to share with a suicidal acquaintance? Third, are there other healing tools that you have used or could use that might make a difference in the quality of your own life or the lives of others?

TOOLS FOR EXPERIENCING AND EXPRESSING OUR HUMANITY

The first tool available to all of us is *exercise*. Whether it is something as simple as gardening or something much more demanding like running a marathon, exercise is important. Kostrubala (1977), who wrote the *Joy of Running,* says that if we can get the heart pumping at 75% of cardiac output for one hour, three times a week, it changes the brain chemistry, increasing the levels of neurotransmitters such as serotonin. We know that the changes in brain chemistry caused by exercise include the release of pain-killing substances (endorphins) that cause people to experience a "natural high." We do not fully understand why, but we know that those who exercise regularly are less likely to stay depressed. Perhaps something as simple as walking with a depressed friend or acquaintance on a daily basis might prove a valuable tool in fighting depression.

Second, there is an expanding arsenal of *mental tools* that can be used as adjuncts to therapy. Meditation, imagery, and self-hypnosis are all becoming very popular tools for helping people attain and maintain a mental state of equilibrium. Evidence collected over at least two decades supports the assertion that such activities produce beneficial physiological changes, including decreased heart rate and oxygen consumption as well as brain wave alteration and increased feelings of well-being (Wallace, 1970; Seligman, 1990). Most of these tools can be learned for very little expense of time or money, and once learned they require only discipline to become valuable parts of self-help routines. They are easy to share with depressed people to help them regain at least some sense of control over their lives.

Third, *learn something new.* The need to learn is basic to our nature. It is the reason we have called ourselves "homo sapiens" (wise ones). Mastering a new field, learning a new skill, brings zest back into life, fuels our self-esteem, and takes our minds off ourselves. Like the competency training discussed in chapter 8, new learning brings multiple mental health benefits. It may be something simple like learning the names of wildflowers or something more complicated like learning to weave cloth, fix a car engine, or use a computer. Whatever it is, new learning helps depressed people feel better by diverting their attention from themselves and increasing their self-confidence and self-esteem as they gain skill, knowledge, and/or insight.

Fourth, *fall in love with something.* Whether it is music or collecting or growing things, become passionate about something. Healthy people tend to feel there are so many things they want to do that one lifetime is not nearly time enough. Suicidal individuals feel that there is nothing in life worth doing. Sometimes merely including them in activities that you are passionate about may spark them to develop a similar interest.

Fifth, *laugh!* Seek out laughter. Norman Cousins (1979) laughed his way back to health—so can depressives. Laughing decenters us—we cannot focus only on the negatives if we can laugh. Some therapists give homework assignments as part of their approach, asking suicidal people to find cartoons or jokes or to record how many times they laugh between visits. In effect, they use laughter as their assistant therapist. If you can find ways to help others smile or laugh, you will be making a real difference in the lives of suicidal people.

Sixth, *get in touch with the earth and the seasons.* It is easy to forget in this modern age that we are creatures of the earth, just like the birds and other animals, and we lose contact with its rhythms at our own peril. The spring makes us feel hopeful with the promise of new beginnings. The summer reminds us of the richness of our home. The fall brings a special beauty into our lives and teaches us lessons about harvesting what we have sown and giving thanks for it. The winter brings a special kind of peace and reminds us that even in the coldest of the seasons, the seeds of new life are there, awaiting reawakening. We need to note these seasons and allow ourselves to appreciate each in its turn. They serve as powerful metaphors for our lives. Sometimes, just urging a depressed person to walk after a snowfall or to watch a sunset with you may reawaken an appreciation for the beauty of our planet and the life it supports.

Seventh, give of yourself to others. People who reach out to help others who are in pain or who need education or food find they cannot long keep their own troubles uppermost in their minds. The world is full of need. There are always people and causes that need our help. If we are successful in helping

La Danse, **Jean-Baptiste Carpeaux, 1865–69. Ecaillon stone (h.330). (Musee d'Or-say, Paris.)**

suicidal people become involved with those who need them, we break the feelings of essential loneliness and disconnection that are part of the suicidal state.

Eighth, *explore new and old ways of seeking meaning*. Humans have a need to search for meaning actively. The world's great religions attest to the powerful need to find ways to express our spiritual nature. Whether it is through religion or some more individual pathway, we need to be active in trying to find the meaning for our lives. While you may not feel comfortable advocating a particular religion, you can remind suicidal people that we all have spiritual needs and encourage them to explore the spiritual dimensions in their lives.

Ninth, *focus on the uniqueness of each person*. Every individual is a miracle. Helping depressed friends understand this reality may make their self-hatred less powerful. Help them to realize their essential uniqueness. At conception, one of millions of sperm fertilized the one egg out of some 400,000 that might have ripened at that particular time. If any other sperm had been quicker or if any other egg had ripened that month, we would not be the person we are. Perhaps we would be taller or shorter; perhaps our coloring would be different. We might even have been born as a member of the opposite sex. Clearly, the statistical probabilities surrounding the uniqueness of each individual are astronomical. Being a living miracle brings with it responsibility, challenge, and joy. Use that insight as an aid to reach your depressed friends.

Tenth, *express your uniqueness creatively*. You do not have to have a major talent to find release in creative expression. Writing a poem or keeping a diary are creative acts that help us to know ourselves better whether they lead to publication or not. Painting a picture or sculpting a figure allow for self-expression regardless of the quality of the product. Participating in musical or dramatic performances helps us understand the universality of the human condition through the notes and words of others. Weaving a cloth or throwing a pot are acts of creation that reaffirm our ties with past generations and permit us to take pride in producing a unique product. Moreover, all of these actions reaffirm our role as producers and actors rather than as consumers and passive participants.

Eleventh, *develop a sense of history*. Humankind is arguably the only creature mindful of the past and able to conceptualize the future. Seeing ourselves as one link in a long chain of human endeavors that go back through time unimaginable and forward into the unseeable future helps us to develop a sense of perspective and increased objectivity. As personal history becomes one with the history of the species, we find ourselves growing calmer and more able to handle the problems of the day. Reading history and ancient philosophy helps us build ties to the fine minds of the past and permits us to share in those studies most central to our species.

Finally, *celebrate the process of living*. Meaning can be found in the process of becoming. We each have a certain time in life, some shorter, some longer, to discover who we will be. The very process of going from infancy to old age brings meaning to our lives, if we do not abort it. Work with that innate sense of adventure we all have when young. Life is very short when compared to eternity. Remind clients as you can that life is the scarcest, most precious commodity in the universe and therefore deserves utmost respect. Suicide is not respectful. Because life is short at best, we all need to maximize our time and talents. Reaching out to others is one way to do that.

We congratulate you on completing this book. We hope that what you have learned will make a difference in your own lives and in the lives of others with whom you come in contact. We wish you the very best as you travel through your own life's journey and trust that you will be better equipped to reach out to others you may meet who might be considering making premature exits.

References

Ackerly, W. C. (1967). Latency-age children who threaten or attempt to kill themselves. *Journal of the American Academy of Child Psychiatry, 6,* 242–261.

Adam, K. S., Bouckoms, A., & Streiner, D. L. (1982). Parental loss and family stability in attempted suicide. *Archives of General Psychiatry, 39,* 1081–1085.

Adams-Tucker, C. (1982). Proximate effects of sexual abuse in childhood: A report in 28 children. *American Journal of Psychiatry, 139,* 1252–1256.

Akiskal, H. S., & McKinney, W. T. (1973). Depressive disorders: Toward a unified hypothesis. *Science, 218,* 20–29.

Alsop, R. (1984, April 24). As early retirement grows in popularity, some have misgivings. *The Wall Street Journal,* 1.

Alschuler, R., & Hattwick, L. B. W. (1947). *Painting and personality: A study of young children.* Chicago: University of Chicago Press.

Alvarez, A. (1970). *The savage god: A study of suicide.* New York: Random House.

American Humane Association. (1987). *Highlights of official child neglect and reporting, 1985.* Denver, CO: Author.

American Nurses Association (1992). *Position Statement on Assisted Suicide.* Washington, DC: The Author.

American Psychiatric Association (1987). *Diagnostic and Statistical Manual of Mental Disorders* (ed. III-R). Washington, DC: American Psychiatric Association Press.

Anderson, O. (1987). *Suicide in Victorian and Edwardian England.* Oxford: Clarendon Press.

Angle, C., O'Brien, T., & McIntire, M. (1983). Adolescent self-poisoning: A nine year follow up. *Developmental and Behavioral Pediatrics, 4,* 83–87.

Apter, A., Bleich, A., Plutchik, R., Mendelsohn, S., & Tyano, S. (1988). Suicidal behavior, depression, conduct disorder in hospitalized adolescents. *Journal of the American Academy of Child and Adolescent Psychiatry, 27,* 696–699.

Aquinas, T. (1975). *Summa theologica* (Vol. 38). London: Blackfriars. (Original work written 1265–1272)

Aries, P. (1981). *The hour of our death.* New York: Knopf.

Asarnow, J. R. (1992). Suicidal ideation and attempts during middle childhood: Associations with perceived family stress and depression among child psychiatric inpatients. *Journal of Clinical Child Psychology, 21,* 35–40.

Asarnow, J. R., & Guthrie, D. (1989). Suicidal behavior, depression, and hopelessness in child psychiatric inpatients: A replication and extension. *Journal of Clinical and Child Psychology, 18,* 129–136.

Asberg, M., Nordstrom, P., & Traskman-Bendz, L. (1986, December). Cerebrospinal fluid studies in suicide. *Annals of the New York Academy of Sciences, 487,* 243–255.

Asberg, M., & Traskman, L. (1981). Studies of CSF 5-HIAA in depression and suicidal behavior. *Experiments in Medical Biology, 133,* 739–752.

Asberg, M., Traskman, L., & Thoren, P. (1976). 5-HIAA in the cerebrospinal fluid: A biochemical suicide predictor. *Archives of General Psychiatry, 33,* 1193–1197.

Atchley, R. C. (1976). *The sociology of retirement.* New York: Halstead Press.

Axline, V. A. (1947). *Play therapy: The inner dynamics of childhood* (L. Carmichael, Ed.). Boston: Houghton Mifflin.

Baker, P. M. (1985). The status of age: Preliminary results. *Journal of Gerontology, 40,* 506–508.

Baker, S. P., O'Neill, B. D., & Karpf, R. S. (1984). *The injury fact book.* Lexington, MA: Heath.

Bandura, A. (1977). *Social learning theory.* Englewood Cliffs, NJ: Prentice-Hall.

Bandura, A. & Walters, R. H. (1963). *Social learning and personality development.* New York: Holt, Rinehart, and Winston.

Banki, C. M., & Arato, M. (1983). Amine metabolites, neuroendocrine findings, and personality dimension as correlates of suicidal behavior. *Psychiatry Research, 10,* 253–261.

Bardwick, J. (1971). *The psychology of women: A study of bio-cultural conflicts.* New York: Harper & Row.

Baron, C. H. (1980, April). Termination of life support systems in the elderly. Discussion: To die

303

before the gods please: Legal issues surrounding euthanasia and the elderly. Paper presented at a Scientific Meeting of the Boston Society for Gerontologic Psychiatry.

Barraclough, B. M. (1971). Suicide in the elderly. In D. W. Kay & A. Walk (Eds.), *Recent developments in psychogeriatrics* (pp. 89–97). Kent, England: Headly Brothers.

Barraclough, B. (1987). *Suicide: Clinical and epidemiological studies*. London: Croom Helm.

Barraclough, B., Bunch, J., & Nelson, B. (1974). A hundred cases of suicide: Clinical aspects. *British Journal of Psychiatry, 125,* 355–373.

Barraclough, B. M., & Hughes, J. (1987). *Suicide*. London: Croom Helm.

Barraclough, B., & Shepherd, D. (1994). A necessary neologism: The origin and uses of suicide. *Suicide and Life-Threatening Behavior, 24,* 113–126.

Barrett, C. J. (1979). Women in widowhood. In J. H. Williams (Ed.) *Psychology of women: Selected readings* (pp. 506–596). New York: Norton.

Barry, B. (1984). Perceptions of suicide. *Death Studies (Supplement), 8,* 17–26.

Barry, B. (1989). Suicide: The ultimate escape. *Death Studies, 13,* 185–190.

Barry, M. P. (1984). The concept of rational suicide. In E. Shneidman (Ed.), *Death: Current perspectives* (3rd ed., pp. 297–320). Palo Alto, CA: Mayfield.

Battin, M. P. (1994). *The least worth death: Essays in bioethics on the end of life.* New York: Oxford University Press.

Battin, M. P. (1995a). *Ethical issues in suicide.* Englewood Cliffs, NJ: Prentice-Hall.

Bayatpour, M., Wells, R. D., & Holoford, S. (1992). Physical and sexual abuse as predictors of substance use and suicide among pregnant teenagers. *Journal of Adolescent Health, 13,* 128–132.

Beck. A. T. (1967). *Depression: Clinical, experimental, and theoretical aspects.* New York: Hoeber.

Beck, A. T. (1987). Cognitive therapy. In J. K. Zeig (Ed.), *The evolution of psychotherapy* (pp. 149–178). New York: Brunner/Mazel.

Beck, A. T., Kovacs, M., & Weissman, A. (1979). Assessment of suicide ideation: The scale for suicide ideators. *Journal of Consulting and Clinical Psychology, 47,* 343–352.

Beck, A. T., Rush, A., Show, B., & Emery, G. (1979). *Cognitive therapy of depression.* New York: Guilford Press.

Beck, A. T., Steer, R. A., Kovacs, M., & Garrison, B. (1985). Hopelessness and eventual suicide: A 10-year prospective study of patients hospitalized with suicidal ideation. *American Journal of Psychiatry, 142,* 559–563.

Belcher, G. (1972). The death of the Russian novel. *New American Review, 14,* p. 147.

Benjaminsen, S. (1981). Stressful life events preceding the onset of neurotic depression. *Psychological Medicine, 11,* 369–378.

Benson, R. A., & Brodie, D. C. (1975). Suicide by overdose of medicines among the aged. *Journal of the American Geriatrics Society, 23,* 304–308.

Berardo, F. M. (1968). Widowhood status in the United States: Perspective on a neglected aspect of the family life-cycle. *The Family Coordinator, 17,* 191–203.

Berardo, D. H. (1988). Bereavement and mourning. In H. Wass, F. M. Berardo, & R. A. Neimeyer (Eds.), *Dying: Facing the facts* (pp. 279–300). Washington, DC: Hemisphere.

Berger, M. (1984). Intervention with potential suicides. In N. Linzer, (Ed.), *Suicide: The will to live vs. the will to die* (pp. 55–70). New York: Human Sciences Press.

Berglund, M. (1984). Suicide in alcoholism—a prospective study of 88 alcoholics: The multidimensional diagnosis at first admission. *Archives of General Psychiatry, 41,* 888–891.

Bergquist, W. H., Greenberg, E. M., & Klaum, G. A. (1993). *In our fifties: Voices of men and women reinventing their lives.* San Francisco: Jossey-Bass.

Berman, A. L. (1987, November). *Suicide prevention: A critical need and a critical perspective.* Paper presented at the First National Conference on Suicide Prevention and the Public Schools, Orlando, FL.

Berman, A. L. (1988). Playing the suicide game. *Readings: A Journal of Reviews and Commentary in Mental Health, 3,* 20–23.

Berman, A. (1993). Adolescent suicide: An update. Paper presented at the 26th Annual Conference of the American Association of Suicidology, San Francisco, CA.

Berman, A. L., & Carroll, T. A. (1984). Adolescent suicide: A critical review. *Death Education, 8,* 53–64.

Berman, A. L., & Jobes, D. A. (1991). *Adolescent suicide: Assessment and intervention.* Washington, DC: American Psychological Association.

Bernard, J. (1981). *The female world.* New York: Free Press.

Berne, E. (1964). *Games people play.* New York: Grove Press.

Bettelheim, B. (1976). *The uses of enchantment.* New York: Knopf.

Bettes, B. A., & Walker. E. (1986). Symptoms associated with suicidal behavior in childhood and adolescence. *Journal of Abnormal Child Psychology, 14,* 591–604.

Bezchlibnyk-Butler, K. Z., Jeffries, J. J., & Martin, B. A. (1994). *Clinical Handbook of Psychotropic Drugs.* Seattle: Hogrefettluber Publishers.

Blackwell, P. L., & Gessner, J. C. (1983). Fear and trembling: An inquiry into adolescent perceptions of living in the nuclear age. *Youth and Society, 15*(2), 237–255.

Bloom, A. D. (1987). *The closing of the American mind: How higher education has failed democracy and impoverished the souls of today's students.* New York: Simon and Schuster.

Blum, J. E., Clark, E. T., & Jarvik, L. F. (1973). The New York State Psychiatric Institute Study of Aging Twins. In L. F. Jarvik, C. Eisdorfer, & J. E. Blum (Eds.), *Intellectual functioning in adults: Psychological and biological influences* (pp. 13–20). New York: Springer.

Blumenthal, S. J., & Kupfer, D. J. (1986). Generalizable treatment strategies for suicidal behavior. In J. J. Mann & M. Stanley (Eds.), *Psychobiology of suicidal behavior* (pp. 327–340). New York: New York Academy of Sciences.

Bock, E. W., & Webber, I. L. (1972a). Social status and relational systems of elderly suicides: A reexamination of the Henry-Short Thesis. *Suicide and Life-Threatening Behavior, 2,* 145–159.

Bock, E. W., & Webber, I. L. (1972b, February). Suicide among the elderly: Isolating widowhood and mitigating alternatives. *Journal of Marriage and the Family,* pp. 24–31.

Boldt, M. (1982). Normative evaluations of suicide and death: A cross-generational study. *Omega, 13,* 145–157.

Bolger, N., Downey, G., Walker, E., & Steininger, P. (1989). The onset of suicidal ideation in childhood and adolescence. *Journal of Youth and Adolescence, 18,* 175–189.

Bollen, K. A., & Phillips, D. P. (1982). Imitative suicides: A national study of the effects of television news stories. *American Sociological Review, 47,* 802–809.

Borg, S. E., & Stahl, M. (1982). A prospective study of suicides and controls among psychiatric patients. *Acta Psychiatrica Scandinavica, 65,* 221–232.

Borst, S. R., & Noam, G. (1991). Adolescent suicidality: A clinical-developmental approach. *Journal of the American Academy of Child and Adolescent Psychiatry, 30,* 796–803.

Bowen, M. (1978). *Family therapy in clinical practice.* New York: Jason Aronson.

Bowlby, J. (1980). *Attachment and loss: Loss, sadness, and depression.* Vol. III. New York: Basic Books.

Brazelton, B. (1969). *Infants and mothers.* New York: Delacorte Press.

Breed, W. (1963). Occupational mobility and suicide among white males. *American Sociological Review, 28,* 179–188.

Breed, W., & Huffine, C. (1979). Sex differences in suicide among older white Americans: A role and developmental approach. In O. J. Kaplan (Ed.), *Psychopathology of Aging* (pp. 289–309). New York: Academic Press.

Brent, D. A., Kalis, R., Edelbrock, C., Costello, A., Dulcan, M. K., & Conover, N. (1986). Psychopathology and its relationship to suicidal ideation in childhood and adolescence. *Journal of the American Academy of Child Psychology, 25,* 666–673.

Brent, D. A., Preper, J. A., Moritz, G., Bauger, M., Roth, C., Balach, L., & Schweers, J. (1993). Stressful life events, psychopathology, and adolescent suicide: A case control study. *Suicide and Life-Threatening Behavior, 23,* 179–187.

Briere, J., Evans, D., Runtz, M., & Wall, T. (1988). Symptomology in men who were molested as children: A comparison study. *American Journal of Orthopsychiatry, 58,* 457–461.

Brody, H. (1995, March) From New Jersey to Oregon, by way of Michigan: The evolution of the "right to die" issue in the U.S. Presentation to the National Health Forum, "Physician-Assisted Death: Implications for patients, care providers, and society." Sponsored by the University of Florida, Amelia Island.

Bromberg, S., & Cassel, C. K. (1983). Suicide in the elderly: The limits of paternalism. *Journal of the American Geriatrics Society, 31*(11), 698–703.

Bronisch, T., & Hecht, H. (1987). Comparison of depressed patients with and without suicide attempts in their past history. *Acta Psychiatrica Scandinavica, 76,* 438–449.

Brown, G. W., & Harris, T. (1978). *Social origins of depression.* London: Tavistock.

Buehler, J. W., Devine, O. J., Berkelman, R. L., & Chevarley, F. M. (1990). Impact of the human immunodeficiency virus epidemic on mortality trends in young men in the United States. *American Journal of Public Health, 80,* 1080–1086.

Buhler, C. (1961). Old age and fulfillment of life with consideration of the use of time in old age. *Acta Psychologica, 19,* 126–148.

Butler, R. N., & Lewis, M. I. (1977). *Aging and mental health: Positive psychological approaches.* St. Louis, MO: Mosby.

Butler, R. N., & Lewis, M. I. (1982). *Aging and mental health: Positive psychosocial and biomedical approaches* (3rd ed.). St. Louis: Mosby.

Cain, A. C. (Ed.) (1972). *Survivors of suicide.* Springfield, IL: Charles C. Thomas.

Cain, A. C., & Fast, I. (1972). Children's disturbed reaction to parent suicide: Distortions of guilt, communication, and identification. In A. C. Cain (Ed.), *Survivors of suicide* (pp. 93–111). Springfield, IL: Charles C. Thomas.

Calhoun, L. G., Selby, J. W., & Faulstich, M. E. (1980). Reactions to the parents of the child suicide: A study of social impression. *Journal of Consulting and Clinical Psychology, 48,* 535–536.

Calhoun, L. G., Selby, J. W., & Faulstich, M. E. (1982). The aftermath of child suicide: Influences on the perceptions of parents. *Journal of Community Psychology, 10,* 250–254.

Callahan, D. (1992). When self-determination runs amok. *Hastings Center Report, 22(2),* 52–55.

Campbell, C. (1995). When medicine lost its moral conscience: Oregon Measure 16. *BioLaw, 11(1)* 5:1–5:16.

Canadian Medical Association (1995). CMA Policy Summery. *Physician Assisted Death.* Ottawa Ontario: Canadian Medical Association.

Canetto, S. S. (1994). Gender issues in the treatment of Suicidal individuals. In A. A. Leenaars, J. T. Maltsberger, & R. H. Neimeyer (Eds.), *Treatment of Suicidal People* (pp. 115–126). Washington, DC: Taylor and Francis.

Canetto, S. S. (1992). Gender and suicide in the elderly. *Suicide and Life-Threatening Behavior, 22,* 80–97.

Cantor, P. (1987, November). *During and after a suicidal crisis: What educators need to know.* Paper presented at the First National Conference on Suicide Prevention and the Public Schools, Orlando, FL.

Carlson, G. A., Asarnow, J. R., & Orbach, I. (1987). Developmental aspects of suicidal behavior in children, Part I. *Journal of the American Academy of Child and Adolescent Psychiatry, 26,* 186–192.

Carlson, G. A., Asarnow, J. R., & Orbach, I. (1994). Developmental aspects of suicidal behavior in children and developmentally delayed adolescents. In G. G. Noam & S. Borst (Eds) *Children, Youth, and Suicide: Developmental Perspectives.* San Francisco: Jossey-Bass.

Carlson, G. A., & Cantwell, D. P. (1982). Suicidal behavior and depression in children and adolescents. *Journal of the American Academy of Child Psychiatry, 21,* 361–368.

Carter, B. F., & Brooks, A. (1990). Suicide postvention: Crisis or opportunity? *The School Counselor, 37,* 378–390.

Cassem, N. H. (1980, April). Termination of life support systems in the elderly: Clinical issues. Paper presented at the Scientific Meeting of the Boston Society for Gerontologic Psychiatry.

Cattell, H. R. (1988). Elderly suicide in London: An analysis of coroners' inquests. *International Journal of Geriatric Psychiatry, 3,* 251–261.

Cattell, R. B. (1963). Theory of fluid and crystallized intelligence: A critical experiment. *Journal of Educational Psychology, 54,* 1–22.

Celis, W. (1994). Schools getting tough on guns in the classroom. *The New York Times, 143,* A1, B8.

Centers for Disease Control (1986). *Mortality and Morbidity Weekly Report, 35(22).*

Chapin, H. & Chapin, S. (1974). Cats in the cradle. Story Songs Ltd.

Chesler, P. (1972). *Women and madness.* Garden City, NY: Doubleday.

Chesnais, J. C. (1992). The history of violence: Homicide and suicide through the ages. *International Social Science Journal, 44,* 217–234.

Clark, D. C. (1993). Narcissistic crises of aging and suicidal despair. *Suicide and Life-Threatening Behavior, 23,* 21–26.

Clarkin, J. F., Friedman, R. C., Hurt, S. W., Corn, R., & Aronoff, M. (1984). Affective and character pathology of suicidal adolescents and young adult inpatients. *Journal of Clinical Psychiatry, 45*(1), 19–22.

Clausen, J. A. (1981). Men's occupational careers in the middle years. In D. H. Eichoun, J. A. Clausen, N. Haan, M. P. Honzik, & P. Mussen (Eds.), *Present and past in middle life* (pp. 321–351). New York: Academic Press.

Clum, G., Patsiokas, A., & Luscomb, R. (1979). Empirically based comprehensive treatment program for parasuicide. *Journal of Consulting and Clinical Psychology, 47,* 937–945.

Cohen, J. (1961). A study of suicide pacts. *Medical Legal Journal, 29,* 144–151.

Cohen-Sandler, R., Berman, A. L., & King, R. A. (1982). Life stress and symptomatology: Determinants of suicidal behavior in children. *Journal of the American Academy of Child Psychiatry, 21,* 178–186.

Cohn, H. (1976). Suicide in Jewish legal and religious tradition. *Mental Health and Society, 3,* 129–136.

Cole, D. A. (1989). Psychopathology of adolescent suicide: Hopelessness, coping beliefs, and depression. *Journal of Abnormal Psychology, 98,* 248–255.

Coleman, L. (1987). *Suicide clusters.* Boston: Faber & Faber.

Connell, H. M. (1972). Attempted suicide in school children. *Medical Journal of Australia, 1,* 686–690.

Conwell, Y. (1994). Suicide in elderly patients. In L. S. Schneider, C. F. Reynolds, B. D. Lebowitz, & A. J. Friedhoff (Eds.) *Diagnosis and treatment of depression in late life* (pp. 397–418). Washington, DC: American Psychiatric Press.

Corder, B. F., & Haizlip, T. M. (1984). Environmental and personality similarities in case histories of suicide and self-poisoning in children under ten. *Suicide and Life-Threatening Behavior, 14,* 59–66.

Corder, B. F., Shorr, W., & Corder, R. F. (1974). A study of social and psychological characteristics of adolescent suicide attempters in an urban disadvantaged area. *Adolescence, 9,* 1–16.

Corey, G. (1991). *Theory and practice of counseling and psychotherapy.* Pacific Grove, CA: Brooks/Cole.

Cote, T. R., Biggar, R. J., & Dannenberg, A. L. (1992). Risk of suicide among persons with AIDS. *Journal of the American Medical Association, 268,* 2066–2068.

Cottone, R. R. (1992). *Theories and paradigms of counseling and psychotherapy.* Boston: Allyn and Bacon.

Cousins, N. (1979). *Anatomy of an illness as perceived by the patient: Reflections on healing and regeneration.* New York: Norton.

Curphey, T. J. (1961). The role of the social scientist in the medicological certification of death from suicide. In N. L. Farberow & E. S. Shneidman (Eds.), *The cry for help* (pp. 110–117). New York: McGraw-Hill.

Curran, D. K. (1987). *Adolescent suicidal behavior.* Washington, DC: Hemisphere.

Darbonne, A. R. (1969). Suicide and age: A suicide note analysis. *Journal of Consulting and Clinical Psychology, 33,* 46–50.

Davidson, L. E., Rosenberg, M. L., Mercy, J. A., Franklin, J., & Simmons, J. T. (1989). An epidemiological study of risk factors in two teenage suicide clusters. *Journal of the American Medical Association, 262,* 2687–2692.

Deluty, R. (1988). Physical illness, psychiatric illness, and the acceptability of suicide. *Omega, 19,* 79–91

Deluty, R. H. (1989). Factors affecting the acceptability of suicide. *Omega, 19,* 315–326.

Demi, A. S., & Miles, M. S. (1988). Suicide bereaved parents: Emotional distress and physical problems. *Death Studies, 12,* 297–307.

DeRose, N., & Page, S. (1985). Attitudes of professional and community groups toward male and female suicide. *Canadian Journal of Community Mental Health, 4,* 51–64.

Derryberry, D., & Rothbart, M. K. (1984). Emotion, attention, and temperament. In C. E. Izard, J. Kagan, & R. B. Zajonc (Eds.), *Emotions, cognition, and behavior* (pp. 132–167). Cambridge: Cambridge University Press.

DeWild, E. J., Kienhorst, I. C., Diekstra R. F., & Wolters, W. H. (1993). The specificity of psychological characteristics in adolescent suicide attempters. *Journal of the American Academy of Child and Adolescent Psychiatry, 32,* 51–59.

Domino, G. (1990). Popular misconceptions about suicide: How popular are they? *Omega, 21,* 167–175.

Domino, G., Domino, V., & Berry, T. (1986/87). Childrens' attitudes toward suicide. *Omega, 17,* 279–287.

Domino, G., MacGregor, J. C., & Hannah, M. T. (1989). Collegiate attitudes toward suicide: New Zealand and United States. *Omega, 19,* 351–364.

Domino, G., Moore, D., Westlake, L., & Gibson, L. (1982). Attitudes toward suicide: A factor analytic approach. *Journal of Clinical Psychology, 38*(2), 257–262.

Domino, G., & Swain, B. (1985–86). Recognition of suicide lethality and attitudes toward suicide in mental health professionals. *Omega, 16,* 301–308.

Donne, J. (1982). *Biathanatos* (M. Rudick & M. P. Battin, Trans.). New York: Garland. (Original work published 1644)

Dorpat, T. L., Anderson, W. F., & Ripley, H. S. (1968). The relationship of physical illness to suicide. In H. L. P. Resnik (Ed.), *Suicide: Diagnosis and management* (pp. 209–219). Boston: Little, Brown.

Dorpat, T. L., & Ripley, H. S. (1960). A study of suicide in the Seattle area. *Comprehensive Psychiatry, 1,* 349–359.

Downey, A. (1990). The impact of drug abuse upon adolescent suicide. *Omega, 22,* 261–275.

Doyle, J. A. (1983). *The male experience.* Dubuque, IA: Brown.

Droogas, A., Siiter, R., & O'Connell, A. N. (1982). Effects of personal and situational factors on attitudes toward suicide. *Omega, 13,* 127–144.

Duberstein, P. R., Conwell, Y., & Caine, E. D. (1993). Interpersonal stressors, substance abuse, and suicide. *Journal of Nervous and Mental Disease, 181,* 80–85.

Dunn, R. G., & Morrish-Vidners, D. (1987). The psychological and social experience of suicide survivors. *Omega, 18,* 175–215.

Dunne-Maxim, (1994, March). *Impact of Suicide on the professional in training.* Featured panel presentation at the American Association of Suicidology, New York.

Durkheim, E. (1951). *Le Suicide* (J. A. Spaulding & G. Simpson, Trans.). Glencoe, IL: Free Press. (Original work published 1897)

Dyck, R. J. (1991). System-entry issues in school suicide prevention education programs. In A. A. Leenaars & S. Wenckstern, (Eds.), *Suicide prevention in schools.* New York: Hemisphere.

Easterlin, R. A., Macdonald, C., & Macunovich, D. J. (1990). Retirement prospects of the baby boom generation: A different perspective. *Gerontologist, 30,* 776–783.

Eisenberg, L. (1980). Adolescent suicide: On taking arms against a sea of troubles. *Pediatrics, 66,* 315–321.

Ekerdt, D. J., Bosse, R., Levkov, S. (1985). An empirical test of phases of retirement: Findings from the normative aging study. *Journal of Gerontology, 40,* 95–101.

Elkind, D. (1967). Egocentrism in adolescence. *Child Development, 38,* 1025–1034.

Elkind, D., & Bowen, R. (1979). Imaginary audience behavior in children and adolescents. *Developmental Psychology, 15,* 38–44.

Ellis, A. (1962). *Reason and emotion in psychotherapy.* New York: Lyle Stuart.

Ellis, A. (1973). Rational psychotherapy. In M. R. Goldfried & M. Merbaum (Eds.), *Behavior change through self-control.* NY: Holt Rinehart and Winston.

Ellis, A. (1974). *Humanistic psychotherapy: The rational-emotive approach.* New York: McGraw-Hill.

Ellis, A., & Bernard, M. E. (1986). What is rational-emotive therapy (RET)? In A. Ellis & R. Grieger (Eds.), *Handbook of rational-emotive therapy: Vol. 2* (pp. 3–30). New York: Springer.

Erikson, E. H. (1959). *Identity and the life cycle.* New York: International Universities Press.

Erikson, E. H. (1968). *Identity: Youth and crisis.* New York: Norton.

Erikson, E. H. (1980). *Identity and the life cycle.* New York: Norton.

Farberow, N. L. (Ed.). (1975). *Suicide in different cultures.* Baltimore, MD: University Park Press.

Farberow, N. L. (1991). Preparatory and prior suicidal behavior factors. In L. Davidson and M. Linnoila (Eds.), *Risk Factors in Youth Suicide.* New York: Hemisphere.

Farberow, N. L., & Moriwaki, S. Y. (1975, August). Self-destructive crisis in the older person. *The Gerontologist,* pp. 333–337.

Farberow, N. L., & Shneidman, E. (1961). *The cry for help.* New York: McGraw-Hill.

Favazza, A. R. (1989). Why patients mutilate themselves. *Hospital and Community Psychiatry, 40,* 137–145.

Fillenbaum, G. G., George, L. K., & Palmore, E. B. (1985). Determinants and consequences of retirement among men of different races and economic levels. *Journal of Gerontology, 40,* 85–94.

Flavin, D. K., Franklin, J. K., & Frances, R. J. (1986). The acquired immune deficiency syndrome (AIDS) and suicidal behavior in alcohol-dependent homosexual men. *American Journal of Psychiatry, 143,* 1440–1442.

Fox, R. (1984). The Samaritans: An alternative approach to suicide prevention. In N. Linzer (Ed.), *Suicide: The will to live vs. the will to die.* (pp. 43–53). New York: Human Sciences Press.

Frankish, C. J. (1994). Crisis Centers and their role in treatment: Suicide prevention versus health promotion. In A. A. Leenaars, J. T. Maltsberger, & R. A. Neimeyer (Eds.), *Treatment of Suicidal People* (pp. 33–43). Washington, DC: Taylor & Francis.

Frankl, V. E. (1963). *Man's search for meaning: An introduction to logotherapy* (I. Lasch, Trans.). New York: Washington Square Press.

Frederick, C., & Resnik, H. (1971). How suicideal behaviors are learned. *American Journal of Psychotherapy, 25,* 37–55.

Frenkel-Brunswik, E. (1963). Adjustments and reorientation in the course of the life span. In R. G. Kuhlen & G. G. Thompson (Eds.), *Psychological studies of human development* (pp. 554–564). New York: Appleton-Century-Crofts.

Freud, S. (1953). *The standard edition of the complete psychological works.* J. Strachey (Ed.). London: Hogarth Press.

Freud, S. (1961a). *Mourning and melancholia.* In J. Strachey (Ed. and Trans.), *The standard edition of the complete psychological works of Sigmund Freud* (Vol. 14, pp. 243–258). London: Hogarth Press. (Original work published 1917)

Freud, S. (1961b). *The ego and the id.* In J. Strachey (Ed. and Trans.) *The standard edition of the complete psychological works of Sigmund Freud* (Vol. 19, pp. 3–66). London: Hogarth Press. (Original work published in 1923)

Freud, S. (1961c). *Beyond the pleasure principle.* In J. Strachey (Ed. and Trans.) *The standard edition of the complete psychological works of Sigmund Freud* (Vol. 18, pp. 7–64). London: Hogarth Press. (Original work published 1920)

Freud, S. (1961d). *Civilization and its discontents.* In J. Strachey (Ed. and Trans.). *The standard edition of the complete psychological works of Sigmund Freud* (Vol. 21, pp. 64–145). London: Hogarth Press. (Original work published in 1930)

Frierson, R. L., & Lippman, S. B. (1988). Suicide and AIDS. *Psychosomatics, 29,* 226–231.

Fryer, J. (1987). AIDS and suicide. In J. D. Morgan (Ed.) Proceedings of the *Suicide: Helping those at risk* Conference. (pp. 193–200). Kings College, London: Ontario.

Garfinkel, B. D., Froese, A., & Hood, J. (1982). Suicide attempts in children and adolescents. *American Journal of Psychiatry, 139,* 1257–1261.

Garland, A. (1987, November). *Prevention programs: Evaluation guidelines.* Paper presented at the First National Conference on Suicide Prevention and the Schools, Orlando, FL.

Gartley, W., & Bernasconi, M. (1967). The concept of death in children. *Journal of Genetic Psychology, 110,* 71–85.

Gendreau, P., & Suboski, M. D. (1971). Intelligence and age in discrimination conditioning of eyelid response. *Journal of Experimental Psychology, 89,* 379–382.

Gesell, A. (1940). *The first five years of life.* New York: Harper.

Gibbs, J. P., & Martin, W. T. (1964). *Status integration and suicide.* Eugene, OR: University of Oregon Press.

Gibbs, J. T. (1984). Black adolescents and youth: An endangered species. *American Journal of Orthopsychiatry, 57,* 6–21.

Giles, J. (1994). Generation X. *Newsweek,* June 6, 62–72.

Glick, I. O., Parkes, C. M., & Weiss, R. (1975). *The first year of bereavement.* New York: Basic Books.

Gold, M. S. (1986). *Good news about depression.* New York: Bantam Books.

Goldberg, E. L. (1981). Depression and suicide ideation in the young adult. *American Journal of Psychiatry, 138,* 35–40.

Goldberg, H. (1977). *The hazards of being male: Surviving the myth of masculine privilege.* New York: New American Library.

Goldney, R. D. (1981). Attempted suicide in young women: Correlate of lethality. *British Journal of Psychiatry, 139,* 382–390.

Goldney, R. D., & Katsikitis, M. (1983). Cohort analysis of suicide rates in Australia. *Archives of General Psychiatry, 40*(1), 71–74.

Golombek, H., & Marton, P. (1989). Disturbed affect and suicidal behavior during adolescence: Personality considerations. *Israel Journal of Psychiatry and Related Sciences, 26*, 30–36.

Goode, T. L., & Brophy, J. E. (1984). *Looing in classrooms*. New York: Harper & Row.

Goodwin, D. (1973). Alcohol in suicide and homicide. *Quarterly Journal of Studies of Alcohol, 34*, 144–156.

Gould, M. S., & Shaffer, D. (1986). The impact of suicide in television movies: Evidence of imitation. *New England Journal of Medicine, 315*, 690–694.

Gould, R. E. (1965). Suicide problems in children and adolescents. *American Journal of Psychotherapy, 19*, 228–245.

Gould, R. L. (1978). *Transformations: Growth and change in adult life*. New York: Simon & Schuster.

Gove, W. R., & Tudor, J. F. (1973). Adult sex roles and mental illness. *American Journal of Sociology, 78*, 812–35.

Goy, R. W., & Resko, J. A. (1972). Gonadal hormones and behavior of normal and pseudohermaphrodetic non-human female primates. In E. Astwood (Ed.), *Recent Progress in hormone research*. New York: Academic Press.

Gray, D., & Hudson, L. (1984). Formal operations and the imaginary audience. *Developmental Psychology, 20*, 619–627.

Green, A. H. (1978). Self-destructive behavior in battered children. *American Journal of Psychiatry, 135*, 579–582.

Greer, G. (1992). *The change: Women, aging and the menopause*. New York: Knopf.

Greuling, J., & DeBlassie, R. (1980). Adolescent suicide. *Adolescence, 15*, 589–601.

Guze, S. B., & Robins, E. (1970). Suicide and primary affective disorder. *British Journal of Psychiatry, 117*, 437–438.

Haan, N. (1981). Common dimensions of personality development: Early adolescence to middle life. In D. H. Eichoun, J. A. Clausen, N. Haan, M. P. Honzik, & P. Mussen (Eds.), *Present and past in middle life* (pp. 117–151). New York: Academic Press.

Haas, A. P., & Hendin, H. (1983). Suicide among older people: Projections for the future. *Suicide and Life-Threatening Behavior, 13*, 147–154.

Hafen, B. Q., & Frandsen, K. J. (1986). *Youth suicide: Depression and loneliness*. Evergreen, Colorado: Cordillera Press.

Hall, G. S. (1904). *Adolescence* (Vol. 1). New York: Appleton.

Haas, A. P., & Hendin, H. (1983). Suicide among older people: Projections for the future. *Suicide and Life-Threatening Behavior, 13*, 147–154.

Harmet, A. R. (Ed.), (1984). *The World Book Encyclopedia* (Vol. 18, p. 770). Chicago: World Book.

Harris, T. A. (1969). *I'm OK, You're OK*. New York: Harper & Row.

Harrison, P. A., Hoffman, N. G., & Edwall, G. E. (1989). Sexual abuse correlates: Similarities between male and female adolescents in chemical dependency treatment. *Journal of Adolescent Research, 4*, 385–399.

Harry, J. (1983). Parasuicide, gender, and gender deviance. *Journal of Health and Social Behavior, 24*, 350–361.

Hawton, K. (1982). Annotation: Attempted suicide in children and adolescents. *Journal of Child Psychology and Psychiatry, 23*, 497–503.

Health and Welfare Canada (1987). *Suicide in Canada: Report of the National Task Force on Suicide in Canada*. Ottawa: Department of National Health and Welfare.

Hendin, H. (1995). Assisted suicide, euthanasia, and suicide prevention: The implications of the Dutch experience. *Suicide and Life-Threatening Behavior, 25*(1), Spring.

Hirschfield, R. M. A., & Blumenthal, S. J. (1986). Personality, life events, and other psychosocial factors in adolescent depression and suicide. In G. L. Klerman (Ed.), *Suicide and depression among adolescents and young adults.* (pp. 213–254). Washington, DC: American Psychiatric Press.

Hirschfield, R. M. A., & Cross, C. K. (1982). Epidemiology of affective disorders: Psychosocial risk factors. *Archives of General Psychiatry, 39*, 35–46.

Holinger, P. C. (1979). Violent deaths among the young: Recent trends in suicide, homicide and accidents. *American Journal of Psychiatry, 139*, 1144–1147.

Holinger, P. C., & Offer, C. (1982). The prediction of adolescent suicide: A population model. *American Journal of Psychiatry, 139,* 302–307.

Holinger, P. C., & Offer, D. (1991). Sociodemographic, epidemiologic, and individual attributes. In L. Davidson and M. Linnoila (Eds), *Risk Factors in Youth Suicide.* New York: Hemisphere.

Holinger, P. C., Offer, D., Barter, J. T., & Bell, C. C. (1994). *Suicide and homicide among adolescents.* New York: Guilford Press.

Holinger, P. C., Offer, D., & Zola, M. A. (1988). A prediction model of suicide among youth. *The Journal of Nervous and Mental Disease, 176,* 275–279.

Holmes, T. H., & Rahe, R. H. (1967). The social readjustment rating scale. *Journal of Psychosomatic Research, 11,* 213–218.

The Holy Bible. (1949). (King James edition). New York: American Bible Society.

Horn, J. L. (1982). The theory of fluid and crystallized in relation to concepts of cognitive psychology and aging in adulthood. In F. J. M. Craik and S. Trehub (Eds.), *Aging and cognitive processes.* New York: Plenum.

Hostetter, C. (1988, April). AIDS: Its impact on the nation, the community, the family and the individual. Paper presented at the meeting of the Association for Death Education and Counseling, Orlando, FL.

Hoyenga, K. B., & Hoyenga, K. T. (1979). *The question of sex differences.* Boston: Little Brown.

Hudgens, R. W. (1983). Preventing suicide. *New England Journal of Medicine, 308,* 897–898.

Hull, D. (1979), Migration, adaptation, and illness: A review. *Social Science and Medicine, 13A,* 25–36.

Hume, D. (1929). *An essay on suicide.* Yellow Springs, OH: Kahoe. (Original work published 1783)

Humphrey, D. (1991). *Final exit: The practicalities of self-deliverance and assisted suicide for the dying.* Eugene, OR: The Hemlock Society.

Hutton, C. L., & Valente, S. M. (1984). *Suicide: Assessment and intervention* (2nd ed.). Norwalk, CT: Appleton-Century-Crofts.

Illfeld, F. W. (1977). Current social stressors and symptoms of depression. *American Journal of Psychiatry, 135,* 161–166.

Inhelder, B., & Piaget, J. (1958). *The growth of logical thinking from childhood to adolescence.* New York: Basic Books.

Jaco, R. M. (1987). Suicide-proofing youth: A survival technique for the eighties. In J. D. Morgan (Ed.), *Suicide: Helping those at risk. Proceedings of the Conference* (pp. 103–111). London, Ontario: King's College.

Jacobs, J. (1971). *Adolescent suicide.* New York: Wiley Interscience.

Jacobziner, H. (1960). Attempted suicide in children. *Journal of Pediatrics, 56,* 519–525.

Jacobziner, H. (1965). Attempted suicide in adolescence. *Journal of the American Medical Association, 10,* 22–36.

Jaques, E. (1965). Death and the mid-life crisis. *International Journal of Psychoanalysis, 146,* 502–514.

Jennings, C., Barraclough, B., & Moss, J. (1978). Have the Samaritans lowered the suicide rate? A controlled study. *Psychological Medicine, 8,* 413–422.

Jobes, D. A., Berman, A. L., & Josselsen, A. R. (1986). The impact of psychological autopsies of medical examiners' determination of manner of death. *Journal of Forensic Science, 32*(1), 177–189.

Joffe, R. T., & Offord, D. R. (1983). A review: Suicidal behavior in childhood. *Canadian Journal of Psychiatry, 28,* 57–63.

Joffe, R. T., & Offord, D. R. (1990). Epidemiology. In G. MacLean (Ed.), *Suicide in children and adolescents* (pp. 1–39). Toronto: Hogrefe & Huber.

Joffe, R. T., Offord, D. R., & Boyle, M. H. (1988). Ontario child health study: Suicidal behavior in youth age 12–16 years. *American Journal of Psychiatry, 145,* 1420–1423.

Johansson, B., Zarit, S. H., & Berg, S. (1992). Changes in cognitive functioning of the oldest old. *Journal of Gerontology: Psychological Sciences, 47,* 75–80.

Jones, J. S., Stanley, B., Mann, J. J., Frances, A. J., Guido, J. R., Traskman-Bendz, L., Winchel, R., Brown, R. P., & Stanley, M. (1990). CSF 5-HIAA and HVA concentrations in elderly depressed patients who attempted suicide. *American Journal of Psychiatry, 147,* 1225–1227.

Jong, E. (1994). *Fear of fifty: A midlife memoir.* New York: HarperCollins.

Jorgenson, D. E., & Neubecker, R. C. (1981). Euthanasia: A national survey of attitudes toward voluntary termination of life. *Omega, 11,* 281–291.

Josepho, S. A., & Plutchik, R. (1994). Stress, coping, and suicide risk in psychiatric in-patients. *Suicide and Life-Threatening Behavior, 24,* 48–57.

Judd, S. (1995). Oregon's measure 16 blocked. *Timelines: The Newsletter of the Hemlock Society USA,* January-February.

Jung, C. G. (1960). *The structure and dynamics of the psyche* (R. F. C. Hull, Trans.). In G. Adler (Ed.), *The collected works of C. G. Jung* (Bollingen Series 20, Vol. 8, pp. 749–795). Princeton, NJ: Princeton University Press.

Kalish, R. A. (1963). Variables in death attitudes. *The Journal of Social Psychology, 59,* 137–145.

Kalish, R. A. (1975). *Late adulthood: Perspectives on human development.* Monterey, CA: Brooks/Cole.

Kalish, R. A., Reynolds, D. K., & Farberow, N. L. (1974). Community attitudes toward suicide. *Community Mental Health Journal, 10,* 301–308.

Kart, C. S. (1981). *The realities of aging.* Boston: Allyn & Bacon.

Kazdin, A. E., French, N. H., Unis, A. S., Esveldt-Dawson, K., & Sherick, R. B. (1983). Helplessness, depression, and suicidal intent among psychiatrically disturbed inpatient children. *Journal of Consulting and Clinical Psychology, 51,* 504–510.

Kellerman, A., Rivara, F, Somes, G., Reay, D., Francisco, J., Banton, J., Prodzinski, J., Fligner, C., & Hackman, B. (1992). Suicide in the home in relation to gun ownership. *The New England Journal of Medicine, 327*(7), 467–472.

Kelly, G. A. (1955). *The psychology of personal constructs.* New York: Norton.

Kelson v. City of Springfield, Oregon, 767 F.2d 651 (Ninth Circuit 1985)

Kessler, R. C., Downey, G. D., Milavsky, J. R., & Stipp, H. (1988). Clustering of teenage suicides after television news stories about suicides: A reconsideration. *American Journal of Psychiatry, 145,* 1379–1383.

Khan, A. U. (1987). Heterogeneity of suicidal adolescents. *Journal of the American Academy of Child and Adolescent Psychiatry, 26,* 92–96.

Kienhorst, C. W., DeWilde, E. J., Diekstra, R. F., & Wolters, W. H. (1992). Difference between adolescent suicide attempters and depressed adolescents. *Acta Psychiatrica Scandinavica, 85,* 222–228.

Kiev, A. (1984). Suicide and depression. In N. Linzer (Ed.), *Suicide: The will to live vs. the will to die* (pp. 23–34). New York: Human Sciences Press.

Kizer, K. W., Green, M., Perkins, C. I., Doebbert, G., & Hughes, M. J. (1988). AIDS and suicide in California. *Journal of the American Medical Association, 260,* 1881.

Kleemeier, R. W. (1962). Intellectual change in the senium. *Proceedings of the Social Statistics Section of the American Statistical Association* (pp. 290–295).

Kohlberg, L. (1966). A cognitive-development analysis of children's sex-role concepts and attitudes. In E. Maccoby (Ed.), *The development of sex differences.* Stanford, California: Stanford University Press.

Kohlberg, L. (1976). Moral stages and moralization: Cognitive-development approach. In T. Lickona (Ed.), *Moral development and behavior: Theory, research, and social issues* (pp. 31–53). New York: Holt, Rinehart and Winston.

Koocher, G. P. (1973). Childhood, death, and child development. *Developmental Psychology, 9,* 369–375.

Kosky, P. (1982). Childhood suicidal behavior. *Journal of Child Psychology and Psychiatry and Allied Disciplines, 24,* 457–467.

Kostrubala, T. (1977). *The Joy of Running.* New York: Pocket Books.

Kral, M. J., & Sakinofsky, I. (1994). A clinical model for suicide risk assessment. In A. A. Leenaars, J. T. Maltsberger, & R. A. Neimeyer (Eds.), *Treatment of suicidal people* (pp. 19–31). Washington, DC: Taylor & Francis.

Kubler-Ross, E. (1969). *On death and dying.* New York: Macmillan.

Lampert, D. I., Bourque, L. B., & Kraus, J. F. (1984). Occupational status and suicide. *Suicide and Life-Threatening Behavior, 14,* 254–269.

Lavin, M., Roy, A., Dunne-Maxim, K., & Slaby, A. (1994). *Impact of suicide on the professional in training.* Featured Panel at the American Association of Suicidology, New York.

Lecky, P. (1945). *Self-consistency: A theory of personality*. Fort Myers Beach, FL: Island Press.

Lecky, P. (1973). *Self-consistency: A Theory of personality*. Fort Myers Beach, FL: Island Press.

Leenaars, A. A. (1992). Suicide notes of the older adult. *Suicide and Life-Threatening Behavior, 22*, 62–79.

Leenaars, A. A., Balance, W. D., Pellarin, S., Aversano, G., Magli, A., & Wenckstern, S. (1988). Facts and myths of suicide in Canada. *Death Studies, 12*, 195–206.

Leenaars, A. L., & Wenckstern, S. (1991). *Suicide prevention in the schools*. Washington, DC: Hemisphere.

Lester, D. (1969). Suicide as a positive act. *Psychology, 6*(3), 43–48.

Lester, D. (1970). The concept of an appropriate death. *Psychology, 7*(4), 61–66.

Lester, D. (1971). The evaluation of suicide prevention centers. *International Behavioral Scientist, 3*(2), 40–47.

Lester, D. (1986). Genetics, twin studies, and suicide. In R. Maris (Ed.), *Biology of suicide*. New York: Guilford Press.

Lester, D. (1987). Preventing suicide: Past failures and future hopes. In J. D. Morgan (Ed.), *Suicide: Helping those at risk. Proceedings of the conference* (pp. 69–78). London, Ontario: King's College.

Lester, D. (1994). A comparison of 15 theories of suicide. *Suicide and Life-Threatening Behavior, 24*(1), 80–88.

Lester, D. (1994). Suicide in the elderly: An overview. In D. Lester & M. Talmer, *Now I lay me down: Suicide in the elderly*. Philadelphia: The Charles Press.

Lester, D., Beck, A. T., & Mitchell, B. (1979). Extrapolation from attempted suicides to completed suicides: A test. *Journal of Abnormal Psychology, 88*, 78–80.

LeUnes, A. D., Nations, J. R., & Turley, N. M. (1980). Male-female performance in learned helplessness. *Journal of Psychology, 104*, 255–258.

Levenson, M., & Neuringer, C. (1971). Problem-solving behavior in suicidal adolescents. *Journal of Consulting and Clinical Psychology, 37*, 433–436.

Levinson, A. J. (1980, April). Termination of life support systems in the elderly: Ethical issues. Paper presented at the Scientific Meeting of the Boston Society for Gerontologic Psychiatry.

Levinson, D. J., Darrow, D., Klein, E., Levinson, M., & McKee, B. (1978). *The seasons of a man's life*. New York: Knopf.

Lewis, S. A., Johnson, J., Cohen, P., Garcia, M., & Velez, C. N. (1988). Attempted suicide in youth: Its relationship to school achievement, educational goals, and socioeconomic status. *Journal of Abnormal Child Psychology, 16*, 459–471.

Limbacher, M., & Domino, G. (1985–86). Attitudes toward suicide among attempters, contemplators, and nonattempters. *Omega, 16*, 319–328.

Lindeman, E. (1944). Symptomatology and management of acute grief. *American Journal of Psychiatry, 101*, 141–148.

Linehan, M. M. (1971). Towards a theory of sex differences in suicidal behavior. *Crisis Intervention, 3*, 93–101.

Linehan, M. M. (1973). Suicide and attempted suicide: Study of perceived sex differences. *Perceptual and Motor Skills, 37*, 31–34.

Linehan, M. M. (1981). A social behavioral analysis of suicide and parasuicide. Implications for clinical assessment and treatment. In J. F. Clarkin & H. I. Glazer (Eds.), *Depression: Behavioral and directive intervention strategies*. New York: Garland Press.

Linnoila, R., Erwin, C., Ramm, D., Cleveland, P., & Brendle, A. (1980). Effects of alcohol on psychomotor performance of women: Interaction with menstrual cycle. *Alcoholism: Clinical and Experimental Research, 4*, 302–305.

Long, V. O. (1987). The pursuit of happiness: Feeling good about yourself, problems and prescriptions. *Counseling Interview, 19*, 15–17.

Lopata, H. (1973). Self-identity in marriage and widowhood. *The Sociological Quarterly, 14*, 407–418.

Lore, R. K., & Schultz, L. A. (1993). Control of human aggression: A comparative perspective. *American Psychologist, 48*, 16–25.

Lowenthal, M. F., Thurnher, D. C., & Associates (1975). *Four stages of life*. San Francisco: Jossey-Bass.

The luckiest generation (1954). *Life Magazine,* January 4, 1954 (pp. 27–29).

Lyons, M. J. (1984). Suicide in later life: Some putative causes with implications for prevention. *Journal of Community Psychology, 12,* 379–388.

Maccoby, E. E., & Jacklin, C. N. (1974). *The psychology of sex differences.* Stanford, CA: Stanford University Press.

Maclay, E. (1990). Losses. In E. Maclay (Ed.) *Green Winter* (p. 69). New York: Henry Holt.

MacMahon, B., & Pugh, T. F. (1965). Suicide in the widowed. *American Journal of Epidemiology, 81,* 23–31.

Malcolm, A. H. (1990, June 1). *Giving death a hand: Rending issue.* New York Times, A6.

Manton, K. G., Blazer, D. G. & Woodbury, M. A. (1987). Suicide in middle age and later life: Sex and race specific life table and cohort analyses. *Journal of Gerontology, 42,* 219–227.

Maris, R. W. (1971). Deviance as therapy: The paradox of the self-destructive female. *Journal of Health and Social Behavior, 12,* 113–124.

Maris, R. W. (1981). *Pathways to suicide: A survey of self-destructive behaviors.* Baltimore: Johns Hopkins University Press.

Maris, R. W. (1989). Suicide intervention: The existential and biomedical perspectives. In D. Jacobs & H. N. Brown (Eds.), *Suicide: Understanding and responding.* Madison, CT: International Universities Press.

Marks, A. (1989). Structural parameters of sex, race, age, and education and their influence on attitudes toward suicide. *Omega, 19,* 327–336.

Marshall, J. R. (1978). Changes in aged white male suicide: 1948–1972. *Journal of Gerontology, 33,* 763–768.

Marzuk, P. M., Tierney, H., Tardiff, K., Gross, E. M., Morgan, E. B., Hsu, M., & Mann, J. J. (1988). Increased risk of suicide in persons with AIDS. *Journal of the American Medical Association, 259,* 1333–1337.

Maslow, A. H. (1954). *Motivation and personality.* New York: Harper & Row.

Maslow, A. H. (1971). *The farther reaches of human nature.* New York: Viking Press.

Masters, W. H., & Johnson, V. E. (1966). *Human sexual response.* Boston: Little, Brown.

Mathieu, J., & Peterson, J. (1970, November). Some social psychological dimensions of aging. Paper presented at the annual meeting of the Gerontological Society, Ontario, Canada.

Matter, D. E., & Matter, R. M. (1984, April). Suicide among elementary school children. *Elementary School Guidance and Counseling,* pp. 260, 267.

Mattisson, A., Hawkins, J. W., & Seese, L. R. (1969). Suicidal behavior as a child psychiatric emergency. *Archives of General Psychiatry, 20,* 100–109.

McAnarney, E. R. (1979). Adolescent and the young adult suicide in the United States—a reflection of social unrest? *Adolescence, 14,* 765–774.

McBrien, R. J. (1983). Are you thinking of killing yourself? Confronting students' suicidal thoughts. *The School Counselor, 31,* 75–82.

McCall, P. L. (1991). Adolescent and elderly white male suicide trends: Evidence of changing well-being? *Journal of Gerontology, 46,* S43–S51.

McClure, G. M. G. (1984). Recent trends in suicide amongst the young. *British Journal of Psychiatry, 144,* 134–138.

McConkie, B. R. (1966). *Mormon doctrine* (2nd ed.). Salt Lake City: Bookcraft.

McDowell, E. E. (1985). Sex differences in suicidal behavior. *Forum Newsletter, 8,* 9–11.

McDowell, E. E., & Stillion, J. M. (1994). Suicide across the phases of life. In G. G. Noam & S. Borst (Eds.), *Children, youth, and suicide: Developmental perspectives.* San Francisco: Jossey-Bass.

McGinnis, J. M. (1987). Suicide in America: Moving up the public health agenda. *Suicide and Life-Threatening Behavior, 17,* 18–32.

McGraw, K. O. (1987). *Developmental Psychology.* New York: Harcourt, Brace, Jovannovich.

McIntire, M. S., & Angle, C. R. (1971). Suicide as seen in a poison control center. *Pediatrics, 48,* 914–922.

McIntire, M. S., & Angle, C. R. (1973). Psychological "biopsy" in self-poisoning of children and adolescents. *American Journal of Diseases of Children, 126,* 42–46.

McIntire, M. S., & Angle, C. R., & Struempler, L. J. (1972). The concept of death in midwestern children and youth. *American Journal of Diseases of Children, 123,* 527–532.

McIntosh, J. L. (1983). Suicide among the elderly. *American Journal of Orthopsychiatry, 55,* 288–293.

McIntosh, J. L. (1984). Components of the decline in elderly suicide: Suicide among the young-old and old-old by race and sex. *Death Education, 8,* 113–124.

McIntosh, J. L. (1985). Suicide among the elderly: Levels and trends. *American Journal of Orthopsychiatry, 35,* 288–293.

McIntosh, J. L. (1990). Older adults: The next suicide epidemic? Presented at the meeting of the American Association of Suicidology, New Orleans.

McIntosh, J. L. (1992). Epidemiology of suicide among the elderly. *Suicide and Life-Threatening Behavior, 22,* 15–35.

McIntosh, J. L. (1994). Generational analyses of suicide: Baby boomers and 13ers. *Suicide and Life-Threatening Behavior, 24,* 334–342.

McIntosh, J. L., Hubbard, R. W., & Santos, J. F. (1981). Suicide among the elderly: A review of issues with case studies. *Journal of Gerontological Social Work, 4,* 63–74.

McIntosh, J. L., Hubbard, R. W., & Santos, J. F. (1985). Suicide facts and myths: A study of prevalence. *Death Studies, 9,* 267–281.

McIntosh, J. L., & Jewell, B. L. (1986). Sex difference trends in completed suicide. *Suicide and Life-Threatening Behavior, 16,* 16–27.

McKenry, P. C., Tishler, C. L., & Kelly, C. (1983). The role of drugs in adolescent suicide attempts. *Suicide and Life-Threatening Behavior, 13,* 166–175.

McKusick, L. (1993). Riding the HIV roller coaster: Counseling and care in later-stage illness. *HIV Frontline, 11,* 1–8.

McLaren, J., & Brown, R. E. (1989). Childhood problems associated with abuse and neglect. *Canada's Mental Health,* 1–6.

McLean, P., & Taylor, S. (1994). Family therapy for suicidal people. In A. A. Leenaars, J. T. Maltsberger, & R. A. Neimeyer (Eds.), *Treatment of suicidal people* (pp. 75–88). Washington, DC: Taylor & Francis.

McRae, R. R., & Costa, P. T., Jr. (1983). Psychological maturity and subjective well-being: Toward a new synthesis. *Developmental Psychology, 19,* 243–248.

Mehta, D., Mathew, P., & Mehta, S. (1978). Suicide pact in a depressed elderly couple: Case report. *Journal of the American Geriatrics Society, 26,* 136–138.

Meichenbaum, D. (1985). *Stress inoculation training.* Elmsford, NY: Pergamon.

Memory, J. M. (1988). *Juvenile suicides in secure detention facilities: Correction of published rates.* Unpublished manuscript.

Merian, J. (1763). Sur la crainte de la mort, sur le mepris de la mort, sur le suicide, memoire [About the fear of death, about contempt for death, about suicide, recollection]. In *Histoire de l'Academie Royale des Sciences et Belles-Lettres de Berlin* (Vol. 19).

Miles, C. (1977). Conditions predisposing to suicide: A review. *Journal of Nervous and Mental Disease, 164,* 231–246.

Miller, L. (1994). *Reliability and Validity of the Multi-dimensional Suicide Attitude Scale: An instrument for assessing attitudes toward suicide.* Unpublished master's thesis, Western Carolina University.

Miller, K. E., King, C. A., Shain, B. N., & Naylor, M. W. (1992). Suicidal adolescents' perceptions of their family environment. *Suicide and Life-Threatening Behavior, 22,* 226–239.

Miller, M. (1978a). Geriatric suicide: The Arizona study. *The Gerontologists, 18,* 488–495.

Miller, M. (1978b). Note: Toward a profile of the older white male suicide. *The Gerontologists, 18,* 80–82.

Miller, M. (1979). *Suicide after sixty: The final alternative.* New York: Springer.

Minear, J. D., & Brush, L. R. (1981). The correlations of attitudes toward suicide with death anxiety, religiosity, and personal closeness to suicide. *Omega, 11,* 317–324.

Minkoff, K., Bergman, E., Beck, A. T., & Beck, R. (1973). Hopelessness, depression, and attempted suicide. *American Journal of Psychiatry, 130,* 455–459.

Mitchell, G. (1979). *Sex differences in non-human primates.* New York: Van Nostrand Reinhold.

Money, J., & Ehrhardt, A. (1972). *Man and woman, boy and girl.* Baltimore: Johns Hopkins University Press.

Morano, C. D., Cisler, R. A., & Lemerond, J. (1993). Risk factors for adolescent suicidal behavior: Loss, insufficient familial support, and hopelessness. *Adolescence, 28,* 851–865.

Morgan, J. P. (1994). Bereavement in older adults. *Journal of Mental Health Counseling, 16,* 318–326.

Morrison, G. C., & Collier, J. G. (1969). Family treatment approaches to suicidal children and adolescents. *Journal of the American Academy of Child Psychiatry, 8,* 140–153.

Murphy, G. E., Armstrong, J., Hermele, S., Fisher, J., & Clendenin, W. (1979). Suicide and alcoholism. *Archives of General Psychiatry, 36,* 65–69.

Murphy, G. E., & Wetzel, R. D. (1982). Family history of suicidal behavior among suicide attempters. *Journal of Nervous and Mental Disease, 170,* 86–90.

Murray, H. A. (1938). *Explorations in personality.* New York: Oxford University Press.

Mussen, P. H., Conger, J. J., & Kagan, J. (1974). *Child development and personality* (4th ed.). New York: Harper & Row.

Myers, K., McCauley, E., Calderon, R., & Treder, R. (1991). The three-year longitudinal course of suicidality and predictive factors for subsequent suicidality in youths with major depressive disorder. *Journal of the American Academy of Child and Adolescent Psychiatry, 30,* 804–810.

Nagy, M. (1948). The child's theories concerning death. *Journal of Genetic Psychology, 73,* 3–27.

National Association of Social Workers (1994). Client self-determination in end-of-life decisions. *Social Work Speaks* (3rd. ed.), 58–61. Washington, DC: NASW Press.

National Center for Health Statistics (1994). Advanced report of final mortality statistics. *Monthly Vital Statistics Report.* Washington, DC: U.S. Government Printing Office.

National Hospice Organization (1990). *Resolution approved by the delegates of the National Hospice Organization,* Annual Meeting, November 8, 1990, Detroit, Michigan.

National Hospice Organization. *Statement of the National Hospice Organization Opposing the Legalization of Euthanasia and Assisted Suicide.*

Nelson, F. L. (1984). Suicide: Issues of prevention, intervention, and facilitation. *Journal of Clinical Psychology, 40,* 1328–1333.

Neugarten, B. L. (1968). The awareness of middle age. In B. L. Neugarten (Ed.), *Middle age and aging: A reader in social psychology* (pp. 93–98). Chicago: University of Chicago Press.

Neugarten, B. L., Havighurst, R. J., & Tobin, S. S. (1961). The measurement of life satisfaction. *Journal of Gerontology, 16,* 168–174.

Nichols, S. F. (1987). Emotional aspects of AIDS: Implications for care providers. *Journal of Substance Abuse Treatment, 4,* 137–140.

Nolen-Hoeksema, S. (1987). Sex differences in unipolar depression: Evidence and theory. *Psychological Bulletin, 101,* 259–282.

Nolen-Hoeksema, S. (1990). *Sex differences in depression.* Stanford, CA: Stanford University Press.

Nolen-Hoeksema, S. (1991). Responses to depression and their effects on the duration of depressive episodes. *Journal of Abnormal Psychology, 100, 4,* 569–582.

Nordstrom, P., Samuelsson, M., Asberg, M., Traskman-Bendn, L., Aberg-Wisdedt, A., Nordin, C., & Bertilsson, L. (1994). CSF5-HIAA predicts suicide risk after attempted suicide. *Suicide and Life Threatening Behavior, 24,* 1–9.

Noyes, R. (1970). Shall we prevent suicide? *Comparative Psychiatry, 11,* 361–370.

Noyes, R., Frye, S. J., & Hartford, C. E. (1977). Conjugal suicide pact. *Journal of Nervous and Mental Disorders, 165,* 72–75.

O'Carroll, P. (1993). Suicide causation: Pies, paths, and pointless polemics. *Suicide and Life-Threatening Behavior, 23*(1).

Offord, D. R., Boyle, M. H., Szatmari, P., Rae-Grant, N. I., Links, P. S., Cadman, D. T., Byles, J. A., Crawford, J. W., Blum, H. M., Byrne, C., Thomas, H., & Woodward, C. A. (1987). Ontario Child Health Study, II: Six month prevalence of disorder and rates of service utilization. *Archives of General Psychiatry, 44,* 831–835.

Orbach, I. (1984). Personality characteristics, life circumstances, and dynamics of suicidal children. *Death Education, 8,* 37–52.

Orbach, I. (1988). *Children who don't want to live: Understanding and treating the suicidal child.* San Francisco: Jossey-Bass.

Orbach, I., Freshbach, S., Carlson, G., & Ellenberg, L. (1984). Attitudes towards life and death in suicidal, normal, and chronically ill children: An extended replication. *Journal of Consulting and Clinical Psychology, 52,* 1020–1027.

Orbach, I., & Glaubman, H. (1979). The concept of death and suicidal behavior in young children: Three case studies. *Journal of the American Academy of Child Psychiatry, 18,* 668–678.

Orbach, I., Gross, Y., & Glaubman, H. (1981). Some common characteristics of latency-age suicidal children: A tentative model based on case study analyses. *Suicide and Life-Threatening Behavior, 11,* 180–190.

Osgood, N. J. (1985). *Suicide in the elderly: A practitioner's guide to diagnosis and mental health intervention.* Rockville, MD: Aspen.

Osgood, N. J. (1992). *Suicide in later life: Recognizing the warning signs.* New York: Lexington Books.

Osgood, N. J., Brant, B. A., & Lipman, A. (1988–1989). Patterns of suicidal behavior in long-term care facilities: A preliminary report on an ongoing study. *Omega, 16,* 69–77.

Osgood, C., Suci, G., & Tannenbaum, P. (1969). *The measurement of meaning.* Urbana, Ill: University of Illinois Press.

Osterweis, M., Solomon, F., & Green, M. (Eds.) (1984). *Bereavement: Reactions, consequences, and care.* Washington, DC: National Academy Press.

Parkes, C. M. (1972). *Bereavement: Studies of grief in adult life.* New York: International Universities Press.

Patros, P. G., & Shamoo, T. K. (1989). *Depression and suicide in children and adolescents.* Boston: Allyn and Bacon.

Paulson, J. J., & Stone, D. (1974). Suicidal behavior of latency-age children. *Journal of Clinical Child Psychology, 3,* 50–53.

Pavlov, I. (1927). *Conditioned reflexes.* London: Oxford University Press.

Paykel, E. S., Prusoff, B. A., Myers, J. K. (1975). Suicide attempts and recent life events: A controlled comparison. *Archives of General Psychiatry, 32,* 327–333.

Peck, D. L. (1987). Social psychological correlates of adolescent and youthful suicide. *Adolescence, 22,* 863–878.

Peck. R. C. (1968). Psychological developments in the second half of life. In B. L. Neugarten (Ed.), *Middle age and aging: A reader in social psychology* (pp. 88–92). Chicago: University of Chicago Press.

Pettifor, J., Perry, D., Plowman, B., & Pitcher, S. (1983). Risk factors predicting child and adolescent suicide. *Journal of Child Care, 1,* 17–50.

Pfeffer, C. R. (1981a). Suicidal behavior of children: A review with implications for research and practice. *American Journal of Psychiatry, 138,* 154–159.

Pfeffer, C. R. (1981b). The family system of suicidal children. *American Journal of Psychotherapy, 35,* 330–341.

Pfeffer, C. R. (1982). Intervention for suicidal children and their parents. *Suicide and Life-Threatening Behavior, 12,* 240–248.

Pfeffer, C. R. (1984a). Death preoccupations and survival behavior in children. In H. Wass & C. A. Corr (Eds.), *Childhood and death* (pp. 261–278). Washington, DC: Hemisphere.

Pfeffer, C. R. (1984b). Recognizing and treating suicidal youngsters. In N. Linzer (Ed.), *Suicide: The will to live vs. the will to die* (pp. 87–100). New York: Human Sciences Press.

Pfeffer, C. R. (1984c). Death preoccupations and suicidal behavior in children. In H. Wass & C. Corr (Eds.), *Childhood and death* (pp. 261–279). Washington, DC: Hemisphere.

Pfeffer, C. R. (1986). *The suicidal child.* New York: Guilford Press.

Pfeffer, C. R. (1990). Manifestation of risk factors. In G. McLean (Ed.), *Suicide in Children and Adolescents* (pp. 65–88). Toronto: Hogrefe & Huber.

Pfeffer, C. R. (1991). Family characteristics and support systems as risk factors for youth suicidal behavior. In L. Davidson and M. Linnoila (Eds.), *Risk Factors in Youth Suicide.* New York: Hemisphere.

Pfeffer, C. R., Conte, H. R., Plutchik, R., & Jerrett, I. (1979). Suicidal behavior in latency-age children: An empirical study. *Journal of the American Academy of Child Psychiatry, 18,* 679–692.

Pfeffer, C. R., Conte, H. R., Plutchik, R., & Jerrett, I. (1980). Suicidal behavior in latency-age children: An outpatient population. *Journal of the American Academy of Child Psychiatry, 18,* 703–710.

Pfeffer, C. R., Plutchik, R., & Mizruchi, M. S. (1983). Suicidal and assaultive behavior in children: Classification, measurement, and intervention. *American Journal of Psychiatry, 140,* 154–157.

Pfeffer, C. R., Solomon, G., Plutchik, R., Mizruchi, M. S., & Weiner, A. (1982). Suicidal behavior in latency-age psychiatric inpatients: A replication and cross validation. *Journal of the American Academy of Child Psychiatry, 21*, 564–569.

Pfeffer, C. R., & Trad, P. V. (1988). Sadness and suicidal tendencies in preschool children. *Developmental and Behavioral Pediatrics, 9*, 86–88.

Pfeffer, C. R., Zuckerman, S., Plutchik, R., Mizruchi, M. S. (1984). Suicidal behavior in normal school children: A comparison with psychiatric inpatients. *Journal of the American Academy of Child Psychiatry, 23*, 416–423.

Phillips, D. P. (1979). Suicide, motor vehicle fatalities and the mass media: Substantive and theoretical implications of the Werther effect. *American Sociological Review, 39*, 340–354.

Phillips, D. P. (1993). Gender, suicide, and AIDS. Paper presented at the 26th Annual Conference of the American Association of Suicidology, San Francisco, April 14, 1993.

Phillips, D. P., & Carstensen, L. L. (1986). Clustering of teenage suicides after television news stories about suicide. *New England Journal of Medicine, 315*, 685–689.

Phillips, D. P. & Paight, D. J. (1987). The impact of televised movies about suicide: A replicative study. *New England Journal of Medicine, 317*, 809–811.

Piaget, J. (1926). *The language and thought of the child.* New York: Harcourt Brace.

Piaget, J., & Inhelder, B. (1969). *The psychology of the child.* New York: Basic Books.

Platz, C., & Kendell, R. E. (1988). A matched control follow up and family study of "peripheral psychosis." *British Journal of Psychiatry, 153*, 90–94.

Pommereau, X., Delile, J. M., & Caule, E. (1987). Hypnotic overdoses and fairy tales: Snow White and the uses of disenchantment. *Suicide and Life-Threatening Behavior, 17*, 326–334.

Potter, L. B., Powell, K. E., & Kachur, S. P. (1995). Suicide prevention from a public health perspective. *Suicide and Life-Threatening Behavior, 25*(1), 82–91.

Powell, E. H. (1958). Occupation, status, and suicide. Toward a redefinition of anomie. *American Sociological Review, 23*, 131–139.

Quill, T. E. (1991). Death and dignity: A case of individualized decision making. *New England Journal of Medicine, 325*, 691–694.

Quill, T. E. (1993). *Death and Dignity: Making choices and taking charge.* New York: W. W. Norton.

Rachels, J. (1975). Active and passive euthanasia. *New England Journal of Medicine, 292*, 78–80.

Rachlis, D. (1970, Fall). Suicide and loss adjustment in aging. *Bulletin of Suicidology, 7*, 23–26.

Rajs, J., & Fugelstad, A. (1992). Suicide related to human immunodeficiency virus infection in Stockholm. *Acta Psychiatrica Scandanavia, 85*, 234–239.

Rando, T. A. (1985). *Loss and anticipatory grief,* Lexington, MA: Lexington Books.

Raphael, B. (1983). *The anatomy of bereavement.* New York: Basic Books.

Ray, L. Y., & Johnson, N. (1983, November). Adolescent suicide. *The Personnel and Guidance Journal,* 131–135.

Reich, T., Rice, J., & Mullaney, J. (1986). Genetic risk factors for the affective disorders. In G. L. Klerman (Ed.), *Suicide and depression among adolescents and young adults* (pp. 77–104). Washington, DC: American Psychiatric Press.

Remafedi, G. (1987). Adolescent homosexuality: Psychosocial and medical implications. *Pediatrics, 79*, 331–337.

Resnik, H. L. P., & Cantor, J. M. (1970). Suicide and aging. *Journal of the American Geriatrics Society, 18*, 152–158.

Richman, J. (1981). Suicide and the family: Affective disturbances and their implications for understanding, diagnosis, and treatment. In M. R. Lansky (Ed.), *Family therapy and major psychopathology* (pp. 145–160). New York: Grune & Stratton.

Rifai, A. H., Reynolds, C. F., & Mann, J. J. (1992). Biology of elderly suicide. *Suicide and Life-Threatening Behavior, 22*, 48–61.

Rifkin, J., & Howard, T. (1980). *Entropy: A new world view.* New York: Bantam.

Robins, L. N., West, P. A., & Murphy, J.G.E. (1977). The high rate of suicide in older white men: A study testing ten hypotheses. *Social Psychiatry, 12*, 1–20.

Rockwell, D., & O'Brien, W. (1973). Physicians' knowledge and attitudes about suicide. *Journal of the American Medical Association, 225*, 1347–1349.

Roesler, T., & Deisher, R. W. (1972). Youthful male homosexuality. *Journal of the American Medical Association, 219*, 1018–1023.

Rogers, C. R. (1961). *On becoming a person.* Boston: Houghton Mifflin.

Rogers, C. (1980). *A way of being*. Boston: Houghton Mifflin.

Rosenbaum, M. (1983). Crime and punishment: The suicide pact. *Archives of General Psychiatry, 40*, 979–982.

Rosenberg, D. (1995). Death at an early age. *Newsweek*, June 12, 69.

Rosenberg, P. H., & Latimer, R. (1966). Suicide attempts by children. *Mental Hygiene, 50*, 354–359.

Rosenn, D. W. (1982). Suicidal behavior in children and adolescents. In E. L. Bassuk, S. C. Schoonover, & A. D. Gill (Eds.), *Lifelines: Clinical perspectives on suicide* (pp. 195–224). New York: Plenum Press.

Rosenthal, M. J. (1981). Sexual differences in the suicidal behavior of young people. *Adolescent Psychiatry, 9*, 422–442.

Rosenthal, P. A., & Rosenthal, S. (1984). Suicidal behavior by preschool children. *American Journal of Psychiatry, 141*, 520–525.

Rossman, M. L. (1984). Imagine health: Imagery in medical self-care. In A. A. Sheikh, (Ed.), *Imagination and Healing*. New York: Baywood.

Rothblum, E. D. (1990). Depression among lesbians: An invisible and unresearched phenomenon. *Journal of Gay and Lesbian Psychotherapy, 1*, 67–87.

Rotheram-Borus, M. J., & Trautman, P. D. (1988). Hopelessness, depression, and suicide intent among adolescent suicide attempters. *Journal of the Academy of Child and Adolescent Psychiatry, 27*, 700–704.

Rotheram-Borus, M., Trautman, P., Dopkins, S., & Shrout, P. (1990). Cognitive styles and pleasant activities among female adolescent suicide attempters. *Journal of Consulting and Clinical Psychology, 58*, 554–561.

Roy, A. (1982). Risk factors for suicide in psychiatric patients. *Archives of General Psychiatry, 39*, 1089–1095.

Roy, A. (1994). Recent biological studies on suicide. *Suicide and Life-Threatening Behavior, 24*, 10–14.

Roy, A. (1994). Biology of elderly suicide. Paper presented at the American Association of Suicidology meeting, New York.

Roy, A., & Linnoila, M. (1986). Alcoholism and suicide. In R. Maris (Ed.), *Biology of suicide* (pp. 162–191). New York: Guilford Press.

Ruark, J. E., Raffin, T. A., & The Stanford University Medical Center Committee on Ethics (1988). Initiating and withdrawing life support: Principles and practices in adult medicine. *New England Journal of Medicine, 318*, 25–30.

Rubenstein, D. H. (1983). Epidemic suicide among Micronesian adolescents. *Social Science Medicine, 17*, 657–665.

Rudestam, K. (1977). Physical and psychological responses to suicide in the family. *Journal of Consulting and Clinical Psychology, 45*(2), 162–170.

Rudestam, K., & Imbroll, D. (1983). Societal reactions to the child's death by suicide. *Journal of Consulting and Clinical Psychology, 51*, 461–462.

Runeson, B. S., & Rich, C. L. (1992). Diagnostic co-morbidity of mental disorders among young suicides. *International Review of Psychiatry, 4*, 197–203.

Rupp, M. T. (1995). *Drug use in assisted suicide and euthanasia: Issues for Pharmacists*. Paper presented at the national Health Forum on Physician Assisted death (March 9–12). Amelia Island, Fla.

Rushing, W. (1969). Suicide and the interaction of alcoholism (liver cirrhosis) with the social situation. *Quarterly Journal of Studies on Alcohol, 30*, 93–103.

Rygnestad, T. K. (1982). A prospective study of social and psychiatric aspects of self-poisoned patients. *Acta Psychiatrica Scandinavica, 66*, 139–153.

Sabbath, J. C. (1969). The suicidal adolescent: The expendable child. *Journal of the American Academy of Child Psychiatry, 8*, 272–289.

Sabo, D. (1994). "Pigskin, patriarchy and pain." In M. S. Kimmel, & M. A. Messner (Ed.), *Men's Lives* (2nd ed.). New York: Macmillan.

Sainsbury, P., Jenkins, J., & Levy, A. (1980). The social correlates of suicide in Europe. In R. D. T. Farmer & S. R. Hirsch (Eds.), *The suicide syndrome* (pp. 38–53). London: Croom Helm.

Sansonnet-Hayden, H., Haley, G., Marriage, K., & Fine, S. (1987). Sexual abuse and psychopathology in hospitalized adolescents. *Journal of the American Academy of Child and Adolescent Psychiatry, 26*, 753–757.

Santrock, J. W. (1985). *Adult development and aging*. Dubuque, IA: William C. Brown.

Santy, P. A. (1982). Observations on double suicide: Review of the literature and two case reports. *American Journal of Psychotherapy, 36*, 23–31.

Satir, V. (1967). *Conjoint family therapy*. Palo Alto, CA: Science and Behavior Books.

Sawyer, D., & Sobal, J. (1987). Public attitudes toward suicide: Demographic and ideological correlates. *Public Opinion Quarterly, 51*, 92–101.

Schaie, K. W., & Willis, S. L. (1986). *Adult development and aging* (2nd ed.). Boston: Little, Brown.

Schaie, K. W., & Willis, S. L. (1993). Age difference patterns of psychometric intelligence in adulthood: Generalizations within and across ability domains. *Psychology and Aging, 8*, 44–55.

Schenck, C. H., Mandell, M., & Lewis, G. M. (1992). A case of monthly unipolar psychotic depression with suicide attempt by self burning: Selective response to bupropion treatment. *Comprehensive Psychiatry, 33*, 353–356.

Schildkraut, J. J. (1965). The catecholamine hypothesis of affective disorders: A review of supporting evidence. *American Journal of Psychiatry, 122*, 509–522.

Schneider, S. G., Farberow, N. L., Kruks, G. N. (1989). Suicidal behavior in adolescent and young gay men. *Suicide and Life-Threatening Behavior, 19*, 381–394.

Schneider, S. G., Taylor, S. E., Kemeny, M. E., & Hammen, C. (1991). AIDS-related factors predictive of suicidal ideation of low and high intent among gay and bisexual men. *Suicide and Life-Threatening Behavior, 21*, 313–328.

Schonfield, A. E. D. (1980). Learning, memory, and aging. In J. E. Birren & R. B. Sloone (Eds.), *Handbook of mental age and aging*. Englewood Cliffs, NJ: Prentice-Hall.

Schoonover, S. C. (1982). Crisis therapies. In E. L. Bassuk, S. C. Schoonover, & A. D. Gill (Eds.), *Lifelines: Clinical perspectives on suicide* (pp. 49–57). New York: Plenum Press.

Schuckit, M. A., & Schuckit, J. J. (1991). Substance use and abuse: A risk factor in youth suicide. In L. Davidson & M. Linnoila (Eds.), *Risk Factors in Youth Suicide*. New York: Hemisphere.

Schulz, R., & Bewen, R. (1993). *Adult development and aging*. New York: MacMillan.

Schultz, K. D. (1984). The use of imagery in alleviating depression. *Imagery and Healing*. New York: Baywood Publishing.

Sears, R. (1977). Sources of life satisfaction of the Terman gifted men. *American Psychologist, 32*, 119–128.

Seiden, R. H. (1981). Mellowing with age: Factors influencing the nonwhite suicide rate. *International Journal of Aging and Human Development, 13*, 265–284.

Seiden, R. H. (1983). Death in the West: A spatial analysis of the youthful suicide rate. *Western Journal of Medicine, 139*, 783–795.

Seligman, M. E. P. (1975). *Helplessness: On depression, development, and death*. San Francisco: Freeman.

Seligman, M. E. P. (1991). *Learned Optimism: How to change your mind and your life*. New York: Pocket Books.

Seligmann, J. (1994). Menopause. *Newsweek*, May 25.

Selkin, J. (1983). The legacy of Emile Durkheim. *Suicide and Life-Threatening Behavior, 13* (1), 3–14.

Sendbuehler, J. M., & Goldstein, S. (1977). Attempted suicide among the aged. *Journal of the American Geriatrics Society*, 245–248.

Serafin, J. D., Thornton, G., & Roberson, D. U. (1988, April). The social stigma of suicide. Paper presented at the meeting of the Association for Death Education and Counseling, Orlando, FL.

Shaffer, D. (1974). Suicide in childhood and early adolescence. *Journal of Child Psychology and Psychiatry, 15*, 275–291.

Shaffer, D., & Fisher, P. (1981). The epidemiology of suicide in children and adolescents. *Journal of the American Academy of Child Psychiatry, 21*, 545–566.

Shaffer, D., Garland, A., Gould, M., Fisher, P., & Trautman, P. (1988). Preventing teenage suicide: A critical review. *Journal of the American Academy of Child and Adolescent Psychiatry, 27*, 675–687.

Shafii, M., Carrigan, S., Whittinghill, J. R., & Derrick, A. (1985). Psychological autopsy of completed suicide in children and adolescents. *American Journal of Psychiatry, 142*, 1061–1064.

Shafii, M., Steltz-Lenarsky, J., Derrick, A. M., Beckner, C., & Whittinghill, J. R. (1988). Comorbidity in mental disorders in the post-mortem diagnosis of completed suicide in children and adolescents. *Journal of Affective Disorders, 15,* 227–233.

Shaughnessy, M. F., & Nystul, M. S. (1985). Preventing the greatest loss—suicide. *The Creative Child and Adult Quarterly, 10*(3), 164–169.

Shaunesey, K., Cohen, J. L., Plummer, B., & Berman, A. (1993). Suicidality in hospitalized adolescents: Relationships to prior abuse. *American Journal of Orthopsychiatry, 63,* 113–119.

Sheehy, G. (1976). *Passages: Predictable crises of adult life.* New York: Dutton.

Sheehy, G. (1991). *The silent passage: Menopause.* New York: Random House.

Sheehy, G. (1995). *New Passages: Mapping Your Life Across Time.* New York: Random House.

Sheskin, A., & Wallace, S. (1976). Differing bereavements: Suicide, natural and accidental death. *Omega, 7,* 229–242.

Shneidman, E. S. (Ed.). (1967). *Essays in self-destruction.* New York: Science House.

Shneidman, E. S. (1971). Suicide among the gifted. *Suicide and Life-Threatening Behavior, 1,* 23–45.

Shneidman. E. S. (1973). Suicide. In *Encyclopedia Britannica,* 14ᵗʰ ed., vol. 21, pp. 383–386. Chicago: Willam Benton.

Shneidman, E. S. (1976). A psychological theory of suicide. The components of suicide. *Psychiatric Annals, 6,* 51–66.

Shneidman, E. S. (1984). Postvention and the survivor-victim. In E. Schneidman (Ed.), *Death: Current perspectives* (3rd ed., pp. 412–419). (Reprinted from Shneidman, E. S., *Deaths of Man,* 1973).

Shneidman, E. S. (1985). *Definition of suicide.* New York: Wiley.

Shneidman, E. S. (1993). Suicide as Psychache. *Journal of Nervous and Mental Disease, 181,* 147–149.

Shneidman, E., Farberow, N., & Litman, R. (1961). The suicide prevention center. In N. Farberow & E. Shneidman (Eds.), *The cry for help* (pp. 6–18). New York: McGraw Hill.

Siegel, K. (1986). Psychosocial aspects of rational suicide. *American Journal of Psychotherapy, 40,* 405–418.

Siehl, P. (1990). Suicide postvention: A new disaster plan—what a school should do when faced with a suicide. *The School Counselor, 38,* 52–57.

Sigelman, C. K., & Shaffer, D. R. (1995). *Lifespan human development.* Pacific Grove, CA: Brooks/Cole.

Silver, M. A., Bohnert, M., Beck, A. T., & Marcus, D. (1971). Relation of depression of attempted suicide and seriousness of intent. *Archives of General Psychiatry, 25,* 573–576.

Silverman, M. M., & Felner, R. D. (1995). Suicide prevention programs: Issues of design, implementation, feasibility, and developmental appropriateness. *Suicide and Life Threatening Behavior, 25(1).*

Skinner, B. F. (1953). *Science and human behavior.* New York: Macmillan.

Slap, G. B., Vorters, D. F., Chaudhuri, S., & Centor, R. M. (1989). Risk factors for attempted suicide during adolescence. *Pediatrics, 84,* 762–772.

Slater, J., & Depue, R. A. (1981). The contribution of environmental events and social support to serious suicide attempts in primary depressive disorder. *Journal of Abnormal Psychology, 40,* 275–285.

Smith, J. (1991). Suicide intervention in schools: General considerations. In A. A. Leenaars & S. Wenckstern, *Suicide prevention in schools.* New York: Hemisphere.

Smith, K., Eyman, J., Dyck, R., & Ryerson, D. (1987, December). *Report of a survey of school-related suicide programs.* Paper prepared for the American Association of Suicidology, Denver, CO.

Speece, M. W., & Brent, S. B. (1984). Children's understanding of death: A review of three components of a death concept. *Child Development, 55,* 1671–1686.

Spirito, A., Overholser, J., & Stark, L. J. (1989). Common problems and coping strategies II: Findings from adolescent suicide attempts. *Journal of Abnormal Child Psychology, 17,* 213–221.

Stack, S. (1991). Social correlates of suicide by age. In A. A. Leenaars (Ed.), *Life span perspectives of suicide* (pp. 187–213). New York: Plenum.

Stafford, M. C., & Weisheit, R. A. (1988). Changing age patterns of U.S. male and female suicide rates, 1934–1983. *Suicide and Life-Threatening Behavior, 18,* 149–163.

Stenback, A. (1980). Depression and suicidal behavior in old age. In J. C. Birren & R. B. Sloane (Eds.), *Handbook of mental health aging*. Englewood Cliffs, NJ: Prentice-Hall.

Stephens, J. B. (1985). Suicidal women and their relationships with husbands, boyfriends, and lovers. *Suicide and Life-Threatening Behavior, 15*, 77–89.

Stillion, J. M. (1984). Women and widowhood: The suffering beyond grief. In J. Freeman (Ed.), *Women: A feminist perspective* (p. 282–296). Palo Alto, CA: Mayfield.

Stillion, J. M. (1985a). *Death and the sexes: An examination of differential longevity, attitudes, behaviors, and coping skills*. Washington, DC: Hemisphere.

Stillion, J. M. (1985b). *Exploring coping techniques among ninth grade academically gifted students*. Unpublished raw data.

Stillion, J. M. (1986a). Examining the shadow: Gifted children respond to the nuclear threat. *Death Studies, 10*, 27–41.

Stillion, J. M. (1986b). The demise of dualism: Toward a convergence of brain research and therapy. *Death Studies, 10(4)*, 313–330.

Stillion, J. M. (1995). The true bottom line: Male longevity and violent death. In D. Sabo (Ed.), *Men's Health and Illness: Gender, Power and the Body*. Newbury Park, CA: Sage.

Stillion, J. M., Goodrow, H., Klingman, A., Laughlin, M., Morgan, J. D., Sandsberg, S., Walton, M., & Warren, W. G. (1988). Dimensions of the shadow: Children of six nations respond to the nuclear threat. *Death Studies, 12(3)*, 227–251.

Stillion, J. M., & McDowell, E. E. (1991). Examining suicide from a life span perspective. *Death Studies, 15*, 327–354.

Stillion, J. M., McDowell, E. E., & May, J. H. (1984). Developmental trends and sex differences in adolescent attitudes toward suicide. *Death Education, 8*, 81–90.

Stillion, J. M., McDowell, E. E., & May, M. J. (1989). *Suicide across the life span: Premature exits*. New York: Hemisphere.

Stillion, J. M., McDowell, E. E., & Shamblin, J. B. (1984). The suicide attitude vignette experience: A method for measuring adolescent attitudes toward suicide. *Death Education, 8*, 65–80.

Stillion, J. M., McDowell, E. E., Smith, R. T., & McCoy, P. A. (1986). Relationships between suicide attitudes and indicators of mental health among adolescents. *Death Studies, 10*, 289–296.

Stillion, J. M., & Wass, H. (1979). Children and death. In H. Wass (Ed.), *Dying: Facing the facts* (pp. 208–235). Washington, DC: Hemisphere.

Stillion, J. M., White, H., McDowell, E. E., & Edwards, P. (1989). Ageism and sexism in suicide attitudes. *Death Studies, 13(3)*, 247–261.

Stivers, C. (1991). Promotion of self-esteem in the prevention of suicide. In A. A. Leenaars & S. Wenckstern, *Suicide prevention in schools*. New York: Hemisphere.

Strauss, W., & Howe, N. (1991). *Generations: The history of America's future, 1584–2069*. New York: Morrow.

Streiner, D. L., & Adam, K. S. (1987). Evaluation of the effectiveness of suicide prevention programs: A methodological perspective. *Suicide and Life-Threatening Behavior, 17*, 93–106.

Styron, W. (1990). *Darkness visible: A memoir of madness*. New York: Random House.

Sudak, H. S., Ford, A. B., & Rushforth, N. B. (1984). Adolescent suicide: An overview. *American Journal of Psychotherapy, 38*, 350–363.

Suter, B. (1976). Suicide and women. In B. B. Wolman & K. H. Krass (Eds.), *Between survival and suicide* (pp. 129–161). New York: Gardner Press.

Svare, B., & Gandelman, R. (1975). Aggressive behavior of juvenile mice: Influence of androgen and olfactory stimuli. *Developmental Psychobiology, 8*, 405–415.

Swain, B. J., & Domino, G. L. (1985). Attitudes toward suicide among mental health professionals. *Death Studies, 9*, 455–468.

Swain, H. L. (1979). Childhood views of death. *Death Education, 2*, 341–358.

Syer-Solursh, D. (1985, April). Suicide in Canada—task force report summary. Paper presented at the Conference of the American Association of Suicidology, Toronto, Canada.

Szasz, T. S. (1976) The ethics of suicide. In B. B. Wolman (Ed.), Between survival and suicide (pp. 163–185). New York: Gardner Press.

Szasz, T. (1986). The case against suicide prevention. *American Psychologist, 41*, 806–812.

Tallmer, M. (1994). Symptoms and assessment of suicide in the elderly patient. In D. Lester and M. Tallmer (Eds.), *Now I lay me down: Suicide in the elderly*. Philadelphia: The Charles Press.

Tanney, B. (1995). Suicide prevention in Canada: A national perspective highlighting progress and problems. *Suicide and Life-Threatening Behavior, 25*(1), 105–122.

Taylor, S. (1982). *Durkheim and the study of suicide.* New York: St. Martin's Press.

Terenzini, P. T. (1987, November). A review of selected theoretical models of student development and collegiate impact. Paper presented at the meeting of the Association for the Study of Higher Education, Baltimore.

Teuting, P., Kaslow, S. H., & Hirshfeld, R. M. A. (1981). Special report on depression research. In *Science reports.* Rockville, MD: National Institute of Mental Health.

Thomas, R. M. (1979). *Comparing Theories of Child Development.* Belmont, CA: Wadsworth.

Tishler, C. L., & McKenry, P. C. (1983). Intrapsychic symptoms dimensions of adolescent suicide attempters. *Journal of Family Practice, 16,* 731–734.

Tishler, C. L., McKenry, P. C., & Morgan, K. C. (1981). Adolescent suicide attempts: Some significant factors. *Suicide and Life-Threatening Behavior, 11,* 86–92.

Toolan, J. M. (1962). Suicide and suicidal attempts in children and adolescents. *American Journal of Psychiatry, 118,* 719–723.

Toolan, J. M. (1975). Suicide in children and adolescents. *American Journal of Psychotherapy, 29,* 339–344.

Topol, P., & Reznikoff, M. (1982). Perceived peer and family relationships, hopelessness, locus of control as factors in adolescent suicide attempts. *Suicide and Life-Threatening Behavior, 12,* 141–150.

Toynbee, A. (1984). The relationship between life and death, living and dying. In E. S. Shneidman (Ed.), *Current perspectives* (3rd ed., pp. 8–14). Palo Alto, CA: Mayfield.

Turkington, C. (1983, May). Child suicide: An unspoken tragedy. *APA Monitor,* p. 15.

Unger, (1979). *Female and male psychological perspectives.* New York: Harper & Row.

U.S. Bureau of the Census (1970). *Statistical Abstract of the United States.* Washington, DC: U.S. Government Printing Office.

U.S. Bureau of the Census (1994). *Statistical Abstract of the United States: 1992* (114th Edition). Washington, DC: U.S. Government Printing Office.

Useui, W. M., Keil, T. J., & Durig, K. R. (1985). Socioeconomic comparisons and life satisfaction of elderly adults. *Journal of Gerontology, 40,* 110–114.

Vaillant, G. E. (1977). *Adaptation to life.* Boston: Little, Brown.

Van Fossen, D. (1985, June). Preventing youth suicide. *Health Link,* pp. 7–10.

Van Hoof, A. J. L. (1990). *From Autothanasia to suicide: Self-killing in classical antiquity.* London and New York: Routledge.

Victoroff, V. M. (1983). *The suicidal patient: Recognition, intervention, management.* Oradell, NJ: Medical Economics Books.

Viorst, J. (1986). *Necessary losses.* New York: Fawcett.

Walker, W. L. (1980) Intentional self-injury in school age children. *Journal of Adolescence, 3,* 217–228.

Wallace, R. K. (1970). Physiological effects of transcendental meditation. *Science, 167,* 1751–1754.

Walsh, P. B. (1983). *Growth through time: An introduction to adult development.* Monterey, CA: Brooks/Cole.

Warren, L. W., & Tomlinson-Keasey, C. (1987). The context of suicide. *American Journal of Orthopsychiatry, 57,* 41–48.

Wass, H. (1977). Views and opinions of elderly persons concerning death. *Educational Gerontology, 2,* 15–26.

Wass, H. (1979). Death and the elderly. In H. Wass (Ed.), *Dying: Facing the facts.* Washington, DC: Hemisphere.

Wass, H. (1984). Concepts of death: A developmental perspective. In H. Wass & C. A. Corr (Eds.), *Childhood and death* (pp. 3–24). Washington, DC: Hemisphere.

Wass, H. (1995). Death in the lives of children and adolescents. In H. Wass & R. A. Neimeyer (Eds.), *Dying: Facing the Facts* (3rd Ed.) (pp. 269–302). Washington, D.C.: Taylor & Francis.

Wass, H., & Stillion, J. M. (1988). Death in the lives of children and adolescents. In H. Wass, F. M. Berardo, & R. A. Neimeyer (Eds.), *Dying: Facing the facts* (pp. 201–208). Washington, DC: Hemisphere.

Webb, N. B. (1986). Before and after suicide: A preventive outreach program for colleges. *Suicide and Life-Threatening Behavior, 16* (4), 469–480.

Weisman, A. (1972). *On dying and denying: A psychiatric study of terminality.* New York: Behavioral Publications

Weissman, M. M. (1974). The epidemiology of suicide attempts, 1960 to 1971. *Archives of General Psychiatry, 30,* 737–746.

Weissman, M. M. (1978). Psychotherapy and its relevance to the pharmacotherapy of affective disorders: From ideology to evidence. In M. A. Lipton, A. DiMascio, & K. F. Killam (Eds.), *Psychopharmacology: A generation of progress.* New York: Raven Press.

Weissman, M. M. (1986). Being young and female: Risk factors for major depression. In G. L. Klerman (Ed.), *Suicide and depression among adolescents and young adults* (pp. 105–30). Washington, DC: American Psychiatric Press.

Wellman, M. M., & Wellman, R. J. (1986). Sex differences in peer responsiveness to suicide ideation. *Suicide and Life Threatening Behavior, 16,* 360–377.

Wenckstern, S., & Leenaars, A. A. (1991). Suicide postvention: A case illustration in a secondary school. In A. A. Leenaars & S. Wenckstern (Eds.), *Suicide prevention in schools.* New York: Hemisphere, pp. 181–195.

Werth, J. L., Jr. (1992). Rational suicide and AIDS: Considerations for the psychotherapist. *Counseling Psychologist, 20,* 645–659.

Werth, J. L., Jr. (1994b). Psychotherapists' attitudes toward suicide. *Psychotherapy: Theory, Research and Practice, 31,* 440–448.

Werth, J. L., Jr. (1996). *Rational suicide?* Implications for mental health professionals. *Death Studies.*

Werth, J. L. (Jr.) & Liddle, B. J. (1994). Psychotherapists' attitudes toward suicide. *Psychotherapy, 31(3),* 440–448.

Westermark, E. (1906–1908). *The origin and development of the moral ideas.* London: MacMillan.

Wetzel, R. D. (1976). Hopelessness, depression, and suicide intent. *Archives of General Psychiatry, 33,* 1069–1073.

White, H., & Stillion, J. M. (1988). Sex differences in attitudes toward suicide: Do males stigmatize males? *Psychology of Women Quarterly, 12,* 357–366.

Whiteford, H. A., & Csernasky, J. G. (1986). Psychiatric aspects of acquired immune deficiency syndrome (AIDS). *Australian and New Zealand Journal of Psychiatry, 20,* 399–403.

Whiting, B. B., & Whiting, J. W. (1975). *Children of six cultures: A psychocultural analysis.* Cambridge, MA: Harvard University Press.

Wiley, J. (1987). *Report to the Children's Services Commission regarding teenage suicide.* Unpublished report of the Missouri Children's Services Commission, Columbia, MO.

Worden, J. W. (1982). *Grief counseling and grief therapy: A handbook for the mental health practitioner.* New York: Springer.

Worden, J. W. (1991). Grief counseling and grief therapy: A handbook for the mental health practitioner, Second Edition. New York: Springer Publishing Co.

Worsnop, R. L. (1992). Assisted Suicide, *C.Q. Researcher, 2(7)* 145–168.

Wrobleski, A. (1984). The suicide survivors grief group. *Omega, 15,* 173–184.

Yalom, I. (1975). *The theory and practice of group psychotherapy* (2nd ed.). New York: Basic Books.

Yalom, I. D. (1980). *Existential psychotherapy.* New York: Basic Books.

Young, D., Rich, C. L., & Fowler, R. C. (1984). Double suicides: Four model cases. *Journal of Clinical Psychiatry, 45,* 470–472.

Index